I0128366

JUNG AND THE EPIC OF TRANSFORMATION

Vol. 2

Goethe's "Faust" as a Text of Transformation

by Paul Bishop

CHIRON PUBLICATIONS • ASHEVILLE, NORTH CAROLINA

© 2025 by Chiron Publications. All rights reserved. No part of this publication may be reproduced, stored in a retrieval system, or transmitted, in any form by any means, electronic, mechanical, photocopying, recording, or otherwise, without the prior written permission of the publisher, Chiron Publications, P.O. Box 19690, Asheville, N.C. 28815-1690.

This work may not be used without permission for artificial intelligence training or development of machine learning language models.

www.ChironPublications.com

Interior and cover design by Danijela Mijailovic
Printed primarily in the United States of America.

ISBN 978-1-68503-595-2 paperback
ISBN 978-1-68503-596-9 hardcover
ISBN 978-1-68503-597-6 electronic
ISBN 978-1-68503-598-3 limited edition paperback
ISBN 978-1-68503-599-0 limited edition hardcover

Library of Congress Cataloging-in-Publication Data Pending

Contents

List of Abbreviations

BB = C.G. Jung, *The Black Books, 1913-1932: Notebooks of Transformation*, ed. Sonu Shamdasani, trans. Martin Liebscher, John Peck, and Sonu Shamdasani, 7 vols. (New York and London: Norton, 2020).

CW = C.G. Jung, *Collected Works*, ed. Sir Herbert Read, Michael Fordham, Gerhard Adler, and William McGuire, 20 vols. (London: Routledge & Kegan Paul, 1953-1983). Cited in the text with volume number and paragraph reference.

DKV = Wolfram von Eschenbach, *Parzival*, ed. Eberhard Nellmann, trans. Dieter Kühn, 2 vols. (Frankfurt am Main: Deutscher Klassiker Verlag, 2006).

ETG = *Erinnerungen, Träume Gedanken von C.G. Jung*, ed. Aniela Jaffé (Olten und Freiburg im Breisgau: Walter-Verlag, 1990).

H = *The Holy Bible, according to the Douay and Rheimish Version* [1859], ed. George Leo Haydock (Duarte, CA: Catholic Treasures, 2006).

L = C.G. Jung, *Letters*, ed. Gerhard Adler and Aniela Jaffé, trans. R.F.C. Hull, 2 vols. (Princeton, NJ: Princeton University Press, 1973-1975).

MDR = *Memories, Dreams, Reflections of C.G. Jung*, ed. Aniela Jaffé, trans. Richard and Clara Winston (London: Routledge & Kegan Paul, 1963).

NJB = *The New Jerusalem Bible*, general ed. Henry Wansbrough (London: Darton, Longman & Todd, 1985).

PU = Jung, *Psychology of the Unconscious: A Study of the Transformations and Symbolisms of the Libido: A Contribution to the History of the Evolution of Thought*, trans. Beatrice M. Hinkle (London: Moffat, Yard, and Co., 1916) (cited with paragraph references as reprinted [London: Routledge, 1991]).

RB = C.G. Jung, *The Red Book: Liber Novus* [Reader's Edition], ed. Sonu Shamdasani, trans. Mark Kyburz, John Peck, and Sonu Shamdasani (New York and London: Norton, 2012).

SE = Sigmund Freud, *The Standard Edition of the Complete Works of Sigmund Freud*, general eds. James Strachey and Anna Freud, 24 vols (London: Hogarth Press, 1953-1974).

SNZ = C.G. Jung, *Nietzsche's "Zarathustra": Notes of the Seminar given in 1935-1939*, ed. James L. Jarrett, 2 vols. (London: Routledge, 1989).

Editions of translations cited

Wolfram von Eschenbach, *Parzival: A Knightly Epic*, trans. Jessie L. Weston [1894], 2 vols. (New York: Stechert, 1912).

Johann Wolfgang Goethe, *Faust: Parts I and II*, trans. Albert G. Latham (London; New York: Dent; Dutton, 1908).

Friedrich Nietzsche, *Thus Spake Zarathustra: A Book for All and None* [*Complete Works of Friedrich Nietzsche*, ed. Oskar Levy, vol. 4], trans. Thomas Common (Edinburgh and London: Foulis, 1909).

A note on translation

Goethe's *Faust* is cited here from the translation published in 1909 by Albert George Latham (1864-1940), who was the first Professor of Modern Languages at Newcastle University. It has been chosen, not simply because it is out of copyright, but because it has been described as the version most familiar to English-speaking readers in the early twentieth century, and hence the period when Jung was developing his Analytical Psychology.

Faust editions and commentaries

Goethe, Johann Wolfgang, *Faust: Der Tragödie erster Teil*, ed. Lothar J. Scheithauer (Stuttgart: Reclam, 1971).

Goethe, Johann Wolfgang, *Faust: Der Tragödie zweiter Teil*, ed. Lothar J. Scheithauer (Stuttgart: Reclam, 1971).

Theodor Friedrich and Lothar J. Scheithauer, *Kommentar zu Goethes Faust* [1959] (Stuttgart: Reclam, 1974; 1980).

Goethe, *Faust*, ed. Erich Trunz = *Werke* [Hamburger Ausgabe], vol. 9 [1949] (Munich: Beck, 1972).

HA = *Werke* [*Hamburger Ausgabe*], ed. Erich Trunz, 14 vols. (Hamburg: Wegner, 1948-1960).

WA = *Werke* [*Weimarer Ausgabe*], 133 vols. in 143 (Weimar: Böhlau, 1887-1919).

Bishop = *A Companion to Goethe's "Faust": Parts I and II*, ed. Paul Bishop (Rochester, NY, and Woodbridge, UK: Camden House, 2001).

Gernot Böhme, *Goethes Faust als philosophischer Text* (Zug: Die Graue Edition, 2005).

Jane K. Brown, Meredith Lee, Thomas P. Saine et al. (eds), *Interpreting Goethe's "Faust" Today* (Columbia, SC: Camden House, 1994).

Wilhelm Emrich, *Die Symbolik von Faust II: Sinn und Vorformen* (Frankfurt am Main: Athenäum, 1957; [3]1964).

Gaier = Johann Wolfgang Goethe, *Faust-Dichtungen*, ed. Ulrich Gaier, 3 vols (*Texte, Kommentar I, Kommentar II*) (Stuttgart and Leipzig: Reclam, 1999).

Hamlin = Johann Wolfgang von Goethe, *Faust: A Tragedy*, trans. Walter Arndt, ed. Cyrus Hamlin, 2nd edn. (New York and London: Norton, 2001).

Kaufmann = *Goethe's "Faust": The Original German and a New Translation*, trans. Walter Kaufmann (New York: Anchor Books, 1963). [A German-English parallel text of the entirety of Part One with selections from Part Two]

Charlotte Lee (ed.), *Goethe in Context* (Cambridge and New York, NY: Cambridge University Press, 2024).

Eudo C. Mason, *Goethe's "Faust": Its Genesis and Purport* (Berkeley and Los Angeles: University of California Press, 1967).

Kurt May, *Faust II. Teil: In der Sprachform gedeutet* (Munich: Hanser, 1962).

Heinrich Rickert, *Goethes Faust: Die dramatische Einheit der Dichtung* (Tübingen: Mohr (Siebeck), 1932).

Schöne = Johann Wolfgang Goethe, *Faust: Kommentare*, ed. Albrecht Schöne, 2 vols. (*Texte, Kommentare*) (Frankfurt am Main: Deutscher Klassiker Verlag, 2005).

Hans Schulte, John Noyes, and Pia Kleber (eds.), *Goethe's "Faust": Theatre of Modernity* (Cambridge: Cambridge University Press, 2011).

Rudolf Steiner, *Geisteswissenschaftliche Erläuterungen zu Goethes «Faust»*, 2 vols. (Dornach: Rudolf Steiner Verlag, 1982).

John R. Williams, *Goethe's "Faust"* (London: Allen & Unwin, 1987).

Works on Goethean life (in chronological order):

Robert d'Harcourt, *Goethe et l'art de vivre* (Paris: Payot, 1935).

Frank Nager, *Der heilkundige Dichter: Goethe und die Medizin* (Zurich and Munich: Artemis & Winkler, 1990).

Julie D. Prandi, *"Dare to Be Happy!": A Study Goethe's Ethics* (Lanham, New York, and London: University Press of America, 1993).

Heinrich Schipperges, *Goethe–seine Kunst zu Leben: Betrachtungen aus der Sicht eines Arztes* (Frankfurt am Main: Knecht, 1996).

John Armstrong, *Love, Life, Goethe: How to Be Happy in an Imperfect World* (London: Allen Lane, 2006).

Pierre Hadot, *N'oublie pas de vivre: Goethe et la tradition des exercices spirituels* (Paris: Albin Michel, 2008).

Peter Schraud, *Mein Freund fürs Leben: Goethe als Partner der Selbsterkenntnis und Selbsterziehung* (Neukirchen: Novalis Verlag, 2014).

Works on Goethean aesthetics (in chronological order):

Elizabeth M. Wilkinson and L.A. Willoughby, *Goethe: Poet and Thinker* (London: Edward Arnold, 1962).

R.H. Stephenson, *Goethe's Wisdom Literature: A Study in Aesthetic Transmutation* (Bern, Frankfurt am Main, New York: Peter Lang, 1983).

Elizabeth M. Wilkinson (ed.), *Goethe Revisited: A Collection of Essays* (London; New York: John Calder; Riverrun Press, 1984).

R.H. Stephenson, *Goethe's Conception of Knowledge and Science* (Edinburgh: Edinburgh University Press, 1995).

Elizabeth M. Wilkinson and L.A. Willoughby, *Models of Wholeness: Some Attitudes to Language, Art and Life in the Age of Goethe*, ed. Jeremy Adler, Martin Swales, and Ann Weaver (Oxford, Bern, Berlin: Peter Lang, 2002).

R.H. Stephenson, *Studies in Weimar Classicism: Writing as Symbolic Form* (Oxford, Bern, Berlin: Peter Lang, 2010).

Jungian/alchemical readings of *Faust* (in chronological order):

Ronald D. Gray, *Goethe the Alchemist: A Study of Alchemical Symbolism in Goethe's Literary and Scientific Works* (Cambridge: Cambridge University Press, 1952).

Gottfried Diener, *Fausts Weg zu Helena: Urphänomen und Archetypus: Darstellung und Deutung einer symbolischen Szenenfolge aus Goethes Faust* (Stuttgart: Klett, 1961).

Alice Raphael, *Goethe and the Philosophers' Stone: Symbolical Patterns in "The Parable" and the Second Part of "Faust"* (New York: Garrett Publications, 1965).

Edward F. Edinger, *Goethe's "Faust": Notes for a Jungian Commentary* (Toronto: Inner City Books, 1990).

Irene Gerber-Münch, *Goethes Faust: Eine tiefenpsychologische Studie über den Mythos des modernen Menschen* [*Jungiana: Beiträge zur Psychologie von C.G. Jung*, Reihe B, Band 6] (Küsnacht: Stiftung für Jung'sche Psychologie, 1997).

Jeffrey Raff, *Jung and the Alchemical Imagination* (Lake Worth, FL: Nicolas-Hays, 2000).

Jack Herbert, *The German Tradition: Uniting the Opposites: Goethe, Jung & Rilke* (London: Temenos Academy, 2001).

Stephen Cross and Jack Herbert, *Inward Lies the Way: German Thought and the Nature of Mind* (London: Temenos Academy, 2008).

Stephen Y. Wilkerson, *A Most Mysterious Union: The Role of Alchemy in Goethe's "Faust"* (Asheville, NC: Chiron, 2018).

Audiovisual recommendations

Faust: Der Tragödie erster Teil [in der Gründgens-Inszenierung des Düsseldorfer Schauspielhauses], Deutsche Grammophon 1954. 2 CDs. ISBN 0-2845-99122.

Faust: Der Tragödie zweiter Teil [in der Gründgens-Inszenierung des Düsseldorfer Schauspielhauses], Deutsche Grammophon 1959. 2 CDs. ISBN 0-2894-99152.

Faust: Der Tragödie zweiter Teil, read by Peter Stein [Bayerischer Rundfunk, 2000]. 7 CDs. Der Hörverlag. ISBN 3-89584-852-2.

Peter Stein inszeniert Faust [ZDF, 2005]. 4 DVDs. Die Theater Edition. 7-000000-621918.

Acknowledgements

I should like to thank colleagues at Chiron Press, especially Len Cruz and Steve Buser, for their interest in this project at an early stage and for their support in turning it into a reality; many thanks to Jennifer Fitzgerald for her invaluable contribution to managing the project, and to Robert Mikulak for his careful copyediting.

I am extremely grateful to the Academic Sub-Committee of the IAAP for its financial support for this project, without which it would have not been possible to bring it to publication. And I should like to thank Joe Cambray for his advice and support, for which I am likewise extremely grateful.

Over the years, I have incurred a number of debts to innumerable colleagues in *Germanistik* and Jung Studies alike. It was a pleasure and a privilege to work at the University of Glasgow with one of the leading figures (nationally and internationally) of Goethe scholarship, Roger Stephenson; Murray Stein's kind invitation to give the Zurich Lecture Series in Analytical Psychology in 2010 offered me an opportunity to examine Goethe's late, great work *Urworte. Orphisch* ("Primal Words. Orphic") at a length and in a depth which is rare, or even nonexistent, in academia these days; and I am grateful to Stephen Farah, CEO of the Centre for Applied Jungian Studies, for his invitations to contribute a seminar on "The Faustian Myth and its Significance for Jung" to an online course titled *Mythos: Myth and Metamorphosis* in 2021 and a seminar on "Goethe on *das Dämonische* in life and in art" to an online lecture series on the *Art of Individuation* in 2022, as well as to Jakob Lusensky for his invitation to join him for an episode of his *Psychology & The Cross* podcast titled *"Imitatio Faust*: Jung, Goethe and the question of secular redemption" in 2021; and to Stefano Capani for his invitation to contribute a lecture on "Jungian Psychology and 21st-Century Socio-Cultural Challenges: Living in a Faustian Age?" to the *Contemporary Analytical Psychology and Neo-Jungian Studies* program at Pacifica Graduate Institute in 2024. Finally, I am grateful to the C.G. Jung Institute of New York for its invitation to join its faculty and present a Readings Course on *Faust I* in the Fall of 2024 (with the prospect of a follow-up course on *Faust II* in 2025).

In addition, I should like to thank Jim Walker (at Camden House), especially for his invitation to edit *A Companion to Goethe's "Faust": Parts I and II* for Camden House, those students in the School of Modern Languages and Cultures (SMLC) at the University of Glasgow who chose the Honours Option "Faust: Text of Transformation," and the training analysts at the C.G. Jung Institute of New York on the *Faust* Reading Course, as well as Alan Cardew; Terence Dawson; Leslie Gardner; Phil Goss; Lucy Huskinson; Peter Kingsley; Laura London; Christiana Ludwig; Martin Liebscher; Roderick Main; Catriona Miller; Susan Rowland; Andrew Samuels (and other colleagues at the Department of Psychosocial and Psychoanalytic Studies, formerly the Centre for Psychoanalytic Studies, at the University of Essex); and Sonu Shamdasani.

Above all, I am grateful as always for love and support from Helen, and how could I forget Ruben?

Preface

The Amfortas wound and the Faustian split in the Germanic individual are still not healed: his unconscious is still loaded with contents that must first be made conscious before he can be free of them.
("Commentary on 'The Secret of the Golden Flower'" [1929])

As far as Jung was concerned, there was no doubt that Goethe's *Faust* was one of the greatest works of all time. In a letter to Max Rychner of 28 February 1932, Jung described *Faust* as "the most recent pillar in that bridge of the spirit which spans the morass of world history, beginning with the Gilgamesh epic, the *I Ching*, the Upanishads, the *Tao-Te-King*, the fragments of Heraclitus, and continuing in the Gospel of St John, the letters of St Paul, in Meister Eckhart and in Dante," and he concluded that "one cannot meditate enough about *Faust*," for many of "the mysteries" of Part Two are "still unfathomed" (L1, 89). And he went on to say that *Faust* is "out of this world and therefore it transports you," for it is "as much the future as the past and therefore the most living present [*lebendigste Gegenwart*]" (L1, 89)! As usual, Jung was right.

In a survey of leading professionals, academics, and intellectuals conducted by the German weekly newspaper *Die Zeit* in the spring of 1997, nearly everyone questioned put Goethe's *Faust* at the top of the books they considered the most important.[1]

---

[1] "Was sollen Schüler lesen? Prominente beantworten die ZEIT-Umfrage nach einem neuen Literatur-Kanon," *Die Zeit*, 16 May 1997.

On the 250th anniversary of the birth of Goethe, a computerized analysis of the holdings of the Library of Congress (published in the *Washington Post* on 12 September 1999) revealed that, after (in descending order) Jesus, Shakespeare, Lenin, Abraham Lincoln, Napeolon Bonaparte, Karl Marx, and the Virgin Mary, in eighth position in terms of the number of books written about them was — Goethe. In the meantime, very little has changed, even if Goethe is probably actually read less than previously. In the end, Goethe's *Faust* was — and is — *the* big book of German literature, and by the same token it was — and is — *the* great epic of transformation.[2]

In linguistic terms, many of the quotations from *Faust* have become proverbial; in this respect, its status for German culture can be compared to Shakespeare's *Hamlet* for the English language. And it is a work which, as we shall see, occupied the life of Goethe who himself, along with Luther *before* him and Nietzsche *after* him, operated a decisive change in the use of German as a literary language. After *Faust*, nothing was the same; and by the same token, after we have read and if we have understood *Faust*, nothing will be the same for us again.

In recent years, the very notion of a literary canon has become contested;[3] yet, simply because the notion of the canon is contested, this does not mean that the canon does not exist. In his masterful guide to the canon, the American critic Harold Bloom naturally includes a chapter on *Faust*, in which he rightly emphasizes the idiosyncratic nature of this work. And in *The Western Canon* (1994), Bloom goes on to write that *Faust* is "a banquet of sense, though doubtless too replete with scarcely healthy viands. As a sexual nightmare or

---

[2] For an analysis of *Faust* which places transformation at the heart of its discussion, see Johannes Anderegg, *Transformationen: Über Himmlisches und Teuflisches in Goethes Faust* (Bielefeld: Aisthesis, 2011). See my review of this study in *Monatshefte*, vol. 103, no. 4 (Winter 2011), 668-670.

[3] See, for instance, Nicholas Saul and Ricarda Schmidt (eds), *Literarische Wertung und Kanonbildung* (Würzburg: Könighausen & Neumann, 2007).

erotic fantasy, it has no rival, and one understands why the shocked Coleridge declined to translate the poem" —:[4] although Paul M. Zall in a paper given in 1971 and then Frederick Burwick and James C. McKusick in 2007 have made the case that Samuel Taylor Coleridge (1772-1834) did indeed translate *Faust*, publishing it in 1821 — but anonymously.[5] As Bloom goes on to write, *Faust* is "certainly a work about what, if anything, will suffice, and Goethe finds myriad ways of showing us that sexuality by itself will not," adding that "even more obsessively, *Faust* teaches us that, without an active sexuality, absolutely nothing will suffice."[6] (In an episode of the program called *Nachtstudio* broadcast on Bavarian Radio as part of the Faust-Festival in Munich on 12 March 2018, the premise of its title was that eroticism had very much helped Goethe to write his drama of murder, devil-worship, and sex.)[7]

The centrality of *Faust*'s place in Goethe's life and work is illustrated by the timetable of composition included in David Luke's translations of *Faust*,[8] the most important dates in which are given below:

1768	Traveling players perform the Faust puppet-play in Frankfurt
1769	Traveling players perform the Faust puppet-play in Strassburg

---

[4] Harold Bloom, *The Western Canon: The Books and School of the Ages* (New York: Harcourt & Brace, 1995), p. 211.
[5] Paul M. Zall, "Coleridge's Translation of *Faust*?", Philological Association of the Pacific Coast, 27 November 1971; and Frederick Burwick and James C. McKusick, *Faustus From the German of Goethe Translated by Samuel Taylor Coleridge* (Oxford: Oxford University Press, 2007).
[6] Bloom, *The Western Canon*, p. 210.
[7] Bayerischer Rundfunk, *Nachtstudio*, "Goethes Faust: Erotik half Goethe beim Schreiben," broadcast on 12 March 2018.
[8] See "Synopsis of the Composition of *Faust* Part One" and "Chronological Summary of the Composition and Publication of *Faust* Part Two," in Johann Wolfgang von Goethe, *Faust: Part One*, ed. and trans. David Luke (Oxford: Oxford University Press, 1987), pp. lvi-lvii and Johann Wolfgang von Goethe, *Faust: Part Two*, ed. and trans. David Luke (Oxford: Oxford University Press, 1994), pp. lxxxi-lxxxii.

1772-1775	Goethe begins to work on a *Faust* drama (known as the *Urfaust* = first period of composition)
1778	Goethe resumes work on *Faust* (= second period of composition)
1790	Publication of *Faust: A Fragment*
1797	With the encouragement of Schiller, Goethe resumes work on *Faust* (= third period of composition)
1808	Publication of *Faust: The First Part of the Tragedy*
1825-1831	Goethe completes *Faust: The Second Part of the Tragedy*
1827	Publication of Act III under the title *Helena: A Classical-Romantic Phantasmagoria*
1828	Publication of part of Act I
1832	Death of Goethe (on 22 March). Posthumous publication of *Faust: Part Two*
1887	Erich Schmidt discovers Fräulein von Göchhausen's transcript (c. 1775-1776) of the *Urfaust* and publishes it as *Goethe's Faust in its Original Form*

(For a detailed discussion of the composition of *Faust*, the reader is advised to consult Eudo C. Mason's study.)[9] To pick up on a couple of remarks made by Goethe in his correspondence with Schiller: In his letter of 27 June 1797, in which he described *Faust* as "this barbarous composition" — here, a term with positive connotations he himself applied to Shakespeare and Calderón — Goethe told Schiller that "in the poem itself, which will ever remain a fragment, I may apply our new theory of the epic poem" —: an allusion to their essay "On Epic and Dramatic Poetry" of that same year (which was discussed in Volume 1, Chapter 1, pp. 17-21. And elsewhere, Goethe described progress on the work — in a letter to Schiller of 1 July 1797, i.e., shortly before his departure for Italy — as "shooting up like a great family of mushrooms out of the earth, to the wonder

---

[9] Eudo C. Mason, *Goethe's Faust: Its Genesis and Purport* (Berkeley and Los Angeles: University of California Press, 1967).

and terror of many," or it would "if I only had now a quiet month at my disposal," while in his letters to Schiller of 18 June 1795 and 6 December 1797, he described *Faust* as a "tragelaph," that is, the legendary creature (also known as a hircocervus), imagined as being a hybrid that was half-goat, half-stag.

Finally, in a diary entry for 22 June 1831, Goethe noted: "Das Hauptgeschäft zu Stande gebracht. Letztes Mundum. Alles rein Geschriebene eingeheftet" (i.e., "Main business achieved. Final version. All pages of fair copy fastened together"),[10] thus recording the completion of *Faust II* in the form of 386 handwritten pages, now bound together. In what sense, however, was *Faust* actually Goethe's "main business"? After all, a glance at the chronology of the composition of *Faust* suggests how the various compositional phases are interwoven with Goethe's other activities and literary productions, including the publication of *The Sorrows of Young Werther* (in 1774); his ministerial duties, his growing interest in natural sciences, his relationship with Charlotte von Stein, and the ending of his earlier *Sturm und Drang* phase, marked by his work on such classical dramas as *Iphigenia in Tauris* and *Torquato Tasso* (from 1775 to 1786); his first Italian journey (from September 1786 to June 1788); his relationship with Christiana Vulpius, whom he met on his return to Weimar in 1788 and married in 1806; his work on the *Roman Elegies* (1788-1790); the beginning (in 1794) of his friendship with Schiller, in the course of which an extensive correspondence over a thousand letters would be exchanged; the publication in 1795 of the *Roman Elegies*, in 1795-1796 of *Wilhelm Meister's Apprenticeship*, and in 1797 of *Hermann und Dorothea*; the publication in 1809 of *Elective Affinities*, in 1819 of the *West-Eastern Divan*, and in 1821 of *Wilhelm Meister's Journeyman Years* (and its second edition in 1829); and between 1823 and 1832 his conversations with Johann Peter Eckermann (1792-1854).

---

[10] Cf. WA III, vol. 13 , p. 112 .

In fact, it is in his conversations with Eckermann that we find a concept that is helpful in defining the relation between *Faust* and Goethe's life; namely, the notion of "anticipation" (or, in German, *Antizipation*). In their conversation of 26 February 1824, Goethe told Eckermann:

> The region of love, hate, hope, despair, or by whatever other names you may call the moods and passions of the soul, is innate with the poet, and he succeeds in representing it. But it is not born with him to know by instinct how courts are held, or how a parliament or a coronation is managed; and if he will not offend against truth, while treating such subjects, he must have recourse to experience or tradition. Thus, in *Faust*, I could, by anticipation, know how to describe my hero's gloomy weariness of life, and the emotions which love excites in the heart of Gretchen; but the lines,
>
> > *Wie traurig steigt die unvollkommne Scheibe*
> > *Des späten Monds mit feuchter Glut heran!*
>
> > How gloomy does the imperfect disc
> > Of the late moon with humid glow arise!
>
> required some observation of nature.[11]

"Yet," Eckermann thoughtfully responds, "every line of *Faust* bears marks, not to be mistaken, of a careful study of life and the world; nor does one for a moment suppose otherwise than that the whole is only the result of the amplest experience." In response, Goethe confirms this analysis:

---

[11] Johann Peter Eckermann, *Conversations of Goethe*, ed. J.K. Moorhead, trans. John Oxenford [1930] (New York: Da Capo Press, 1998).

"Perhaps so," replied Goethe; "yet, had I not the world already in my soul through anticipation, I should have remained blind with seeing eyes, and all experience and observation would have been dead, unproductive labour. The light is there, and the colours surround us; but, if we had no light and no colours in our own eyes, we should not perceive the outward phenomena." (48)

In other words, Goethe is telling Eckermann that human experience is not confined to what we know through *actual experience*; rather, a knowledge of fundamental and universal situations is something we carry within us (or is, in Jungian terms, *archetypal*); what the poet, in particular, can do is to project by means of *Antizipation* this image of the world within into the work of art. Thus, it is by "anticipation" that Goethe can, in *Faust*, conjure up out of his own inner consciousness both the depths of the hero's despair and the heights of Gretchen's love.[12]

Elsewhere in his conversations with Eckermann, Goethe addresses the question of the *poetic unity* of this work — published in two parts, the composition of which extended from 1772 (or earlier) to 1831. For instance, on 6 May 1827, Goethe tells Eckermann, "It would have been a fine thing, indeed, if I had strung so rich, varied, and highly diversified a life as I have brought to view in *Faust* upon the slender string of one pervading idea."[13] And yet Goethe had earlier, in his conversation with the historian Heinrich Luden (1778-1847) in 1806, observed that *Faust* "has a higher interest," that is, "the idea which animated the poet, and which links the single elements together to a whole, governing them as a law and

---

[12] For further discussion, see Elizabeth M. Wilkinson and L.A. Willoughby, *Goethe: Poet and Thinker* (London: Arnold, 1962), pp. 153-154.
[13] Eckermann, *Conversations of Goethe*, p. 205.

conferring their significance upon them."[14] In so remarking, Goethe was responding to Luden's thesis that, as he explained to Goethe (in highly Hegelian terms), "the spirit of the entire history of the world will find itself represented here in this tragedy [i.e., *Faust*], should it ever be completed; the latter will prove a true image of the life of humanity itself, effectively embracing the past, the present and the future," and adding: "Humankind has been idealised in the figure of Faust; he is the very representative of humanity [*der Repräsentant der Menschheit*]".[15] What Luden told Goethe recalls the remark of the great Swiss historian Jacob Burckhardt (1818-1897) about how "every Greek of the classical era carried in himself a fragment of the Oedipus, just as every German carries a fragment of Faust,"[16] or as Jung put it, "every Greek of the classical era carried in himself a fragment of Oedipus, just as every German carries a fragment of Faust" (PU §56, fn. 42).

What is the origin of the Faust legend?[17] Around 1480, a figure known as Georg or Johann Faust was born in Knittlingen,

---

[14] Heinrich Luden, *Rückblicke in mein Leben* (Jena: Luden, 1847), p. 37.

[15] Luden, *Rückblicke in mein Leben*, pp. 24-25; translated in Rüdiger Bubner, *Innovations of Idealism*, trans. Nicholas Walker (Cambridge: Cambridge University Press, 2003), p. 256.

[16] In a footnote, Jung invites us to consider Burckhardt's letter to Albert Brenner of 11 November 1855: "I have absolutely nothing stored away for the special interpretation of Faust. You are well provided with commentaries of all sorts. Hark! let us at once take the whole foolish pack back to the reading-room from whence they have come. What you are destined to find in Faust, that you will find by intuition. Faust is nothing else than pure and legitimate myth, a great primitive conception, so to speak, in which everyone can divine in his own way his own nature and destiny. Allow me to make a comparison: What would the ancient Greeks have said had a commentator interposed himself between them and the Oedipus legend? There was a chord of the Oedipus legend in every Greek which longed to be touched directly and respond in its own way. And thus it is with the German nation and Faust" (PU §56; see Hans Brenner-Eglinger, "Briefe Jakob Burckhardts an Albert Brenner," *Basler Jahrbuch 1901*, 87-110 [p. 92]).

[17] For a comprehensive account of the Faust legend, see Elizabeth M. Butler's trilogy, *The Myth of the Magus*, *Ritual Magic*, and *The Fortunes of Faust* (Cambridge: Cambridge University Press, 1948-1952); as well as Osman Durrani, *Faust: Icon of Modern Culture* (Mountfield: Helm Information, 2004), and Sara Munson Deats,

a small town in the Enz district of Baden-Württemberg in south Germany. This Faust died in around 1540, and by 1548 various reports of his legendary exploits had begun to circulate. (For example, in a letter of 1507, Johannes Trithemius (1462-1516), a German Benedictine abbot whose students included Heinrich Cornelius Agrippa and Paracelsus, described the historical Faust as being "able to do what Christ did, as often and whenever he wanted.")[18] But often these accounts draw on material from a much earlier epoch, and the figure who came to be known as Faust (or Faustus) goes back, in fact, to the origins of Christianity itself and to the origins of Christian heresy. For in the Acts of the Apostles, Chapter 8, we read of the supposed first Gnostic, Simon Magus of Samaria. On this biblical account, Simon Magus tried to buy from the apostles the gift of the power of the Holy Spirit and the ability of perform miracles, but Peter refuses (8:9-24). (In fact, the sin of trying to sell Church positions for profit is, to this day, known as simony.) When he later went to Rome, he acquired the name of *Faustus*, i.e., "the favored one."[19]

Earlier on, Simon had come across a prostitute in the ancient Phoenician city of Tyre (today in part of Libya) and had proclaimed this woman to be the fallen Thought of God (or *Ennoia*) and to have been (in one of her previous incarnations) none other than Helen of Troy. (Helen of Troy was, of course, the beautiful woman in whose name many a ship had set sail to bring her back when

---

The Faust Legend: From Marlow and Goethe to Contemporary Drama and Film (Cambridge and New York: Cambridge University Press, 2019).

[18] Johannes Trithemius, *Opera historica*, vol. 2 [1601] (Frankfurt am Main: Minerva, 1966), p. 560; cited in Schöne, *Kommentare*, p. 183; cf. Rudolf Steiner, *Geisteswissenschaftliche Erläuterungen zu Goethes «Faust»*, 2 vols (Dornach: Rudolf Steiner Verlag, 1982), vol. 1, p. 64.

[19] For further discussion, see Philip Mason Palmer and Robert Pattison More, *The Sources of the Faust Tradition: From Simon Magus to Lessing* [1936] (London and New York: Routledge, 2013); and Ramona Fradon, *The Gnostic Faustus: The Secret Teachings Behind the Classic Text* (Rochester, VT: Inner Traditions, 2007).

she had been captured by Paris: the story of Homer's *Iliad*, and Helen also returns in *Faust II*.) In the biblical account, Peter says to Simon Magus, "Do penance, therefore, for this thy wickedness: and pray to God, if perhaps this thought [*epinoia*] of thy heart may be forgiven thee" (Acts 8:22), and Gert Lüdemann has suggested that Luke's reference to the state of Simon's heart (ἡ ἐπίνοια τῆς καρδίας) may be an ironic reference to Helen as Simon's *epinoia* (ἐπίνοια) or *ennoia* (ἔννοια).[20] If so, then two core elements of Gnostic thought (and, in particular, Simonianism) can be found in this episode from Acts: the reference to the godlike status of Simon, and of his syzygos, ἐπίνοια.[21] On a related note, it is worth recalling that, in Stoicism, a clenched fist is a metaphor for "understanding" or "comprehension."[22]

The heretical scandal of Simon Magus provided the distant source for the legend of Faust, which later became attached to an actual individual — the mysterious Georg or Johann Faust, an early 16th-century wandering confidence man and astrologer who died in around 1540. As such, Faust is also a Renaissance figure, a figure of the period of the Reformation (above all, in Germany, the Lutheran Reformation) and the scientific revolution. His contemporaries would have included such seminal figures as Leonardo da Vinci

---

[20] Gerd Lüdemann, *Early Christianity according to the Traditions in Acts: A Commentary* (Minneapolis: Fortress Press, 1989), pp. 96-98.

[21] Lüdemann, *Early Christianity according to the Traditions in Acts*, pp. 100-191; cf. Stephen Charles Haar, *Simon Magus: The First Gnostic?* (Berlin and New York: de Gruyter, 2003), p. 82.

[22] "Zeno professed to illustrate this by a piece of action; for when he stretched out his fingers, and showed the palm of his hand, 'Perception,' said he, 'is a thing like this.' Then, when he had a little closed his fingers, 'Assent is like this.' Afterwards, when he had completely closed his hand, and held forth his fist, that, he said, was comprehension. From which simile he also gave that state a name which it had not before, and called it κατάληψις [katalepsis]. But when he brought his left hand against his right, and with it took a firm and tight hold of his fist, knowledge, he said, was of that character; and that was what none but a wise man possessed" (Cicero, *Academica*, book 2, §XLVII; in Cicero, *The Academic Questions, Treatise de Finibus, and Tusculan Disputations*, trans. C.D. Yonge (London: Bohn, 1853), p. 91).

(1452-1519), Columbus (1451-1506), Machiavelli (1469-1527), Erasmus (c. 1466-1536), Copernicus (1473-1543), Luther (1483-1546), Paracelsus (c. 1493-1541), and Vesalius (1514-1564) (the Flemish founder of modern anatomy). In turn, these figures can be seen as paving the way to the Enlightenment, and it is no surprise that, for the Marxist political theorist Marshall Berman (1940-2013) in his study titled — with an allusion to a phrase in *The Communist Manifesto* — *All That Is Solid Melts into Air* (1982), the figure of Faust stands as a powerful symbol of the "experience of modernity."[23]

Yet the story of Faust can be placed in another historico-cultural context as well. For, according to astrological symbolism, something important happened in the 16th century in the constellation of Pisces, a configuration of stars consisting of two fish (i.e., *pisces*) joined by a cord of stars.[24] While one fish, Pisces 1, swims vertically, the other fish, Pisces 2, swims parallel to the ecliptic, the plane of the Earth's orbit around the sun. The place on the ecliptic where the sun crosses equator, making day and night equal in length, around 21 March is known as the vernal (or spring) equinox point. Every year, the vernal equinox moves westward along the ecliptic relative to the fixed stars, a movement known as the precession of the equinoxes. Is there, Jung wondered in *Aion* (1951), a correlation between, on the one hand, the alignment of the vernal equinox with the constellation of Pisces and, on the other, the rise and decline of Christianity? After all, the birth of Christ, heralded by the appearance of the star of Bethlehem in 7 B.C.E., coincides with the alignment of the vernal equinox with the star marking the knot in the cord linking the two fishes and hence the point where the first fish begins.

---

[23] Marshall Berman, *All That Is Solid Melts into Air: The Experience of Modernity* (New York: Penguin, 1982).
[24] See Maggie Hyde, *Jung and Astrology* (London: Aquarian Press; Thorson's, 1992), pp. 16-18.

As Jung put it, the connection between "the figure of Christ and the inception of the astrological age of the fishes" — or, more precisely, "the simultaneity of the fish symbolism of the Redeemer with the astrological symbol of the new aeon" — is reflected in the coincidence between the move of the vernal equinox point through the precession of the equinoxes, into the sign of Pisces, thus inaugurating a new age, and the fact that the sign of the fish was used to designate the God-become-Man, who (a) was born as the first fish of the Pisces era and sacrificed as the last ram or lamb of the previous era of Aries era; (b) had fishermen for disciples and designated them "fishers of men"; (c) fed the multitude with miraculously multiplying fishes; (d) was himself as eaten as a fish, a "holier food" or "more sacred diet" (*sanctior cibus*);[25] and (d) had disciples who were known as *pisculi,* or little fishes (CW 9 §148; cf. §147). This astrological approach to Christianity is summarized by Maggie Hyde as follows:

> Looking at the constellation of Pisces [...], we see that the two fish are bound by a cord at the star alpha, known to the Arabs as Al Rischa, the Knot. They swim in different directions, the eastern fish moving vertically north from the ecliptic, the western fish swimming horizontally along the ecliptic. This is understood to represent a dual nature in the sign, a vertical and a horizontal, two opposite qualities, which cross but are forever bound up with each other. They are the fish of spirit and the fish of matter, and the crucifixion of the Messiah of the Piscean Age is indicated by the symbolism of this crossing. Christ, the first fish of spirit, is crucified on the cross of matter. The great themes of Christianity — sacrifice, renunciation and

---

[25] See Tertullian, *Adversus Marcionem* (*Against Marcion*), Book 1, Chapter 14.

redemption — are also the defining qualities of the sign of Pisces. For Jung, the duality inherent in the fish of Pisces reflects Christianity's irreconcilable opposites. Theistic religious systems have to reconcile the "dual" nature of God; God in manifestation as both positive and negative, male and female, spirit and matter. God is often seen as that principle which unites opposites but Christianity has a difficulty in reconciling this dualism. This manifests in the European intellect as the "Good versus Evil" problem and in the challenging question of how an all-good God can create evil [...].[26]

Yet if the movement of the vernal equinox point along the ecliptic in alignment with the stars of Pisces 1 corresponds to the origin and spread of Christianity (i.e., the birth of Christ, the Edict of Milan in 313, which marked the end of persecution of Christians, and the Edict of Thessalonica in 380, which made the Catholicism of the Nicene Creed the official doctrine of the state Church of the Roman Empire), the passage of the vernal equinox along the cord uniting the two fish in the constellation towards Pisces 2 marks a shift *away* from Christianity. In this period, heretical doctrines come into being and flourish, the Reformation and violent religious conflict begin to affect Europe (leading to the Thirty Years' War and other European wars of religion). As Christianity moves into the Renaissance age of voyage, discovery, science, and the revival of paganism, so Christianity starts to disintegrate.[27]

---

[26] Hyde, *Jung and Astrology*, p. 18.

[27] For discussion of Jung's understanding of the Zodiac in relation to the millenarian thought of Joachim of Fiore, see Riccardo Bernardini's insightful analysis of the steganographic inscription in the second panel of the nave floor in the Basilica of San Miniato al Monte (*Simboli de rinascita nella Basilica di San Miniato al Monte de Firenze: Da Gioacchino da Fiore a C.G. Jung/Rebirth Symbols in the Basilica of San Miniato al Monte in Florence: From Joachim of Fiore to C.G. Jung* (Bergamo: Moretti & Vitali, 2022), pp. 149-167).

Seen in this light, Faust as a black magician (or someone who claimed to be one), practicing the arts of astrology and soothsaying and pretending to have all kinds of academic qualifications he did not actually have, is really quite an apt figure for this age of cultural and religious upheaval. Just as, on one level, the whole Christian fish symbolism seems to have happened "fortuitously and without premeditation" (CW 9 §148), so the rise of the Faust legend in the 16th century coincides (as the vernal equinox moves along the southern edge of Pisces 2 and into the constellation of Aquarius) with the Reformation, the Renaissance, the modern age (*die Moderne*), and — ultimately — the age of Antichrist and the end of time (CW 9 §149). Here resides, in Jung's view, the "deep significance" of Goethe's *Faust*: it formulates a problem that has been (as he put it in *Transformations and Symbols of the Libido*) "turning in restless slumber since the Renaissance, just as was done by the drama of Oedipus for the Hellenic sphere of culture" (PU §141) — or, as he rephrased it in *Symbols of Transformation*, a problem that "had been brewing for centuries" (CW 5 §121) — , namely: the way out between "the Scylla of the renunciation of the world and the Charybdis of its acceptance" — as well as the way out between every other kind of opposition, including faith and knowledge, spirit and matter, good and evil.

Jung's argument as set out in *Aion* has subsequently been taken up and developed by Richard Tarnas in *Cosmos and Psyche* (2006), which presents an account of human culture structured around an apparently remarkable correspondence between planetary alignments and the archetypal patterns of history. Seen in this light, *Faust* turns out to be a paradigmatic work of art which — given the presence of Mephistopheles as Faust's shadow and as the tempter from hell who is the "spirit who always negates" — illustrates the alignment of Saturn (as the structural-limiting) and Pluto (as the biological-instinctual): a symbol of an archetypal complex associated with such themes as "harsh oppression and constraint, crime and punishment, sin and judgment, trauma and retribution, rigid control and dark consequences, intensely challenging contradictions and tensions, the depths of shadow and moral discernment."[28] Even those who are not convinced by the grand scheme of this kind of archetypal cosmology might, however, be more comfortable with Tarnas's earlier assessment in *The Passion of the Western Mind* (1991) that the "complex matrix" of the Renaissance gave rise to two "distinct streams of culture": one which emerged in the Scientific Revolution and the Enlightenment, emphasizing "rationality, empirical science, and a skeptical secularism," and another which is its "polar complement," sharing "common roots" in the Renaissance and in classical Greco-Roman culture (and in the Reformation) while tending to express "those aspects of human experience suppressed by the Enlightenment's overriding spirit of rationalism."[29] This side of the Western sensibility can be found in Jean-Jacques Rousseau, then in Goethe (as well as in Friedrich Schiller, Johann Gottfried Herder, and German Romanticism). Yet how had the Faust legend been mediated to Goethe in the first place?

The story of Faust was initially told and spread through various chapbooks, a "chapbook" being a book or a pamphlet of a popular type hawked by itinerant dealers called chapmen; the first known of these, the *Historia of Doctor Johann Faust, the infamous magician and necromancer*, was published in Frankfurt in 1587; written by an anonymous author, it is thought to be based on an earlier version which has become lost.[30] The second *Faustbuch* in a version by Georg Rudolf Widmann was published in Hamburg in 1599, the third in a version by Nikolaus Pfitzer was published in Nuremberg

---

[28] Richard Tarnas, *Cosmos and Psyche: Intimations of a New World View* (New York: Plume, 2007), pp. 273 and 268.
[29] Richard Tarnas, *The Passion of the Western Mind: Understanding the Ideas that have shaped our World View* (London: Pimlico, 1996), p. 366.
[30] See H.G. Haile (ed.), *The History of Doctor Johann Faustus* (Urbana: University of Illinois Press, 1965). This version forms the basis of Ramona Fradon's "Gnostic" reading of the Faust legend (see above, p. xxv, fn. 19).

in 1674, and the fourth, with the title *History of the universally notorious arch-necromancer and sorcerer Doctor Johann Faust, his alliance with the devil* — the version known to Goethe — was published in 1725. A translation of the first chapbook was soon published in England, and it provided the basis for the drama by Christopher Marlowe. (Marlowe's play, with its intensely dramatic concluding scene, remains for many English speakers almost as well-known, or even more well-known, than Goethe's *Faust*.)

The story was also performed as a puppet play, and it was in this form that Goethe first encountered it. As he wrote in *Dichtung und Wahrheit* (Part Two, Book 10), the biography of *Faust* "had seized my inmost heart" and "the figure of a rude, well-meaning self-helper, in a wild anarchical time, awakened my deepest sympathy":

> The significant puppet-show fable of the latter resounded and vibrated many-toned within me. I had also wandered about in all sorts of science, and had early enough been led to see its vanity. I had, moreover, tried all sorts of ways in real life, and had always returned more unsatisfied and troubled. Now these things, as well as many others, I carried about with me, and delighted myself with them during my solitary hours, but without writing anything down.[31]

(This sense of being in some way directly addressed — one might say, directly *interpellated* — by the story of Faust was also a characteristic of Jung's own response to Goethe's version, as we shall see in Chapter 3.)

---

[31] Goethe, *The Autobiography of Goethe: Truth and Poetry: From My Own Life*, trans. John Oxenford, revised edn (London: Bell, 1897), pp. 356-357.

For all its myriad variants, the basic story of Faust can be reduced to the following elements:

- Faust involves himself in the study and practice of magic
- He conjures up the Devil and concludes a pact, according to which — in return for the Devil's services — he stakes his soul
- He sets off on a series of fantastic travels and adventures, using his newly acquired magic powers, and encountering all sorts of weird and wonderful (and not so wonderful ...) people, including great historical figures
- He falls in love with Helen of Troy
- Finally, at the end of his time, Faust perishes in a strange and terrible way; and, under the terms of the pact, the Devil claims his soul.

(So runs the basic Faust legend, and the British scholar, E.M. Butler (1885-1939), identified some 50 different versions of the legend in her study, *The Fortunes of Faust*.)

It would be impossible (and otiose) to survey all these versions here, but other early treatments include a version by another Sturm und Drang writer, Friedrich von Klinger (1752-1831), *Fausts Leben, Thaten und Höllenfahrt* (1791); and a version by the Romantic poet, Nikolaus Lenau (1802-1850), *Faust: Ein Gedicht* (1836). After its publication, Goethe's *Faust* served as the basis of numerous musical settings, including Berlioz's *La Damnation de Faust* (1846); Schumann's settings of scene from both part of *Faust* (1853); Liszt's *A Faust Symphony* (1855); Gounod's opera, *Faust* (based on Part One); Arrigo Boito's opera, *Mefistofele* (1868); and Ferruccio Busoni's opera, *Doctor Faust* (1925). A memorable setting of the final scene of *Faust II* constitutes the second part of Gustav Mahler's Eighth Symphony (written in 1906 and first performed in 1910), known as the "Symphony of a Thousand" because of the enormous vocal and instrumental forces required for its performance (a bit like performing *Faust II* itself — see below). In a different musical register, the Austrian songwriter Wolfgang Ambrose wrote his own version of the Faust legend, titled *Fäustchen*.

Under the pseudonym Deutobold Symbolizetti Allegorio-witisch Mystifizinsky, the German novelist, playwright, and aesthetician Friedrich Theodor Vischer (1807-1887) published in 1862 a parody of *Faust* that claimed to be the *Third Part of the Tragedy*! Of all the modern treatments of *Faust*, however, arguably the most significant is Thomas Mann's great Modernist novel, *Doctor Faustus* (1947), a reckoning with Goethe, with Nietzsche, and with the German tradition as a whole. These great musical and literary responses to *Faust* prompt the question: What about performances of the work itself? In 1829, the first public performance of *Faust*, Part One, was put on in Brunswick, but it was not until 1876 that the first production of *Faust*, Parts One and Two, took place, directed by Otto Devrient, in Weimar. Max Reinhard's productions of *Faust* at the Salzburg Festivals between 1933 and 1937 acquired legendary status, as did Gustav Gründgens's *Faust* productions in Hamburg in 1957 to 1958. Despite Goethe's own occasional skepticism about the performability of *Faust* (see, for example, his conversations with Anton Eduard Odyniec of 29 August 1829 and with Friedrich Christoph Förster of May 1829), in 2000, the German director Peter Stein was responsible for staging the entire work at the Expo 2000 site in Hanover, organized to follow up the celebrations of the 250th birthday of Goethe in 1999. (In total, the play lasted approximately 21 hours and was performed during a marathon weekend, and over six evenings.) In addition, Stein released a CD-collection of him reading aloud *Faust II* — a bravura performance, and highly recommended to anyone wishing the experience the power of Goethe's language at first hand.[32]

---

[32] *Faust: Der Tragödie zweiter Teil*, read by Peter Stein [Bayerischer Rundfunk, 2000]. 7 CDs. Der Hörverlag. ISBN 3-89584-852-2.

Aside from Stein's performance, however, Goethe's *Faust* has been regularly performed *in its totality* at the Goetheanum in Dornach (just outside Basel in Switzerland), the center of the school of anthroposophy founded by Rudolf Steiner (1861-1925). The first uncut production of the work was performed in 1938 under the direction of Marie Steiner (*née* von Sivers), lasting almost 23 hours over a series of days, and *Faust* was subsequently performed in its totality at the Goetheanum in 1939, 1947, 1949, 1952, 1959, and 1963. Steiner himself frequently gave lectures on the interpretation of *Faust*, claiming to illuminate the work from "the standpoint of spiritual science" (1910) and examining "the problem of *Faust*" in a series of lectures given at Dornach between 1916 and 1919.[33] The Dornach productions are based on the technique called *eurythmy*, developed by Steiner as a method for use in performance art, education (at Waldorf schools), and anthroposophical medicine. (The relation between Steiner's anthroposophy and Jung's Analytical Psychology still remains a topic for future research.)[34]

As is clear from the summary above, on one level the legend of Faust is about

- theology
- knowledge
- and power

But there is another level as well, for early versions of the Faust story, both popular and poetic, demonstrate an inclination to associate Faust with another legendary figure — Don Juan, the

---

[33] See Rudolf Steiner, *Anthroposophy in the Light of Goethe's "Faust": Volume One of Spiritual-Scientific Commentaries on Goethe's "Faust"* [*Collected Works*, vol. 272], introd. Frederick Amrine, trans. Burley Channer (Hudson, NY: Steiner Books, 2014); and *Goethe's "Faust" in the Light of Anthroposophy: Volume Two of Spiritual-Scientific Commentaries on Goethe's "Faust"* [Collected Works, vol. 273], introd. Frederick Amrine, trans. Burley Channer (Hudson, NY: Steiner Books, 2016).
[34] For further discussion, see Gerhard Wehr, *Jung & Steiner: The Birth of a New Psychology* [*C.G. Jung und Rudolf Steiner: Konfrontation und Synopse*, 1990], trans. Magdalene Jaeckel (Hudson, NY: Anthroposophic Press, 2003).

famous libertine and lover of ladies. Indeed, both traditions have much in common:

- Both are heroes but, at the same time, villains
- Both are interested in occult (i.e., hidden or forbidden) knowledge
- Both are interested in the secret of *sexuality*
- Both are subject to erotic delusions and fantasies
- Both follow a trajectory from *desire* to *excess* to damnation.

(Both these legends merge in the figure of Byron, and this is why, in *Faust II*, Goethe links the traditions of Faust and Don Juan with reference to Byron in the figure of Euphorion.[35] In Greek mythology, Euphorion — whose name means "the abundant one" — was the son of Achilles and Helen, born of them in the Land of the Blessed and struck down by Zeus after an attempt to fly to heaven; in Goethe's *Faust*, Euphorion is the son of Faust and Helena, and he suffers a similarly Icaruslike fate.)

So we can discern two overarching thematic levels in *Faust*:

- Knowledge, theology, and power
- Sexuality and eroticism

Or, put even more succinctly, Faust represents the point where the esoteric meets the erotic. Of course, these two thematic levels are linked — as reflected, for instance, in the biblical expression "to know," which can mean both cognition and sexual congress. And

---

[35] For Goethe's appreciation of Byron, see, for example, his conversation with Eckermann of 5 July 1827 (Eckermann, *Conversations of Goethe*, pp. 210-211); and for the identification of Euphorion as an "allegorical being," representing "poetry personified," see his conversation of 20 December 1829 (pp. 337-338). As Benjamin Bennett has noted, the "ubiquity" of Byron in Part Two "should not surprise us": "From 1816 on, he had, in Goethe's view, more or less appropriated *Faust*, especially with his *Manfred*. See e.g. Goethe's letters to Eichstädt (4 June 1816), to Knebel (13 October 1817), to Boisserée (1 May 1818). And when Goethe writes to Wilhelm von Humboldt (22 October 1826) that the 3,000-year historical scope of Faust ends with the fall of Missolunghi, surely he is thinking more of Byron's death than of the Greek-Turkish conflict" (Benjamin Bennett, "Histrionic Nationality: Implications of the Verse in *Faust*," *Goethe Yearbook*, vol. 17 (2010), 21-30 (p. 29).

eroticism is, after all, related to power. Yet there is also a third level, linking these two other levels:

- Language

After all, language is both a means of communication for our ideas *and* an important realm for the expression of sexual desire as well. And, as we know from Lacan, the unconscious itself is "structured like a language" (*l'inconscient est structuré comme un langage*).[36]

As a result, *Faust* is full of learned references and allusions, intellectual playfulness and scholarly jokes; on one occasion, Goethe himself referred to *Faust* as *diese sehr ernsten Scherze* ("these very serious jests") and as *dieses seltsame Gebäu* ("this strange edifice").[37] (The phrase about "serious jests" is a striking one, because it seems to echo the title of the *Jocus Severus* (1617), a baroque fable which counts as Count Michael Maier's first "Rosicrucian" work.)[38] Yet arguably it is also written in places in the language of the people, with the result that, although it is one of the great "classical" works of German literature, it is also full of vigor and energy, colloquial language and even bad language and swearing. It is, as Harold Bloom says, a very strange work!

At the same time, it is a work about themes that are current today: the role of power in sexual relationships; the dynamics between men and women; transgender identities (Phorkyas!); single-parent mothers; and, above all, the desire to go on, to go

---

[36] Jacques Lacan, *The Seminar: Book XI: The Four Fundamental Concepts of Psychoanalysis, 1964*, trans. Alan Sheridan (London: Hogarth Press; Institute of Psycho-Analysis, 1977), p. 20. For further discussion, see John Gasperoni, "The Unconscious is structured like a language," *Qui Parle*, vol. 9, no. 2 (Special Issue on Lacan) (Spring/Summer 1996), 77-104; and Ross Skelton, "Is the Unconscious structured like a language?", *International Forum of Psychoanalysis*, vol. 4, no. 3 (1995), 168-178.

[37] See Goethe's letter to Wilhelm von Humboldt of 17 March 1832; Goethe, *Briefe*, ed. Karl Robert Mandelkow, 4 vols (Hamburg: Wegner, 1962-1967), vol. 4, p. 481.

[38] See Hereward Tilton, *The Quest for the Phoenix: Spiritual Alchemy and Rosicrucianism in the Work of Count Michael Maier (1569-1622)* (Berlin and New York: de Gruyter, 2003), pp. 130-139.

further, to go faster ... In this sense, then, Faust stands as an icon of the Western individual: straining and yearning toward the future, always wanting more, always believing in better ... In particular, Faust is a figure associated with modernity and with the Enlightenment, and their faith in technological solutions, and as such Faust is a culturally specific figure for an attitude that is arguably still characteristic of the West compared to other cultures. In other words, Faust is a symbol of *our* culture, and in each of us there is a part which is just like Faust.

No wonder, then, Faust is an important figure for psychoanalysis and Analytical Psychology. In "Leonardo da Vinci and a Memory of his Childhood" (1910), Freud compared Faust to Leonardo, hailing the Italian genius — the very embodiment of "Renaissance Man" — as "the Italian Faust," and describing "the possible transformation of the instinct to investigate back into an enjoyment of life" (*die mögliche Rückverwandlung des Forschertriebs in Lebenslust*) as being "fundamental in the tragedy of Faust" (SE 11, 75). Here already, Freud sounds the note of *transformation* that is, as we shall argue, central to its significance as an epic; and, in his introduction to *Transformations and Symbols of the Libido* (1911-1912), Jung cited Freud's essay on Leonardo as a methodological exemplar of his *own* study, speaking of the need to "broaden the analysis of the individual problems by a comparative study of historical materials relating to them," just as Freud, "in a masterly manner in his book on *Leonardo da Vinci*," had "already done" (PU §5).

At the same time, however, Jung seems to have been more alert than Freud was to the major shift operated by Goethe in his treatment of the Faust legend. For at the core of the original story with its pro-Christian, anti-Gnostic and anti-pagan perspective, lies the fact that, in the end, Faust is damned. It is this aspect of the "tragicall historie" of the life and death of Doctor Faustus that is so memorably portrayed in Marlowe's treatment of the story. In his final hour, Faust is confronted with the ineluctability of his fate:

Ah, Faustus,
Now hast thou but one bare hour to live,
And then thou must be damn'd perpetually!
Stand still, you ever-moving spheres of heaven,
That time may cease, and midnight never come;
Fair Nature's eye, rise, rise again, and make
Perpetual day; or let this hour be but
A year, a month, a week, a natural day,
That Faustus may repent and save his soul!
O lente, lente currite, noctis equi!
The stars move still, time runs, the clock will strike,
The devil will come, and Faustus must be damn'd.
O, I'll leap up to my God! — Who pulls me down? —
See, see, where Christ's blood streams in the firmament!
One drop would save my soul, half a drop: ah, my Christ! —
Ah, rend not my heart for naming of my Christ!
Yet will I call on him: O, spare me, Lucifer!—
Where is it now? 'tis gone: and see, where God
Stretcheth out his arm, and bends his ireful brows!
Mountains and hills, come, come, and fall on me,
And hide me from the heavy wrath of God!
No, no!
Then will I headlong run into the earth:
Earth, gape! O, no, it will not harbour me!
You stars that reign'd at my nativity,
Whose influence hath allotted death and hell,
Now draw up Faustus, like a foggy mist.
Into the entrails of yon labouring cloud[s],
That, when you vomit forth into the air,
My limbs may issue from your smoky mouths,
So that my soul may but ascend to heaven!
[*The clock strikes the half-hour.*]
Ah, half the hour is past! 'twill all be past anon

O God,
If thou wilt not have mercy on my soul,
Yet for Christ's sake, whose blood hath ransom'd me,
Impose some end to my incessant pain;
Let Faustus live in hell a thousand years,
A hundred thousand, and at last be sav'd!
O, no end is limited to damned souls!
Why wert thou not a creature wanting soul?
Or why is this immortal that thou hast?
Ah, Pythagoras' metempsychosis, were that true,
This soul should fly from me, and I be chang'd
Unto some brutish beast!
All beasts are happy, for, when they die,
Their souls are soon dissolv'd in elements;
But mine must live still to be plagu'd in hell.
Curs'd be the parents that engender'd me!
No, Faustus, curse thyself, curse Lucifer
That hath depriv'd thee of the joys of heaven.
[*The clock strikes twelve.*]
O, it strikes, it strikes! Now, body, turn to air,
Or Lucifer will bear thee quick to hell!
[*Thunder and lightning.*]
O soul, be chang'd into little water-drops,
And fall into the ocean, ne'er be found!
Enter DEVILS.

My God, my God, look not so fierce on me!
Adders and serpents, let me breathe a while!
Ugly hell, gape not! come not, Lucifer!
I'll burn my books! — Ah, Mephistophilis!
[*Exeunt DEVILS with FAUSTUS.*]

The final words belong to the Chorus, which solemnly intones the sententious message of the traditional Faust story:

Cut is the branch that might have grown full straight,
And burnèd is Apollo's laurel-bough,
That sometime grew within this learnèd man.
Faustus is gone: regard his hellish fall,
Whose fiendful fortune may exhort the wise,
Only to wonder at unlawful things,
Whose deepness doth entice such forward wits
To practise more than heavenly power permits.[1]

As Walter Kaufmann remarks, it was this "tragic ending at the price of a religious orthodoxy" that Goethe found "deeply repellent" (16). In stark contrast, in Goethe's treatment of the Faust story, there is a scandalous inversion of the outcome (so scandalous, in fact, that even Jung was shocked by it): for in Goethe's version, *Faust is saved ... redeemed ...* in other words, he is *transformed.*

---

[1] Christopher Marlowe, *The Tragical History of Doctor Faustus*, ed. Israel Gollancz (London: Dent, 1897), pp. 91-93 and 94.

Chapter 1

Goethe's *Faust*, Part One

The first part of *Faust* opens with a scene called "Night," set in a narrow, high-vaulted Gothic chamber where we see Faust sitting, restless, in his armchair by the desk. Except that it doesn't. Because this first scene is preceded by three texts which together form an introductory triptych: the poem "Dedication," the "Prelude in the Theater," and the "Prologue in Heaven," the last of which sets up a theological framework to the work as a whole.

The first of these texts, the poem "Dedication" (*Zueignung*) — not to be confused with the identically named allegorical poem,[1] written by Goethe in 1784 as an introduction to his never-completed verse epic, *The Mysteries* (*Die Geheimnisse*) — was written in 1797 when Goethe resumed his work on *Faust*. "Ye wavering phantoms, yet again my leisure / Ye haunt, as erst ye met my troubled gaze. / Still doth mine heart the old illusion treasure? / Now shall I fix the dream that round me plays? / Ye throng upon me! [...]." In these lines, Goethe addresses the ideas of his own poetic imagination, describing them as "wavering phantoms"

---

[1] See Johann Wolfgang von Goethe, *Selected Poems*, ed. Christopher Middleton [*Goethe Edition*, vol. 1] (Boston: Suhrkamp/Insel Publishers, 1983), pp. 88-95; and Goethe, *Selected Poems*, trans. John Whaley (London: Dent, 1998), pp. 48-53. For further discussion, see Paul Bishop, "Psyche and Imagination in Goethe and Jung: Or, How to Live Your Life and Love It, Too," in Susan Rowland (ed.), *Psyche and the Arts: Jungian Approaches to Music, Architecture, Literature, Painting and Film* (London and New York: Routledge, 2008), pp.107-116. For a translation and interpretation of Goethe's *Die Geheimnisse*, see Rudolf Steiner, *The Mysteries: A Poem for Christmas and Easter by J.W. v. Goethe*, trans. Marianne H. Luedeking (Great Barrington: SteinerBooks, 2014).

(*schwankende Gestalten*),[2] echoing what he says toward the end of the "Prologue in Heaven" when he addresses the "sons of God" (*Göttersöhne*) and encourages them, "In wavering apparition [*in schwankender Erscheinung*] what doth float, / Bodied in thought [*mit dauernden Gedanken*] unperishing uphold you" (ll. 348-349). In this dedicatory poem, Goethe foregrounds the part that *Faust* played in his own artistic trajectory and the *personal* dimension of the work. At the same time, the poem also highlights key ideas in the epic it introduces: the motif of rejuvenation ("My bosom by the magic breath is [youthfully = *jugendlich*] shaken, / That breathing round your train, old dreams doth waken"); the notion of life as a labyrinth ("grief again retraces / Life's labyrinthine course"); and above all, desire ("There seizes me a long unwonted yearning / For yonder silent, solemn spirit-realm") (ll. 1-5, 7-8, 13-14, 25-26).

The second text, the "Prelude in the Theater," consists of a conversation between three figures in a troupe of itinerant players: the Director, the Dramatic Poet, and the Merry Person (not quite a clown or buffoon, like the figure that jumps over the tightrope walker in the Prologue in *Thus Spoke Zarathustra*, but surely distantly related). The tone of these exchanges is essentially ironic; doubly so, given the virtual unperformability of the entirety of Goethe's *Faust*! Once again, central themes in the work itself that follows are adumbrated: for instance, the biblical motif of the strait gate (Matthew 7:13-14), when the Director asks:

Pray, how shall we contrive, that fresh and new
And weighty all may be, yet pleasing too?

---

[2] In his ETH lectures on the history of modern psychology, Jung reads this line as showing how Goethe "crossed the threshold," adding: "Here we are in the shadow land. Seldom has anyone fathomed nature so well, and seldom has anyone seen so much of the dark world as he did" (C.G. Jung, *History of Modern Psychology: Lectures Delivered at ETH Zurich, 1933-1934*, ed. Ernst Falzeder, trans. Mark Kyburz, John Peck, and Ernst Falzeder (Princeton, NJ, and Oxford: Princeton University Press, 2019), p. 135).

For of a truth the spectacle is stirring,
When to our booth in streams the people press,
And with convulsive throes and oft-recurring,
Thrust themselves through the narrow gate of grace [...].

(ll. 47-52)

This image of the strait gate or *Gnadenpforte* — full of theological resonances (Matthew 7:13-14), and frequently found in Jakob Böhme — is taken up by the Dramatic Poet and associated with the motif of transcendent creativity when he says: "Nay, lead me to that tranquil heavenly region [*zur stillen Himmelsenge*], / Where only blooms the Poet's pure delight' (ll. 63-64); and he touches on the motif of poetic timelessness: "The genuine, posterity will cherish" (*Das Echte bleibt der Nachwelt unverloren*) (l. 74). And the Merry Person touches on theme of reason and the limitations of reason, when he says: "Let Fancy lead her witching train before us, — / Reason and Passion, Sense and Sentiment; / But mark me, let not Folly fail in the chorus" (ll. 86-88). In turn, the Dramatic Poet foregrounds the deep relationship between the raw material of life and the process of poetic creativity that draws on it:

'Tis with the harmony his bosom doth conceive,
That in his heart knits up the ravelled sleave
Of this frayed world! When Nature on her spindle,
Impassive ever, twists her endless thread,
When all things clash discordant, and but kindle
Displeasure in the jarring notes they spread —
Who with the dull, monotonous flow doth mingle
Life, and doth mark it off with rhythmic swing?

(ll. 140-145)

Thus seen, the poet's craft serves as a conduit for the power of humanity itself: "Man's might it is, and in the Bard revealed!" (l.

157). The Merry Person wants to act a play that thrusts its audience into life itself, "So let us give a play, friend Poet! / Take a good handful out of human life" (ll.166-167); emphasizes the rich mixture found in such a work, "Your pictures vague — but crowd your mirror; / A spark of truth — a sea of error. / Thus is the best drink brewed, whereby / All men you will refresh and edify" (ll. 170-173); and foregrounds the theme of *Werden* or becoming: "A heart in growth with gratitude still teems" (*Ein Werdender wird immer dankbar sein*) (l. 183). Recalling his own youth (ll. 1855 ff.) and touching on a dynamic that Nietzsche would later place under the sign of Dionysos and Apollo, "Thirsting for truth [*Den Drang nach Wahrheit*], and in Illusion glad [*und die Lust am Trug*]" (l. 193), the Merry Person conjures up the motif of rejuvenation in his cry, "Ah! give me back my youth again") (l. 197). The final words of this *Vorspiel*, spoke by the Director, presciently evoke the ambitious extent and breadth of the drama that follows when, invoking the traditional metaphor of the *theatrum mundi* or the world as a theater, he says:

> Within our boarded house's narrow bound
> Mete out Creation's spacious round,
> And quickly move, yet thoughtfully as well,
> From Heaven, through the Earth, to Hell. (ll. 239-242)

If "Dedication" placed emphasis on the personal aspect, the *Vorspiel* places it on the performative and the collective dimension of the work.

Theological framework

Yet another dimension is opened up in the third introductory text, the "Prologue in Heaven," which picks up on the image in the closing words spoken by the Director of the sun and the moon (traditionally represented in German theaters on the canopy above the platform stage), describing them as "the great and little light of heaven" (l. 235), and transfers them into the realm of the cosmic or the metaphysical. For in the third of these prologetic texts we are literally in heaven, in the company of the Lord (in German, *der Herr*) and the heavenly host (i.e., the army of angels, mentioned in both the Hebrew Bible and the New Testament, that accompanies Yahweh or Elohim). As the three archangels, belonging to the highest rank of angel, step forward, one of them, Raphael, describes the path of the sun, "The sun, with many a sister-sphere, / Still sings the rival psalm of wonder, / And still his fore-ordained career / Accomplishes, with tread of thunder" (ll. 243-246), thus evoking the Pythagorean notion of the music or harmony of the spheres (*musica universalis*) as well as the biblical line from God's address out of the whirlwind in the biblical Book of Job, "When the morning stars praised me together, and all the sons of God made a joyful melody" (Job 38:7). And the echo of Job is not accidental, for this entire Prologue in Heaven is strongly reminiscent of the premise of the Book of Job: namely, that God and the Devil talk to each other.

The Book of Job can fairly be described as the "literary masterpiece" of the wisdom movement, a form of literature that flourished throughout the ancient East and is reflected in five books in the Ketuvim ("Writings") section of the Hebrew Bible or the Old Testament: Job, Proverbs, Ecclesiastes (or Qoheleth), Ecclesiasticus (or Ben Sira), and Wisdom (NJB, OT, 753 and 749).[3] The Book of Job opens with a prose narrative that recounts how Job, a rich and happy man as well as a faithful servant of God, is allowed by God to be tested by Satan to see if, amid misfortune, he

---

[3] For further discussion, see Robert Alter, *The Wisdom Books: Job, Proverbs, and Ecclesiastes: A Translation with Commentary* (New York and London: Norton, 2010); and Katharine J. Dell, Suzanna R. Millar, and Arthur Jan Keefer (eds), *The Cambridge Companion to Biblical Wisdom Literature* (Cambridge: Cambridge University Press, 2022).

will remain faithful. (The Hebrew term *śāṭān* means "accuser" or "adversary"; in Goethe's version, the role of Satan is occupied by Mephistopheles, a figure closely associated with the Faust legend and whose name has been variously interpreted as meaning: (a) someone who does not love the light [*mē* = not + φίλος, i.e., *philos* = love + φῶς, φωτός, i.e., *phōs, photós* = light]; (b) someone who does not love Faust [*mē* = not + *philos* = love + φως το, i.e., *phosto* = Faust]; (c) someone who loves the stench of the earth [*mephitis* = poisonous vapors rising from the earth + *philos* = love].) In its commentary on the biblical figure of Satan, the NJB describes him as an "equivocal figure, distinct from the sons of God" — i.e., the angels, as the Septuagint expresses it — "sceptical as regards human beings, anxious to find fault in them, capable of unleashing all sorts of disaster on them and even of impelling them into sin" (NJB, OT, 757). It adds that, "behind the cynicism and cold, malicious sarcasm" — qualities shared with Goethe's Mephistopheles — there "lurks a pessimistic being, whose hostility to human beings is based on envy" (757).

As in the Book of Job, where Yahweh singles out Job for special mention to Satan, in the "Prologue in Heaven" it is the Lord who draws the attention of Mephistopheles to Faust, his "servant" (*Knecht*). Whereas the biblical Job is said by Satan to serve God because of his wealth and his good health, Goethe's Faust is said by Mephistopheles to serve the Lord in an unusual way: namely, through his almost fanatical thirst for knowledge. The Lord responds to this by conceding, "Though now his service be as a tangled skein, / Yet will I lead him soon to perfect vision" (*Wenn er mir jetzt auch nur verworren dient, / So werd ich ihn bald in die Klarheit führen*) (ll. 308-309). Indeed, the Lord goes so far as to declare as a maxim, "Whilst still man strives, still must he stray" (*Er irrt der Mensch, solang er strebt*), thus introducing the notion of driving (*Streben*) and giving expression to the Goethean doctrine of the beneficial aspect of error: "Error is related to truth as sleep to waking. I have observed that on awakening from error a man turns again to truth as with new vigour" (*Maxims and Reflections*, §391). Or as the Lord Himself says in another aphoristic formulation, "That a good man, by his dim impulse driven, / Of the right way hath ever consciousness" (*Ein guter Mensch in seinem dunklen Drange / Ist sich des rechten Wesens wohl bewußt*) (ll. 328-329).

And as in the Book of Job, where Satan is permitted by Yahweh to destroy his livestock, his servants, and even members of his family, so Mephistopheles is permitted by the Lord to tempt Faust; in fact, Mephistopheles and the Lord embark on a wager — on a contractual arrangement that anticipates the wager that Mephistopheles will conclude with Faust: "What will you wager? Give me but permission / To lead him gently on my way, / I'll win him from you to perdition" (ll. 312-314). Not only does the Lord give Mephistopheles free license (or at least license to appear to be free: *Du darfst auch da nur frei erscheinen*) (l. 336),[4] He even admits to a kind of affection for Mephisto: "Of all the Spirits of Denial [*Von allen Geistern, die verneinen*], / Irks Me the least the mischievous buffoon [*der Schalk*]" (ll. 337-339). Whereas in *Thus Spoke Zarathustra* the clown or buffoon appears as a sinister, even dangerous (or, in Jungian terms, tricksterish) figure, in Goethe's universe there is, it seems, still room for him. In fact, the Lord goes on to articulate another Goethean doctrine: namely, that there is a functional reason for evil to exist in the world:

> Man's efforts lightly flag, and seek too low a level.
> Soon doth he pine for all-untrammelled sloth.
> Wherefore a mate I give him, nothing loth,
> Who spurs, and shapes and must create though Devil.
>   (ll. 340-343)

---

[4] In this line, as in its counterpart in the concluding scene of Part Two (l. 12104-12105), much depends on the meaning of this deceptively simple little word — *nur*, which is used both as a scalar particle with a restrictive sense and as a modal particle with an intensifying sense.

(Or, in the discourse of anthroposophy, "in Goethe's Mephistopheles, the two different kinds of qualities, Luciferic and Ahrimanic, are mingled.").[5]

It is this conception of evil that not only Jung found shocking (see MDR, 78-79). As Peter Kreeft has realized, Goethe has taken the traditional moral story of Faust and turned it 180 degrees: Whereas the story was traditionally a cautionary tale about damnation, an exploration of the question, "For what shall it profit a man, if he gain the whole world, and suffer the loss of his soul?" (Mark 8:36), in Goethe's version the whole point and purpose of the story is turned into its opposite, for Faust is "not damned at all but enlightened [...] not punished but rewarded for disobeying the moral law."[6]

In the concluding words of the Lord, before the heavens close and the archangels disperse, evoke two central themes of *Faust* — beauty and becoming:

> But ye, God's sons in love and duty,
> Rejoice ye in the living wealth of beauty.
> Eternal Growth, that works and faileth not,
> Within Love's golden bars ever enfold you.
>
> (ll. 344-347)

The final lines, "In wavering apparition what doth float, / Bodied in thought unperishing uphold you" (*Und was in schwankender*

---

[5] Rudolf Steiner, *Goethe's Standard of the Soul* [*Goethes Geistesart in ihrer Offenbarung durch seinen Faust und durch das Märchen von der Schlange und der Lilie*, 1918], trans. D.S. Osmond (New York: Anthroposophic Press, 1925), p. 40.

[6] Peter Kreeft, *The Platonic Tradition* (South Bend, IN: St Augustine's Press, 2018), p. 103. For further discussion, see Alan P. Cottrell, *Goethe's View of Evil: and the Search for a New Image of Man in our Time* (Edinburgh: Floris Books, 1982); and John Whiton, "Reading Goethe's *Faust* from a Catholic Perspective," *Faith & Reason: The Journal of Christendom College*, vol. 22, nos. 1-2 (Spring-Summer 1996), 1-6.

Erscheinung schwebt, / Befestiget mit dauernden Gedanken) (ll. 348-349), articulates a position that would evolve into the insight of the Chorus Mysticus at the end of Part Two.[7] And in a final ironic flourish, Mephistopheles mutters to himself: "I like to see the Ancient now and then, / And shun a breach, for truly 'tis most civil / In such a mighty personage, to deign / To chat so affably, e'en with the very Devil" (ll. 350-353). Leaving this joke aside, however, we should note (as M.H. Abrams has done) that "the compulsion to Faust's spiritual and geographical journey is objectified as a person who represents the 'great drivewheels' of *Polarität* and *Steigerung*" — in themselves, Hermetic and alchemical terms — "which are Goethe's version of the contrariety and sublimation in the dialectic of his philosophical contemporaries" (and, specifically, in F.W.J. Schelling and in G.W.F. Hegel).[8]

The "Prologue in Heaven" thus creates a theological framework that governs the work as a whole and finds its corresponding scene at the end of the work in the "Mountain Gorges" scene with which *Faust II* concludes. Now how seriously are we to take this framework? On the one hand, the ironic and parodic tone of the "Prologue in Heaven" (and, *mutatis mutandis*, the "Mountain Gorges" scene) is not to be overlooked. On the other, the "Prologue" makes a serious metaphysical and psychological point, as commentators from Jung to Peter Kreeft have realized. For his part, Jung wrote that in Goethe's *Faust* he had at last found confirmation that "there were or had been people who saw evil and

---

[7] Or as Steiner puts it, "Goethe, as a young man, could not of course realise that in the course of his life he would rise to the conception which at the end of *Faust* in the 'Chorus Mysticus' he was able to express [...]," for "at the end of Goethe's life the Eternal element in existence [*was im Dasein ewig ist*] was revealed to him in a sense other than he could have dreamed in 1797, when he allows the Lord to speak to the Archangels of this Eternal element [*dieses Ewige*] [...]" (*Goethe's Standard of the Soul*, p. 5).

[8] M.H. Abrams, *Natural Supernaturalism: Tradition and Revolution in Romantic Literature* (New York and London: Norton, 1973), p. 244.

its universal power, and — more important — the mysterious role it played in delivering humankind from darkness and suffering"; and so, in Jung's eyes, Goethe became "a prophet" (MDR, 78-79). For his part, Kreeft emphasizes the epochal significance in the shift made by Goethe between the moral and religious lesson of the moral story of Faust, the man who sold his soul to the Devil, and his own antitraditional, antimoral retelling:

> [Goethe] sided with the devil, or the devil in Faust; Faust incorporates his own devil as well as his God, Faust accepts evil as well as good, he is told that he must become "better *and more evil*" [cf. *Zarathustra*, "The Convalescent"], and the true God turns out to be not the Judeo-Christian God but [...] half evil and half good. [...] In *Faust* God and the Devil turn out to be allies, because they both move Faust up the ladder of enlightenment and maturity and away from his earlier moralistic innocence. (103)

Despite the fact that he is not a Germanist (or perhaps rather *because* he is not one), Kreeft realizes the full significance of the change Goethe made to the traditional tale. Noting the proximity between Goethe's outlook and Nietzsche's later motto of going "beyond good and evil," Kreeft goes on to say that Goethe shows us "the world where heaven and hell, God and the devil, good and evil, are ultimately one" — a world which is, in Kreeft's assessment, "the most Nihilistic world of all because there is no ultimate choice [...] and no ultimate tragedy of meaninglessness [...], and therefore no ultimate drama in life" (103-104). And here Kreeft touches on an important aspect of Goethe's work, for "even though *Faust* is a great drama literarily, ultimately there *is* no drama in life if Goethe's worldview is true because there is no real difference between heaven and hell, good and evil" (104).[9] Against this view, one might argue that, although *Faust* does not involve the dramatic choice between good and evil, it exemplifies and embodies a different kind of drama — the drama of self-transformation, of "becoming" (in Nietzsche's words) "who one is."

The evident parallels between the "Prologue in Heaven" and the Book of Job might prompt us to consider more carefully the importance of the figure of Job for Jung. In the recollection of Jung's school days in *Memories, Dreams, Reflections*, his reflections on the role of the secret in his younger years conclude by recalling that the "conventional 'edifying' interpretation" of Job had prevented him from taking a deeper interest in this book; a missed opportunity, he concludes, inasmuch as he would have found "consolation" in it, especially in such lines as "If I be washed, as it were, with snow-waters [...]: Yet thou shalt plunge me in filth" (9:30-31), a passage which inverts the traditional topos that it is God who purifies the sinner and instead imagines Him as plunging the sinner "into the mire" (or, in Greek, "into the dung"; in Hebrew, "into the pit") (MDR, 59).

In *Memories, Dreams, Reflections*, our attention is drawn to two works in which the theme of Job is prominent. In 1951, Jung published *Aion*, giving his study as a subtitle "Researches into the Phenomenology of the Self." The theme of this work, as Jung himself explained in his foreword, was an investigation of the idea of the Aeon (i.e., Αἰών = *aion*), and specifically the "change of psychic situation" in the Christian aeon as reflected in Christian, Gnostic, and alchemical symbols of the self. In Hellenistic religion, Aion is a deity associated with cyclical time (as opposed to the linear, historical time associated with Chronos), but within various Gnostic systems the term Aion is associated with certain

---

[9] Kreeft expands this point into a general cultural observation, suggesting that "only cultures that have believed in the great choice between some kind of heaven and hell have produced great drama," which explains why the West, rooted in classical and Judeo-Christian thinking, has produced so much greater drama than the East (104).

emanations from God leading to the creation of the phenomenal world. On some accounts, the first Aion is the source of all being, within which another inner being, Ennoia (ἔννοια, i.e., "thought") dwells, thus dividing the perfect being and conceiving a second Aion, Nous (νοῦς, i.e., "mind"). Further hierarchies of Aions are produced, constituting the noumenal or intelligible world known as the Pleroma (i.e., "fullness"), and below which lies the material world known as the Creatura. (This Gnostic cosmology informs the sermons of Philemon, known as the *Septem Sermones ad mortuos*, as found in *The Red Book*.)

From its inception, Jung argues, the Christian tradition was not only strongly influenced by Persian and Jewish notions about a beginning and end of time but envisaged "a kind of enantiodromian reversal of dominants" — or, in other words, the problem of Christ and Antichrist. Here is the point of contact with the astrological symbolism of the two fishes discussed above (pp. xxvii-xxx), or Jung's description of the Pieces aeon as "the synchronistic concomitant of two thousand years of Christian development" (CW 9/ii p. ix). On this account, there is a significant coincidence between the astrological conception of the "Platonic month" of the Fishes and the end of the Christian aeon in the form of the appearance of the Antichrist and the Second Coming.

In Chapter 5 of *Aion*, Jung returned to the problem of the Antichrist and described it as a "hard nut to crack" for anyone who had a positive attitude toward Christianity (CW 9/ii §77). As late as the Book of Job, he observes, the Devil was "still one of God's sons and on familiar terms with Yahweh," referring for further discussion of this topic to the study by one of his followers, Rivkah Schärf Kluger (1907-1987), titled "The Figure of Satan in the Old Testament" (1953).[10] It was only with the rise of Christianity, Jung

---

[10] See Rivkah Schärf, "Die Gestalt des Satans im Alten Testament," in C.G. Jung, *Symbolik des Geistes* (Zurich: Rascher, 1953), pp. 151-319; and Rivkah Schärf Kluger, *Satan in the Old Testament*, trans. Hildegard Nagel (Evanston, IL: Northwestern University Press, 1967).

noted, that the Devil attained his "true stature" as "the adversary of Christ, and hence of God" (§77). Yet Jung made clear that he was approaching the problem not *theologically*, but *psychologically*: Beside the "sublime and spotless" dogmatic figure of Christ, everything else "turns dark" (§77). In fact, this very one-sided perfection is said to demand "a psychic complement to restore the balance" (§77). And this "inevitable opposition" is said to have led to the doctrine (espoused, for instance, by the Gnostic sect known as the Bogomils) that there were in fact two sons of God, Jesus and an elder son called Satanaël (§77). Seen in this light, the coming of the Antichrist is "not just a prophetic prediction," but rather "an inexorable psychological law" — a law whose existence, even if not known to the author of the Epistles attributed to John, nevertheless brought him "a sure knowledge of the impending enantiodromia" (§77). In Jung's view, there was a clear correlation between "every intensified differentiation of the Christ-image" and its "corresponding accentuation of its unconscious complement," a dynamic that brought about an ever-increasing tension between "above and below" (§77).

According to Jung, it is thus "in accordance with psychological law" (and not through the "obscure workings of chance") that the "Christian disposition [...] leads inevitably to a reversal of its spirit" (CW 9/i §78). This clash between, on the one hand, "the ideal of spirituality striving for the heights" and, on the other, "the materialistic earth-bound passion to conquer matter and master the world" (§77) — or, in Jung's words elsewhere, "the Scylla of the renunciation of the world and the Charybdis of its acceptance" (PU §141; cf. CW 5 §121) — emerged in the Renaissance, that is, in the age of Faust, and is reflected in the architecture of the time: in the shift from the vertical, Gothic style to a horizontal perspective (voyages of discovery, exploration of the world and of nature) (CW 9/ii §78). Following on the Renaissance came the Enlightenment and the French Revolution, paving the way to our own "antichristian" time — or "end of time." Thus, with the coming of Christ, those "opposites" that had hitherto been *latent* now became *manifest*; and, alluding to the words of Nietzsche's Zarathustra, "But it is the same with man as with the tree. / The more he seeketh to rise into the height and light, the more vigorously do his roots struggle earthward, downward, into the dark and deep — into the evil" (Z I 8), Jung concludes that "the double meaning of this movement lies in the nature of the pendulum": Christ is "without spot, but right at the beginning of his career" — namely, in his temptation in the desert — there occurs "the encounter with Satan, the Adversary, who represents the counterpole of that tremendous tension in the world psyche which Christ's advent signified" (§78).

In Jung's eyes, Christ is "our nearest analogy of the self" (CW 9/i §79). And yet it is in some ways an imperfect analogy, for although such attributes as consubstantiality with the Father, coeternity, filiation, parthenogenesis, crucifixion, being a lamb sacrificed between opposites, being One divided into Many, etc., are said to mark Christ out as an "embodiment of the self," he nevertheless corresponds to "only one half of the archetype," the other half of which appears as the Antichrist, the manifestation of the "dark aspect" of the self. Hence *both* are "Christian symbols," which tells us the same thing as we are told by the image of the Savior crucified between the two thieves: namely, that "the progressive development and differentiation of consciousness leads to an ever more menacing awareness of the conflict" — i.e., of the opposites — "and involves nothing less than a crucifixion of the ego, its agonizing suspension between irreconcilable opposites" (§79). On this point, Jung quotes no less an authority than Origen: "It was proper, moreover, that the one of these extremes, and the best of the two, should be styled the Son of God, on account of His pre-eminence; and the other, who is diametrically opposite, be termed the son of the wicked demon, and of Satan, and of the devil" (*Contra Celsum*, Book 6, §45). And later in *The Red Book*, the crucifixion of the self becomes one of the great symbols in that work (RB, 197-198 and 388-389).

Thus, on Jung's account the figure of Christ, as the Christian "image of the self," is in an important respect fundamentally *lacking*, for it "lacks the shadow that properly belongs to it" (and this is Jung's quarrel with the theological doctrine of the *summum bonum*) (CW 9/i §79-§80). In *Memories, Dreams, Reflections,* Jung describes Job as "a kind of prefiguration of Christ," the link between the two figures being "the idea of suffering" (MDR, 243). Just as Christ was the "suffering servant" of God, so too was Job, and in the case of Christ the cause of his suffering is said to be the sins of the world: But who is really responsible for these sins? "In the final analysis," it is argued, the responsibility rests with God, for He "created the world and its sins, [...] and therefore became Christ in order to suffer the fate of humanity" (242). In *Aion,* Jung refers to "the bright and dark side" of the divine image, to the notion of the "wrath of God," to the commandment to "fear God," and to the petition in the Lord's Prayer (recently revised by Pope Francis), "And lead us not into temptation" (or "Do not let us fall into temptation") (243). Here lies the link between Jung's thought and the Book of Job — and its "ambivalent God-image," for Job "expects that God will, in a sense, stand by him against God," and in this expression ("with God ... against God") we have "a picture of God's tragic contradictoriness" (243). Yet here, too, lies a link to Goethe's *Faust,* and to the wager struck between the Lord and Mephistopheles in the "Prologue in Heaven"; to Mephistopheles as the shadow-side of Faust himself; and to the frankly post-Christian notion of redemption in the work, according to which Faust, for all the suffering he has caused — especially to Gretchen in Part One and to Philemon and Baucis in Part Two — is, in the end, redeemed.

This theme of the tragic contradictoriness is taken up, as Jung points out in *Memories, Dreams, Reflections*, in 1952 in *Answer to Job* (MDR, 243). In this work, which evidently constitutes a response to the biblical book, Jung applies the Gnostic model of fissure and emanation to what he calls the "Christian myth of salvation."[11] As the Creator is whole, so is His creature — His son — whole, but within that wholeness a splitting ensued, and a realm of light and a realm of darkness emerged (MDR, 365). On Jung's account, this development had been prefigured in the sixth century B.C.E. in the experience described in the Book of Job and in the third or second centuries B.C.E. in the apocryphal Book of Enoch, part of which (the so-called Book of Parables) belongs to immediate pre-Christian times. In Christianity, this metaphysical split had come to the fore, with the result that Satan, previously part of the immediate entourage of Yahweh, now turned into His diametrical opposite (MDR, 365). Not surprisingly, the view emerged at the beginning of the 11th century that it was not God, but the Devil, who had created the world — as the medieval Cathars are said to have believed (CW 9/ii §225-§226). This view is said to have sounded the keynote for the second Christian millennium (i.e., the second half of the Christian aeon); and the essentially paradoxical nature of the God-image is captured by the "visionary genius" of Jakob Böhme (1575-1624) in his mandala found in his *XL Questions concerning the Soule* (1620). In the English translation of this mandala, titled "The Philosophical Globe, or Eye of the Wonders of Eternity," an outer circle contains the quaternity of *Father*, *Holy Ghost*, *Sonne*, and *Earth*, while the inner circle is divided into two semicircles standing back-to-back rather than closing (MDR, 366; CW 9/i §534, **Fig. 1**).

---

[11] For further discussion, see Paul Bishop, *Jung's "Answer to Job": A Commentary* (Hove and New York: Brunner-Routledge, 2002).

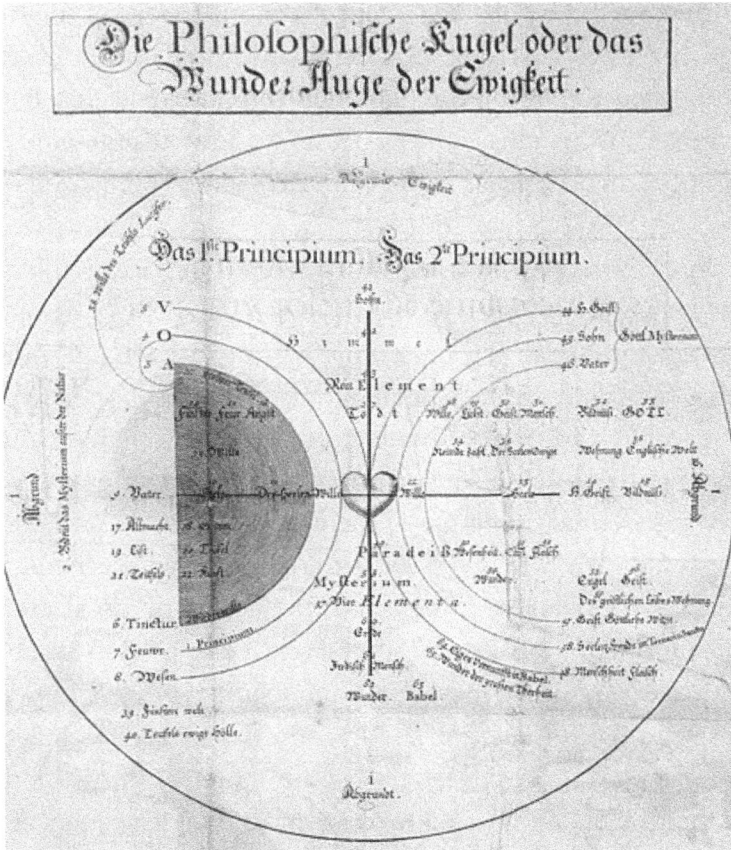

Figure 1: Böhme's mandala. Image in the public domain.

If, as Jung had argued in *Aion*, the appearance of Christ had coincided with the beginning of a new aeon, the age of the Fishes, the constellation under which the next aeon would stand is Aquarius, coinciding with the time when the *complexio oppositorum* of the God-image enters into humankind — not as unity but as conflict, as the dark half of the image (as represented in Böhme's diagram) comes into opposition with the conventional Christian view that "God is Light" (MDR, 366) — a key idea in the New Testament, reflected in the First Letter of John, "God is light, and in him there is no darkness" (1 John 1:5), and a central theme in Wolfram's *Parzival*, where Trevrizent tells Parzival in Book 9 how Plato and the Sibyl had foretold the redemption to come, and that Parzival must repent of his sins — "For He is a Light all-lightening, and never His faith doth cease" (§465, l. 19-28 and §466, ll. 1-4; vol. 1, pp. 268) (MDR, 248 and 366).

In *Memories, Dreams, Reflections*, Jung says that this process was *taking place in his own time*; and, if so, it must be taking place *a fortiori* in our own. One might even call our own age the Faustian age, inasmuch as the theological framework of Goethe's drama apparently encompasses a shift from the traditional Judeo-Christian view of the opening "Prologue in Heaven" to the mysterious Eternal Feminine of the concluding scene in Part Two. At the center of *Faust* (with its "Prologue in Heaven") and at the center of *Answer to Job* alike stands the notion of transformation: the transformation of Faust from his service to God in an obscure or confused way (*verworren dient*) into clarity (*in die Klarheit*) (ll. 308-309) in the former, and the transformation of the God-image and of humankind in the latter — "the future birth of the divine child" or "the metaphysical process [...] known to the psychology of the unconscious as the individuation process" (CW 11 §755), the transformation of God into humankind and of humankind into God. The former ends with the Eternal Feminine who *zieht uns heran* ("draws us onward and upward"), the latter with an evocation of "the One who dwells within [...], whose form has no knowable boundaries, who encompasses [us] on all sides, fathomless as the abysms of the earth and vast as the sky" (CW 11 §758).

Faust I

After these three prologetic texts, the drama itself begins, as we have said, with Faust seated in his armchair by the desk in his study, a narrow, high-vaulted Gothic chamber. He is experiencing what one could fairly describe as a midlife crisis, realizing that all his studies — "Philosophy, / And Jurisprudence, and Medicine too, / And saddest of all, Theology" — have got him nowhere: "And here I stick, as wise, poor fool, / As when my steps first turned to school" (ll. 353-355 and 358-359). His chief insight is a nihilistic one: "And know that in truth we can know — naught!" (l. 364). Faust's ignorance is a kind of anti-Socratic ignorance: realizing as Socrates does that he knows nothing,[12] Faust does not draw the Socratic conclusion that one must use the path of philosophical dialectic to attain the Idea of the Good.

(In this respect, Faust's dilemma is at once a personal and a universal one: Here, in the middle of the Enlightenment, a warning is sounded that Enlightenment might, as Max Horkheimer and Theodor W. Adorno were later to show, contain another kind of dialectic — one that would undermine Enlightenment and turn it (back) into myth.[13] Equally, within the anthroposophical tradition, Faust — and, through him, Goethe — are seen as crying — much as Heidegger in *What Is Thinking?* saw Nietzsche in the poem "The desert grows ..." as crying —[14] "for the sources of life:" "It is also the cry [*der Schrei*] of a contemporary humankind which still fully deserves this name, which has not anaesthetized its humanity through the noise of the machines and the pressure of soul-destroying mechanics," and which "should perceive again this cry in poetry in its shattering force, let it stir things up inside it, react

---

[12] See Richard Bett, "Socratic Ignorance," in Donald R. Morrison (ed.), *The Cambridge Companion to Socrates* (Cambridge and New York: Cambridge University Press, 2010), pp. 215-236.

[13] "Just as myths already entail enlightenment, with every step enlightenment entangles itself more deeply in mythology" (Theodor W. Adorno and Max Horkheimer, *Dialectic of Enlightenment: Philosophical Fragments* [1947], ed. Gunzelin Schmid Noerr, trans. Edmund Jephcott (Stanford, CA: Stanford University Press, 2002), p. 8).

[14] Martin Heidegger, *What Is Called Thinking?* [1951/1952], trans. J. Glenn Gray (New York: Harper & Row, 1968), pp. 48-49.

to it."[15] And as Jung remarks in "Individual Dream Symbolism in Relation to Alchemy," the "skull soliloquies" of Faust and Hamlet alike are "reminders of the appalling senselessness of human life when 'sicklied o'er with the pale cast of thought'" [CW 12 §108].)

And yet Faust's thirst for knowledge remains unquenched; and so, in order to satisfy this epistemological thirst, he has had recourse — as Jung, in his *Red Book*, will also — to magic (*Magie*):

> So I've turned me to magic in my need,
> If haply spirit-power and speech
> May many a hidden mystery teach,
> That I with bitter labour so
> No more need say what I do not know;
> That I the mighty inmost tether
> May know, that binds the world together
> [*Daß ich erkenne, was die Welt*
> *Im Innersten zusammenhält*];[16]
> All germs, all forces that lifewards struggle,
> And with vain words no longer juggle.
>
> (ll. 377-385)[17]

---

[15] Marie Steiner, "Vorwort" [1931], in Rudolf Steiner, *Geisteswissenschaftliche Erläuterungen zu Goethes «Faust»*, 2 vols (Dornach: Rudolf Steiner Verlag, 1982), vol. 1, p. 10.

[16] This phrase appears to echo the Breviary hymn for None ascribed to St. Ambrose, *Rerum, Deus, tenax vigor*, and its opening lines in German translation, *Du starker Gott, der diese Welt / im Innersten zusammenhält, / du Angelpunkt, der unbewegt / den Wandel aller Zeiten trägt* ("O Strength and Stay upholding all creation, / Whoever dost Thyself unmoved abide"); in reality, however, it more likely shows how Goethe's language has itself acquired an almost sacral dimension.

[17] In these words, Faust expresses a fundamentally Platonic view of the world, as found in the *Statesman* and the *Philebus* and their emphasis on measure, limit, and proportion as essentials of goodness and *kālos*, and summarized by W.K.C. Guthrie as follows: "The cosmos, though not perfect, is the best and most lasting of all created living things. It cannot therefore have been thrown together haphazard, but was planned as an organism in which the various components *are blended with the most exquisite delicacy and prevision*" (*A History of Greek Philosophy*, vol. 5, *The Later Plato and the Academy* (Cambridge: Cambridge University Press, 1978),

Faust's impassioned cry recapitulates the warning issued by the alchemists, namely: "Rend the books, lest your hearts be rent asunder" (*Rumpite libros, ne corda vestra rumpantur*), and glossed by Jung in his "Epilogue" to *Psychology and Alchemy* as follows: "Not for nothing did alchemy style itself an 'art' [*»Kunst«*], feeling — and rightly so — that it was concerned with creative processes [*Gestaltungsvorgänge*] that can be truly grasped only by experience [*im Erleben*], even if intellect can give them a name. [...] It is experience [*das Erlebnis*] that brings us close to understanding [*Verstehen*]" (CW 12 §564). In fact, Faust is searching for the kind of knowledge which, for Jung, can be indexed to the name of Paracelsus: namely, a knowledge to which one can only accede if one "opens wide the eyes of the soul and the spirit [*die Augen der Seele und des Geistes*] and observes and recognizes by means of the inner light [*mit dem inneren Lichte*]," a light which from the beginning God has lit "in nature as well as in our hearts" (CW 12 §431).[18]

Precisely what kind of magic Faust is trying to use is, however, unclear; there are echoes of Nostradamus in the reference to "this book of mystic Gramarye, / The work of Nostradamus' hand," of Swedenborg in the reference to the sign of the Macrocosm, and of Böhme's *Morgenröte im Aufgang* in the lines, "The spirit-world shuts not its portal; / Thine heart is dead, thy senses sleep; / Up! in the crimson dayspring, mortal, / All undismayed, thy bosom steep!"

---

pp. 277-278). If, in the *Timaeus*, cosmic and wholeness and unity are achieved by proportionate blending of all its components in bonds of amity or φιλία (32d-33a), in the *Phaedo* Socrates seeks an explanation of the cosmos which can demonstrate how it is held together by the power of the good and right (99c) (ibid., 278).

[18] Or in Goethean terms, we learn to see "with the eyes of the spirit" (*mit Augen des Geistes sehen*) (*On Morphology*) or to see with "spirit-eyes" (*Geistes-Augen*) ("A Few Remarks"), using a terminology found in Johann Gottlieb Fichte, Leonardo da Vinci, St Augustine, and St Ambrose. For further discussion, see Paul Bishop, *Analytical Psychology and German Classical Aesthetics*, vol. 2, *The Constellation of the Self* (London and New York: Routledge, 2009), pp. 34-36 and 45-47.

(ll. 443-446).[19] Whichever kind of magic he is trying to use, Faust finds himself unable to overcome his sense of profound alienation from nature:

> A glorious pageant! yet a pageant merely!
> Thou boundless Nature, where shall I grasp thee clearly?[20]
> Where you, ye breasts, founts of all life that fail not,
> At which both Heaven and Earth are nursed?
> For ye the withered breast doth thirst —
> Ye well, ye slake, I faint, yet ye avail not!
>   (ll. 454-459)

And then — he sees the sign of the Earth Spirit, and suddenly everything looks different:

> Full-steeled to tread the world I feel my mettle,
> Earth's woe, Earth's bliss, my soul can not unsettle,

---

[19] For further discussion of the sign of the Macrocosm and its function, see Neil M. Flax, "The Presence of the Sign in Goethe's *Faust*," *Publications of the Modern Languages Association*, vol. 98, no. 2 (March 1983), 183-203. For Rudolf Steiner, the sign of the Macrocosm is "a sense picture of the Universe, — a picture of the sun itself, of the earth in connection with the other planets of the solar system, and of the activity of the single heavenly bodies as a revelation of the Divine Being guiding movement and reciprocal interplay": "This is not a mechanical heaven, but a cosmic weaving of spiritual hierarchies whose effluence is the life of the world. Into this life man is placed, and he comes forth as the apotheosis of the work of all these Beings. Faust, however, cannot find in his soul the experience for which he is seeking even in the vision of this universal harmony. We can sense the yearning that gnaws in the depths of this soul: 'How do I become Man in the true sense of the word?' The soul longs to experience what makes man consciously truly Man. In the sense image hovering there, the soul cannot call up from the depths of being that profound experience which would make it able to realise itself as the epitome of all that is there as the sign of the macrocosm. For this is the "knowledge" that can be transformed through intense inner experience, into 'Self-Knowledge'" (Steiner, *Goethe's Standard of the Soul*, pp. 33-34).

[20] In his ETH lectures on the history of modern psychology, Jung uses this line to express the idea that we are "at a loss" fully to understand Goethe, adding: "Here one actually does not know where to set the highest point. His light has shone on the whole *orbis terrarum*" (Jung, *History of Modern Psychology*, p. 134).

I would not blench with storms to battle,
Nor quail amidst the shipwreck's crash and rattle! —

(ll. 464-467)

When he conjures up the Earth Spirit itself, however, things do not go entirely to plan. True, the Earth Spirit conjures up a vision of the world as a place of *becoming*, "In floods of being, in action's storm, / Up and down I wave, / To and fro I flee, / Birth and the grave, / An infinite sea, / A changeful weaving, / An ardent living; / The ringing loom of Time is my care, / And I weave God's living garment there" (ll. 501-507), echoing (as Rudolf Steiner points out) the "all-embracing conception of Nature" which we find in a fragmentary prose poem attributed to Goethe (but probably written by Georg Christoph Tobler),[21] but the Spirit also mocks Faust, asking him, "What mortal dread, thou man of more than mortal essence, / Gets hold on thee? Where now the outcry of thy soul?" (ll. 489-490. By the word translated here as "man of more than mortal essence" there is introduced into the discourse of German thought a key term to which Nietzsche will later attach such importance — *Übermensch*.[22] Dismissing Faust's claim to be his equal, the Earth

---

[21] See "Nature," in *Scientific Studies*, ed. and trans. Douglas Miller [Goethe Edition, vol. 12] (New York: Suhrkamp Publishers, 1988), pp. 3-5; cf. Steiner, *Goethe's Standard of the Soul*, p. 9.

[22] For further discussion of this term, which reaches back to the early Christian notion of the *super humanus* or *super homines* as an expression for the "exalted" and perfected individual and beyond to the *hyperanthropos* of Lucian of Samosata's dialogue *The Journey to the Underworld or The Tyrant* and to other classical sources, see Katharina Grätz, *Kommentar zu Nietzsches "Also sprach Zarathustra" I und II* [NK, vol. 4/1] (Berlin and Boston: de Gruyter, 2024), pp. 121-126; Ernst Benz (ed.), *Der Übermensch: Eine Diskussion* (Zurich and Stuttgart: Rhein-Verlag, 1961); Volker Gerhardt, "Übermensch," in Joachim Ritter, Karlfried Gründer, and Gottfried Gabriel (eds), *Historisches Wörterbuch der Philosophie*, vol. 11 (Basel: Schwabe, 2001), cols. 46-50; and Babette Babich, "Nietzsche's Zarathustra and Parodic Style: On Lucian's *Hyperanthropos* and Nietzsche's *Übermensch*," *Diogenes*, vol. 58, no. 4 (2012), 58-74). Other important (and Goethean) sources for Nietzsche's idea of the *Übermensch* are his allegorical poem "Dedication" (*Zueignung*) and its line, "So glaubst du dich schon Übermensch genug" ("You think you are some sort of

Spirit describes Faust as being "a timorous, writhing worm" (l. 498) and tells him, "Thou'rt like the Spirit thou graspest with thy mind, / Thou'rt not like me" (ll. 512-513) — and promptly disappears.

Faust is interrupted in these magical proceedings by Wagner, his famulus, or academic servant, a well-meaning — but ultimately ridiculous — figure who represents a type of scientific inquiry that lacks all conviction and passion. Faust tries to convince Wagner of the need for the soul (*die Seele*) or the heart (*das Herz*), telling him how to teach: "You must feel it first, your end to capture. / Unless from out the soul [*aus der Seele*] it well," he says, "But heart to heart ye will not sway and fashion, / Save in your heart ye feel it first," repeating this plea for pedagogical passion thus: "All unrefreshed the soul still sickens, / Till from the soul itself [*aus eigner Seele*] the fountain burst" (ll. 534-535, 544-545, and 568-569). Responding to Wagner's observation about the delights of intellectual-historical curiosity and that "the joy well be courted, / Into the spirit of the times [*den Geist der Zeiten*] transported" (ll. 570-571], Faust seizes on the phrase "Spirit of the Times" (*den Geist der Zeiten*), coining an expression that Jung will later pick up and repurpose in the opening opposition in "The Way of What Is to Come" in *The Red Book* between the "spirit of this time" (*der Geist dieser Zeit*) and the "spirit of the depths" (*der Geist der Tiefe*) (RB, 119).

Superman"), and the famous passage in *Dichtung und Wahrheit* (Part 4, Book 16) where it is linked to the figure of Spinoza. "Our physical as well as our social life, manners, customs, worldly wisdom, philosophy, religion, and many an accidental event, all call upon us, *to deny ourselves* [*daß wir* entsagen *sollen*]," Goethe writes, yet as individuals we often renounce one thing only to pursue another, "we are continually putting one passion in the place of another; [...] — we try them all, only to exclaim at last, All is vanity." Spinoza, on the other hand, appears to be one of those rare individuals who "convince themselves of the Eternal, the Necessary, and of Immutable Law, and seek to form to themselves ideas which are incorruptible, nay which observation of the Perishable does not shake, but rather confirms": "But since in this there is something superhuman [*etwas Übermenschliches*], such persons are commonly esteemed *in-human* [*Unmenschen*], without a God and without a World" (*The Autobiography of Goethe: Truth and Poetry: From My Own Life*, trans. John Oxenford (London: Bell, 1897), pp. 583-584).

After Wagner has left, Faust reflects ironically on his ambition to be "God's own image" (1. 614, cf. 1. 516), to be — in a phrase borrowed from Jakob Böhme — "the mirror [...] of truth eternal" (1. 615),[23] and to be "higher than the angels" (*mehr als Cherub*) (1. 618). He sinks into deep depression, meditating on how "deep in the heart nests Care [*Sorge*], a guest unbidden" (11. 643-644); on the truth of the Earth Spirit's assertion that, far from being godlike, he is more like a worm (11. 652-655); and on the problem of the transmission of knowledge, when he observes:

> What from thy sires thou hast, make thine indeed,
> Ere that amongst thy goods thou number!
> We use alone the tool framed by the moment's need
>   [*was der Augenblick erschafft*];
> The rest, all that we use not, is but lumber.
>
>   (11. 682-685)

Here the fateful word, "moment," or *der Augenblick*, anticipates the wager with Mephistopheles that Faust will before very long be

---

[23] "Of all whatever this world is an earthly type and resemblance [*ein jrrdisch gleichnuß vnd Spiegel*], that is in the divine kingdom in great perfection in the spiritual essence; not only spirit, as a will, or thought, but essence, corporeal essence, sap and power; but as incomprehensible [*vnbegreifflich*] in reference to the outward world," Böhme declares, and he continues: "For this visible world was generated and created out of the same spiritual essence in which the pure element is; and also out of the dark essence in the mystery of the wrath (being the original of the eternal manifest essence from whence the properties arise) as an out-spoken breath out of the Being of all beings" (Jacob Boehme, *The Signature of All Things* [*De Signatura rerum*, 1622], trans. Clifford Bax (London; Toronto: Dent; Dutton, 1912), pp. 213-214 = chapter 16, §16; cf. Jacob Böhme, *Werke: Morgenröte; De Signatura rerum*, ed. Ferdinand van Ingen (Frankfurt am Main: Deutscher Klassiker Verlag, 2009), p. 779); cf. Steiner, *Goethe's Standard of the Soul*, pp. 14-15. As Steiner shrewdly goes on to note, however, "for the sake of those who love truisms let it be observed that it is not in any sense correct to state that Goethe had precisely this passage of Jacob Boehme in his mind when he wrote the words quoted above. What he had in his mind was the mystical knowledge which finds expression in Boehme's sentences. Goethe lived in this mystical knowledge and it grew riper and riper within him. He created from the kind of knowledge possessed by the mystics" (p. 15).

signing. Spotting a phial full of poison, Faust even contemplates suicide, expressed in lines that had a special significance for Jung: on the one hand, Faust feels as if pulled to an upward trajectory, while on the other he steels himself to descend to the underworld:

> A flaming car floats down on wafting pinions
> Hither to me. Ready to cleave am I
> On pathways new, the ethereal dominions,
> Borne to new spheres of pure activity.
> That life divine, that bliss of God-like being,
> Dar'st thou, but now a worm, make it thy goal?
> Aye, thou hast but to turn thy face from seeing
> The Earth's sweet sun, with dauntless soul!
> Be bold to wrench the brazen gates asunder,
> Past which no mortal but is fain to slink!
> 'Tis time by deeds to show that e'en not under
> The majesty of Gods, Man's dignity need shrink.
> To face yon gloomy cavern never tremble,
> Where Fancy dooms herself but self-bred torments to,
> And though all Hell its flames assemble
> About the narrow mouth, press boldly through;
> Blench not, but blithely let the step be taken,
> Were it with jeopardy, ne'er from the Naught to waken
> *[ins Nichts dahin zu fließen]*! —
> (ll. 702-719)

These lines and others (ll. 1070-1083) deploy the motif of the Solar Myth in a way which will intrigue Jung in *Transformations and Symbols of the Libido* (as we shall see in Chapter 3). For in an extensive footnote in Chapter 6 of that work, he is prompted by a detail in this passage (l. 71: *nach jenem Durchgang*) to posit a parallel between the Hercules myth and the journey of the sun to the Western sea, where Hercules "discovered the straits of Gibraltar

[…], and with the ship of Helios set out towards Erythia" (PU §461, fn. 36). And in *Memories, Dreams, Reflections*, Jung again recalls this passage when he cites the lines, "Now let me dare to open wide the gate / Past which men's steps have never flinching trod," in the context of the experiences that led to *The Red Book*, describing "the uncertain path that leads into the depths of the unconscious" as "the path of error, of equivocation and misunderstanding" (*ein Pfad des Irrtums, der Zweideutigkeit und des Mißverständnisses*) (MDR, 213). Jung thus not only subscribes to the Goethean doctrine of the beneficial aspect of error, but he believes that such error is necessary to enable the "confrontation with the unconscious."

Later, in *The Red Book*, Jung will open a new perspective on these lines when he introduces the theme of the poison (*Gift*) as "science" (*die Wissenschaft*), as laming Izdubar "to the marrow," and as being "cooked" by "the enlightened" in such a way that leaves them "totally paralyzed," "wrapped in brown poisonous vapor," and unable to move without "artificial means" (RB, 279 and 295) — a predicament from which Izdubar can only be rescued by singing incantations "in the ancient manner" (*nach uralter Weise*) (RB, 298). Here as elsewhere, Jung picks up the motif of being a "worm" (*Wurm*) (see RB, 278 and 279; cf. 285, 290, 297) to which Faust — accused by the Earth Spirit of being a "timorous, writhing worm" (1. 498) — himself has repeated recourse, echoing the biblical narrative of Genesis 3 ("Not like the gods am I! Into the quick 'tis thrust! / I'm like the worm, that wriggles through the dust, / Which, as in dust it lives and dust consumes, / The passing foot annihilates and entombs" [ll. 652-655]) (cf. 1. 707). At the same time, the reference to "ebbing into nothingness" (*ins Nichts dahinzufließen*) (1. 719; trans. Arndt) anticipates, or looks forward to, the Mothers Scene in Part Two, where Mephisto tells Faust that in the realm of the Mothers "Naught wilt thou see i' the ever-empty Far" (*Nichts wirst du sehn in ewig leerer Ferne*) (1. 6246), to which

27

Faust responds: "For in thy Naught I trust to find the All" (*In deinem Nichts hoff ich das All zu finden*) (1. 6256).

Faust is on the point of lifting the glass vessel to his mouth to drink the poison when a burst of angelic song and the sound of church bells signal the arrival of Easter Day, the commemoration of the Resurrection of Christ. (By contrast, the liturgical season of Holy Week and, in particular, Good Friday plays a similarly significant part in *Parzival*. Both *Parzival* and *Faust*, while by no means religious works, foreground the cultural and symbolic significance of Christianity for the West.) The sound of the Easter message revives Faust's faith, or rather his nostalgia for the time when he believed: "I hear the tale ye tell, but Faith lends no approval," he says, "And Miracle is Faith's most cherished child' (ll. 765-766). Yet something has stirred in Faust: "With childlike feelings now hath memory withholden / Back from the last grim step, the man," and so he calls out, "Chime on, ye sweet angelic songs that thrall me! / My tears well forth, to earth again ye call me!" (ll. 781-784). If Faust's faith experiences a kind of renaissance, however, a counteraction in the form of the meeting with Mephistopheles is not far off.

Just how down to earth Faust has come is underscored by the following scene, "Outside the City Gate," a setting in which Plato's dialogue called the *Phaedrus* also takes place.[24] In the case of this dialogue, Ernst Cassirer (1874-1945) argued, this setting — over which "a glamour and fragrance well-nigh unequaled in classical descriptions of nature" is said to lie —[25] enables Phaedrus to raise the question of the veracity of mythology (*Phaedrus*, 229d ff.). In the case of Goethe's *Faust*, this setting enables Goethe to present a thumbnail sketch of social life in the 16th century; to show

---

[24] R.E. Wycherley, "The Scene of Plato's 'Phaidros,'" *Phoenix*, vol. 17, no. 2 (Summer 1963), 88-98.
[25] Ernst Cassirer, *Language and Myth*, trans. Susanne K. Langer (New York: Dover, 1953), p. 1.

Faust's sensitivity to nature and its seasons; and to prompt Faust to confess to Wagner the catastrophic results of his father's alchemical experiments:

> Thus have we wrought among these hills and valleys,
> With hellish letuaries, worse havoc than the malice
> Of that same desolating pest.
> Myself to thousands have the poison given;
> They pined away — and yet my fame has thriven,
> Till I must hear their shameless murderers blessed.
>
> (ll. 1050-1055)

In turn, these memories prompt Faust to further self-disclosures, and in particular the famous confession of his sense of psychic fissure, expressed in terms of the "two souls" that are said to persist within him:[26]

> Two souls, alas! within my breast abide,
> The one to quit the other ever burning.
> *This*, in a lusty passion of delight,
> Cleaves to the world with organs tightly-clinging;
> Fain from the dust would *that* its strenuous flight
> To realms of loftier sires be winging.
>
> (ll. 1112-1117)

These lines expose the full extent of Faust's crisis: Not only is he in a state of deep epistemological despair, he is in the grip of existential self-alienation as well. And as if in recognition of this fact, Faust's inferior nature externalizes itself in symbolic form as a black dog

---

[26] In his ETH lectures on the history of modern psychology, Jung reads these preceding lines, spoken by Faust to Wagner, "One only passion is thy bosom's guide, / Seek not to know the other yearning!" (ll. 1110-1111), as expressing Goethe's "polar tension" (Jung, *History of Modern Psychology*, p. 135).

(*Pudel*) running around behind them and gradually coming closer. (Cyrus Hamlin has suggested that the motif of Mephistopheles's manifestation in canine form could be adapted from one of the early chapbook sources, in which Faustus was the owner of a black dog with demonic powers called Praestigiar; while, according to Walter Kaufmann, the Lutheran reformer Philip Melanchthon was among those who believed the Devil accompanied Faust in the shape of a dog.)[27] Accompanied by their new four-legged friend (or — in reality — fiend), Faust and Wagner return to the city gate.

The next scene takes us back to Faust's study, which he enters accompanied by the black dog. The walk in the countryside has improved Faust's mood, and he says that "In us the better soul doth waken, / With a presaging, holy thrill' (*Mit ahnungsvollem, heil'gem Grauen / In uns die beßre Seele weckt*) (ll. 1180-1181):

> Now stress of deed and storm of yearning [*wilde Triebe /*
> *Mit jedem ungestümen Tun*]
> Sleep, at her all-compelling nod;
> The love of man now bright is burning,
> And burning bright the love of God.
> (ll. 1182-1185)

So Faust sets about trying to translate the majestic opening of the Gospel of St. John, "In the beginning was the Word," wondering whether *logos* is best translated into German as "word" (*Wort*), "meaning" (*Sinn*), "power" (*Kraft*) — or "deed" (*Tat*). (This final version echoes Faust's ambition in Part One to ascend to "new spheres of pure activity [*Tätigkeit*]" [l. 7059] and his aspiration in Act 5 of Part Two for the reclaimed land to allow millions of people to live "not safely, but in free resilience [*tätig-frei*]" [l. 11564].) On hearing Faust translate *logos* — a word whose significance

---

[27] Hamlin, p. 33; Kaufmann, p. 14.

Jung ponders deeply in "The Anchorite" and "First Day" (RB, 245-247 and 287-288) — as "deed," the dog responds by barking, and then suddenly and rapidly expanding in size. (In fact, we are told it becomes as large as a hippopotamus [l. 1254] or an elephant [l. 1311]!) Spirits can be heard in the hallway; Faust, alarmed, flicks urgently through his alchemical books for a spell, alighting on the *Clavicula Salomonis* (or "Greater Key of Solomon") and conjuring up elemental forces in the personified forms of salamanders (fire), undines (water), sylphs (air), and goblins (earth).

As in his previous attempts at magic, his efforts are to no avail: and vapors fill in the room, revealing — when they clear — Mephistopheles, dressed like a medieval traveling student. ("It is by no means for nothing," as Jordan Peterson has shrewdly observed, "that the cloak of choice for Mephistopheles is that of a 'Traveling Scholar'"!)[28] *Das war also des Pudels Kern*, says Faust, coining a proverbial expression: so that's what was really in the dog! Asked by Faust to reveal his name (and thus potentially to give away power over himself ...), Mephistopheles identifies himself in paradoxical terms as "Part of that Power that would / Ever the Evil do, and ever does the Good" (*Ein Teil von jener Kraft, / Die stets das Böse will und stets das Gute schafft*) (ll. 1335-1336),[29] and at

---

[28] Jordan B. Peterson, *We Who Wrestle with God: Perceptions of the Divine* (London: Allen Lane, 2024), p. 63.

[29] This self-definition by Mephistopheles represents a (characteristically, for Goethe, optimistic) reworking of the famous lines in Milton's *Paradise Lost* (1667), where Satan declares:

> To do aught good never will be our task,
> But ever to do ill our sole delight,
> As being the contrary to his high will
> Whom we resist. If then his Providence
> Out of our evil seek to bring forth good,
> Our labour must be to pervert that end,
> And out of good still to find means of evil

(Book 1, ll. 160-165; in Milton, *Paradise Lost*, ed. Alastair Fowler, 2nd edn (Harlow: Longman, 1998), p. 70.

Faust's request he expands on this definition as follows:

> I am the Spirit that Denies!
> [*Ich bin der Geist, der stets verneint!*]
> And rightly so, for all that from the Void
> Wins into life, deserves to be destroyed;
> Thus it were better nothing life should win.
> And so is all that you as Sin,
> Destruction, in a word, as Evil represent,
> My own peculiar element.
>
> (ll. 1337-1344)

In so saying, Mephistopheles insists on the essential negativity of his character, and his destructiveness which, while evil (*das Böse*), can nevertheless contribute to positive outcomes. Mephistopheles explains this paradox by describing himself further as being a part of the primordial darkness from which the light emerged; whatever the origins of this cosmogony, it is certainly not biblical, but it is eminently Goethean in its emphasis on striving:

> Part am I of that Part that once was Everything;
> Part of the Darkness, whence the Light did spring —
> The arrogant Light, which now for Space doth joust,
> And Mother Night from her old rank would oust.
> And yet its aim not all its toil achieves.
> Fettered to bodies still it cleaves; [...]
>
> (ll. 1349-1354)

What Mephistopheles unfolds here is nothing less than a cosmogony *in nuce*; echoes of this description of the world in terms of wholeness (Pleroma) and division (Creatura) will recur in the Gnostic worldview expounded by Philemon in his *Seven Sermons to the Dead* ... Perhaps not surprisingly, Faust (for all his learning) struggles to understand the theological and metaphysical implications of what he is hearing, hailing Mephistopheles as "thou fantastic Son of Chaos" (*Des Chaos wunderlicher Sohn*) (1. 1384).[30] Mephistopheles begs Faust to release him; he is trapped within the pentagram that Faust has drawn on the floor! Faust marvels that he should have power over the Devil; but Mephistopheles is resourceful. Summoning again the spirits, their song lulls Faust to sleep; and Mephistopheles gets a rat to gnaw a hole in the pentagram, through which he can escape. And so he does: When Faust awakes, both the Devil and the black dog alike have disappeared: Could it all have been only a dream?

The next scene is set in Faust's study; and with a knock at the door (in fact, three knocks), Mephistopheles — dressed this time as a Spanish cavalier — enters again. (Why, one might wonder, are there two "Study" scenes one after the other, rather than just one? The answer is that Goethe had intended to write a disputation scene to go in between these two "Study" scenes, but never actually did; one of the functions of this unwritten scene, apart from its satire at the expense of the academy, being to explain Faust's shift of mood from his Easter-inspired optimism back to the pessimistic despair we saw in the opening "Night" scene.) Faust now pours out his soul to Mephistopheles, lamenting: "Alas! I am too old to trifle, / Too

---

[30] For Jung's view of evil, see his essay "Good and Evil in Analytical Psychology" (1959), where he remarks that "evil is terribly real, for each and every individual," and "if you regard the principle of evil as a reality you can just as well call it the devil" (CW 10 §879); and his letter to Bill Wilson of 30 January 1961, in which he speaks of an experience which can only happen if "you walk on a path, which leads you to a higher understanding and "you might be led to that goal by an act of grace or through a personal and honest contact with friends, or through a higher education of the mind beyond the confines of mere rationalism," adding: "I am strongly convinced that the evil principle prevailing in this world, leads the unrecognized spiritual need into perdition, if it is not counteracted either by a real religious insight or by the protective wall of human community. An ordinary man, not protected by an action from above and isolated in society cannot resist the power of evil, which is called very aptly the Devil." For further discussion, see C.G. Jung, *Jung on Evil*, ed. Murray Stein (London and New York: Routledge, 1995).

young, no yearning wish to nurse. / What hath the world to tempt a trial? / But self-denial, self-denial!" (ll. 1546-1549) and concluding as follows: "And so to me existence is a burden, / Hateful is Life, and Death a longed-for guerdon" (ll. 1570-1571). These are dangerous words to say to the Devil, but Faust cannot pull himself back from the brink: In a speech that recalls his earlier conjuring-up of the Earth Spirit, his temptation to commit suicide, and his response to the Easter Chorus that leads him to set the phial of poison aside, Faust now utters a series of curses:

> Cursed be the grape-vine's sweet effusion!
> Cursed that last favour Love doth seek!
> Cursed be Hope's vision, Faith's delusion,
> And cursed, thrice cursed, be Patience meek!
>   (ll. 1603-1606)

In these lines Faust announces his abandonment of two of the three theological virtues, namely, Hope and Faith, while tellingly replacing the third (love or charity) with Patience. (By tradition, despair is the one sin that cannot be forgiven, since it repudiates God's capacity to save; in a theological sense, then, Faust is already damned, before he even embarks on his wager with the Devil.) An invisible Chorus of Spirits cries out that, in so cursing, Faust has lived up to the meaning of his name in German (*Faust* = fist) and smashed to pieces "the beautiful world" (*die schöne Welt*), which has become "beauty destroyed" (*die verlorne Schöne*).[31]

    This, then, is Faust's state of mind — or, we might say, the state of his soul — when Mephistopheles makes his strategic move and lures Faust into accepting the wager. The language in this pact scene deserves to be carefully scrutinized: What is it exactly that

---

[31] For further discussion of these lines, see Ulrich Wesche, "The Spirits' Chorus in *Faust*: A Jungian Reading," *Germanic Notes*, vol. 14, no. 4 (1983), 49-51.

Faust signs up to? At the core of the wager lies Faust's rejection of *Ruhe* or rest:

> If on the bed of sloth I loll contented ever,
> Then with that moment end my race!
> Canst thou delude me with thy glozing
> Self-pleased, to put my grief away,
> Canst thou my soul with pleasures cozen,
> Then be that day my life's last day!
> That is the wager.
>
> (ll. 1692-1697)

It is important to note that it is Faust, not Mephistopheles, who proposes the exact terms of the wager, going on to rephrase and reformulate it in these famous words:

> When to the moment fleeting past me,
> Tarry! I cry, so fair thou art !
> [*Werd ich zum Augenblicke sagen:*
> *Verweile doch! du bist so schön!*]
> Then into fetters mayst thou cast me,
> Then let come doom, with all my heart!
> Then toll the death-bell, do not linger,
> Then be thy bondage o'er and done,
> Let the clock stop, let fall the finger,
> Let Time for me be past and gone!
>
> (ll. 1699-1705)

(The term *der Augenblick*, as used by Martin Heidegger, recalls the Greek term *exaiphnes* [ἐξαίφνης], as defined by Plato and later found in Plotinus and in Pseudo-Dionysius the Areopagite, and translatable as "the instant," "the moment," or "the sudden"; in *The Concept of Anxiety*, Søren Kierkegaard explicitly connects the "moment" and *exaiphanes*, and the latter term has distinct theological overtones [see Luke 2:13; Mark 13:33-36; cf. 1 Corinthians 15:52, "in the twinkling of an eye"].)[32] in Goethe's drama, what Faust is signing up to here is permanent, perpetual activism: Eschewing rest, he embraces ceaseless activity, expressed in the form that he ought never say to the "moment" (*Augenblick*), "Tarry a while! You are so fair!", and that, should he ever say this, he will have lost the wager. Much critical ink has been spilled over whether, at the end of *Faust II*, Mephistopheles really does win the wager on the terms that it is proposed here; but for now, the ink that matters is the fresh drop of blood with which Faust signs the deal. And he insists again on the exact nature of what the wager involves: This is not a quest for pleasure; it is in a sense a quest to become a Jungian Self — to become total, universal, all-encompassing, even at the cost of ultimately failing therein:

> You hear! No dreams of joy am I caressing!
> The giddy whirl be mine, with agonized delight,
> With loving hatred, quickening despite.
> My bosom, healed now from the lust of learning,
> Henceforth unto no pain shall close its portals;
> And in myself I'll gratify each yearning,
> Assigned in sum to the whole race of mortals.
> All heights and depths my mind shall compass single;
> All weal and woe within my breast shall mingle;
> Till mine own self to mankind's self expanded,
> Like it at last upon Time's reef be stranded.
>
> (ll. 1765-1775)

---

[32] See Plato, *Parmenides*, 156d-e; Plotinus, *Enneads*, V.3.17; Pseudo-Dionysius, Letter 3; Søren Kierkegaard, *The Concept of Anxiety* [*Writings*, vol. 8], ed. and trans. Reidar Thomte (Princeton, NJ: Princeton University Press, 1980), pp. 87-88; and Martin Heidegger, *Being and Time*, §68 (a). For further discussion, see John Panteleimon Manoussakis, *God After Metaphysics: A Theological Aesthetic* (Bloomington and Indianapolis: Indiana University Press, 2007), pp. 57-70.

In so saying, Faust is turning his back on the quest for knowledge that had hitherto been the guiding principle of his existence and is instead embarking on the quest for experience. It is this quest for experience that will initiate Faust's process of self-transformation and in this sense will lead to his (Goethean — and, in a way, anti-Christian) redemption.

Faust goes off to prepare to set off on his journey with Mephistopheles, and into his study stumbles one of Faust's students. Dressed in Faust's academic robes, Mephistopheles gives the hapless student an impromptu lesson in the ways of the world in a scene that has justly become famous as one of the most acerbic satirical takes in the academic world — a satire whose biting wit has, in the intervening centuries, become more, not less, appropriate and relevant. After the student has left, Faust returns, and Mephistopheles promises him, "The little world and then the great we'll see" (*Wir sehn die kleine, dann die große Welt*) (l. 2052), a formula that could be read as accurately summarizing the scope of Faust itself, Parts One and Two! (In effect, Faust is following the advice offered to the psychologist by Jung in "New Paths in Psychology" (1912) to "put away his scholar's gown, bid farewell to his study, and wander with human heart through the world," for it is there, "in the horrors of prisons, lunatic asylums and hospitals, in drab, suburban pubs, in brothels and gambling-hells, in the salons of the elegant, the Stock Exchanges, Socialist meetings, churches, revivalist gatherings and ecstatic sects"; it is, Jung insists, "through love and hate, through the experience of passion in every form in his own body" — that the psychologist would "reap richer stores of knowledge than text-books a foot thick could give him" [CW 7 §409]. Faust's journey is, in a sense, Jung's journey, and in particular the journey he undertakes in *The Red Book*.) Traveling, not by coach and horse, but on Mephistopheles's magic mantle, Faust and Mephisto set off — for Leipzig, and for Auerbach's Tavern.

Nowadays, Auerbachs Keller is very firmly on the tourist route for visitors to Saxony's largest city, and it is Leipzig's second-oldest but arguably most famous restaurant. A wine bar on the site of the present-day restaurant is recorded as early as 1438, and it is said to have been Goethe's favorite drinking establishment during his time as a student in Leipzig (1765-1768). In fact, one of its wooden panels depicted two scenes from the Faust legend: the doctor drinking with students; and riding out of the bar astride a wine barrel. So by setting a scene in Auerbachs Keller, Goethe is both remaining true to the story of Faust and paying homage to one of his favorite haunts. The scene itself is a mixture of contemporary political satire and crude humor at the expense of the four inebriated students — Frosch, Brander, Siebel, and Altmayer. Into it further elements of the Faust legend are woven: Mephisto's trick of creating a wine cask that magically serves up different sorts of wine; and the hypnotizing of the drunken students who imagine themselves transported to a beautiful vineyard.

The following scene is set in the Witch's Kitchen. At the end of the pact scene, Faust had lamented his old age, and in particular his long beard (ll. 2055-2060). So, the first of the transformations he must undergo is to be rejuvenated, and Mephisto's chosen method for doing this is to pay a visit to a witch. (The Witch's Kitchen scene caught the attention of Freud, who wrote in "Analysis Terminable and Interminable" (1937) with regard to psychoanalysis's aim of bringing the instinct into harmony with the ego: "If we are asked by what methods and means this result is achieved, [...] we can only say: 'So muss denn doch die Hexe dran!' [i.e., 'We must call the Witch to our help, after all!'] — the Witch Metapsychology," for "without metapsychological spevulation and theorizing — I had almost said 'phantasying' [*Phantasieren*] — we shall not get another step forward.")[33] But why *must* Faust call on the Witch? As Faust himself protests, why cannot Mephisto brew the rejuvenating potion (ll. 2366-2367)?

Part of the answer lies in the way this episode operates with the 18th-century "doctrine of indirection," as found in Schiller's treatise *On the Aesthetic Education of Humankind* (1794). On this account, there is no direct path between feeling and thinking, but an intermediate stage is required: a "step backward," a *reculer pour mieux sauter*, or a condition which Schiller describes in Letter 20, §3-§4, as the *aesthetic*.[34] For "from time to time," as Elizabeth M. Wilkinson and L.A. Willoughby explain, we need to "abandon the inevitable 'one-sidedness' of all goal-oriented activity and return to that state of pure potentiality in which all our powers are at full stretch and in equal play," and this "recurrent 'regression' to the active determinability of the aesthetic state is indispensable to the creative living" of the "whole [individual]."[35]

This "step backwards" corresponds to what Freud calls "phantasy" (*Phantasieren*) or what Jung describes as "an *introversion into the unconscious*" (CW 6 §186). Thus a structural parallel can be detected between the two parts of *Faust*: Whereas, in Part One, the episode in Auerbachs Keller is followed by the visit to the Witch's Kitchen and then the tragic story of Faust's affair with Gretchen, in Part Two the Carnival (in the "Spacious Hall" scene

---

[33] Freud, SE, vol. 23, p. 225. For further discussion, see Sabine Prokhoris, *The Witch's Kitchen: Freud, "Faust," and the Transference* [1988], trans. G.M. Goshgarian (Ithaca and London: Cornell University Press, 1995). Note Freud's emphasis here on a Jungian category — *Phantasie* (see CW 6 §711-§722).

[34] Friedrich Schiller, *On the Aesthetic Education of Man*, ed. and trans. Elizabeth M. Wilkinson and L.A. Willoughby, 2nd edn. (Oxford: Clarendon Press, 1982), pp. 138-143, cf. pp. lxxxi-lxxxii and 262. For further discussion of Schiller's argument in *Psychological Types*, see Jung CW 6 §185-§188.

[35] Elizabeth M. Wilkinson and L.A. Willoughby, "'The Whole Man' in Schiller's Theory of Culture and Society" [1969], in *Models of Wholeness: Some Attitudes to Language, Art and Life in the Age of Goethe*, ed. Jeremy Adler, Martin Swales, and Ann Weaver (Oxford: Lang, 2002), pp. 233-268 (p. 243).

of Act I) is followed by the Mothers Scene (in the "Dark Gallery" scene of Act I), and then the tragic story of Faust's quest for Helena (in the "Hall of Chivalry" scene of Act I and in Act III). In Part One, this regression to the aesthetic/unconscious is presented in a parodic form against the chaotic backdrop of the Witch's Kitchen; in Part Two, it is presented in a different parodic sense by being beyond any intelligible description.

Another part of the answer lies in the deliberate strategy of retardation being practiced by Mephisto. In one of his existential laments before he signs the wager, Faust — as we saw above — curses "hope," "faith," and — above all — "patience" (*Geduld*) (ll. 1605-1606). Here Mephisto tells him, "Not skill nor lore suffice to brew / The draught. There must be patience [*Geduld*] too" (ll. 2370-2371). After signing the wager, Mephisto — wearing Faust's academic robe — describes Faust as having been given by Destiny "a spirit […] / That all unbridled, ever forward sweeps," so instead he will give Faust the "wildest life" (*das wilde Leben*) and "vapid insignificancy" (*flache Unbedeutenheit*) (ll. 1856-1857 and 1860-1861). The creatures in the drunken songs of the previous scene — the poisoned rat (ll. 2126-2149) and the "giant flea" (ll. 2211-2240) — and the animals in the witch's kitchen — the family of monkeys, which run around and serve her as a desk when she begins to cast her spell — represent, in Mephisto's words, "bestiality / […] revealed in guise most glorious" (ll. 2297-2298). If Mephistopheles represents the shadow of Faust, do the drunken students — like their simian counterparts in the kitchen — represent the shadow of Mephistopheles, i.e., the shadow of the shadow?

In the context of the dramatic economy of *Faust I*, the Witch's Kitchen scene advances the plot in two respects: first, by bringing about the rejuvenation of Faust; and second, by introducing the figure of the feminine, whose image Faust sees in a magic mirror.[36] Faust is transfixed by this sight, which he describes as one of overwhelming beauty:

> What see I here? What vision heavenly bright
> Within this magic glass? Thy fleetest pinion
> Now lend me, Love, and into her dominion
> Lead thou my swift, unerring flight!
> Ah! if upon this spot I bide not — fate inhuman!
> If near I venture, as my heart doth list,
> I see her only through a veil of mist!
> The fairest vision of a woman!
> Is't possible? So fair can woman be?
> Or in this couched form see I what no man
> Hath ever seen, all heaven's epitome?
> Is there on earth so fair a being?
>
> (ll. 2429-2440)

Does Faust see Gretchen in the mirror? If so, his imminent obsession with Gretchen is in part erotic, but in even larger part aesthetic. Indeed, it would be no exaggeration to say that Faust clearly falls in love with an ideal, although to be sure it is an ideal that is indexed to the feminine. Even after he has been rejuvenated, thanks to the witch's magic spell (the "Hexen-Einmal-Eins"),[37] it is clear that

---

[36] For further discussion of mirrors in magic and alchemy as well as in Jung's extensive study of the symbols connected to mirrors in relation to his analysis of Wolfgang Pauli's dreams in *Psychology and Alchemy*, see Giovanni B. Caputo, "Archetypal-Imaging and Mirror-Gazing," *Behavioral Sciences*, 4 (2014), 4, 1-13;

[37] For further discussion, see Gustav Siebert, *Das Hexeneinmaleins, der Schlüssel zu Goethes Faust* (Münster: Aschendorff, 1914), drawing on the number mysticism of Kabbalah with a view to reveal the spell as "the profound world edifice, clothed in wonderful symbolism and wrapped in the robe of magic, of the theosophy or mysticism of Israel created by the rabbis" (p. 5); Holger Vietor, "Das Hexen-Einmaleins — der Weg zur Entschlüsselung," *Goethe-Jahrbuch*, 122 (2005), 325-327; and Wilhelm Resenhöfft, *Goethes Rätseldichtung im "Faust": Mit Hexenküche*

the real transformation that Faust has undergone is his emotional-aesthetic attachment to Gretchen. "Let me but glance in the glass that lovely form doth swim in, / That vision of fair womanhood!" (ll. 2599-2600), Faust begs, to which Mephisto responds in an ironic aside that links Gretchen to the archetypal image of beauty itself, Helen of Troy: "Thy body so this philter dwell in, / In every wench thou'lt see a Helen!" (ll. 2603-2604).

No sooner has Mephisto promised Faust that he will see "the paragon of women / Before thee soon in flesh and blood" (ll. 2601-2602) than in the very next scene, "Street," he does! When Gretchen deftly knocks back Faust's overtures to her, he tells Mephisto, "Hear, get me that young wench" (l. 2619), to which Mephisto's response suggests — not for the first time (the pentagram, the need to knock three times at the door) — that his powers are actually very limited: "I have no power over her" (l. 2626). As Faust insists, however, it becomes clear that Mephisto's methods to help introduce Faust to Gretchen are going to be primarily psychological. For we see in a short scene set that evening in her neat and tidy bedroom that Gretchen has not forgotten her brief encounter with the handsome stranger and is quite intrigued by him.

When she leaves, Mephistopheles and Faust enter. Faust is full of almost fetishistic delight at being in Gretchen's room and is overwhelmed by his feelings; Mephisto, by contrast, remains detached and cynical, saying, "True, lass is lass, and jest is jest" (*Zwar Kind ist Kind, und Spiel ist Spiel*) (l. 2737). As if mindful of Marilyn Monroe's principle that diamonds are a girl's best friend, Mephisto produces a casket of jewels that he leaves for Gretchen to discover. When she returns and does, it is her turn to look in the mirror: Trying on the jewels, Gretchen admires herself in them. Before she does so, Gretchen sings to herself a ballad titled "The

---

und Hexen-Einmal-Eins in soziologischer Deutung (Berne: Lang, 1972). In its use of number symbolism, the "Hexen-Einmal-Eins" looks forward to the numerological play on the numbers 3, 4, and 7 in the Cabiri Scene of Part Two.

King of Thule." This ballad casts an ironic light on what is going to happen, as it tells the story of an ancient Nordic king who remains faithful to his mistress, whereas Gretchen is going to experience an utter lack of fidelity. (This ballad has been memorably set to music by Schubert.) And her closing words in this scene reveal the harsh socio-economic reality that underlies the tragedy that is about to unfold: 'For gold all throng, / On gold all hang, / Alas! we poor!" (ll. 2802-2804).

Yet Goethe was no crude materialistic determinist. In the following scene, Mephisto curses Gretchen's mother who, discovering the jewelry and rightly suspecting its provenance, has ordered Gretchen to give the casket and its contents to a priest for the Church! Gretchen is proving a hard nut for Mephisto to crack, so a more elaborate plan is called for: one involving Gretchen's recently widowed next-door neighbor, Marthe. She is going to play the traditional role of the matchmaker in Mephisto's campaign to get Gretchen and Faust together: In fact, Mephisto describes her to Faust as "an arrant go-between" (l. 3030). That night Mephisto and Faust are going to go to Marthe's house where Faust will meet Gretchen. Faust — not for the first time, and not for the last — is unsettled by Mephisto's methods, and he accuses him of being "a liar and a sophist" (l. 3050). Instead, Faust insists on the authenticity of his feelings for Gretchen, using words that — in retrospect — hint at the figure of the Eternal and the Feminine, i.e., the Eternal-Feminine, at the end of Part Two:

> If I this passion,
> This maelstrom of emotion try
> To name, yet vainly, then Creation
> From end to end I range with all my powers,
> Grasp at each word that loftiest towers,
> This fire within my bosom flaming,
> Eternal, endless, endless [*Unendlich, ewig, ewig*] naming,
> Is that a devilish, juggling lie?
>
> (ll. 3059-3066)

In these lines the entire moral dimension of the *Gretchentragödie* comes to the fore: Faust claims (and may even actually believe) that he will be faithful to Gretchen, but Mephistopheles knows better. And in the end Mephistopheles, not Faust, will be proved right.

In the next scene, set in a garden, we see Gretchen on Faust's arm and Marthe with Mephistopheles, strolling to and fro. We learn more about Gretchen's background and personal circumstances: Her father is dead, her brother is a soldier, and her younger sister is also dead. Gretchen's memories of caring for her younger sister uncannily prefigures the later infanticide when Gretchen will drown her own child. Plucking the leaves from a forget-me-not, Gretchen pulls a final leaf that coincides with "he loves me!" and this message in the language of flowers (*Blumenwort*) prompts Faust to seize her by the hand and to promise his undying love:

> O shudder not, but let this glance,
> Let thou this hand-clasp say to thee
> What is unspeakable [*unaussprechlich*].
> 'Tis self-surrender, 'tis to feel a rapture
> Which surely is eternal [*ewig*]!
> Eternal [*Ewig!*]! Aye, an end would be despair!
> Nay, no end! no end!
>
> (ll. 3188-3194)

(Here, too, this emphasis on what is "inexpressible" and, echoing ll. 3064-3065, "unending" or "eternal," again anticipates the language of the concluding scene of Part Two, as well as reminding us of the terms and conditions of the wager with Mephisto.) Gretchen again resists and runs away; but Marthe has noticed that Faust seems fond of Gretchen, while Mephisto remarks that *she* is also fond of *him*, and "that's how it ever was" (l. 3205), he cynically adds.

Faust pursues Gretchen to a garden pavilion, where she teasingly hides and is discovered; the pair embrace. Gretchen confesses her love for Faust but, to Faust's immense fury, Mephistopheles turns up and tells Faust that it is time to go. The deteriorating relationship between Faust and Mephistopheles forms the background to the next scene, "Forest and Cave," which opens with Faust on his own. In an impassioned monologue addressed to the *erhabener Geist*, conventionally identified with the Earth Spirit from an earlier scene, Faust expresses his gratitude for the insights that he had been afforded into nature as well as into himself. By contrast, he expresses his bitter regret that he is involved with Mephistopheles — and his utter distaste for his character:

> Oh! now I feel there falls to mortals' lot
> No perfect gift! Thou gavest with this rapture
> Which brings me near and nearer to the Gods,
> The comrade whom I now no more can spare,
> Though he abases, cold and insolent,
> Myself before myself, and with a word
> Breathed from his mouth, thy gifts to naught he withers.
> Within my heart with busy zeal he fans
> A fire devouring for yon beauteous form;
> And so from longing to delight I reel,
> And even in delight I pine for longing.
>
> (ll. 3240-3250)

Faust now realizes that his reliance on Mephistopheles has fatefully compromised the integrity of his relationship with Gretchen, and he also understands that, in falling in love with Gretchen and seducing her, he will also bring about her ruin:

> Outlawed and homeless, man no more I wander!
> I have no goal, I have no peace!
> I am the cataract! From crag to crag I thunder
> With hungry frenzy, headlong to the abyss.

And sideways she, with childlike clouded senses
Her shieling hath, on the small Alpine mead,
Her little world, within whose fences
Her homely cares are limited.
And I, the God-abhorred —
It sated not my lust
To seize the craggy forehead
And dash it into dust.
Her and her peace — I needs must undermine them!
Thou Hell, to be thy victim didst design them!
The time of anguish, Devil, help to shorten,
What must be, let it quickly be!
Upon my head come crashing down her fortune,
One ruin whelm both her and me!

(ll. 3348-3365)

The sense of inevitability underscores the tragic dimension of Goethe's work, at least in Part One. (The status of the entire work as a tragedy is another controversial issue among the critics.)[38]

Gretchen's sense of confusion and her disquiet at her feelings for Faust are expressed in ballad form as she sits at her spinning wheel. (This ballad has also been set to music by Schubert.) Yet it is significant that, at this crucial moment in the unfolding of the *Gretchentragödie*, Goethe returns in the scene set in Marthe's garden to an eminently theological theme. For here Gretchen asks Faust *the* question that has become known proverbially as the *Gretchenfrage*: *Wie hast du's mit der Religion?*, "How is't with

---

[38] Goethe himself highlighted the problematic status of Faust as a tragic work when he wrote to Carl Friedrich Zelter on 31 October 1831: "I was not born to be a tragic poet, for my nature is conciliatory; consequently, a purely tragic incident cannot interest me, for it must be essentially irreconcilable, and to me, in the exceeding flatness of this world, the irreconcilable seems an utter absurdity" (HA *Briefe*, vol. 3, p. 458). For further discussion, see Nicholas Boyle, "Goethe's Theory of Tragedy," *The Modern Language Review*, vol. 105, no. 4 (October 2010), 1072-1086.

thy religion, pray?" (l. 3415). The opening of this dialogue runs as follows:

MARGARET.
Tell me, how is't with thy religion, pray?
Thou art a good and kindly man,
And yet, I think, small heed thereto dost pay.

FAUST.
Enough, dear child! I love thee, thou dost feel.
For those I love, my life, my blood I'd spill,
Nor of his faith, his church, would any man bereave.

MARGARET.
That is not right! We must believe!

FAUST.
Must we?
(ll. 3415-3422)

In the great discourse that follows as part of this exchange, Faust makes a crucial intellectual move when he replaces *belief* in God with *feeling*: while acknowledging (in an almost Job-like way...) the argument for God's existence from the splendour of the natural universe, Faust psychologizes its conclusion, equating "God" with "heart" and "love," prefiguring the soft and fluffy pseudoreligion of our own times:

Who can name Him?
Who thus proclaim Him:
I believe Him?
Who that hath feeling
His bosom steeling,

Can say: I believe Him not?
The All-embracing,
The All-sustaining,
Clasps and sustains He not
Thee, me, Himself?
Springs not the vault of Heaven above us?
Lieth not Earth firm-stablished 'neath our feet?
And with a cheerful twinkling
Climb not eternal stars the sky?
Eye into eye gaze I not upon thee?
Surgeth not all
To head and heart within thee?
And floats in endless mystery
Invisible visible around thee?
Great though it be, fill thou there from thine heart,
And when in the feeling wholly blest thou art,
Call it then what thou wilt!
Call it Bliss! Heart! Love! God!
I have no name for it!
Feeling is all in all!
Name is but sound and reek,
A mist round the glow of Heaven!

(ll. 3432-3458)

These words — spoken, after all, by a man who is literally in league with the Devil! — record a major shift in Christian belief that took place in the Enlightenment and in Romanticism and that arguably had begun in the age associated with the story of Faust: namely, its gradual disintegration.

While the notion that religious belief is really a question of feeling has been aligned by some critics (and not without good reason) with the thought of Friedrich Schleiermacher's *Über die Religion*

(1799; ²1806; ³1821),³⁹ Faust's renunciation of intellect in this scene might also be seen to have been part and parcel of coming face to face with his own unconscious in the form of Mephistopheles rather than espousing any particular theological line of thought. Parzival's question was, *weh, was ist Gott*: and for Wolfram, it turns out to be that God is light *and* dark; for Goethe's Faust, it turns out that God is really a feeling; and for Nietzsche's Zarathustra, it will turn out that God is dead. (As an inheritor of this tradition, Jung will try and evolve his own answer to this question about the nature of God.)

This theological conversation dissolves into the background again as Faust persuades Gretchen to give her mother a sleeping potion so that she will not be disturbed when Faust comes to visit Gretchen tonight. (Given Faust's previous track record of involvement in the production of dodgy potions by his father, Gretchen is right to be cautious; as it turns out, this sleeping potion is going to kill her mother.) In the scene "At the Well" with her friend Lieschen, Gretchen learns that their mutual friend, Bärbelchen, has now got an illegitimate child. (The figure of Lieschen will reappear in the opening scenes of *Faust*, Part Three; written, not by Goethe, but by Deutobold Symbolizetti Allegorowitsch Mystifizinsky, the pseudonym of Friedrich Theodor Vischer.) Reflecting on her own, Gretchen realizes — in a kind of counterpoint to Faust's realization in "Forest and Cave" of the path of destruction on which he has embarked— that she herself is now in danger of exposing herself to sin, and yet — "all that urged me into it / Was oh! so dear, and oh! so sweet" (ll. 3585). Or as the saying has it, the road to hell is paved with good intentions ...

The narrative of the *Gretchentragödie* and the theological background intersect briefly, yet powerfully, for one more time in the next scene where we see Gretchen putting fresh flowers into

---

³⁹ See Friedrich Schleiermacher, *Über die Religion: Reden an die Gebildeten unter ihren Verächtern*, ed. Rudolf Otto [1899] (Göttingen: Vandenhoeck & Ruprecht, 2002).

the jars standing in front of an image of the Virgin Mary as the Mater Dolorosa (the Sorrowing Mother), placed in a shrine located in a niche in the city wall. The opening words of her prayer to the Virgin, "Ah, bow / Thy gracious brow, / Mother of Woes, to the woebegone!" (ll. 3587-3589), are later recalled in her prayer in the final scene of *Faust II*, where they are addressed on this second occasion, however, to the Mater Gloriosa.

The "shame and death" from which Gretchen begs the Virgin to save her begin to become reality when her brother Valentin, who has learned of his sister's affair, decides to come and confront Faust in person. The situation rapidly spins out of control, and Faust — urged on and assisted by Mephisto — kills Valentin with his sword. Gretchen's nightmare grows when, in the requiem service for her now-dead mother, she is tormented in the cathedral itself by an evil spirit, causing her to swoon. (In this scene Goethe deftly interweaves the mocking threats of the evil spirit with biblical paraphrase and lines from the Latin Requiem Mass — a powerful combination that attracted the musical interest of Schubert and Schumann alike.) While one might imagine that this manifestation of evil is visible only to Gretchen, evil takes on a much more tangible form in the Walpurgis Night scene. Previously, shortly before Faust murders Valentin, Mephistopheles had expressed his enthusiasm for the imminent celebration, "Already thrills my body thorough / The glorious Walpurgis-night! / We keep it in the morrow's morrow" (ll. 3660-3662). And now the feast day of Saint Walpurga, traditionally celebrated on the night before 1 May, has arrived, and Mephisto has taken Faust to the Harz Mountains to witness for himself the dark, supernatural world of witches and demons as represented in the Nordic imagination.[40] Guided through the countryside of the Brocken, the highest peak in the Harz Mountains and traditionally

---

[40] For further discussion of the pagan origins of Walpurgis Night, see Christian Rätsch, *Walpurgisnacht: Von fliegenden Hexen und ekstatischen Tänzen* (Baden: AT Verlag, 2005).

believed to have been the site of the annual witches' sabbath, by a will-o'-the-wisp, Faust is warned, "the mount is magic-mad to-day" (*der Berg ist heute zaubertoll*) (l. 3868) — a line that would inspire the title of Thomas Mann's second novel, *The Magic Mountain*.

Although the witches at this celebration are all very Nordic, the reference by a chorus of them to old Baubo (ll. 3962-3965), a nurse who (according to classical mythology) tried to use lewd humor to bring comfort to Demeter after Hades had carried off her daughter, Persephone, points forward to the very different ambience of the Classical Walpurgis Night in *Faust II*.[41] At the same time, this Walpurgis Night is characterized by its emphasis on the feminine, reflected in a sequence of female figures: (a) Lilith, a primordial she-demon in Judaic mythology, said to have been the first wife of Adam (l. 4119); (b) an attractive young witch, with whom Faust dances — until a red mouse jumps out of her mouth (a detail Goethe borrows from *Anthropodemus Plutonicus, das ist, Eine Neue Weltbeschreibung* (1666) by Johannes Praetorius [1630-1680]); and finally (c) a pale, beautiful child who recalls Gretchen to Faust. Mephisto dismisses her as a wraith, as a lifeless counterfeit, and reminds Faust of the Medusa myth — one of the Gorgons whose face turned those who looked at her to stone. Yet this is no Medusa, Faust insists: Her eyes are lifeless, while her breasts and her enchanting body recall Gretchen to him. Her neck is marked by a thin, red line: for Mephisto, a reminder of how Perseus cut off the head of the Medusa, while in the drama the mark stands

---

[41] The figure of Baubo is invoked by Nietzsche in his Preface to the second edition of *The Gay Science*: "'Is it true that God is present everywhere?' a little girl asked her mother: 'I think that's indecent' — a hint for philosophers! One should have more respect for the bashfulness with which nature has hidden behind riddles and iridescent uncertainties. Perhaps truth is a woman who has reasons for not letting us see her reasons. Perhaps her name is — to speak Greek — *Baubo*?" (GS Preface §4). In Greek, the name Baubo (Βαυβώ) means "vagina" or "vulva" (see Sebastian Kaufmann, *Kommentar zu Nietzsches "Die fröhliche Wissenschaft"* [NK, vol. 3/2.1] (Berlin and Boston: de Gruyter 2022), pp. 153-157). See also below, pp. 209-210.

proleptically for the death sentence soon to be pronounced on Gretchen.

At this point, an intermezzo titled "Walpurgis Night's Dream, or the Golden Wedding of Oberon and Titania" brings the Walpurgis Night to a close. This mixture of Shakespearean parody and contemporary satire in the form of a series of epigrams often seems out of place, even irrelevant, to readers today, although Cyrus Hamlin has argued that it is precisely because the intermezzo has nothing in common either with the human world of Faust or with the daimonic domain of Mephisto, it nevertheless — by virtue of contrast — reflects on both, inasmuch as Goethe "affirms a positive and creative order to the natural world, as demonstrated both in the human setting of the Gretchen story and in the demonic setting of the 'Walpurgis Night'" (387). Underlying this affirmation is a crucial point about the theme of salvation or redemption in *Faust* as a whole:

> Yet [Goethe] also knew that the May Day rites celebrated in Shakespeare's play, where all strife between Oberon and Titania is resolved, were essentially identical with the traditional pagan festival of the Walpurgis Night itself [...] and that the essential meaning of this festival is not sexual debauch but rather the regeneration and renewal of life and spirit in the natural world. Indeed, the festival signifies a secular form of salvation, both in the sense of redemption [...] and in the sense of new life in nature [...]. (387)

If the redemptive meaning of salvation (in a theological sense) can be found in the words of the Voice from Above at the end of Part One (see below), salvation in the sense of new life in nature is subsequently "performed poetically and musically by the elfin chorus directed by Ariel at the outset of Part Two" (387). If nothing else, this interpretation reminds us of the ways in which the theme of redemption — and the associated, overarching theme of transformation — is woven as much into the granular detail of the work as it is into its overall structure. In fact, Ariel — the spirit of the air from Shakespeare's play *The Tempest* — is the penultimate speaker in this intermezzo, but he returns in full vocal splendor in the opening scene of Part Two, "Charming Landscape," where the theme of transformation moves to the fore.

The contrast between the exuberance of the lighthearted epigrams in the Walpurgis Night intermezzo and the mood of the following scene, "Dreary Day" set in "A Field," could not be greater.[42] For a start, because the scene is in prose, as if the resources of versification were exhausted. And for another, because in the meantime the stages of the *Gretchentragödie* have advanced further toward its tragic end. Faust rails against the news of Gretchen's despair and her recent imprisonment. He curses Mephistopheles for keeping the news from him, and the latter's response, "She is not the first!" (*Sie ist die erste nicht*) is chilling in its horrific simplicity and cynicism. (This phrase is taken over verbatim from the legal documents relating to the trial of Susanna Margaretha Brandt, who was executed on the guillotine for infanticide in Frankfurt in 1772.) Faust appeals to the Earth Spirit but to no avail, and Mephisto reminds Faust of who bears the real responsibility: "Who was it plunged her into ruin, I or thou?" prompting Faust to glance around him furiously. He orders Mephisto take him to the prison where Gretchen is awaiting her execution, and the pair ride off on black steeds, passing the so-called raven-stone — the place where Gretchen is to be executed at dawn and around which a cabal of witches is gathered, suggesting that evil is never far away.

---

[42] As if Goethe was aware of this problematic transition, the *Paralipomena* to *Faust* contain a series of sketches for scenes involving the figure of Satan, surrounded by "smelly," "stinking" billy goats and nanny goats (Gaier, vol. 1 = *Texte*, pp. 624-627; cf. Schöne, *Texte*, pp. 552-559).

And so we arrive at the harrowing conclusion to Part One, set in a dungeon. We see Gretchen, wearing chains and lying on straw, driven half-mad by what has happened to her: her double murder of her mother (thanks to Faust's sleeping potion) and her illegitimate child. Although modeled on Ophelia in Shakespeare's *Hamlet*, Gretchen's madness is expressed in a very Germanic way through an adaptation of a song from the Grimms' fairy tale "The Juniper Tree." Gretchen initially mistakes Faust for her executioner, but then she recognizes him in a double sense: When she kisses him but discovers his lips are cold, she realizes he no longer loves her; and when she sees Faust is accompanied by Mephistopheles, she shrinks away: "Heinrich! I shudder at thee!" (*Heinrich! Mir graut's vor dir*) (l. 4610). In the final words of Part One, Gretchen prays to God to save her (*Rette mich!*); Mephisto declares that she is condemned (*Sie ist gerichtet*); a Voice from Above responds that she is "redeemed" (*Ist gerettet!*), and Mephisto calls to Faust to follow him — *Her zu mir!* — and they disappear, as Gretchen's voice from within cries out, "Heinrich! Heinrich!" (l. 4612).[43] While this final line echoes the traditional ending of the Faust legend and its proclamation of eternal damnation against Faust (*Fauste! Fauste! In aeternum damnatus est!*), the end of Part One marks the end of just the first stage of Faust's self-transformative adventure. For who, one wonders, has the Voice from Above declared to be redeemed — Gretchen? Or Faust? And what does the notion of redemption itself in such a work as Goethe's *Faust* really mean?

---

[43] In Mephisto's cry, *Her zu mir!*, at the exact same moment as the Voice from Above speaks, Rudolf Steiner saw an indication that Mephisto now in some sense owns Faust: "We know from this conclusion to Part One where Faust has come. He has come to Mephistopheles" (*Erläuterungen*, vol. 1, p. 105).

Chapter 2

Goethe's *Faust*, Part Two

Act I

Part One closes with Faust and Mephistopheles hastening away from the dungeon where Gretchen is languishing, awaiting execution; Part Two opens in what is literally another world. In a "Charming Landscape," we see Faust lying on flower-covered grass, weary and restless, while above him a ring of spirits as graceful little shapes gently floats and weaves.[1] Accompanied by Aeolian harps, the spirit Ariel — a figure from Shakespeare's *The Tempest* who had concluded the intermezzo of the "Walpurgis Night's Dream" — sings of how the elves and fairies will wipe Faust's conscience clear, for "good or evil be his nature / Pity they the luckless man" (ll. 4619-4620). (The figure of Ariel, whose name in Hebrew means "lion of God," derives from the biblical Book of Isaiah, where Ariel serves as another name for Jerusalem [see Isaiah 29:1-2].) Thus, *Faust II* establishes itself as a very different work from its previous part — a difference which Jung captured with admirable concision when he said that "in the first part of *Faust* Goethe has shown us what it means to accept instinct and

---

[1] To what extent can we even say this is the same figure whom we saw in Part One? Rudolf Steiner puts his finger on a significant shift in the identity of Faust when he writes that "at the beginning of the second part the person who speaks is not the same Faust whom we know from the first part, but he who speaks is another, a second nature, who only externally bears Faust's shape and can feel its way into what as something spiritual pervades the external world" (Rudolf Steiner, *Geisteswissenschaftliche Erläuterungen zu Goethes «Faust»*, 2 vols. (Dornach: Rudolf Steiner Verlag, 1982), vol. 1, *Faust, der strebende Mensch*, p. 107).

in this second part what it means to accept the ego and its weird unconscious world" (CW 7 §43).

Whereas Part One is located in pre-Reformation Germany, Part Two is located everywhere and nowhere; whereas Part One pursued two main narrative themes, the *Gelehrtentragödie* (or "scholar's tragedy") and the *Gretchentragödie* (or "Gretchen tragedy"), Part Two involves a plurality of narratives; whereas Part One involved identifiably human characters (including Wagner, Marthe, Valentin, and Gretchen herself), Part Two introduces a host of mythological figures of various sorts. These include numerous kinds of "little people," such as the elves in the opening scene, the gnomes in the Carnival, the ants on the Upper Peneios, and the pygmies who fight with the cranes in the same scene, and the masked dwarfs before the palace of Menelaus at Sparta, not to mention the figure of Homunculus (as a "little man") and the mysterious Cabiri in the Classical Walpurgis Night. These figures, like those of fairies, daimons, or other "elusive, contradictory, shape-shifting" beings in general, can be read as "root metaphors for certain central aspects of modern Western culture," which are excluded from it and yet continue to appear in our culture in different forms.[2] Their frequent appearance in Part Two of *Faust* signals the way in which this work as a whole seeks to engage with some of the most profound themes of Western culture.

A good example of how these themes are woven in the structure of Goethe's play is given by Faust's monologue, spoken in *terza rima* — a rhyming verse form associated with Dante, and one of the many classical verse forms eschewed in Part One in favor of *Knittelvers*, a Germanic verse meter involving lines of four stresses in rhyming pairs (aa, bb, etc.).[3] Thanks to the magical intervention

---

[2] Patrick Harpur, *The Philosophers' Secret Fire: A History of the Imagination* (Harmondsworth: Penguin, 2002), p. 7.

[3] For an analytical table showing the different metrical forms used in *Faust* (as well the dates of composition), see Hamlin's Norton edition, pp. 508-513. For further discussion of metrical considerations in *Faust*, see Kurt May, *Faust II. Teil: In der*

of the elves, Faust finds himself once again rejuvenated and renewed: "Life's pulses newly-quickened now awaken," he says (l. 4679).[4] The source of this rejuvenative power, however, is not this time, as it had been in Part One, the witch's magic spell as cast at the instigation of the Devil, but rather the Earth: "Thou girdest me about with gladness," Faust says, "priming / My soul to stern resolve and strenuous keeping, / Onward to strive, to highest life still climbing" (*Zum höchsten Dasein immerfort zu streben*) (ll. 4684-4685), thus restating the great Faustian themes of striving (*Streben*) and intensification (*Steigerung*).

In this refreshed and renewed state, the natural world around now seems paradisiacal to Faust: "A very Paradise about me lightens!" (l. 4694), although later on, Faust will try to use technological means to make a paradise out of the earth in his great land reclamation project. *Hinaufgeschaut!* — "Look up," says Faust, just as he will not just *look up* but be *pulled up* toward the Mater Gloriosa in the final scene. The radiance of the sun, whose approach had earlier in the scene made a stupendous clangor — an acoustic recapitulation of the "far-thundering progression" attributed to its "appointed round" in the words of the archangel Raphael that open the "Prologue in Heaven" — causes Faust to be "blinded" (l. 4702), anticipating the way he will later be blinded in Act V by Care (*Sorge*). What Empedocles saw as a pair of opposites,

---

Sprachform gedeutet (Munich: Hanser, 1962); Anthony Phelan, "Deconstructing Classicism: Goethe's *Helena* and the Need to Rhyme," in Richard Sheppard (ed.), *New Ways in Germanistik* (Oxford: Berg, 1990), pp. 192-210; and Benjamin Bennett, "Histrionic Nationality: Implications of the Verse in *Faust*," *Goethe Yearbook*, vol. 17 (2010), pp. 21-30.

[4] In one of his lectures published as part of his *Geisteswissenschaftliche Erläuterungen zu Goethes «Faust»*, Rudolf Steiner described this scene as Faust's "initiation with the spirits of the earth." In this lecture given at Dornach on 22 May 1915, Steiner tried to draw a link — despite the disastrous global situation — between the liturgical season (that is, Pentecost) and this opening scene of Part Two: "This Pentecostal mood is having an effect on Faust. And afterwards he continues on his life's journey" (*Erläuterungen*, vol. 1, p. 105).

love (*philotes* = φιλότης) and strife (*neikos*=νεῖκος) —[5] and the theme of the opposites will become one of the overriding concerns (or even obsessions) of Jung in *The Red Book* — are here understood by Faust as reciprocally related, as a *Wechselwirkung*: "Is't Love? Is't Hate? that yonder glowing spindle / In bliss and bale alternating [*wechselnd*] tremendous / About us twines, till we the dazed beholders / To veil our gaze in Earth's fresh mantle wend us" (ll. 4711-4714). Whereas, in the "Forest and Cave" scene in Part One, Faust had compared *himself* to a waterfall, "roar[ing] in cataracts from cliff to boulder" (l. 3350), here the waterfall is seen as something external, through which the sun shines in order to compose a phenomenon that is as symbolic as it is meteorological — a rainbow:

> Nay then, the sun shall bide behind my shoulders!
> The cataract, that through the gorge doth thunder
> I'll watch with growing rapture, 'mid the boulders
> From plunge to plunge down-rolling, rent asunder
> In thousand thousand streams, aloft that shower
> Foam upon hissing foam, the depths from under.
> Yet blossoms from this storm a radiant flower;
> The painted rainbow bends its changeful being,
> Now lost in air, now limned with clearest power,
> Shedding this fragrant coolness round us fleeing.
> Its rays an image of man's efforts render;
> Think, and more clearly wilt thou grasp it, seeing
> Life in the many-hued, reflected splendour.
> [*Am farbigen Abglanz haben wir das Leben*].
>   (ll. 4715-4727)

---

[5] See Empedocles (DK 31 B 26 and DK 31 B 35). For further discussion of the relation between Presocratic thought and psychoanalysis, see Arthur M. Arkin, "A Short Note on Empedocles and Freud," *American Imago*, vol. 6, no. 3 (September 1949), 197-203; and Garfield Tourney, "Empedocles and Freud, Heraclitus and Jung," *Bulletin of the History of Medicine*, vol. 30 no. 2 (March-April 1956), 109-123.

In his lectures on *Dream Interpretation Ancient & Modern* (given in 1936-1941), Jung quoted this final line, suggesting that in it Goethe expresses "approximately the same opinion as that of the Romantics," namely: that "reflection is a reality, illusion is reality."[6] (According to Jung, this notion "corresponds exactly to the Eastern conception of *maya*," and he takes issue with the translation of *maya* simply as "illusion": rather, we should say "real illusion, which emanates from something unknowable.") Perhaps (for once) more tellingly, Rudolf Steiner comments that "after this night Faust has reached the point where he no longer wants, like the Faust of the first part, to hurl himself into life, just as it has thrown him into guilt and into evil, but he turns to its *many-hued, reflected splendour*," adding: "It is the same *many-hued, reflected splendour* which we call *Geisteswissenschaft*, which only appears to him as a *many-hued, reflected splendour*, and by means of which we gradually raise ourselves to experience reality."[7] (The scene is beautifully evoked in music by Robert Schumann in his *Scenes from Goethe's Faust*.) In so many ways, this opening scene of Act I of Part Two signals and foreshadows many of the themes and motifs that are to follow.

And herein lies a methodological problem for any commentator on Goethe's *Faust*. The sheer exuberance and richness of the material means that one has necessarily to be selective in the aspects that one highlights. Nevertheless, stepping back from the granular detail of the work also allows its central motif — the motif of transformation — to stand out more clearly. For each of the

---

[6] C.G. Jung, *Dream Interpretation Ancient & Modern: Notes from the Seminar Given in 1936-1941*, ed. John Peck, Lorenz Jung, and Maria Meyer-Grass, trans. Ernst Falzeder and Tony Woolfson (Princeton, NJ, and Oxford: Princeton University Press, 2014), p. 80. Cf. Jung's allusion to this line in relation to the figure of Ka: "Ka was the one who made everything real [*wirklich*], but who veiled the kingfisher spirit, the meaning [*den Sinn*]" — i.e., Philemon — "or replaced it by beauty, the 'eternal reflection' [*«ewigen Abglanz»*]" (MDR, 209-210).

[7] Steiner, *Erläuterungen*, vol. 1, p. 116.

five Acts of *Faust II*, like the entirety of *Faust I* before it, displays a structure of crisis and (partial) resolution, or what Benjamin Bennet called "interrupted tragedy."[8] In each Act (arguably with the exception of Act V), the "interruption" takes the form of some kind of catastrophic event: in Act I, the explosion when Faust tries to seize hold of Helena, causing a backlash which knocks him to the ground and makes the spirits of Paris and Helena disappear into mist, before the entire scene comes to an abrupt end in darkness and tumult; in Act II, the festival at the Aegean Sea comes to a fiery as well as a watery conclusion as Homunculus crashes into Galatea's throne and is shattered; in Act III, Euphorion launches himself into the air, his shining head leaving a trail of light in his wake, before plunging down to the feet of Faust and Helena, only for his corporeal body to vanish and his aureole to rise like a meteor to the sky, leaving behind his robe, cloak, and lyre; Helena herself then vanishes, leaving her robe and veil in Faust's arms; and the Chorus celebrates a Bacchic feast or Dionysian orgy; while in Act IV, a series of magical interventions orchestrated by Mephisto's ravens in the battle between the opposing forces of the Emperor and the Rival Emperor in the form of the illusion of a massive flood (created by water-sprites) and daimonic summer lightning (produced by fire made in their smithy by mountain dwarf-folk) culminate in the sound effects of loud "Pan-icky" (*panisch*) noise resounding from the the echo chamber of empty armor, reflected in the sounds of "warlike tumult" (*Kriegstumult*) in the orchestra. (This

---

[8] Benjamin Bennett, "Interrupted Tragedy as the Structure of Goethe's *Faust*," *Mosaic: An Interdisciplinary Critical Journal*, vol. 11, no. 1 (Fall, 1977), 37-51; reprinted in *Goethe's Theory of Poetry: "Faust" and the Regeneration of Language* (Ithaca and London: Cornell University Press, 1986), pp. 19-49. For his part, Harold Bloom enthusiastically agrees with Bennett's argument that these interruptions should be interpreted as "progressively subtle suggestions of masturbatory climaxes" (Harold Bloom, *The Western Canon: The Books and School of the Ages* (New York: Harcourt & Brace, 1995), p. 224), but this seems an unduly reductionist (and Freudian) reading.

tumult eventually resolves into cheerful martial airs, and it remains a matter of debate whether in the scene in the Rival Emperor's tent that follows — written in the classical alexandrines of neoclassical French drama, and the last part of *Faust* composed by Goethe — an order of some kind is restored, or a disorder of another kind prevails as the Archbishop demands from the Emperor "a formal deed of transfer" to the Church of land and the construction of an elaborate cathedral as an expensive penance for collusion with Satanic powers.)

This structural principle of "interrupted tragedy" is perhaps what Jung was trying to get at when, in *Psychology and Alchemy*, he identified "the body of the *lapis*" (or the philosopher's stone who is "endowed with spirit and life") with "that strange Faustian figure" who "bursts into flame" three times (or, more precisely, is dispersed in some way or another): a figure who recurs in the Boy Charioteer, in Homunculus, and in Euphorion, whose common fate is said to symbolize "a dissolution of the 'centre' into its unconscious elements" (*Auflösung der "Mitte" ins Unbewußte*) (CW 12 §243; cf. §558; cf. CW 14 §200).[9] Certainly this structural approach is more convincing than arguing, as some critics have suggested that Jung is trying to do, that each of these figures has a specific alchemical significance (Boy Charioteer = earth, Homunculus = water, Euphorion = fire), for instance. In respect of the principle of "interrupted tragedy," Act V succeeds where the others fail, as the **entelechy** of Faust is pulled onward and upward toward the Mater Gloriosa.[10]

---

[9] In his conversation with Eckermann of 20 December 1829, Goethe himself identifies the Boy Charioteer of Act 1 with Euphorion in Act 3, because he is "not a human, but an allegorical being" (Johann Peter Eckermann, *Conversations of Goethe*, ed. J.K. Moorhead, trans. John Oxenford [1930] (New York: Da Capo Press, 1998), p. 337).

[10] The Aristotelian notion of *entelechy*, from the ancient Greek ἐντελέχεια (*entelékheia*), meaning "having the aim in itself" (in the way that, for instance, a chestnut tree grows from a chestnut, but not an oak tree), can also be understood as "persona" (named

In keeping with the principle enunciated by Mephisto in Part One, "The little world and then the great we'll see" (*Wir sehn die kleine, dann die große Welt*) (l. 2052), and the constant shifting in space and time that characterizes Part Two, Faust moves from the idyllic natural world of "Charming Landscape" to the Throne Room in the Imperial Residence of the Holy Roman Emperor, identifiable in the story of the historical Faustus as Maximilian I (even if in Goethe's drama the Emperor has no exact historical counterpart). Although Faust's involvement in the world of the Holy Roman Emperor — or, to give him his full title, the *Kaiser des Heiligen Römischen Reiches deutscher Nation* — was part of this original legend and, according to Goethe's plan for the composition of Part Two, it had always been intended that Faust's encounter with him would form part of his drama, it is Mephistopheles who takes the lead in the opening lines of this scene, where he assumes the role of the replacement Fool at the court.

The *große Welt* of Part Two allows Goethe more opportunities for political satire than had Part One (with the exception of the scene in Auerbach's cellar and the intermezzo of the Walpurgis Night's dream), and it quickly emerges that the Emperor's state finances are in a bad way. The solution to the Emperor's financial crisis is proposed by Mephistopheles: The Emperor's territories contain buried gold, on the basis of which — as we subsequently learn in the scene set in the *Lustgarten* or Pleasance — paper money (i.e., certificates of credit) has been printed with great success, leading to Faust and Mephisto being placed in charge of the treasury. (The significance of this economic satire has been explored at length by Hans Christoph Binswanger in *Money and Magic* (1985), which offers a critique of the modern economy in the light of Goethe's

---

after the mask worn by a Greek actor on the stage) or something "sounding through" (as a creature can make known a person) or something "individual"/"indivisible" (in the sense of individuality), as explained in Henk van Oort, *Anthroposophy: A Concise Introduction to Rudolf Steiner's Spiritual Philosophy* (Forest Row: Temple Lodge, 2008). For further discussion of *entelechy*, see below, pp. 177-179.

Faust.)[11] It is in this economic context, rather than in an alchemical one, that *Faust's* repeated references to gold might perhaps most profitably be read. In fact, the presence of the Astrologer and in particular his speech in response to the muttering of the crowd, which is spoken to promptings by Mephistopheles (ll. 4955-4970), are self-evidently satirical: While the references to Mercury, to Sol and Luna (the sun and the moon), and to Mars, Jupiter, and Saturn might correspond to traditional astrological or alchemical lore, the speech as a whole is surely deliberate mystification.[12]

In between the scenes in the Throne Room and in the *Lustgarten* is the lengthy Carnival Masque or *Mummenschanz*, which takes place in a Spacious Hall with adjacent apartments. The participants include numerous allegorical figures, including the Boy Charioteer, who explicitly identifies all the figures as allegories, saying to the Herald (who acts as Master of Revels or Lord of Misrule):

> Herald, up! Thine to expound us,
> Ere we flee, to read our stories.
> Thine to paint, to name, to show us,
> For we all are allegories [*Allegorien*],
> Wherefore shouldst thou surely know us.
>
> (ll. 5528-5532)

---

[11] See Hans Christoph Binswanger, *Money and Magic: A Critique of the Modern Economy in the Light of Goethe's "Faust"* [1985], trans. J.E. Harrison (Chicago and London: University of Chicago Press, 1994).

[12] In his seminar on *Dream Interpretation Ancient & Modern* (1936-1941), however, Jung appears to take these astrological references at face value. Here he summarized the Helena story of *Faust II* as follows: Faust "had to descend into deepest hell to find out the secret, which was personified in the figure of Helen. He was confronted by Helen, and then he performed the *coniunctio* with Helen. This is Selene, the moon. He went into the depths as the sun, the *nous*, consciousness, and united with Helen, which was a bit of a blunder, as it were. It should have been different. He should have left that to Paris. So their son [i.e., Euphorion] flew away from him, and was consumed again by the fire" (Jung, *Dream Interpretation Ancient & Modern*, pp. 175-176).

and who identifies himself to the Herald as an allegorical figure of
poetry:

> I am Profusion, Poesy am I;
> [*Bin die Verschwendung, bin die Poesie*]
> The Poet, wrought to perfect measure
> When he his most peculiar treasure
> Doth lavish, rich with wealth untold,
> And Plutus' peer for all his gold.
> I grace and gladden dance and rout,
> And what he lacks, that deal I out.
>   (ll. 5573-5579)

In so speaking, the Boy Charioteer draws attention to the essentially
allegorical nature of much of Part Two, and Cyrus Hamlin has
emphasized the significance of Goethe's allegorical technique for
the whole of Part Two, where "literally everything that happens
participates in an elaborate symbolic action in which Faust himself
no longer holds an exclusive place": accordingly, "the entire world
of the drama assumes Faustian qualities that are represented in
general, even universal terms, which translate all individuality
into generic political or even mythological terms," Hamlin argues,
with two important consequences: First, the role of theater as
spectacle or festival is enhanced to the point that "all historical
and mimetic frames of reference disappear"; and second, Goethe
begins to explore questions relating to politics and economics in
a way that extends "throughout the rest of the drama in the form
of various symbolic transformations," together with "theatrical or
mythological excursions along the way" (Hamlin, 398).

The Boy Charioteer welcomes the figure of Plutus, the god
of wealth in Greek mythology (and, according to some, the son
of Demeter and Iasion, said to have founded the mystic rites on
the island of Samothrace; according to others, the son of Hades

and Persephone; and, according to yet others, the son of Tyche, the goddess of good fortune). Plutus is obviously connected with the Greek and Roman god of the underworld, Pluto, who is (according to Plato) "so called because riches arise from the earth" (*Cratylus*, 403a). In fact, Plutus is Faust himself in disguise, and likewise the figures of Zoilo-Thersites (an amalgamation of Zoilos of Amphipolis, an ancient literary critic known as Homeromastix or the "Homer whipper" because of his scathing criticism of Homer, and of Thersites, a bowlegged and lame, sloping shouldered, and tufty-haired soldier of the Greek army during the Trojan War, who is described in Book 2 of the *Iliad*, where he is brutally suppressed by Odysseus) and of the Skinny Fellow who identifies himself as *Avaritia* (l. 5649) and later as Greed (l. 5665) are, in fact, Mephistopheles in disguise.[13] Just as, in the *Iliad*, Thersites — the ugliest man who ever came to Troy, as Homer calls him —[14] is beaten into a bloody mess by Odysseus for disrupting the rallying of the Greek army, so here he criticizes the goings-on at the Masquerade: "But where aught notable is done / I buckle straight my harness on. / Up with the deep, down with the high, / The crooked straight, the straight awry!" (ll. 5465-5468), prompting the Herald to strike him with his staff as Odysseus struck Thersites. At this point Mephistopheles metamorphoses into a giant egg, from which an adder and a bat are hatched — one of the most bizarre of the many transformations that take place in this text (and a possible precursor for the transformation of Izdubar into an egg in Jung's *Red Book*?).

That there is some kind of relation between the Boy Charioteer and Faust-as-Plutus is suggested by the latter's declaration that the

---

[13] For further discussion, see Alan P. Cottrell, "Zoilo-Thersites: Another 'sehr ernster Scherz' in Goethe's *Faust II*," *Modern Language Quarterly*, vol. 29, no. 1 (March 1968), 29-41.

[14] See Homer, *The Iliad*, Book 2, ll. 246-324; cf. Seth Bernadete, *The Rhetoric of Morality and Philosophy: Plato's "Gorgias" and "Phaedrus"* (Chicago and London: Chicago University Press, 1991), pp. 100-101.

former is "spirit of my spirit" (l. 5623) and his exclamation (in an echo of the Father's words spoken to Christ at the moment of his baptism [Matthew 3:17]), "Beloved son, in thee well-pleased am I!" (l. 5629). Yet the nature of this relation is obscure to say the least, unless it is to hint that, without wealth, there can be no art; and the Boy Charioteer suddenly leaves this episode "with no rational explanation whatsoever," as Hamlin notes (403). Yet Jung is right when he suggests (see above) that the figure of the Boy Charioteer has something in common with Euphorion, the offspring of Faust and Helena in Act III, for Goethe himself identified the two figures as identical in his conversation with Eckermann of 20 December 1829. And what they have in common is fire: The Boy Charioteer is constantly snapping his fingers, sending jewels or flames which transform into insects or butterflies into the crowd and exciting it (ll. 5582-5605). Just before the Boy Charioteer leaves, Faust-as-Plutus descends from his opulent carriage pulled by a float of dragons and lifts onto the stage a huge chest, apparently full of gold, which, however, instantly turns to fire when anyone tries to grab it. Under the guise of the allegorical figure of Greed, Mephistopheles gathers this magical gold and molds it into a giant phallus, frightening the women in the crowd.

Among the Carnival Masquerade are Gnomes, another example of the "little people" from the opening scene of Part Two, in this case elves, hobgoblins, or dwarfs of Germanic folklore (the term *gnomes* was invented in the 16th century by Paracelsus, who derived the term from the Latin *gēnomos*, i.e., "earth-dweller"), who are presented here as miners of precious metals, carrying lanterns.[15] (These figures

---

[15] As Christopher McIntosh has noted, elves and dwarves are part of a rich mythology about the little people of the earth in Germany and are closely connected with such mountainous areas where precious metals are mined as the Harz Mountains (*Occult Germany: Old Gods, Mystics, and Magicians* (Rochester, VT: Inner Traditions, 2024), pp. 46-47). According to the ethnobotanist Wolf-Dieter Storl, garden gnomes or "red-capped plaster dwarfs" may be "scorned by cock-sure intellectuals as the epitome of bourgeois kitsch," but "are, in fact, visual representations of the etheric

anticipate the Cabiri of the Classical Walpurgnis Night, as well as the Cabiri who build the Tower in *The Red Book*.) In the procession the Gnomes are followed by their counterparts, the Giants (or "Wild Men" from the Harz Mountains),[16] who serve as bodyguards to the Emperor himself, who appears in the disguise of the Great Pan. The link between the Emperor and the mining or gold-digging activities of the Gnomes is underscored when a deputation of these diminutive figures approaches the Emperor and addresses him with a ballad full of technical mining terminology, before conducting him to the source of fire that surges up from the depths of the earth. As he stoops down to look, the Emperor's beard catches fire, the hall catches alight, and the entire scene is about to turn into a massive conflagration, when Faust-as-Plautus calls on Mephisto magically to intervene with a fire-quenching sprinkler system of water. The closing words of this scene spoken by Faust, "Thus, if spirit-malice lower, / Magic shall assert its power" (ll. 5985-5986), reinforces the theme of magic (later so important for Jung in *The Red Book*), while structurally the chaos of the imminent conflagration offers the first instance in Part Two of the principle of "interrupted tragedy."

And Faust's question — as he and Mephistopheles, dressed inconspicuously in current fashion, kneel before the Emperor—"You pardon, Sire, the juggling sport of flame [*das Flammengaukelspiel*]?" (l. 5987) anticipates the term *Fratzengeisterspiel* (l. 6546) in the later episode in Act I where the structural principle of "interrupted tragedy" makes itself felt once again. It is the context of Faust's fresh appointment at the court as Master of Revels that the theme

---

forces present in a garden" (*Pflanzendevas* (Aarau: AT-Verlag, 2002), p. 134; trans. McIntosch). For further discussion of Paracelsus and Goethe, see Chapter 4.

[16] As figures inspiring a mixture of "fear, awe, and fascination," these Wild Men — "The Wildwood-men — their name to tell / In the Harz Mountains known full well. / In native nakedness, antique might, / They come, each one of giant height" (ll. 5864-5867) — represent "the unbridled forces of nature, the carnal drives, and a more primitive state of humanity" (McIntosch, *Occult Germany*, p. 50).

of Helena — another part of the traditional Faust legend — is introduced, as Faust takes Mephistopheles aside into a "Dark Gallery" where he asks for his help in conjuring up Paris and Helena for the Emperor's entertainment:[17]

> But I meanwhile must rack my brain
> Urged by the Seneschal and Chamberlain.
> The Emperor wills — and straightway must it be —
> Helen and Paris 'fore his face to see,
> The paragon of men and eke of women
> Distinctly to behold, their mortal trim in.
>
> (ll. 6181-6186)

(Thus, Helena's appearance in *Faust II* is, as Gottfried Diener points out, a dual one: first, as the spirit whom Faust conjures up for the Emperor; and second, as the concubine whom Mephisto delivers into the arms of Faust [37].) Mephisto's unexpectedly serious response to this request from the Emperor highlights a fundamental ambivalence in the way this theme is treated: Is it a matter of mere entertainment, or does it signal a moment of great metaphysical significance?

---

[17] This episode may well find its inspiration in a work by the *Meistersinger* Hans Sachs (1494-1576) relating how a necromancer conjured up Helena at the court of the Holy Roman Emperor Maximilian I (see *Ein wunderbarlich gesicht keiser Maximiliani löblicher gedechtnus von einem nigromanten* [1564]):

> die schönen küngin Helena
> her aus Lacedemonia,
> des künigs Menelai weib,
> die aller schönest frau von leib,
> die im Paris, des künigs sun,
> von Troia het entführen tun […]

Relatedly, in his poem *The Story of Emperor Maximilian with the Alchemist* (*Die Geschicht Keyser Maximiliani mit dem alchamisten*) Sachs recounted an incident in the seventh century involving the alchemist Morienus and Sultan Khalif of Egypt which may have inspired other aspects of the scene at the imperial court.

For Mephistopheles responds that, unlike in the case of the quintessentially Germanic scenes of the "Witch's Kitchen" and of the "Walpurgis Night" in Part One, to access the classical realm of what he dismissively refers to as "the heathen-folk" (*das Heidenvolk*) requires engaging with the figures of the Mothers, whose existence he describes as a "lofty mystery" or "exalted riddle" (*höheres Geheimnis*) which he claims to be reluctant to reveal:

> In solitude throne goddesses sublime,
> Round them no place is, and still less a time.
> Only to speak of them the brain doth swim.
> The *Mothers* are they!
> (ll. 6213-16)

Who or what *are* the Mothers? Much critical ink has been spilled over their identity and nature, and these issues cannot be resolved here;[18] suffice it to say that they have been interpreted variously as Platonic Ideas, as Goethe's own concept of the "type," as the past, or as the world of beauty, and as related to the Eleusinian rites and to the Orphic mysteries and to Plutarch's *Life of Marcellus* (20) or his treatise *De defectu oraculorum* (*On the Obsolescence of Oracles*) (22).[19] (According to Rudolf Steiner, the three

---

[18] For further discussion, see Stuart Atkins, "The Mothers, the Phorcides and the Cabiri in Goethe's 'Faust,'" *Monatshefte*, vol. 45, no. 5 (October 1953), 289-296; Harold Jantz, *The Mothers in "Faust": The Myth of Time and Creativity* (Baltimore: Johns Hopkins Press, 1969); Mohammed Nadeem Niazi, "Faust's Violence against the Mothers," *The German Quarterly*, vol. 72, no. 3 (Summer 1999), 221-231; and John R. Williams, "The Problem of the Mothers," in Paul Bishop (ed.), *A Companion to Goethe's "Faust", Parts I and II* (Woodbridge and Rochester, NY: Camden House, 2001), pp. 122-143.

[19] In his conversation with Eckermann of 10 January 1830, Goethe claimed that he had "found in Plutarch that in ancient Greece mention was made of the Mothers as divinities," and that this was all that he owed to others and the rest was his "own invention" (*Conversations of Goethe*, p. 342). For further discussion, see Paul Bishop, "Plutarch and Goethe," in Sophia Xenophontos and Katerina Oikonomopoulou (eds), *Brill's Companion to the Reception of Plutarch* (Leiden and Boston: Brill, 2019), pp. 528-546; and Diener, *Fausts Weg zu Helena*, pp. 67 and 114.

Mothers are identifiable as Rhea, Demeter, and Persephone, each a mother of the next, and hence correspondingly identifiable as Saturn, sun, and moon.)[20] Faust's own response is immediate and startled: "Mothers!" he says, and in reply to Mephisto he explains his response, "The *Mothers! Mothers!* Nay, it sounds so weird!" (ll. 6216 and 6217). And "weird" (or *wunderlich*) it is, Mephisto confirms, and he goes on to reveal some more about the Mothers:

> And weird it is! Goddesses of you men
> Unknown, whom we to name are none too fain.
> To the uttermost Profound, wherein they tarry
> Mayst burrow [...]
>
> (ll. 6218-6219)

"Whither the way?" Faust asks, and Mephisto replies with an even more riddling response — that there *is* no way:

> No way! To the unexplorable
> Aye unexplored; a way to the unimplorable,
> Aye unimplored! Art thou in the mood?
> No locks are there, no bolts to shoot asunder!
> Through solitudes wilt thou be drifted yonder.
> Dost know what desert is and solitude?
>
> (ll. 6221-6227)

---

[20] Steiner, *Erläuterungen*, vol. 2, *Die romantische und die klassische Walpurgisnacht*, pp. 81 and 89. For further discussion of the Magna Mater, see the edition of the *Eranos-Jahrbücher* dedicated to *Gestalt und Kult der »Großen Mutter«*, especially Charles Picard, "Die Ephesia von Anatolien" and "Die Große Mutter von Kreta bis Eleusis," *Eranos-Jahrbuch*, 6 (1938), 59-90 and 91-119; and V.C.C. Collum, "Die schöpferische Mutter-Göttin der Völker keltischer Sprache," *Eranos-Jahrbuch*, 6 (1938), 221-324; as well as Erich Neumann, *The Great Mother: An Analysis of the Archetype* [1951], trans. Ralph Manheim [1955] (Princeton and Oxford: Princeton University Press, 2015), cf. Camille Paglia, "Erich Neumann: Theorist of the Great Mother," *Arion*, vol. 13 no. 3 (Winter 2006), 1-14.

Faust's irritated response to Mephisto's question about "desert" (*Öd'*) and "solitude" (*Einsamkeit*),[21] "Spare me such speeches by your favour, / That of the Witch's Kitchen savour / After a long, long interlude," reminds us of the fact that, since entering on Mephisto's wager, there is no one more "forlorn and quite forsaken" than he, Faust, is. Yet Mephisto's response suggests that the solitude he is talking about is not at all something social but rather metaphysical:

> And hadst thou swum through Ocean's vasty hollow
> And there beheld the boundless room,
> Yet wouldst thou see on billow billow follow.
> Aye, even shuddering at threatened doom
> Something thou still wouldst see. The emerald gulf in
> Of tranquil seas, wouldst spy the gliding dolphin,
> Wouldst see the clouds drift by, sun, moon and star;
> Naught wilt thou see i' the ever-empty Far,
> Not hear thy footstep where 'tis prest,
> Nor find firm ground whereon to rest.
>
> (ll. 6239-6248)

Not for nothing does Faust accuse Mephisto of playing the part of "mystagogue in chief," but he decides to play along and see where it all leads — in the spirit, he adds, of how, in one of La Fontaine's fables (Book 9, §17), Bertrand the monkey persuades Raton the cat to pull chestnuts out of the fire for him:

> [...] Me thou dost despatch
> Unto the Void, that there I may be able
> Both art and mind to enhance. [...]
> But on, we'll plumb the Deep whate'er befall,

---

[21] For discussion of the significance of *Öd'* and *Einsamkeit*, and the association for Goethe of *Öde* and *Leere* with *Chaos*, see Diener, *Fausts Weg zu Helena*, pp. 83-84.

For in thy Naught I trust to find the All
[In deinem Nichts hoff ich das All zu finden].
(ll. 6251-6252 and 6255-6256)

In his essay "The Spiritual Problem of Modern Man" (1928; ²1931), Jung alluded to the concluding line of this quotation from Faust to express the spiritual devastation of modernity. According to Jung, modern individuals have "become 'unhistorical' in the deepest sense [*im tiefsten Sinne »unhistorisch« geworden*] and have estranged themselves from the mass of human beings who live entirely within the bounds of tradition," adding: "Indeed, they are completely modern only when they have come to the very edge of the world, leaving behind them all that has been discarded and outgrown, and acknowledging that they stand before the Nothing out of which the All may grow [*das zugestandene Nichts, aus dem noch Alles werden kann*]" (CW 10 §150). (Could it be that Jung is thinking of the Lemures in Part Two, Act V, when he goes on to talk about those "worthless people" (*Untauglichen*) who "suddenly appear" by the side of "truly modern human individuals" as "uprooted wraiths, bloodsucking ghosts" (*als Entwurzelte, als vampyrische Gespenster*) and "discredit [those individuals] in [their] hardly enviable loneliness" [CW 10 §151]?)

But what is this Nothing in which Faust hopes to find his all? For some, it would seem to represent what Jung would call the collective unconscious (and Jung for his part would seem to agree), but the question remains: Is this Nothing something psychological or something metaphysical?²² Whatever its ontological status, it

---

²² We should not insist too much on this binary of the psychological and the metaphysical. After all, the notion of the archetype spans these two categories: notably, the archetype of the Mother, both in the sense that "there is nothing in the world which so completely enfolds us as the mother" (PU §700) or that "nothing in the world ever embraces us so completely as the mother" (CW 5 §682) and in the sense of the Platonic *khôra* (or *chora*, χώρα), the receptacle (or "third kind" [*triton genos*], cf. *Timaeus*, 48e) — "And the third kind is space everlasting, admitting not

would seem to be remarkably close to what ΦΙΛΗΜΩΝ in the first of the Sermons to the Dead in *The Red Book* calls the Pleroma — a term which, in its original Greek (πλήρωμα), literally means "fullness." This term can be found in the epistolary literature of the New Testament attributed to St. Paul (see Colossians 1:19; Colossians 2:9; and Ephesians 3:19), as well as in the traditions of Gnosticism attributed to Valentinus among others.

In his first sermon, ΦΙΛΗΜΩΝ announces to the dead that "nothingness is the same as the fullness" and that "we call this nothingness or fullness the *Pleroma*" (RB, 509). According to John M. Dillon, Gnosticism imported its concept of the Pleroma or the ideal realm from Plato's concept of the cosmos and the Demiurge in the *Timaeus* and from Philo's concept of the Noetic cosmos in contrast to the cosmos conceived aesthetically,[23] but in the context of Goethe's *Faust* the "Nothing" which contains the "All" is used in precisely an inverse sense. For the journey to the realm of Mothers will enable Faust (in terms of the dramatic plot) to conjure up Helena, inasmuch as it enables Goethe (through his linguistic resourcefulness) to bring Helena "back to life" in a poetic sense at

---

destruction, but affording place for all things that come into being, itself apprehensible without sensation by a sort of bastard reasoning, hardly matter of belief. It is with this in view that dreaming we say that all which exists must be in some place and filling some space, and that what is neither on earth nor in heaven anywhere is nought" (52a-b) — in which the "Forms" were received from the intelligible realm and were translated into the transitory forms of the sensible realm: "In the same way it behoves that which is fitly to receive many times over its whole extent likenesses of all things, that is of all eternal existences, to be itself naturally without part or lot in any of the forms. Therefore the mother and recipient of creation which is visible and by any sense perceptible we must call neither earth nor air nor fire nor water, nor the combinations of these nor the elements of which they are formed: but we shall not err in affirming it to be a viewless nature and formless, all-receiving, in some manner most bewildering and hard to comprehend partaking of the intelligible" (51b; trans. R.D. Archer-Hind).

[23] John M. Dillon, "*Pleroma* and Noetic Cosmos: A Comparative Study," in Richard T. Wallis and Jay Bregman (eds.), *Neoplatonism and Gnosticism* (Albany, NY: State University of New York Press, 1992), pp. 99-110.

the beginning of Act III. Seen in this light, the pleromatic Nothing-that-is-All *is* the realm of the aesthetic itself.

After all, in *On the Aesthetic Education of Humankind* (1795), Schiller had drawn on the ancient symbol of perfection — the circle — as connoting both 0 (zero) and ∞ (infinity), writing that "in the aesthetic state, [...] the human individual is *Nought*, if we are thinking of any particular result," yet "precisely thereby something Infinite is achieved" (Letter 21, §4 and §5); in other words, "if, [...] in *one* respect the aesthetic mode of the psyche is to be regarded as *Nought* [...] it is in another respect to be looked upon as a state of *Supreme Reality* [*Zustand der höchsten Realität*]" (Letter 22, §1).[24] And Letter 19, §2, as in Letter 21, §3, Schiller uses the term "an empty infinity" (*eine leere Unendlichkeit*), a notion which — as Elizabeth M. Wilkinson and L.A. Willoughby recognize — is "poetically symbolized" by Goethe in this scene in the "endless wastes" through which Faust must pass on his way to the "Mothers," who are themselves, by contrast, an "infinity filled with content" (*eine erfüllte Unendlichkeit*) or the "ground of all potentiality."[25] Is this Naught in which Faust trusts to find the All the Gnostic Pleroma or the Schillerian aesthetic state? Or both?

We never get to see the Mothers; all we know of them is what Mephisto himself seems to suggest in his instructions to Faust about how to gain access to these mysterious Mothers. "Here, take this key," says Mephisto, but Faust immediately balks at it: "That tiny thing!" (ll. 6259). "If tight / Thou grasp it, then its worth thou wilt not slight," retorts Mephisto, and Faust exclaims, "It waxes in

---

[24] Friedrich Schiller, *On the Aesthetic Education of Man*, ed. and trans. Elizabeth M. Wilkinson and L.A. Willoughby, 2nd edn (Oxford: Clarendon Press, 1982), pp. 144-147 and 150-151. Cf. Elizabeth M. Wilkinson and L.A. Willoughby, "'The Whole Man' in Schiller's Theory of Culture and Society" [1969], in *Models of Wholeness: Some Attitudes to Language, Art and Life in the Age of Goethe*, ed. Jeremy Adler, Martin Swales, and Ann Weaver (Oxford: Lang, 2002), pp. 233-268 (p. 248).
[25] Schiller, *On the Aesthetic Education*, pp. 128-129 and 144-145; cf. "Introduction," pp. lxxxi-lxxxii; and "Commentary," pp. 262-263.

my hand, with flames 'tis lit!" (l. 6260-6261).[26] "Follow it down,"
Mephisto promises Faust, "'twill lead thee to the Mothers," and so
it will prove. By now, Faust is impressed, and in lines that attracted
the attention of Pierre Hadot (1922-2010),[27] he declares:

> And yet my weal in torpor seek I not.
> The thrill of awe is still mankind's best lot,
> And though the world not lets him feel it cheaply,
> Yet awe-struck, the stupendous feels he deeply.
>
> (ll. 6271-6274)

Das Schaudern ist der Menschheit bestes Teil — in this phrase
Goethe evokes the motif of "shuddering" as a response that is both
physical and emotional, or (in other words) aesthetic, to the sense
of *das Ungeheure* that we feel when contemplating the world. But
where Mephisto is sending Faust is somewhere that is literally out
of this world, and this is why it is a realm that is neither above nor
below, for it is *outside* space and time:

> Sink then! I might say: Rise! There is no choice,
> For all is one. From the Existent fleeing
> Into the unfettered realm of Form, rejoice
> In that which long hath had no longer being.
> [...]
> At length a glowing tripod wilt thou see,
> Then in the nethermost abyss wilt be.
> The Mothers by its light wilt thou descry,
> Some sitting, standing some, or walking nigh,

---

[26] For further discussion of the symbolic significance of the key, also found in *Wilhelm Meister's Journeyman Years*, see Diener, *Fausts Weg zu Helena*, pp. 95-100.

[27] Pierre Hadot, *La Philosophie comme manière de vivre: Entretiens* (Paris: Albin Michel, 2001), p. 172; and *Philosophy as a Way of Life: Spiritual Exercises from Socrates to Foucault*, ed. Arnold I. Davidson, trans. Michael Chase (Oxford and Malden, MA: Blackwell, 1995), p. 115.

E'en as may chance. Formation, transformation,
The Eternal Mind's eternal recreation,
And round them float forms of all things that be.
They'll see thee not, for wraiths alone they see.
(ll. 6275-6278 and 6283-6290)

(The "glowing tripod" is rich in alchemical and other associations, as Diener discusses in detail [*Fausts Weg zu Helena*, 106-117].) Now enraptured, Faust holds the key and strikes a heroic pose (what Latham translates as "a resolutely imperious attitude" and what Arndt does as "an attitude of peremptory command"). While Mephisto's instructions to Faust to strike the tripod in the midst of the silent Mothers with the magic key could suggest, as Hamlin notes, the possibility of a Freudian reading that interprets the imagery as sexual, what is even more important — and overlooked by many critics — is "the characteristic ironic tone of the entire scene" (410). This ironic dimension is underscored just as much by the fact that Faust's descent to the Mothers is not actually *shown* — an example of what Erich Heller (1911-1990) once called Goethe's "avoidance of the tragic" — [28] as it is by Mephisto's final words in this scene, spoken *ad spectatores*, "I hope the key may profit him, good lack! / I wonder now if ever he'll come back" (ll. 6305-6306). Indeed, this scene is imbued with the ironic, even satirical tone that characterizes much of Goethe's writing in general and *Faust*, Part Two in particular. (This has not, however, prevented such commentators as the anthroposophist Rudolf Steiner from taking Goethe's text fairly and squarely at face value.)[29]

---

[28] See Erich Heller, *The Disinherited Mind: Essays in Modern German Literature and Thought* (Harmondsworth: Penguin, 1961), pp. 33-58.
[29] See Rudolf Steiner, "Faust and the Mothers" in *Erläuterungen*, vol. 2, pp. 81-93. In this lecture given in Dornach on 2 November 1917, Steiner comments as follows: "[Faust] has descended to the Mothers: He has gone through some kind of transformation. Leaving aside what one otherwise knows of the matter and what has been said by us in the course of years, we need reflect only upon how the Greek

Yet this irony would not be irony if there were not *also* something very serious in intent that is going in these lines, and this serious aspect to what is being depicted (or rather what is *not* being depicted, but being described, by Mephistopheles) is twofold. First, the journey to the Mothers and the retrieval of Helena require an emotional response from Faust in the form of courage: "Then pluck a heart up, for the danger's great!" (1. 6291), and this statement, *die Gefahr ist groß*, is one that caught Jung's attention in *Symbols and Transformations of the Libido*, as we shall see in Chapter 3. And second, the conjuring up of Paris and Helena is to be achieved by a procedure that Mephisto expressly describes as magical:

> Calmly thou'lt rise, thee Fortune will upbear,
> And thou'lt be back with it or they are ware.
> Once thou hast brought it hither, thou wilt cite
> Hero and heroine from out the night,
> The first that ever dared the high endeavour.
> It is achieved, and thou art the achiever.
> Then must the incense-mist by magic-process [*nach magischem Behandeln*]
> Shape into gods in instant metamorphosis.
> [*Der Weihrauchsnebel sich in Götter wandeln*].
>
> (ll. 6295-6302)

---

poets, in speaking of the Mysteries, refer to those who were initiated as having learnt to know the three world-Mothers — Rhea, Demeter and Proserpina. These three Mothers, their being, what they essentially are — all this was said to be learnt through direct perception by those initiated into the Mysteries in Greece. When we dwell upon the significant manner in which Goethe speaks in this scene, and also upon what takes place in the next, we shall no longer be in any doubt that in reality Faust has been led into regions, into kingdoms, that Goethe thought to be like that kingdom of the Mothers into which the initiate into the Greek Mysteries was led. By this we are shown how full of import Goethe's meaning is" (vol. 2, pp. 81-82]; trans. George Kaufmann). Such a reading neglects the parodic tone of Goethe's text, or of what he called in his letter to Wilhelm von Humboldt of 17 March 1832 "these very serious jokes" (*diese sehr ernsten Scherze*) (see Goethe, *Briefe*, ed. Karl Robert Mandelkow, 4 vols. (Hamburg: Wegner, 1962-1967), vol. 4, p. 481) — assuming that one can make such an easy distinction between parody and esoteric content.

Once again, the theme of *magic*, which will play a prominent role in Jung's *Red Book*, is in the forefront of the action of Goethe's *Faust*.

That Faust's journey to the Mothers is taken in order to fulfill a request of the Emperor is something of which we are reminded by a remark of the Chamberlain to Mephistopheles at the opening of a short scene set in a "Brightly lit Ballroom." Once again, the theme of magic is foregrounded when Mephisto replies, "The Beautiful, that Treasure, who would raise, / He needs the highest art, the Sage's Magic" (*Denn wer den Schatz, das Schöne, heben will, / Bedarf der höchsten Kunst, Magie der Weisen*) (ll. 6315-6316).[30] As the members of the court gather for the entertainment, Mephisto wonders where Faust has got to, and he cries, "O Mothers! Mothers! Let but Faust go free!" (l. 6366). Around him, the entire court throngs into the spacious Hall of Chivalry, where the illumination is suspiciously dim. Is what we are about to witness really magic, or is it only an illusion? For, as Mephisto puts it, "The ample walls with tapestry are rich, / And decked with armour every nook and niche. / Methought no magic word had here been wanted, / But spirits of themselves the place had haunted!" (ll. 6373-6376).

In the Hall of Chivalry an elaborate stage arrangement has been set up, its walls opening inward to create a deeper space, containing the façade of a Doric temple. Into the prompter's box on the proscenium at the edge of the stage (and thus concealed from the audience) both the Astrologer and Mephistopheles have climbed: "Be opened up, ye walls! / Naught hinders, with us magic doth conspire [*hier ist Magie zur Hand*]," says the Astrologer, but his subsequent words about how the deep-spaced theater contains "A gleam mysterious to light the gloom" (*Geheimnisvoll ein Schein uns zu erhellen*) (l. 6397) hint again at the illusory nature of what

---

[30] For further discussion of the ambitions expressed in these lines, see Diener, *Fausts Weg zu Helena*, p. 93.

is about to unfold. Or is what happens essentially pointing to the artistic magic of aesthetic illusion, as suggested by the Astrologer's further words?

> With reverence hail the star-accorded season,
> Let potent word of magic fetter reason,
> But hither from afar, unshackled-free,
> Resplendent come, audacious Fantasy [*Phantasei*]!
> What boldly ye did covet, mark it well,
> Impossible, therefore most credible.
>
> (ll. 6415-6420)

On the other side of the stage (and visible to the audience) Faust mounts the proscenium: He is dressed in priestly garb and is described by the Astrologer as being "a wondrous man" (*ein Wundermann*) or a man of miracles, a significant variation on how he is described as "the luckless man" (*der Unglücksmann*) by Ariel in the "Charming Landscape" scene at the beginning of Part Two (l. 4620). With "majestic pathos" (*großartig*) Faust invokes the Mothers, recapitulating Mephisto's description of them in the earlier "Dark Gallery" scene:

> In your name, O ye Mothers, ye that throne
> In the Illimitable, ever alone,
> And yet companionably. Restless rife
> Float round ye, lifeless, images of life
> [*Des Lebens Bilder, regsam, ohne Leben*].
> What once hath been, in radiance supernal
> Yonder doth move — for it would be eternal
> [*Was einmal war in allem Glanz und Schein,
> Es regt sich dort; denn es will ewig sein*].
> And ye, almighty Powers, apportion it
> Unto the cope of day, the vault of night.

> Those doth the gracious course of life embrace,
> These the bold wizard seeketh in their place
> [*Des einen faßt des Lebens holder Lauf.*
> *Die andern sucht der kühne Magier auf*]
> And confident and lavish shows to us,
> What all are fain to see, the marvellous
> > [*das Wunderwürdige schaun*].
> > > (ll. 6427-6436)

What are these images of life, *des Lebens Bilder*? Are they archetypes? If so, why are they described as "lifeless" (*ohne Leben*)? And if they are lifeless, why is it that "what was [...] there is astir" (*Was einmal war ... Es regt sich dort*)? The chief conceptual opposition in this passage seems to be one between "being" (*Sein*) and "appearance" (*Schein*), but any attempt to read these lines as a psychological or aesthetic manifesto runs up against the problem of the context in which they are spoken — Faust's excessive posturing as a "bold magician" (*der kühne Magier*) (although in a draft of this passage, Goethe had written *getrost der Dichter*, i.e., "confident the poet," suggesting the true poet is really a magician!).[31] Based on Arndt's translation, but following this manuscript variant, one might translate lines 6435-6436 as follows: "The ones, the lovely course of life embraces, / The others confident the poet traces."

(Thus, on the one hand, this episode enacts the gradual, step-by-step path to the intuitive vision of the realm of the Ideas as outlined in Plato, corresponding to the degree of initiation undergone by the initiate in the Eleusinian Mysteries, as Diener has pointed out: Faust goes from being a "neophyte" [l. 6250], standing on the threshold to initiation, to being a priest of the Mysteries, clad "in priestly garb and wreath" [l. 6421], having achieved the

---

[31] Schöne, *Kommentare*, 486; cf. Schöne, *Texte*, 623. For further discussion of the relationship between poet (*Dichter*) and magician (*Magier*), see Diener, *Fausts Weg zu Helena*, pp. 31 and 166-167.

"full vision of the perfect mysteries" and been "initiated into that mystery which is rightly accounted blessed beyond all others" [*Phaedrus*, 249c and 250b] in the *epopteía* (ἐποπτεία), the mystical vision of the final initiation rite; for Plato, the noetic intuition of the Ideas.[32] On the other, the episode serves as an allegory of the aesthetic and its power to effect a transmutation of the sensible and the intelligible alike.)

In other words, in this first appearance of Helena in Goethe's drama, it is only her likeness, her appearance, her "spirit" that appears — reflected in the choice of verse form in this scene (rhyming couplets) and in the fact that Helena herself never actually speaks. In fact, the order in which things happen is highly significant: as Faust's glowing key touches the rim of the tripod he has brought back from the realm of the Mothers, a cloud billows out from it that will assume the forms of Paris and Helena. First, it is as if the façade of the Doric temple becomes alive and starts to sing:

Lo,

The clouds break into music as they go!

From airy tones a mystic yearning wells,

And as they drift to melody all swells.

The column-shaft, the triglyph is achime,

The temple all bursts into song sublime.

(ll. 6443-6448)

---

[32] Diener, *Fausts Weg zu Helena*, p. 31. Like Plato, who evokes "the ascent and the contemplation of the things above [as] the soul's ascension to the intelligible region" (*Republic*, 517b) and describes "the quest for the universal beauty" as "ever mounting the heavenly ladder, stepping from rung to rung" (*Symposium*, 211c), Goethe uses the imagery of heights or vertical ascension to describe the trajectory of Faust, notably in Act V (Diener, 47).

Second, Paris — in Homer's *Iliad*, the Trojan whose abduction of Helen from Menelaus sparked the Trojan War — steps forth, a beautiful young man whose appearance immediately excites the women in the courtly audience. And it is as the third figure that Helena finally steps forth, provoking an impassioned response from Faust:

> Have I still eyes? Or in my being deep
> Doth Beauty's source in flood outpouréd sweep?
> My pilgrimage of dread brings blessed gain.
> How did the world still worthless, locked remain!
> What is it since my priesthood? Now at last
> Desirable, perdurable, firm-based.
> If from my life I let thee be effaced,
> Then may my life's breath too forsake its duty!
> The goodly form that erst my bosom captured,
> Me in the magic-glass enraptured,
> Was but a foam-wraith of such beauty.
> To thee the play of every power with gladness
> I'll vow, the essence of all passion,
> Liking to thee, love, adoration, madness!
>   (ll. 6487-6500)[33]

The profundity of Faust's response forms an immediate contrast to the response to the sight of the Paris from the court ladies, who behave as they were witnessing a nude wrestler! But has Faust got it all wrong? After all, is this Helena herself whom he has conjured up — or only her appearance?[34] From the prompter's box,

---

[33] Faust's question, "Have I still eyes?" reverses the famous line from Christopher Marlow's *Doctor Faustus* (c. 1590): "Was this the face that launched a thousand ships, and burnt the topless towers of Ilium?"

[34] According to some accounts (such as Euripides and Stesichorus), it was Helen's *eidōlon* (or phantom) that went to Troy, not Helen herself.

Mephistopheles warns Faust not to fall out of his role, "You do forget yourself! Pray you, discretion" (l. 6501). Although one lady of the court compares the sight of Paris and Helena to Endymion and Luna (Endymion was the handsome Aeolian shepherd who was loved by Selene, the Titan goddess of the moon, known to the Romans as Luna), most of the court ladies turn against Helena, making bitchy remarks about her jewelry. When it turns out that Paris is interested in Helena, and that what is being staged is called *The Rape of Helena*, Faust — ignoring Mephisto's advice, "Be still! / Pray, let the phantom do whatever it will" (ll. 6514-6515), and his reminder, "Thyself dost make the phantom-pantomime [*das Fratzengeisterspiel*]!" (l. 6546) — suddenly intervenes in the proceedings and tries to grab hold of Helena:

> Rape, quotha! Am I here for naught then, fellow?
> And hold I not this key here in my hand,
> That hither me, through horror, surge and billow
> Of solitudes, hath led to a sure stand?
> Here foothold is, realities. The spirit
> With spirits here may strive, and by its merit
> The great, the double empire may inherit.
> So far she was, nearer how could she be?
> I save her, doubly she belongs to me.
> I'll do't. Ye Mothers, Mothers, needs must grant her!
> Who once hath known her, never more may want her!
> (ll. 6549-6559)

In so doing, Faust causes the entire vision to collapse: His intervention "with violence" (*mit Gewalt*) causes Helena's "shape" or "form" (*die Gestalt*) to turn cloudy and to disappear. As the vision suddenly vanishes, there is an explosion: Faust is knocked to the ground, the spirits dissolve into mist, and Act I comes to an end in "darkness, tumult."

So, what has really happened here? For all the mysterious description of the Mothers by Mephistopheles, what seems to have taken place is really a kind of projection. As soon as Faust forgets that "the entire spirit show is the projection of his own mind, a dream image that he himself is dreaming" (Hamlin, 414), the show itself collapses. And indeed it is only a (spirit) show, a play within a play, and the entire scene arguably has more to do with theatricality than it has to do with alchemy, despite the references to "the great work" (*das hohe Werk*) (l. 6110), to "cohobation" (l. 6325), and to Luna (ll. 4955-4959 and 6509). But Helena's ghostly appearance in the event leading to the explosive conclusion to Act I is not the last time we shall see her, and Hamlin makes the important point that this spirit show serves as a prefiguration of the "actual encounter" between Faust and Helena that takes place in Act III (414).

At the same time, this episode hints at a link between Faust and Parzival. For in his chapter on the conjunction in *Mysterium Coniunctionis*, Jung warns of the danger of failing to understand that, in analysis, "fantasy" is a "real psychic process" which "is happen[ing] [...] personally" to us (CW 14 §753). Although we "look on" from outside, we are also an "acting and suffering figure" in what Jung calls the "drama of the psyche" (§753). Recognition of this point is "absolutely necessary" and marks an "important advance," for "as long as [we] simply look at the pictures [we are] like the foolish Parzival, who forgot to ask the vital question *because he was not aware of his own participation in the action*" (§753; my italics). We must, Jung insists, "recognize [our] own involvement" by "enter[ing] into the process with [our] personal reactions, just as if [we] were one of the fantasy figures" — or, in other words, "as if the drama being enacted before [our] eyes were real" (§753). After all, he adds, it is a "psychic fact" that this fantasy is happening, and "it is as real as you —as a psychic entity — are real," and if this "crucial operation" does not take place, "all the changes are left to the flow of images" — and we remain "unchanged," that is, untransformed (§753). Faust's mistake is to *overidentify* with the process of conjuring up Paris and Helena and hence loses the double optic which is required. (In his "Epilogue" to *Psychology and Alchemy*, Jung returns to this scene and discusses it in more detail, as we shall see in Chapter 4.)

For now, however, Faust lies unconscious on the floor, and when in Act II he awakens, his first thought will be Helena, and his first question will be, "Where is she?" (ll. 7056 and 7070). "During th[is] unconscious state," as Diener points out, "Helena — or rather that close-to-natural, still vivid world that has long been sunken in the deepest layer of the soul, from which Helena once could arise and under propitious circumstances can perhaps arise again — is the subject of Faust's significant, mysterious dream" (Diener, 222). And, in fact, Faust is asleep during the first scene (set in the narrow, high-vaulted Gothic chamber) and in the second scene (set in the laboratory) of Act II, not reawakening until the beginning of the Classical Walpurgis Night.

Act II

In the first scene of Act II, we find ourselves back in the same narrow, high-vaulted Gothic chamber where we had first seen Faust in Part One. Then, he was sitting in his armchair by the desk; now, he is lying on an antique bed. Nothing has changed, it seems: except that the stained-glass windows are darker, the cobwebs are thicker, and the piles of paper — five-year strategic plans, perhaps, or interim REF impact case-studies? — have grown yellower. The quill pen, with a drop of the blood with which Faust signed the wager, is still there. Nothing has changed, and yet everything has changed, now that Faust has embarked on his self-transformatory journey.

Just as Mephistopheles slipped into Faust's academic gown to bamboozle the student in Part One, so he does again to speak to the Famulus, the academic assistant who has replaced Wagner in this role. Mephistopheles calls for the Famulus by ringing the bell, causing the entire Gothic hall to tremble from the sound and locked, sealed-shut doors to burst open. (In this act there is, Hamlin suggests, an "epochal significance," inasmuch as it symbolizes the liberation from the imprisonment of dead knowledge from which Faust had been suffering [417]. In an extended form, we find a similar imagery in *Zarathustra*, in the dream related in Part Two in "The Prophet" in which one of the many coffins standing in musty vaults in the lonely hill-fortress of death springs open after three loud knocks like thunderbolts at the door [Z II 19] and in the midnight bell at the end of Part Three and Part Four, "an old heavy, heavy booming bell" that "booms out at night up to [Zarathustra's] cave" in "The Second Dance Song" [Z III 15 §2]; the same bell which sounds "from the depths" when all around it has grown "still and mysterious" in "The Drunken Song" [Z IV 19 §2].)

In the meantime, the student of Part One has completed his studies and become a Baccalaureus,[35] while Wagner has finished his doctorate and is now called Doctor Wagner. (In five stanzas of trochaic meter, the Baccalaureus sketches a self-portrait of himself, while the dialogue with Mephistopheles offers a satirical critique of the modern subjectivism of German Idealism.)[36] Not only has Wagner gained his doctoral title, he has clearly been able to access some research funds, for he is working away in a laboratory, full of the latest equipment — the latest equipment, that is, for the medieval setting of the traditional Faust story, so full of "extensive cumbrous sets of apparatus for fantastic purposes." Wagner is embarked on an experiment that is part alchemical, part reminiscent of Mary Shelley's Dr. Frankenstein: he is trying

---

[35] That is, he has a bachelor's degree and thus taken the first step on the academic career ladder; *baccalaureus* derives from *laurus* (= laurel) and *bacca* (= berry), referring to the use of laurels as an award for academic achievement (Diener, *Fausts Weg zu Helena*, p. 232).

[36] For further discussion, see Diener, *Fausts Weg zu Helena*, pp. 233-241.

to create a homunculus.[37] Now the figure of Homunculus has its roots in 16th-century alchemy and in 19th-century fiction alike: meaning, literally, a "little person." In his treatise *De natura rerum* (*On the Nature of Things*) (1537), Paracelsus explains how to make homunculi, although in his lecture titled "The Visions of Zosimos" (given at the Eranos Conference in 1937), Jung suggests that the concept of the homunculus first appeared in the third century in Zosimos's account of an encounter with a priest, who changed "into the opposite of himself, into a mutilated anthroparion" ("The Treatise of Zosimos the Divine concerning the Art," III, I, §2; in CW 13 §86 and fn. 7).[38]

Further details in Zosimos's account lead Jung to the view that "the homunculus [...] stands for the uroboros, which devours itself and gives birth to itself (as though spewing itself forth)" (§111), an example of "'circular' Gnostic thinking" found also in alchemy and Christianity, according to which "the sacrificer is the sacrificed, and the sword that kills is the same as that which is killed" (§110).

---

[37] For further discussion of this figure, see John Fitzell, "Goethe, Jung: Homunculus and Faust," in Alexej Ugrinsky, *Goethe in the Twentieth Century* (New York: Greenwood Press, 1987), pp. 107-115. On the role of Mephistopheles in the creation of Homunculus (and, later, the entire Helena episode), see the conversation of 16 December 1829 where Goethe responds to Eckermann's suggestion that Mephistopheles "has had a secret influence [*heimlich mitgewirkt*] on the production of the Homunculus" and "in the *Helena* he always appears as secretly working [*als heimlich wirkendes Wesen erscheint*]" by agreeing, and considering whether to add some verses expressing this "co-operation" (*Mitwirkung*) (*Conversations of Goethe*, p. 334).

[38] According to Ronald Gray, Homunculus represents the philosopher's stone as the appearance of the carbuncle and the red and white colors suggest, but only as an "embryonic form of perfection" (Ronald D. Gray, *Goethe the Alchemist: A Study of Alchemical Symbolism in Goethe's Literary and Scientific Works* (Cambridge: Cambridge University Press, 1952), p. 214); while Diener suggests that Goethe read Paracelsus's *De generationibus rerum naturalium* (1537) as providing the recipe for the in vitro fertilization of an artificial little man (Diener, *Fausts Weg zu Helena*, p. 248). As the Stone, Homunculus exemplifies Gerhard Dorn's cry, *Transmutemini* [*de lapidibus mortuis*] *in vivos lapides philosophicos!* or "Transmute yourselves [from dead stones] into living philosophical stones!") (cited in CW 12 §187 and §378), but his fate in *Faust* also illustrates a failure to achieve perfection.

Further on in this paper, Jung equates the homunculus as the "inner man" with the *lapis* (or philosopher's stone) as consisting of "body, soul, and spirit," and indeed with Christ, on the basis that the lapis represents the idea of a "transcendent totality which coincides with what analytical psychology calls the self" (§134). Yet in Goethe's *Faust* the Homunculus is a figure who ultimately fails to be constellated as the self: It represents rather a failure successfully to individuate and as such is a further instantiation of the structural principle of "interrupted tragedy" that governs the drama as a whole.[39]

"Soon is achieved a glorious undertaking," Wagner tells Mephistopheles. "What is it, pray?" asks Mephisto more softly, and Wagner, also more softly, replies: "A man is in the making" (ll. 6834-6835). Nowadays this scene is more redolent of modern techniques of in vitro fertilization and genetic engineering rather than alchemical experimentation; an example of the way in which Goethe's *Faust* is a timeless work, that continually adapts itself to the conditions of the world in which it is being performed (or read). Thus, the alembic from which Homunculus speaks is reminiscent of the modern test tube, although even test tubes tend not to do what this one does, when it slips from Wagner's hands and, as a side door opens revealing Faust stretched out on the couch, floats over the sleeping Faust and illuminates him. What now happens recalls another modern technique: that of psychoanalysis, as Homunculus engages with the material of the dream that Faust is dreaming. Once again, however, Goethe's technology is ahead of the game: for Homunculus can actually describe what Faust is seeing in his dream while he is still asleep! What is it that Faust can see in his dream? Homunculus describes it as follows:

---

[39] In his *Homunculus: Modernes Epos in zehn Gesängen* (1888), the Austrian poet Robert Hamerling (1830-1889) used the figure of Homunculus in a modern epic to articulate his social critique of the age (see Steiner, *Erläuterungen*, vol. 2, p. 249).

Limpid waters
In a thick grove! Women, that disarray them!
Most beautiful are they of Beauty's daughters,
Yet radiantly fair doth one outweigh them,
Of highest heroes born, nay, God-born haply.
Her foot she dips the bright pellucid pool in,
The sweet life's flame that warms her form — how
                              shapely! —
Within the waves' enfolding crystal cooling.
But what a rustle of pinions now swift-flashing
Ruffles the polished glass! What rushing, splashing!
Startled the maidens flee; the queen their flight
Shares not, but stands, nor needs with fear to wrestle,
And with a proud and womanly delight
She sees unto her knee the swan-prince nestle,
Importunately tame. Now he grows bolder, —
But suddenly a vaporous cloud
In thickly-woven gauze doth shroud
The fairest scene ere had beholder.

(ll. 6903-6920)

What Homunculus describes is a kind of mythological primal scene — for Faust's dream is a representation of the story of Leda and the swan, and thus a vision of the conception of Helena herself. According to Greek mythology, the god Zeus took the form of a swan, and in this shape he seduced or raped Leda, a daughter of the Aetolian King Thestius who married King Tyndareus of Sparta and was thus queen of Sparta (as well as queen of the nymphs). Consequently, Helena herself emerged from an egg, a birth that is as unconventional as is that of Homunculus himself from the alembic. In the Renaissance, the myth of Leda and the swan became a popular motif, and it is the subject of numerous famous paintings, including ones by Cesare da Sesto copied after a lost original by

Leonardo da Vinci (1515-1520) (in the Uffizi and at Wilton House) and by Correggio (c. 1532) (in the Gemäldegalerie in Berlin and reproduced on the cover of the OUP paperback of the translation of *Faust II* by David Luke).

In this respect, Faust's dream is a very Freudian dream, focused on an act of sexual union which is, in fact, doubly concealed (by the motif of Zeus disguised as a swan and by the misty gauze that suddenly veils the moment of union). At the same time, however, it is a very Jungian dream, as it depicts a scene that transcends the individual dreamer and contains a motif that has become of our collective memory; our *cultural* collective unconscious, so to speak.[40] In the immediate dramatic context, however, the Leda dream has a threefold function: first, it offers comfort to Faust in his present distress, compensating for his currently unfulfilled desire for Helena; second, it revives in Faust the yearning for this highest instantiation of beauty, which acquires an archetypal dimension; and third, it has a prognostic meaning, pointing forward to the epiphany of Helena in Act III (Diener, 265).

How does Homunculus (in his role of impromptu analyst) interpret the dream? He points to the disjunction between Faust's cultural background, embodied in the architecture of the room in which he is sleeping —

---

[40] In "The Meaning of Psychology for Modern Man" (1933; 1934), Jung — in the context of a reference to the Witch's Kitchen scene in *Faust I* — declares that "in dreams we put on the likeness of that more universal, truer, more eternal individual dwelling in the darkness of primordial night. There he is still the whole, and the whole is in him [...]. It is from these all-uniting depths that the dream arises, be it never so childish, grotesque, and immoral. So flowerlike is it in its candour and veracity [...] No wonder that in all the ancient civilizations an impressive dream was accounted a message from the gods! [...] What would become of humankind if nobody had lucky ideas [*Einfälle*] any more? [...] The dream is nothing but a lucky idea [*Einfall*] that comes to us from the dark, all-unifying world of the psyche" (CW 10 §304-§305).

The North thy heritage is,
Thy birth was in the misty ages,
The waste of priesthood and of chivalry,
And how should there thine eye be free?
Thou art at home but in the murky.
Dingy-brown stonework, mouldered, horrid,
And Gothic-arched, ignoble, florid!

— and in the southern, mythological ambiance of his dream:

His dream with sylvan springs beguiled him,
And swans, and naked beauties.
(ll. 6923-6929 and 6932-6933)

In order to reconcile these two opposites — the Christian, courtly world of the North with the pagan, classical South, embodied in personified form in the figures of Faust and Helena — Homunculus recommends that Faust be transported to the Classical Walpurgis Night, an event which is "just now" (*jetzt eben*) taking place: an example of synchronicity, to be sure, as well as "the best thing that could happen" (*das Beste, was begegnen könnte*) (l. 6942). Yet even though Faust is a representative of the Protestant North as opposed to the pagan South, Homunculus describes the Classical Walpurgis Night as bringing Faust "to his own element" (*zu seinem Elemente*) (l. 6943).

In fact, the Classical Walpurgis Night functions as a moment in which a number of opposites are constellated:

• North versus South
• Medieval mist versus classical clarity
• Classical versus Romantic
• Objective versus subjective
• Naïve versus sentimental

- Real versus ideal
- Striving for *Gehalt, Gestalt und Form* versus striving for "free exercise of imagination"
- "Plastic, true, and real" versus "illusory," "unreal, impossible"
- Natural, original versus artificial, exaggerated, excessive
- Organic, harmonious, necessary versus inorganic, lacking in proportion, arbitrary
- "Strong, fresh, cheerful," "healthy and industrious" versus "weak, sickly, and sick"

(Diener, 271-272)

Or as the famous maxim puts it, "the Classical I call healthy, and the Romantic sickly" (*Maxims and Reflections*, §462). (In fact, Goethe's *Faust* itself is a case in point: As a work, does it fall into the category of the Classical or the Romantic? Or does it ultimately transcend this binary, as it transcends all other binaries?)

Since Mephistopheles, as a Northern Devil, is not sure of the way to the Classical Walpurgis Night, Homunculus takes it upon himself to act as their sat-nav, taking them to the river Peneios in Thessaly, where it flows down from the Pindus mountains through the Vale of Tempe — a gorge located between Mount Olympus (to the north) and Mount Ossa (to the south) — and empties in the Aegean Sea. Or as Homunculus himself puts it:

> Southeastward, though, at present are we bound.
> By a great plain, through thicket and through grove
> Peneus flows, in still and humid reaches;
> The champaign to the mountain-gorges stretches,
> And old and new Pharsalus lies above.

(ll. 6951-6955)

At the southern edge of the Thessalian Plain, four kilometres south of the river Enipeas, lies the city of Farsala, known in Antiquity as Pharsalos. It was here that the decisive battle of Caesar's Civil War, the Battle of Pharsalus, was fought on 9 August 48 B.C.E., when Julius Caesar and his allies opposed the army of the Roman Republic under the command of Pompey. Although Pompey enjoyed the backing of a majority of Roman senators and his army significantly outnumbered Caesar's legions, he suffered an overwhelming defeat in a battle which, as Hamlin observes, "marked the transition from the ancient to the modern world" as well as "the death of mythological creatures from the former" (197). It is the annual occasion on which these mythological creatures assemble to commemorate their own demise that constitutes the Classical Walpurgis Night — the title of the next part of Act II.

The Classical Walpurgis Night consists of three scenes, the first being set in darkness on the Pharsalian Fields, just outside the city after which the historical battle is named. On the night before the battle, Sextus Pompeius, the son of Pompey the Great, consulted the witch Erichtho on its likely outcome. According to the account of the civil war between Julius Caesar and the forces of the Roman Senate led by Pompey the Great given by Lucan in *De Bello Civili* (i.e., *On the Civil War*), more usually referred to as the *Pharsalia*, Erichtho chooses a gruesome method to invoke the infernal powers, namely finding a fresh corpse, filling it with a poison in which "was mingled all that Nature wrongly bears" (Book 6, 1. 670) and raising it from the dead; the description by the revived corpse of a civil war that is raging in the underworld leads to prophecy of the fate awaiting Pompey and his kin:

"[…] Sextus, take consolation in this:
the dead look to welcome your father and his house
to a place of peace, keeping a bright region of their
realm for them. Let no short-lived victory trouble

you: cometh the hour that makes all generals equal.
You proud, with your high hearts, hasten to die,
then descend from so pitiful a grave to trample
on the ghosts of the deified Romans. [...]
                    O ill-fated ones,
finding nowhere in the world safer than Pharsalia!"[41]

Both Lucan (in *Pharsalia*, Book 4, l. 507) and Ovid (in *Heroides*, Book 15, l. 139) emphasize the ugliness of Erichtho, but Goethe's Erichtho dismisses their description of her as mere slander. Her soliloquy evokes not just the battle between Pompey and Caesar, but History itself as an essentially circular process: "How oft it hath recurred already, will recur / Through ages everlasting ..." (*Wie oft schon wiederholt' sich's! wird sich immerfort / Ins Ewige wiederholen ...*) (ll. 7012-7013), a kind of anticipation of Nietzsche's doctrine of eternal recurrence. Looking up, Erichtho espies what she takes to be a meteor, but which is, in fact, Faust and Mephistopheles riding through the air on the magic cloak, led by Homunculus in his glass phial and illuminating them with a dazzling light. (The minor detail of this "sphere corporeal" [*körperlichen Ball*] prompts Gottfried Diener to reflect on Goethe's use of the "spherical shape" or *Kugelgestalt* as a symbol for a "perfect, self-contained being," echoing Plato's description in the *Timaeus* of "a rounded and spherical shape, having its bounding surface in all points at an equal distance from the centre" as being "the most perfect and regular shape" [33b].)[42]

---

[41] Lucan, *The Civil War (Pharsalia)*, trans. A.S. Kline (available online HTTP: https://www.poetryintranslation.com/PITBR/Latin/PharsaliaVImaster.php; accessed 15 June 2022).
[42] Diener, *Fausts Weg zu Helena*, p. 293. For further discussion of Jung's numerological symbolism and his understanding of "the dyad, the conjoined two" as potentially representing the "synthesis of opposites," while the Pythagorean tetraktys is an "archetype of order," anticipating the "rotundum or mandala" as a "symbol of the self," that is, of "the archetype of order par excellence" (CW 10 §805), see

Erichtho's soliloquy, the brief exchanges between Homunculus and Mephistopheles (corresponding to Faust's and Mephisto's joint chant with the Will-o'-the-Wisp in the "Walpurgis Night" of Part One) and between Homunculus and Faust, and Faust's monologue expressing excitement at arriving in Greece and his impatience to meet Helena (*Wo ist sie? ... Wo ist sie!*, as he repeatedly asks [ll. 7056, 7070]), form a transition to the rites that will result (in Act III) in the Dream Life Sequence of Faust as a knight living in a castle with Helen of Troy — until the death of their child, Euphorion, shatters the fantasy and Faust returns (until the conclusion of the play) to the physical world.

The next scene, identified by editors as set on the Upper Peneios, stages a meeting between Mephistopheles and Griffins, Sphinxes, and Sirens as well as Giant Ants and the Arimaspians (a tribe of one-eyed people from Northern Scythia who fought with the gold-guarding Griffens for their treasure).[43] (Diener interprets the Shinxes, Griffins, and other mythological beasts as being "symbols of elementary drives and impulses" [334].) Mephistopheles accuses the Sphinxes of being "brazen" (*schamlos*) and the Griffins as "shameless" (*unverschämt*) (l. 7083), presumably because the former (as traditionally represented with the head and upper torso of a woman and the lower body of a lion) appear with naked breasts, and the latter (with the body of a lion and the beak and wings of an eagle) make no secret of the greed with which they stand guard over buried treasure. While Mephistopheles initially appears disconcerted by these creatures, Faust turns up and immediately feels at home with them, declaring (with reference to

---

Paul Bishop, *Reading Plato through Jung: Why must the Third become the Fourth?* (Cham: Palgrave Macmillan, 2022).

[43] On the Giant Ants, see Herodotus, *History*, book 3, §102 and §105; and on the Griffins and the Arimaspians, see his *History*, book 4, §13 and §27 (*The Landmark Herodotus: The Histories*, ed. Robert B. Strassler (London: Quercus, 2008), pp. 257-258 and pp. 287 and 292).

the Sphinxes, the Sirens, the Ants, and the Griffins), "Great are the forms, great memories bring they to me!" (*Gestalten groß, groß die Erinnerungen*) (1. 7190). "Hath one of ye seen Helena, I pray?" he asks the Sphinxes (1. 7196), and while they reply that they are too ancient to have seen her, they suggest that he instead ask Chiron the centaur — advice on which he acts in the following scene (again titled as such by editors), "On the Lower Peneios."

In the conclusion to *this* scene, Mephisto looks up sharply, peeved (*verdrießlich*), when he hears the flapping noise caused by the Stymphalides, the monstrous man-eating birds with iron beaks and claws and sharp metallic feathers, the killing of which was the sixth of Hercules's 12 labors. And he shudders, as if intimidated (*wie verschüchtert*), when he hears a hissing sound: this is being made by the heads of the Lernaean Hydra or Snake which, cut off from the main body by Hercules in the second of his labors, are "still convinced of being" and continue to writhe. This minor detail introduces the motif of the serpent or snake, described by Diener as a "symbol of the material [*des Stoffartigen*], of what lies below [*des »Unteren«*]" (335), which will recur in Nietzsche's *Zarathustra* and come to the fore in *The Red Book* of C.G. Jung.

In "On the Lower Peneios," surrounded by waters and nymphs, Peneios — the Thessalian river god, after whom the river was named — himself speaks, conjuring up the sound of the sedges and reeds (*Schilfgeflüster*), of willows and poplars,[44] as an acoustic accompaniment to interrupted dreams (*unterbrochnen Träumen*):

Wake, ye whispers of the sedges!
Softly breathe, ye reed-fringed edges!

---

[44] For a discussion of this and other settings and locations in *Faust II*, see Richard Busch-Zantner, *Faust-Stätten in Hellas: Topographie und Quellenfrage der griechischen Landschaften in Goethes "Faust"* (Weimar: Böhlaus Nachfolger, 1932), pp. 30-31 (cf. Diener, *Fausts Weg zu Helena*, p. 342).

Rustle, willows of the river!
Lisp, ye poplar-sprays a-quiver,
To my rudely-broken dream!
Me the sultry air doth waken,
Strange all-searching thrill hath shaken
From my sleep and cradling stream.

                    (ll. 7249-7256)

One dream in particular that has been interrupted is, of course, Faust's dream of Leda and the swan as the scene of the procreation of Helena (see above), which he now recapitulates in the waking state — "I am awake!" (*ich wache ja!*), he cries:

          [...] O still resplendent
My sense enthrall, ye forms transcendent,
Such as mine eye doth plant ye there.
Oh, what a wondrous thrill runs through me!
Come ye as dreams — as memories to me?
[*Sind's Träume? Sind's Erinnerungen?*]
Such bliss was once before thy share!
Athwart the cool of softly swaying
Deep shadowy woods, come waters straying:
Not rushing, rippling scarce they glide.
A hundred fountains in one single
Pellucid shallow pool commingle,
For bathing meet, from every side.
The liquid mirror glasses double
Young lusty woman-limbs, that trouble
The eye with rapturous delight.
In fellowship then bathe they blithesome,
Fearsome they wade, swim bold and lithesome,
And end with shrieks and water-fight.
These should content me; these with pleasure

Mine eye should dwell upon at leisure,
Yet forward still my mind doth long.
Pierces my glance where yonder arbour's
Luxuriant wealth of verdure harbours
The lofty queen its shade among.
O the marvel! Swans sedately
With a motion pure and stately
Hither swim from out the bays.
In sweet consort softly sliding,
Moving head and beak and gliding
Proudly conscious of their grace...
One with stately bosom swelling,
In his pride his mates excelling,
Sails through all the throng apace.
Swells his plumage like a pillow;
Billow borne upon the billow
Glides he to the holy place...
His fellows in the glassy roomage
Cruise with unruffled radiant plumage,
Or meet in stirring splendid fray,
Whereby to lure each timid maiden
To quit her office, terror-laden
And save herself, if save she may.

(ll. 7271-7312)

It is strange that Jung never once mentions the centrality of Faust's dream to the action of Part Two, despite this part of the text containing a line (l. 7275) that must surely have struck him as highly suggestive — as the potential name for a set of autobiographical reminscences ...

This account develops and extends the earlier account given by Homunculus of the dream. Here there is a greater emphasis on the setting — the softly swaying rushes, the bathing nymphs mirrored in the water — and on Faust's ambition that his dream may come true. The approach of the swans (including one, Zeus in disguise, destined for Leda) is described as "marvellous" (*wundersam*) (l. 7295), although the punctation in line 7306 marks the moment where the act of union *cannot* be shown and where the scene is *veiled* (just as, in Homunculus's earlier account of Faust's dream, the act of sexual union is concealed by the misty gauze that suddenly descends). Here the dream of the conception of Helena literally involves *Wunder-samen,* or "wondrous seeds/semen," just as in the opening monologue in Part One Faust had expressed the ambition to "view all enactments seed and spring" (*Schau alle Wirkenskraft und Samen*) (l. 384). Yet it is also acknowledged that even if Faust's visual gaze is satisfied (*Mein Auge sollte hier genießen*), his intellect (or sense or mind) strives further (*Doch immer weiter strebt mein Sinn*); nevertheless, however hard his probing gaze seeks to penetrate the covering (*Der Blick dringt scharf nach jener Hülle*), symbolized here by the involucre of the foliage (*Das reiche Laub der grünen Fülle*), the exalted queen (that is, Leda as queen of the nymphs and mother of Helena) will remain hidden (*Verbirgt die hohe Königin*). (We see here the first intimation of the doctrine of *accepting limitations* that will come to play a major role in the conclusion to the play.)

The path to Helena as an "image of the soul" (*Seelenbild*), Gottfried Diener explains, leads Faust — in terms of an analogy proposed by Jung in an early paper from 1927, later published as *Seele und Erde* ("Mind and Earth"), for the "structure of the psyche" — from the "upper storey" of his soul, by means of the memory of deeper strata or lower layers of which one is "barely aware" (*dämmerhaft bewußt*), via the "choked-up cave [*Höhle*] with neolithic tools [...] and remnants of fauna," and yet further below to under the earth's surface, where the archetypal drives and images reside, of which we are otherwise "totally unconscious" (CW 10 §54; cf. Diener, 347). What Goethe in a sketch called the *wichtige Vorwelt* ("important preliminary era") is represented by those Griffins, Sphinxes, and so on; they, together with Helena, represent *ein gebildeteres Zeitalter* ("a more cultivated age"), one which is of *göttlichen Ursprungs* ("divine origin"), and hence his *lebhafte Erinnerung an den Traum Letha und die Schwäne* ("vivid recollection of the dream: Leda and the swan").[45] This Greek landscape, which is at one and the same time an extratemporal landscape of the soul, is characterized (according to Diener) by nature, by life, and by divine transfiguration (348).

This repetition of his earlier vision of Helena's conception is the first of three moments in this scene which dramatize Faust's quest for Helena and move this quest to the thematic foreground of the work. The second is his encounter with Chiron, the centaur — another mythical beast, this time with the upper torso of a human and the lower body and legs of a horse, while Chiron himself was held to be (in Homer's words) the "most righteous of the Centaurs" (Homer, *Iliad*, Book 11, l. 831).[46] The arrival of Chiron is heralded by the sound of his hooves, and the centaur swiftly agrees to carry Faust over the river (the Peneios) and wherever he wants. Faust climbs onto Chiron's back, and as they set off, Chiron gives Faust an impromptu refresher course in Greek mythology, mentioning the heroes he has helped by giving them instruction: Achilles, Jason (the leader of the Argonauts in their quest for the Golden Fleece), Hercules, Orpheus the musician, the Dioscuri (i.e., Castor and Pollux, sons of Leda and twin half-brothers of Helena), the Boreads (sons of the North Wind), and Lynceus (one of the Argonauts who served as the steersman and watchman on their ship, the Argo, and who subsequently appears on two further occasions in Goethe's *Faust*).[47] On one occasion,

---

[45] Schöne, *Texte*, pp. 656-657.

[46] Homer, *The Iliad*, trans. Richmond Lattimore (Chicago and London: Chicago University Press, 1951), p. 256.

[47] See the central section of Act III, where Lynceus serves as Faust's watchman on the lookout for the arrival of Helena, and in Act V, where he is the watchman on the tower of Faust's place, from where he witnesses the murder of Philemon and Baucis. In the mythological tradition, Lynceus was renowned for his keenness of vision, which

Chiron even carried Helena, but he offers a different perspective on Faust's obsession with her. For Chiron dismisses her and her fabled beauty: yet while he rejects feminine beauty, "Woman-beauty hath no savour. / Too oft a statue cold and stiff. / Such being only wins my favour / As wells with fresh and joyous life" (ll. 7399-7402), he embraces her as a kind of Neoplatonic conception of beauty, "Self-blessed is Beauty — cold and listless, / 'Tis grace alone that makes resistless, / Like Helena, when her I bore' (ll. 7403-7405). *Die Schöne bleibt sich selber selig* (translated by Luke as "Beauty remains serene and self-sufficing") — this celebrated line, which looks back to Plato (see *Symposium*, 204d; and *Phaedrus*, 249c-250b)[48] also finds its analogue in G.W.F. Hegel,[49] as well as in Eduard Mörike's poem of 1846 called "Auf eine Lampe" ("On a Lamp") and its famous line, *Was aber schön ist, selig scheint es in ihm selbst* (i.e., "Yet what is beautiful seems blissful [shines blissfully] within itself"), which

---

enabled him to see through solid objects and the ground (hence his association with geology and gold-mining).

[48] "What is it that the lover of the beautiful is longing for?", Diotima asks Socrates, who replies, "He is longing to make the beautiful his own" (Plato, *Collected Dialogues*, ed. Edith Hamilton and Huntington Cairns (Princeton, NJ: Princeton University Press, 1989), p. 556; and Socrates' assertion that "Beauty it was ours to see in all its brightness in those days when [...] we beheld with our eyes that blessed vision" (pp. 496-497).

[49] See G.W.F. Hegel, *Lectures on Aesthetics*, vol. 1, Part I ("The Idea of Artistic Beauty, or the Ideal"), chapter 3 ("The Beauty of Art or the Ideal"), §c: "[...] the Ideal treads into the sensuous and the natural form [of the phenomenal world], yet it still at the same time draws this, like the sphere of the external, back into itself, since art can bring back the apparatus, required by external appearance for its self-preservation, to the limits within which the external can be the manifestation of spiritual freedom. Only by this process does the Ideal exist in externality, self-enclosed, free, self-reliant, as sensuously blessed in itself, enjoying and delighting in its own self [*frei auf sich beruhend da, als sinnlich selig in sich, seiner sich freuend und genießend*]. The ring of this bliss resounds throughout the entire appearance of the Ideal, for however far the external form may extend, the soul of the Ideal never loses itself in it. And precisely as a result of this alone is the Ideal genuinely beautiful, since the beautiful exists only as a total through subjective unity [...]" (Hegel, *Aesthetics: Lectures on Fine Art*, trans. T.M. Knox, vol. 1 (Oxford: Clarendon Press, 1975), p. 157; *Vorlesungen über die Ästhetik*, vol. 1, in: *Werke in zwanzig Bänden*, ed. Eva Moldenhauer and Karl Markus Michel, vol. 13 (Frankfurt am Main: Suhrkamp, 1986), p. 207).

became the occasion of an interpretative dispute between Martin Heidegger (1889-1976) and the Swiss historian and critic Emil Staiger (1908-1987).[50] Whereas Faust's response to hearing about Helena is unbounded enthusiasm, "She is the sum of my desiring' (*Sie ist mein einziges Begehren*) (l. 7412), Chiron is more reserved, even sceptical about classical philologists and their interest in a young woman who was, after all, only 10 years old (!) when she was abducted by Theseus (ll. 7426-7433).[51] Whereas Chiron places emphasis on the action of the philologist or the poet in (re)creating the past, saying, "Abnormal is the heroine of mythology, / She makes her entry at the poet's need [*Der Dichter bringt sie, wie er's braucht, zur Schau*]' (ll. 7438-7439); noting, 'Is never adult, never old, / Still appetising to behold [*Stets appetitlicher Gestalt*], / Is kidnapped young, still wooed beyond her prime' (ll. 7430-7432); and concluding, "Enough, the Poet is not bound by Time" (l. 7433), Faust instead places emphasis on the unlimited and eternal appeal of Helena, that is to say, of Beauty itself: "Her too, then, let not Time have power to bind her!" (*So sei auch sie durch keine Zeit gebunden!*) (l. 7434).

---

[50] See Emil Staiger, "Zu einem Vers von Mörike: Ein Briefwechsel mit Martin Heidegger," *Trivium: Schweizerische Vierteljahrsschrift für Literaturwissenschaft*, vol. 9, no. 1 (1951), 1-16 (reproduced in Martin Heidegger, *Aus der Erfahrung des Denkens, 1910-1976* [*Gesamtausgabe*, vol. I.15], ed. Hermann Heidegger (Frankfurt am Main: Klostermann, 2002), pp. 93-109); and Leo Spitzer, "Wiederum Mörikes Gedicht «Auf eine Lampe»," *Trivium*, vol. 9, no. 3 (1951), 133-147. This debate has been translated as Emil Staiger, Martin Heidegger, Leo Spitzer, "A 1951 Dialogue on Interpretation," trans. Berel Lang and Christine Ebel, *Publications of the Modern Language Association*, vol. 105, no. 3 [Special Topic: The Politics of Critical Language] (May 1990), 409-435. For further discussion, see Benjamin Bennett, "Criticism as Wager: The Politics of the Mörike-Debate and its Object," in *The Defective Art of Poetry: Sappho to Yates* (New York: Palgrave Macmillan, 2014), pp. 147-164.

[51] For the thread of references to Helena's abduction by Theseus and his companion, Pirithous, when they saw the 10-year-old Helena dancing in a temple of Artemis; Theseus's decision to entrust her to his friend Aphidmus in his castle because she was so young; and her subsequent rescue by the Dioscuri, Castor and Pollux, see ll. 6530, 7381-7386, 7415-7426, 8848-8853. To the story of how she is rescued by Castor and Pollux, Goethe has added the detail that Chiron participated in their rescue of Helena — an example of the way that mythology can be endlessly added to and developed?

Indeed, Faust goes on to reactivate another part of the Greek legend as told by Pausanias, according to whom Helena married Achilles and shared the afterlife with him on the island of Leuce, which Goethe transfers to the Thessalian town of Pherae. Here, Faust says, Achilles found Helena, "beyond all time" (*selbst außer Zeit*) (l. 7436), an example of what he describes as "love wrested over and against fate" (*Errungen Liebe gegen das Geschick!*) (l. 7437). And where Achilles could succeed, why should he — Faust — fail? "And should not *I*, with mightiest yearning, charm / Back into life the incomparable form?" (*Und sollt* ich *nicht, sehnsüchtigster Gewalt, / Ins Leben ziehn die einzigste Gestalt?*), he asks (ll. 7438- 7439), using the rhyme on *Gestalt* and *Gewalt* that we encounter on three other occasions in *Faust* (ll. 1251-1252, 3395-3397, 7863- 7864). "My sense, my soul, she weaveth round for ever" (*Nun ist mein Sinn, mein Wesen streng umfangen*), he tells Chiron, "I cannot brook to live, save I achieve her!" (*Ich lebe nicht, kann ich sie nicht erlangen*) (ll. 7444-7445).

We have seen this impetuousness in Faust before. In Part One, he meets Gretchen in the street and tells Mephistopheles, *Hör, du mußt mir die Dirne schaffen* ("Hear, get me that young wench!") (l. 2619). Now, however, there is an almost existential urgency to Faust's desire for Helen, who is not simply the most beautiful woman in the world (or, as formulated by Marlowe in the form of a question, "Was this the face that launched a thousand ships / And burnt the topless towers of Ilium?") but rather — in an archetypal sense — Beauty itself.

The third moment in this scene's dramatization of Faust's quest for Helena arrives when Chiron reponds to this speech by Faust by telling him that he is in luck. For Chiron is on good terms with Manto, the daughter of the prophet Tiresias (or, in Goethe's version, Asclepius, the Greek god of medicine and healing), and he offers to take Faust to Manto so that he may be cured by her (presumably, of his infatuation with Helena).[52] Although Faust retorts that he does not want to be cured and insists that he is of sound mind, Chiron announces that they have arrived at the temple of Apollo, over which Manto presides — not far from the site of the battle of Pydna (168 B.C.E.), where the Romans defeated Perseus, King of Macedonia. (The point of this detail is surely, once again, to suggest how tightly interwoven history and mythology are in the Greek landscape.) Awaking from her state of timeless dreaming, Manto welcomes Faust, who is introduced to her as someone who is, to speak, mad about Helen (*mit verrückten Sinnen* [...] *Helenen will er sich gewinnen*). On hearing this, Faust is hailed by Manto as one who "craves beyond his reach," as someone "whom the impossible doth lure" (*Den lieb ich, der Unmögliches begehrt*) (l. 7488); as someone who says, in the words chosen by Jung to be inscribed above the fireplace in Bollingen, *quaero quod impossibile* ("I seek what is impossible").[53] Manto invites Faust to follow her to the realm of Persephone, the Queen of Hades, and Faust — like Orpheus before him — embarks on a descent to the underworld:

---

[52] For Rudolf Steiner, the "sacred and sublime" moment when Faust appears before Manto is one of three great moments he compares in his lecture "Goetheanism in Place of Homunculism and Mephistophelianism" given in Dornach on 19 January 1919. (The two other moments are the "terrible" scene when Mephistopheles takes on the form of a Phorkyad, "terrible" because we are shown "how something morally impermissible lives in the individual like a sensation that is aesthetically offensive"; and the moment when Homunculus is dashed to pieces against Galatea's shell-chariot, illustrating how "we come from the spiritual world seeking through conception and birth for physical existence." In each case Steiner invited his audience to consider each moment, taken "purely artistically and in terms of feeling" (*künstlerisch empfindungsgemäß*), to underscore his message that "these things are not there merely to be spoken of on Sunday afternoons in the Anthroposophical Society" but are "there as truth, to become gradually known to humankind, so that as impulses they may with their being penetrate what must be accepted in the development of humankind for the future, if we are to advance to what saves and not what destroys" (*Erläuterungen*, vol. 2, pp. 243-247).

[53] As Peter Kingsley has pointed out, this text is the inspiration behind the inscription Jung had carved over the stone fireplace of his retreat at Bollingen, *Quaero quod impossibile* (Kingsley, *Catafalque: Carl Jung and the End of Humanity*, 2 vols (London: Catafalque Press, 2018), vol. 1, p. 104 and vol. 2, pp. 528-529).

Enter, thou shalt be glad, audacious mortal!
Leads to Persephone the gloomy portal.
Within Olympus' hollow foot
She hears by stealth the banned salute.
Here did I smuggle Orpheus in of old.
Use thou it better! In, be bold!
[*They descend.*]

(ll. 7439-94)

Despite making plans for it, Goethe never wrote the scene where Faust encounters Persephone in the underworld and brings back Helena. Of this ambition for this scene, to be titled "Faust as Second Orpheus," Goethe is said to have remarked to Eckermann on 15 January 1817: "Just imagine everything that finds utterance on that mad night! Faust's speech to Proserpina, to move her to relinquish Helena. What a speech that must be, since it moves Proserpina herself to tears!"[54] On this unwritten episode, Hamlin comments that the descent to the underworld that Manto offers Faust "consists primarily in a journey inward, as if to the realm of the unconscious, not unlike the strange journey that Faust earlier made in Act I to the Mothers" (428). In this respect it is important to note that, in both cases, this descent to the unconscious is linked to the feminine — to the Mothers or to Helena, a point that was not lost on Jung, who insisted on the importance of the role of the Great Mother as the object of the descent to the Unconscious.

Faust's descent into Hades anticipates the emblematic scene in Jung's *Red Book* in the chapter titled "Descent into Hell in the Future," with its iconic vision of the submarine cave, the bloody head of a man (Siegfried) on a dark stream, and a large black scarab floating past (RB, 147), followed by the springing up of a stream of thick red blood, while thousands of serpents crowd around

---

[54] Cf. Eckermann, *Conversations of Goethe*, p. 149 (here, trans. Latham).

and veil the sun (RB, 148). Here Jung inserts himself (as Goethe would probably have done, if he had written the scene) into the rich classical tradition of the *katábasis*, the *nekyia*, or the descent of the soul.[55] Jung was, however, not alone in being interested in the motif of the psychic descent: Madame Blavatsky, for instance, wrote about the ancient Mysteries from a theosophical perspective,[56] and even more orthodox scholars, building on the work of W.K.C. Guthrie and Jane E. Harrison, investigated the motif of *katábasis* in relation, for example, to Virgil.[57]

Common to the journey into Hades as found in the stories about Odysseus, Hercules, Theseus and Pirithoos, and (as explicitly mentioned by Manto) Orpheus (cf. l. 7493), is the following constellation of motifs:

- The descent into the underworld
- The "negotiations" with Persephone (or Kore), the daughter of Zeus and Demeter, the Queen of the underworld, and the goddess of the dead
- The return (Diener, 398)

(Later, in 1939-1940, Jung will write a major essay on the figure of Persephone, published in 1941 with two essays by Carl Kerényi in a landmark volume titled *Einführung in das Wesen der Mythologie* and translated in 1949 as *Essays on a Science of Mythology*; while in 1967 Kerényi published *Eleusis: Archetypal Image of Mother and Daughter*, a reconstruction of the Mysteries based on the myth of Demeter's search for her ravished daughter, Persephone.[58]

---

[55] For further discussion, see Paul Bishop, Terence Dawson, and Leslie Gardner (eds), *The Descent of the Soul and the Archaic: Katábasis and Depth Psychology* (London and New York: Routledge, 2023), esp. "Introduction: Is the Only Way Up?" (pp. 1-16).

[56] For further discussion, see Ted G. Davy, *The Descent into Hades* (London: Theosophical Society, 1983).

[57] See Raymond J. Clark, *Catabasis: Vergil and the Wisdom-Tradition* (Amsterdam: Grüner, 1978).

[58] C.G. Jung and Carl Kerényi, *Essays on a Science of Mythology: The Myth of the Divine Child and the Mysteries of Eleusis*, trans. R.F.C. Hull (Princeton, NJ:

Although the figure of Persephone does not feature directly in *The Red Book*, two related figures — Brimo and Triptolemus — are, in different ways, vestigially present.)

At the same time, the journey into Hades can be understood in alchemical — that is to say, psychological — terms. For the *Rosarium Philosophorum* (or *The Rosary of the Philosophers*), an alchemical work published in 1550 and analyzed by Jung in the papers collected in *Psychology and Alchemy* (1944) and *The Psychology of the Transference* (1946), includes an account of an incestuous union between a brother and sister, called Gabricus and Beya. Within the framework of alchemical allegory, they respectively represent body and spirit, while their union produces the soul that holds them together.[59] In the chapter titled "Conjunction or Coupling," which opens with a woodcut featuring Sol and Luna, the alchemical king and queen, as they embrace each other, Arisleus — described in the *Turba Philosophorum* as "begotten of Pythagoras, a disciple of the disciples by the grace of thrice great Hermes, learning from the seat of knowledge, unto all who come after wisheth health and mercy" — cries out in a vision:

Join therefore thy son Gabrick, best beloved of thee among all thy sons, with his sister Beya, who is a fair, sweet and tender damsel. Gabrick is the man and Beya the woman, who gives him all that is hers.

Princeton University Press, 1963); and Carl Kerényi, *Eleusis: Archetypal Image of Mother and Daughter*, trans. Ralph Manheim (Princeton, NJ: Princeton University Press, 1967), earlier versions of which appeared in Dutch (1960) and German (1962).
[59] For a transcription of the 18th-century English translation of the *Rosarium philosophorum*, originally printed as volume 2 of *De Alchemia Opuscula complura veterum philosophorum* (Frankfurt, 1550) with a series of 20 woodcuts, see "The Rosary of the Philosophers," available online HTTP: <http://www.levity.com/alchemy/rosary0.html>. Accessed 22 May 2024. For further discussion, see Thomas Willard, "Beya and Gabricus: Erotic Imagery in German Alchemy," *Mediaevistik*, 28 (2015), 269-281.

O blessed Nature, and blessed is thy operation, because out of an imperfect thing thou makest a perfect thing. Therefore, thou must not take that nature unless pure, clean, raw, pleasant, earthy and right and if thou do otherwise it will not bring forth anything, so that no contrary thing enter in with our Stone and put nothing but that only. Join therefore our ferment with his sweet sister and they will beget a son between them, who shall not be like his parents. And although Gabrick is made more dear to Beya, yet there is no generation made without Gabrick, for the coupling of Gabrick with Beya is presently dead. For Beya ascendeth above Gabrick and includes him in her womb because nothing at all can be seen of him. And she embraceth Gabrick with so great a love that she hath conceived him wholly in his nature and divided him into inseparable parts.

In "Religious Ideas in Alchemy" (1937), Jung recounts the imprisonment by the King in a triple glass house of Arisleus and his companions together with the corpse of the King's son, leaving them captive at the bottom of the sea in the underworld where they languish in an intense heat, exposed to all kinds of terror, for 80 days (CW 12 §437). According to Jung, Arisleus is "in danger of succumbing to the fate of Theseus and Peirithous, who descended into Hades and grew fast to the rocks of the underworld," an episode he interprets as illustrating how "the conscious mind, advancing into the unknown regions of the psyche, is overpowered by the archaic forces of the unconscious" — in Hermetic terms, "a repetition of the cosmic embrace of Nous and Physis" (§438). Placing this episode in the context of the myth of the hero, Jung describes the "purpose of this descent" as being to show that "only in the region of danger" — such as the watery abyss, a cavern, the forest, an island, a castle, etc. — "can one find the 'treasure hard to attain'" — symbolized by a jewel, a virgin, a life-potion, or victory over death (CW 12 §438).

And yet — as thematized in Goethe's *Faust* by Faust's initial reluctance to descend to the Mothers and, indeed, by Goethe's reluctance to write the scene where Faust descends to Persephone — this transformative moment is accompanied by fear, by "the dread and resistance which all natural human beings experience when it comes to delving too deeply into themselves" (CW 12 §439). And Jung continues:

> In actual fact, however, the psychic substratum, that dark realm of the unknown, exercises a fascinating attraction that threatens to become the more overpowering the further we penetrate into it. The psychological danger that arises here is the disintegration of personality into its functional components, i.e., the separate functions of consciousness, the complexes, hereditary factors, etc. Disintegration — which may be functional or occasionally a real schizophrenia — is the fate which overtakes Gabricus (in the *Rosarium* version): he is dissolved into atoms in the body of Beya, this being equivalent to a form of *mortificatio*. (CW12 §439)

In "The Psychology of the Transference," Jung expands on this reading of the figure of Gabricus, aligning his disappearance into the body of his sister Beya and his dissolution into atoms with the "upwelling" of the unconscious psyche found in such other motifs as the danger of the King drowning in the sea, the King's imprisonment under the sea, the drowning of the sun in the mercurial fountain, the sweating of the King in the glass house, and the swallowing of the sun by the green lion (CW 16 §453). Jung reaffirms his reading of the "Vision Arislei" (described above), where the philosophers are incarcerated in a triple glass house, together with the brother-sister pair, at the bottom of the sea, by the *Rex Marinus*, as exemplifying the "night sea journey" or the *descensus ad inferos* as "a descent into Hades and a journey to the land of ghosts somewhere beyond this world, beyond consciousness, hence an immersion in the unconscious" (CW 16 §455), and as recapitulating the Hermetic story of how the Original Man (or Nous) bent down from heaven to earth and became wrapped in the embracing arms of Physis — as found in the first tractate in the *Corpus Hermeticum*, the "Poimandres" (§14), and constituting "a primordial image that runs through the whole of alchemy" (CW 16 §456).

In Hermeticism, alchemy, and in Goethe's *Faust* alike, the epic of transformation hinges on one thing and has but one aim: "the individual's longing for transcendent wholeness" (§456). In the case of *Faust*, as Diener points out, "the highest intensification of vital feeling through the revival of Helena as a psychic image [*als Seelenbild*] is acquired at the cost of the danger of losing one's individual ego when it sees the shapeless and ugly, colossal face of the Medusa," and Faust is "protected from the destructive aspect of the collective unconscious through the 'foresight' [»*Vorsicht*«] of the enlightened prophetess and through her *veil*" (399). This reading makes good sense of those Paralipomena or sketches that constitute all we have of Goethe's thinking on this unwritten episode — his *Red Book*, as it were, that never came to be:

H P157
[Prologue to the third Act.
Secret passageway
Manto and Faust
Introduction of what follows
Head of the Medusa
Further progress.
Persephone veiled.

Manto declaims
The Queen remembering her earthly life.
Conversation from the veiled side, seemingly melodically
                                    articulated but inaudible
Faust wishes to see her unveiled.
Anticipatory delight
Manto leads him quickly back.
Explains the outcome
Honours the antecedents
Helena was already limited to the island of Leuce.
Now she should show herself as living again on Spartan
territory.
Let the suitor earn her favor.
Manto is entrusted with the introduction.]

H P158
FAUST:
What's well-considered, I believe, is just as well expressed
In such serious, long-tailed lines
And if it is the condition of that divine being
To see her, speak to her, to approach her breath on breath
Then if you dare even more Babylonian stuff
To be expected of me, like a schoolchild I'll obey you.
It delights me already to speak of things, with short words
Otherwise easily dealt with, with rhetorical indulgence.
MANTO:
Spare us this, until you come to her who is the oldest
The joy gives a long [time] which one may enjoy
Women love most of all the tragic ones
There every person, aptly, with allusive words
Extensively speaks out what everyone approximately knows.
But silence on this! collected, stand to the side, reserved
One should not jest when Orcus wants to open.

H P159
[MANTO]:
Now go along the path [here] undisturbed
Each person stops short, who hears the incomprehensible
[*Unbegreifliches*].

H P160
[FAUST]:
Look here at the depth of this passageway
It covers up from us a stifling flowery meadow
It seems to me, that something giant, long,
Emerges from the darkness

H P161
FAUST:
Why are you wrapping me in your cloak?
Why are you pushing me violently to the side
MANTO:
I am protecting you from greater agony,
Do honour to your prudent escort.
(Geier, vol. 1 = *Texte*, 650-651; Schöne, *Texte*, 664-665)

From these brief fragments, some in Goethe's handwriting, some in those of his stenographer Ernst Carl Christian John, one can piece together something of the emotional intensity that Goethe would have wished to achieve by and in this scene. And the Helena whom Faust encounters in and recovers from Hades corresponds as an *Erinnerungsbild* to the archetype of the Anima in its dual aspect: first, the Anima as a "quite definite picture" with a "personality character," associated with a "peculiar historical feeling" expressed in a poem by Goethe as "In times gone by you were my wife or sister" (CW 10 §81, §83, §85);[60] and, second, the Anima as a

___

[60] See "To Charlotte von Stein" (1776), in Goethe, *Selected Poems*, ed. Christopher Middleton [Goethe Edition, vol. 1] (Boston: Suhrkamp/Insel, 1983), pp. 60-63; and

"supra-individual image," as "an image of woman that man carries within him eternally" or "the image of woman that [men] carry in their minds" (CW 10 §75, §74, §75) — in this sense, the Anima is indexed to "immortality," even "the divine" (Diener, 405). (In his paper "Mind and Earth" [1927; 1931], as elsewhere, Jung relates the Anima to the figure of Helena in *Faust II*, noting that "the anima-type is presented in the most succinct and pregnant form in the Gnostic legend of Simon Magus, a caricature of whom appears in the Acts of the Apostles" (and in Irenaeus's *Adversus Haereses*, Book 9, §23), adding: "Simon Magus was always accompanied on his travels by a girl, whose name was Helen. He had found her in a brothel in Tyre; she was a reincarnation of Helen of Troy" [CW 10 §75].[61] Was Goethe's Faust-Helen motif, Jung wondered, "consciously derived" from the Simon legend? Or in other words, is Goethe's Helena a reincarnation of a reincarnation?)[62]

Goethe, *Selected Poems*, trans. John Whaley (London: Dent, 1998), pp. 32-35. For further discussion, see Lieselotte E. Kurth-Voigt, *Continued Existence, Reincarnation, and the Power of Sympathy in Classical Weimar* (Rochester, NY, and Woodbridge: Camden House, 1999), pp. 151-154.

[61] For the early Church Fathers (notably St. Irenaeus), the first-century figure of Simon Magus was an opportunistic sorcerer and the father of all heresy; for the Gnostics, however, he was the successor to John the Baptist. For further discussion (and a demonstration of varying approaches), see G.R.S. Mead, *Simon Magus* (London: Theosophical Publishing Society, 1892); and Stephen Charles Haar, *Simon Magus: The First Gnostic?* (Berlin and New York: de Gruyter, 2003).

[62] For the Gnostics, the first-century figure of Helen of Tyre was not just the consort of Simon Magus, she was one of the 30 disciples of John the Baptist; as high priestess of the moon, she was said to possess lunar powers; was a reincarnation of Helen of Troy; and ultimately an incarnated embodiment of Sophia. Henry Wadsworth Longfellow's poem "Helen of Tyre" (in *Ultima Thule*, published in 1880), begins:

> What phantom is this that appears
> Through the purple mist of the years,
> Itself but a mist like these?
> A woman of cloud and of fire;
> It is she; it is Helen of Tyre,
> The town in the midst of the seas.

For further discussion (and a demonstration of varying approaches to the figure of Helen of Troy), see Bettany Hughes, *Helen of Troy: Goddess, Princess, Whore* (New

While Faust descends to Hades in this unwritten scene in which he will persuade Persephone to allow Helena to follow him back to earthly life in Sparta, back on the Upper Peneios, the series of encounters between Mephistopheles and various mythological figures continues. An earthquake caused by Seismos (a personification of an attribute of Poseidon, the god of the sea), introduces the theme of the difference in geological views between the proponents of Vulcanism and Neptunism (the former proposing that rocks and mountains had been formed by volcanic action, and the latter — with whom Goethe was more sympathetic — proposing that the process had involved geological sedimentation arising from the precipitation of water), while the war between Pygmies and Cranes anticipates the political theme of warfare in Act IV. Then, the debate between Homunculus and two Presocratic philosophers, Anaxagoras of Clazomenae and Thales of Miletus, uses these two symbolic intellectual figures as representatives of the two positions of Vulcanism and Neptunism respectively (ll. 7851-7950).[63] On the one hand, Anaxagoras sought to give a scientific account of eclipses and meteors and (according to Pliny) predicted the fall of a meteorite in 467, offering a quasi-atomistic theory of the universe as composed of the "seeds of all things" (DK 59 B4) or (according to Aristotle) *homoiomerien* (ὁμοιομερῆ), that is, things that are homogeneous components,[64] segregated from heterogeneous parts and organized

---

York: Knopf, 2005); and Ruby Blondell, *Helen of Troy: Beauty, Myth, Devastation* (New York: Oxford University Press, 2013).

[63] For an overview of the Vulcanism versus Neptunism debate in relation to Goethe, see W. Scott Baldridge, "The Geological Writings of Goethe: Despite his keen powers of observation, Goethe's ideas on geology reflected the biases of his time," *American Scientist*, vol. 72, no. 2 (March-April 1984), 163-167. For a selection of Goethe's writings on geology, see Goethe, *Scientific Studies*, ed. and trans. Douglas Miller [Goethe Edition, vol. 8] (New York: Suhrkamp, 1988), pp. 131-142.

[64] See *Physics*, Book 3, §4, 203a19-22: "Those who make [the elements] infinite in number, as Anaxagoras and Democritus do, say that the infinite is continuous by contact — compounded of the homogeneous parts according to the one, of the seed mass of the atomic shapes according to the other" (Aristotle, *Complete Works*, ed. Jonathan Barnes, 2 vols. (Princeton, NJ: Princeton University Press, 1984),

into a whole by the work of Mind or Reason (νοῦς). On the other, Thales proposed the cosmological thesis (as reported by Aristotle in his *Metaphysics*, 983 b6 8-11) that the originating principle of all nature was a single material substance, namely, water. (As Goethe reimagined their cosmological positions in political terms: Does change comes about through fire, i.e., revolution, or through water, i.e., gradual change?) Thales, with whom Goethe's sympathies lie, returns in the Cabiri scene (see below).

Finally, Mephistopheles, who, unable to engage successfully (that is, sexually) with the Thessalian witches and left to his own devices by the Lamiae, has been wandering through the classical landscape and apparently climbing around in rocks and cliffs of the Pindus mountains, is directed by the tree nymph Dryad to the cave of the three Phorcyads, otherwise known as the Graiae, or the Grey Sisters. These three sisters, daughters of the primordial sea god Phorcyas, live in a dark and obscure cave, "Sunken in solitude and stillest night" (l. 8000), sharing only one eye and one tooth among them. As the "well-beloved son of Chaos" (l. 8027; cf. l. 1384),[65] Mephistopheles agrees to lend them one of his eyes and

---

vol. 1, p. 345; *On the Heavens*, book 3, §3, 302a28-31: "Now Anaxagoras opposes Empedocles' view of the elements. [...] His elements are the homoeomerous things, viz. flesh, bone, and the like" (vol. 1, p. 495); *On Generation and Corruption*, Book 1, §1, 314a20-21: "Anaxagoras posits as elements the 'homoeomeries'" viz. bone, flesh, marrow, and everything else which is such that part and whole are synonymous" (vol. 1, p. 512); *Metaphysics*, Book 1, §3, 984a12-16: "Anaxagoras of Clazomenae [...] says the principles are infinite in number; for he says almost all things that are homogeneous are generated and destroyed (as water and fire is) only be aggregation and segregation, and are not in any other sense generated or destroyed, but remain eternally" (vol. 2, p. 1556); and *Metaphysics*, Book 1, §7, 988a26-29: "Plato spoke of the great and the small, the Italians [i.e., the Pythagoreans, because Pythagoras founded his society at Croton] of the infinite, Empedocles of fire, earth, water, and air, Anaxagoras of the infinity of homogeneous things" (vol. 2, p. 1562).

[65] On the rich theme of *chaos* as found in the Bible, ancient mythology and philosophy (Hesiod, the Orphics, Empedocles), Paracelsus, and alchemy, and the manifold use of it made by Goethe, see Diener, *Fausts Weg zu Helena*, pp. 470-474. Within the alchemical tradition, Diener distinguishes three different aspects: (a) the primordial, raw, and disordered state of matter or the *chaos confusum*, as in Lactantius's reference to "from the chaos, which is a confused assortment of crude disordered

one tooth, transforming himself in the process into Phorcyas. By appropriating to himself the archetypal ugliness of the Phorcyads, Mephistopheles's transformation into Phorcyas stands as the emblematic opposite to Faust's successful quest for Helena as the embodiment of the ideal of classical beauty — a quest whose fulfilment is expressed in his erotic union with her in Act III. But before that Act, there is the remarkably elaborate scene of the Aegean Sea Festival, set in the rocky inlets of the Aegean Sea.

This scene, described rightly by Hamlin as "the boldest and most obscure poetic sequence in the entire drama," is nevertheless (as he also recognizes) the "symbolic high point" of Goethe's work (433). For, even though it pushes the limits of performability to their utmost and neither Faust nor Mephistopheles is present in its action, this scene does not simply act as a replacement for the

---

matter" (CW 12 §185); (b) from the *chaos confusum* (*massa confusa, materia prima*) arises the Philosopher's Stone, as the "precious substance" or the alchemical "gold" (CW 12 §433, §442, §445); and (c) chaos as the *nigredo* or blackness, i.e., the initial state, either "present from the beginning as a quality of the *prima materia*, the chaos or *massa confusa*" or "produced by the separation [...] of the elements" (CW 12 §334; cf. §433) (Diener, *Fausts Weg zu Helena*, pp. 471-472). Crucial to Jung's understanding of alchemy is the idea that the *lapis*, identified with the "spherical being" which Empedocles describes as the "most serene God" (*eudaimonestatos Theos*), both "arises from, *and constitutes*," the "primal sphere": accordingly, the "initial state is the hidden state, but by the art and grace of God it can be *transmuted into the second, manifest state*" (CW 12 §433; my italics). Order and disorder, chaos and perfection are thus co-implicates for Jung — reciprocally related in a kind of "binary synthesis":

lapis as Philosophers' Stone
(higher [dis]order)

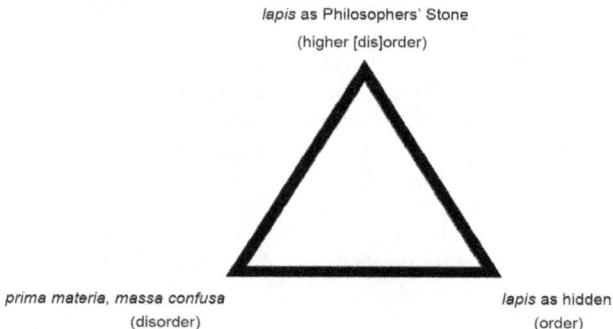

prima materia, massa confusa   *lapis* as hidden
(disorder)   (order)

never-written account of the descent of Faust to the underworld and his visit to Persephone to appeal for the release of Helena, it also foregrounds a number of key themes in the work as a whole: life, love, erotic procreation, and, crucially, the theme of *transformation*. The scene attracted the attention of Carl Kerényi (1897-1973), the classical scholar with whom Jung collaborated on several papers published together under the title *Essays on a Science of Mythology* (1941). In his address on the occasion of the founding of the C.G. Jung Institute on 24 April 1948, Jung hailed Kerényi as "one of the most brilliant philologists of our time" and as having "supplied such a wealth of connections [of psychology] with Greek mythology that the cross-fertilization of the two branches of science can no longer be doubted" (CW 18 §1131 and §1132).

In 1941, Kerényi published a study of the Aegean Festival,[66] and he sent a copy to Jung. Jung was deeply impressed, later claiming that the work had been the stimulus behind writing *Mysterium Coniunctionis* (see CW 14 p. xiii). In that late, great work Jung argued that the "sea journey" as described by Christian Rosencreutz (i.e., by Johannes Valentinus Andreae (1586-1654) in *The Chymical Wedding of Christian Rosenkreutz*) with its essential motif of the "royal marriage" was an alchemical motif that had been taken up by Goethe in *Faust II*, notably in the Aegean Festival scene, whose "archetypal content" had been elaborated by Kerényi in "a brilliant amplificatory interpretation" (CW 14 §658). On Kerényi's account, the bands of nereids on Roman sarcophagi reveal "the epithalmic and the sepulchral element," inasmuch as "the identity of marriage and death on the one hand, and of birth

---

[66] Karl Kerényi, *Das Ägäische Fest: Die Meergötterszene in Goethes Faust II* (Amsterdam and Leipzig: Pantheon, 1941); 3rd edition as *Das Ägäische Fest: Erläuterungen zur Szene "Felsbuchten des Ägäischen Meers" in Goethes Faust II* (Wiesbaden: Limes Verlag, 1950); and in *Humanistische Seelenforschung* (Darmstadt: Wissenschaftliche Buchgesellschaft, 1966), pp. 116-149.

and the eternal resurgence of life from death on the other" is "basic to the antique mysteries" (CW 14 §658).[67]

Indeed, immediately after reading his study on the Aegean Festival, Jung wrote to Kerényi on 19 January 1941 that he had read the work "with great interest" and suggesting that "a terrific lot could be said about it, chiefly from the alchemical side" (L1, 291). Jung confessed that he was particularly fascinated by the figure of Homunculus, whom he assimilates to the threefold figure of the Boy Charioteer (in Act I) and Euphorion (in Act III), as figures who "end up in fire" (291). Yet Jung makes two other important points: First, although the "depth" of Goethe's "alchemical intuition" must have far exceeded those works he had read at the urging of Susanne Katharine von Klettenberg (1723-1774), there was an equally astonishing empathy with Greek mythology; and second, that the scene of the Festival is "without any doubt [...] in accord with the whole plan of the Classical Walpurgisnacht" (291), or in other words, that there is an important *structural* element to be considered. Indeed, Jung noted a certain disjunction between the "feelings" Kerényi's book had "aroused" in him and the picture Kerényi had painted in his book, and Jung claimed that he wanted to avoid "at all costs wrenching out any one detail from that brilliant canvas"; instead, he wanted to "mull over" Kerényi's book some more, and Jung raised the prospect that he might be able to succeed in "arranging" his own "psychological material" in a form that "fits it better" (291-292). Is there a kind of very gentle critique of Kerényi here?

In the stage direction for this scene, we are told that the moon is at rest in the zenith, an indication that the entire festival — the performative climax of the entire mythological Classical Walpurgis Night — takes place in a moment of "suspended time" (Hamlin, 228, n. 1). (A similar astronomical moment is recalled in *Black Book* 6, where Jung recounts a moment in the desert during his visit

---

[67] Kerényi, *Das Ägäische Fest*, p. 55.

to Africa of 1920 when, "in the zenith, there was a large radiant planet exactly at the intersection" — an image which is said to have struck him as "an expression of the mystery of individuation" [BB 6, 227].) The scene opens with the Sirens, who are arrayed on the cliffs above the shore and who act as a chorus throughout the festival, greeting the triumphal procession of mythological creatures (drawn mainly from Benjamin Hederich's *Gründliches mythologisches Lexikon* (1770), a copy of which in its first and in its second edition, edited by Johann Joachim Schwabe, is in Goethe's library). These include the Nereids and Tritons, Nereus (or "the Old Man of the Sea" in the *Iliad*, see Book 1, ll. 358, 538, 556; Book 16, l. 141; Book 20, l. 107; and Book 26, l. 562), Proteus (or another Homeric "Old Man of the Sea," famed for his self-transformative powers),[68] the Telchines (the original inhabitants of the island of Rhodes), the Psylli and the Marsi (the original inhabitants of Cyprus, the island of Aphrodite), and the Dorids. Present at the Festival on the shore are Homunculus and Thales, whose essentially aquatic view of the world is celebrated in the scene as a whole.

At the outset of the Festival, the Nereids and Tritons set off for the island of Samothrace in the north-east Aegean Sea, in search of some very special guests; as the Sirens remark,

> Away in a trice
> To Samothrace as the sea-bird flies
> With favouring breezes they fare,
> But what they would seek is a query
> In the realm of the lofty Kabiri.
> Gods are they, such as were never;
> Themselves engender they ever
> And never know they what they are.
>
> (ll. 8070-8077)

---

[68] In the course of the Aegean Festival, Proteus transforms himself into a giant turtle, a noble shape, and into a dolphin.

Later the Nereids and Tritons return with a gigantic tortoise shell, said to belong to Chelone, a nymph transformed by Hermes into a sea tortoise. In the shell are carried the Cabiri, in an enigmatic scene that draws on Friedrich Creuzer's *Symbolik und Mythologie der alten Völker, besonders der Griechen* (1810-1812; ²1819; ³1837) and F.W.J. Schelling's account of these mysterious gods in his essay of 1815, *Ueber die Gottheiten zu Samothrake* ("On the Divinities of Samothrace") and that proved (as we shall see in Chapter 4) to be of great fascination to Jung:

> SIRENS, *above on the cliffs*:
> Afar what see we furrow
> Its path the surges thorough,
> As by the breeze urged forward
> White sails were gliding shoreward,
> Suffused with light transcendent
> Like mermaidens resplendent?
> Now quickly down be climbing.
> Ye hear their voices chiming!
>
> NEREIDS AND TRITONS:
> We bear in our hands a treasure
> That all shall give you pleasure.
> Chelone's shell gigantic
> Gleams with a group authentic.
> Gods are they that we bring ye,
> Now festal songs come sing ye.
>
> SIRENS:
> Small of height,
> Great of might,
> Helpers when shipwreck rages,
> Gods honoured in primal ages.

NEREIDS AND TRITONS:
We bring ye the Kabiri
With a tranquil feast to cheer ye,
For where they reign auspicious
Is Neptune's sway propitious.

SIRENS:
Aye, that we'll back.
Went a ship to wrack
With might resistless you
Delivered still the crew.

NEREIDS AND TRITONS:
Three have we brought, we could not
The fourth, for come he would not.
Himself the true one call he did,
And said the thinking for all he did.

SIRENS:
A god without a doubt
A god may flout.
All good powers revere ye,
Every mischief fear ye!

NEREIDS AND TRITONS:
Seven are they rightly, marry.

SIRENS:
Where do the three then tarry?

NEREIDS AND TRITONS:
That can my wit not compass!
Enquire within Olympus.
The eighth beeth haply there too,
Whom none hath thought of hereto!

By us as helpers greeted,
But all not yet completed.

These the Unexplainable,
Forward still are yearning,
Hunger-bitten, ever-burning
For the Unattainable.
[*Diese Unvergleichlichen*
Wollen immer weiter,
Sehnsuchtsvolle Hungerleider
Nach dem Unerreichlichen.]

SIRENS:
Wherever may
Be a throne, we pray,
By night and day,
For that doth pay.

NEREIDS AND TRITONS:
How passing high our praise hath shone
That with this feast we cheer ye!

SIRENS:
The heroes of ancient days
Now fail of their praise,
Where and however it shone,
Since they the Golden Fleece have won,
Ye the Kabiri.

TUTTI:
Since they the Golden Fleece have won,
Ye
    the Kabiri.
We

(ll. 8160-8218)

(As we shall see in Chapter 4, Jung argues that, given Goethe's "feeling-toned" nature, the missing fourth Cabiri represents the function of thinking, and *Faust I* illustrates the development that takes place if feeling becomes the "supreme principle" and the function of thinking has to "play an unfavourable role and be submerged" [CW 12 §204].) In these lines the Nereids and the Tritons are celebrated as being superior to the ancient Argonauts, for their achievement in bringing the Cabiri is said to be even greater than that of carrying off the Golden Fleece! What, however, is the significance of these diminutive deities, of whom Homunculus (perhaps inadvertently exemplifying the narcissism of minor differences) somewhat dismissively speaks?

> The uncouth creatures look I on,
> For sorry clay pots I take them.
> Now knock the wise [*die Weisen*] their pates thereon,
> And thick as they are they break them.
>
> (ll. 8219-8222)

In so speaking Homunculus is equally dismissive of the contemporary academic debate about the significance of the Cabiri; Thales tries to draw a line under the debate by remarking aphoristically, "They [i.e., *die Weisen*] would not wish it otherwise. / The canker gives the coin its price" (*Der Rost macht erst die Münze wert*) (ll. 8223-8224). Yet for our purposes here, the importance lies in the way that these figures are reactivated in the work of Jung in two respects: in his discussion of the Cabiri Scene in *Faust II* on several occasions;[69] and in the account of the construction of the Tower in *The Red Book*.

In the context of *Faust II*, the Cabiri as a personification (of sorts) of the striving for self-fulfilment, of "hunger-bitten, ever-

---

[69] For further discussion, see Richard Noll, *Mysteria: Jung and the Ancient Mysteries* (unpublished page proofs, 1994). Available HTTP: <https://www.academia.edu/6698999/Mysteria_Jung_and_the_Ancient_Mysteries_1994_uncorrected_page_proofs_of_a_book_cancelled_prior_to_publication_due_to_objections_by_the_Jung_family_>. Accessed 23 May 2024.

burning / For the Unattainable" (*Sehnsuchtsvolle Hungerleider / Nach dem Unerreichlichen*) embody the essential dynamic motivating Faust himself, while in the background there is Schelling's idea (drawing on the Scholia Parisina to Apollonius of Rhodes's *Argonautica*, Book 1, l. 916, which he describes as "a single account, preserved by exceptional luck") that the four names of the Cabiri as recorded at Samothrace — namely, Axieros, Axiokersa, Axiokersos, and finally Kadmilos — correspond to Demeter, Persephone, Hades (or in its place, Osiris or Dionysos), and finally Hermes (who leads the other gods from the underworld and into heaven), and thus represent a process of spiritual ascent.[70] Because this process involves recapitulating its earlier three stages at a higher heavenly level with Kadmilos/Hermes serving as a mediator between the highest of the gods, Zeus, and the first three gods of the Cabiri, this brings the total number of the Cabiri to seven (although Goethe jokingly suggests in ll. 8194-8199 that there might be an eighth). Thus, despite its satirical tone (here as elsewhere in *Faust II*), the Cabiri Scene symbolizes, as Hamlin points out, the entire "quest journey" for Helena as the realization of the classical ideal of Beauty (438). (Just as, one might add, in Wolfram's *Parzival* the quest was for the Grail ...)

In the Aegean Festival scene, the Cabiri form the ancient counterparts to the more modern figure of Homunculus who, while dismissing them, is in turn described with astonishment by Proteus as "A shining little dwarf!" (*Ein leuchtend Zwerglein!*), the like of which he has never seen before (l. 8245). Climbing onto the back of Proteus, who has transformed himself into a dolphin, Homunculus sets off in search of the fulfilment of his quest for being — which is the dramatic conclusion to the entire Aegean Festival scene.

The iconographical climax of the Festival is achieved with the arrival of the sea-nymph Galatea in her scallop shell chariot. Her

---

[70] Robert F. Brown (ed.), *Schelling's Treatise on "The Deities of Samothrace": A Translation and an Interpretation* (Missoula, MT: Scholars Press, 1974), pp. 16-17.

epiphany has as a visual intertext in the theme of "The Triumph of Galatea," as painted by (among others) Raphael in his fresco completed c. 1512 in the Villa Farnesina in Rome. Just as the conjuring of the Earth Spirit in the opening scene of Part One serves as a *transposition d'art* of Rembrandt's etching of Faust, so Goethe draws here on the lavish details of Raphael's fresco, as well as verbally on the pact of the Wager Scene when Galatea urges the dolphins pulling her shell chariot, "tarry, me rivets the sight" (*verweile, mich fesselt der Blick*) (l. 8425). Galatea's shell is associated with Aphrodite, the goddess of love, in two respects: first, because the scallop shell in which Galatea rides had previously conveyed Aphrodite from her birth at sea to Paphos, the seat of her future cult; and second, Aphrodite's jewel-encrusted, golden chariot was drawn through the sky by a team of doves, and these birds — "Doves are they whom love enflameth, / White as light each quiv'ring wing" (ll. 8341-8342) — here fly ahead of Galatea's shell. (Later, in Nietzsche's *Zarathustra*, the "sign" that Zarathustra's hour has come takes the form of "the laughing lion with the flock of doves" (Z III 12 §1) — doves which will come down on him "as it were a cloud [...] of love," and we shall learn that "whenever a dove whisked over its nose, the lion shook its head and wondered and laughed" [Z IV 20].)

This symbolic presence of Aphrodite at the Aegean Festival represents its culmination — "Now our feast is crowned and fashioned / Unto fullest ravishment" (ll. 8345-8346) — and its celebration of the life-bringing power of nature, and above all the element of water (Diener, 541). The association between Aphrodite and Cyprus as (one of) her birthplace(s) is underpinned by the mythological references to the Ophiogenes, said by Strabo in his *Geography* (§13.1.14) to be akin to a serpent tribe and by Pliny the Elder in his *Natural History* (§7.2.3) to be able to cure snakebites at a touch, while the Psylli and Marsi — "obscure, primeval inhabitants of Cyprus" — were also associated with snakes, in the case of the former by their reputation as a race of snake charmers, and in the case of their latter through their worship of Angitia, an archaic goddess of snakes. (According to

Diener, the taming or charming of snakes served Goethe as a symbol for the "victory of the spirit over 'lower', impersonal strata of the psyche, over lower instinctual drives and a diabolical negation of all that is noble and beautiful" [545].)

So, it is appropriate that Homunculus feels himself erotically attracted to Galatea, and on the back of Proteus as a dolphin he races toward her, shattering the glass of his phial against her shell and dissipating his spiritual flame into the water of the sea (Hamlin, 434). According to Thales, "All things are out of water created, / All by water maintained" (*Alles ist aus dem Wasser entsprungen!! / Alles wird durch das Wasser erhalten!*) (ll. 8435-8436), and hence he is an equally fitting commentator on Homunculus's self-sacrificial act, by means of which he plunges into the sea and embarks upon the process of organic evolution through various stages of metamorphosis which eventually will lead to his emergence as a human being (434). In the words of Thales's final speech to Homunculus:

> Yield to the well-advised hortation
> From the first step to start creation;
> For prompt activity prepare.
> Thou'lt move thee by eternal norms there
> Through thousand and yet thousand forms there,
> And ere thou'rt man there's time to spare.
> [*Da regst du dich nach ewigen Normen,*
> *Durch tausend, abertausend Formen,*
> *Und bis zum Menschen hast du Zeit*].[71]
> (ll. 8322-8326)

---

[71] In his commentary to his translation of *Faust*, Albert G. Latham notes that, in these lines, Goethe sketches his theory of evolution, noting that in his "Metamorphoses of Plants" Goethe had shown how the various parts of the flower are modifications of the leaf type, and how elsewhere he tried to show how the skull is a modification of the upper spinal vertebrae. Latham draws attention to other passages where Goethe embraces a notion of evolution usually associated with Darwin. For instance, in November 1806: "Nature, in order to attain to man, performs a long prelude of beings and forms which still fall far short of man"; in March 1807: "Nature makes no leaps,

In turn, as Homunculus mounts Proteus in his guise as a dolphin, the Old Man of the Sea warns him against his existential ambitions and counsels a kind of anti-Faustian strategy of the avoidance of striving, as he tells him:

> In spirit seek the liquid azure.
> In length and breadth thou'lt live, at pleasure
> Wilt move there, but good counsel hear:
> Strive not to rise, for hast ascended
> To man the scale of being, ended
> For good and all is thy career.
> [*Nur strebe nicht nach höheren Orden;*
> *Denn bist du erst ein Mensch geworden,*
> *Dann ist es völlig aus mit dir*].
> (ll. 8327-8332)

Thus, across Act II we can see how three different strands thematize the motif of transformation and the pattern of ascending creation and self-consciousness (Hamlin, 438):

- Faust's journey to the underworld and his appeal to Persephone for the release of Helena
- The Cabiri as a symbol of hierarchical desire and ascent
- Homunculus's erotic response to Galatea, his self-sacrifice, and his procreative union with the element of water.

All three themes represent the motif of *becoming* and the quintessential Faustian theme of *transformation*, and it is this motif and this theme that are celebrated in the triumphant climax to the Aegean Festival and to Act II as a whole. The dynamic is that of

---

she could, for example, never make a horse, unless all the other animals had gone before, upon which, as upon a ladder, she climbs up to the structure of the horse"; and in November 1810: "All literature is like a process of formation from water to molluscs, polyps and the like, until at last a man comes into existence." In fact, Latham goes so far as to maintain that "it would scarcely be too much to say that evolution is the keynote to the whole Faust drama" (382).

expanding concentric circles (cf. "ring on ring [*Kreis um Kreis*], / File on file now interlacing" and "In drawn-out curving chain [*in gedehnten Kettenkreisen*], [...] The thronging circles swirl and veer" [ll. 8380-8381, 8447 and 8449) and of the snakelike motion of the spiral (cf. "Serpentine meandering" [*Schlangenartig reihenweis*]" and "The thronging circles swirl und veer [*Windet sich die unzählige Schar*]" [ll. 8382 and 8449]), reflecting two aspects of the snakelike spiral in Goethe's thought: first, the image of a circular rotation about a *Mittelpunkt* (as Goethe put it in one of his maxims, "the greatest gift that we have received from God and Nature is life, the rotation of the monad around itself, which knows neither rest nor peace");[72] and second, his description of a "spiral tendency" as the "productive life principle" as found in the botanical world and in the pattern of human development (Diener, 552).

In a conclusion that stages a kind of *coniunctio oppositorum* by uniting not just the opposites of fire and water but of all four elements, at the same time as Homunculus fulfills his quest to achieve life through the creative power of Eros, it is in these final lines as if the entire oceanic world is shuddering in a kind of cosmic orgasm:

SIRENS:
What fiery marvel transfigures the billows
That sparkling shatter them each on its fellows?
So shines it, so surges, sweeps onward in light,
The bodies they burn on their path through the night,
And all round about us in fire is embosomed.
To Eros the empire, whence all things first blossomed!

Hail the Ocean! Hail the Surge!
Girt with holy fire its verge.
Hail the Water! Hail the Fire!
Hail the chance that all admire!

---

[72] Goethe, *Maxims and Reflections*, ed. Hecker, §391 (trans. R.H. Stephenson).

TUTTI:
Hail the breeze that softly swelleth!
Hail the grot where mystery dwelleth!
All we festally adore,
Hail, ye Elements all four!

(ll. 8476-8487)

This all-engendering Eros is the Eros that Ludwig Klages describes as *kosmogonisch*, and he cites these very lines in his study of this "cosmogonic Eros."[73] This Eros is, as Cyrus Hamlin emphasizes, not the "playful Cupid" of later mythology nor even the daimon that we know from Plato's *Symposium* (202d-203a), but rather "a much more ancient, even primal, concept" — "the original creative force that produces life and light out of chaos" (240, fn. 8). Nevertheless, the dynamic associated with this Eros shares with Plato's *Symposium* the step-by-step ascent to the Beautiful, and Gottfried Diener identifies five aspects common to Galatea, to the Beautiful, to Truth, and to life-sustaining, life-enhancing water; that is, common to Helena as the *einzigste Gestalt* and to the Platonic χαλον μονοειδες: (a) Beauty is divine; (b) Truth is divine; (c) in their divine origin, Beauty and Truth are identical; (d) this idea is expressed in the diversity and multiplicity of life (cf. "It is not given to us to grasp the truth, which is identical with the divine, directly. We perceive it only in reflection, in example and symbol, in singular and related appearances. It meets us as a kind of life which is incomprehensible to us, and yet we cannot free ourselves from the desire to comprehend it");[74] and (e) water is the "source of

---

[73] Ludwig Klages, *Vom kosmogonischen Eros*, 2nd edn. (Jena: Diederichs, 1926), p. 202; *Of Cosmogonic Eros*, trans. Mav Kuhn, 2nd edn (Munich: Theion, 2022), p. 18. For further discussion of the Klagesian concept of "cosmogonic Eros," see Paul Bishop and Heinz-Peter Preußer (eds.), *Eros und Sexus in der Philosophie von Ludwig Klages* (Würzburg: Königshausen & Neumann, 2025).

[74] Goethe, *Versuch einer Witterungslehre* (1825). Explicating this statement as a "basic Romantic tenet," Roger Cardinal remarks that "symbolic language thus

the gods" and indeed the "source of all things" (Homer, *Iliad*, Book 14, ll. 201 and 246) (Diener, 563-565).

In short, this Eros is a *vitalist* Eros. And there is a contrast and a continuity with the substance of the Act that follows: on the one hand, a contrast, because while what Act II celebrates in its mythological guise is the world of *nature*, the figure of Helena as the ideal of classical Beauty is all *culture*; and a continuity because, as Kerényi noted, Persephone keeps by her side and preserves "the faithful images of the once-existing, of 'things long since no longer present'" [*des »längst nicht mehr Vorhandenen«*]" (cf. l. 6278), so the question arises as to whether she "lends this origination the likeness [*das Abbild*] of Helena, so that it, with spirit and body united, again becomes alive?"[75] Yet this is, Kerényi avers, an idle question (*müßige Frage*), for at the beginning of Act III, Helena says that she arrives "Still drunken with the unrestful billow's tumultuous / Commotion" (*Noch immer trunken von des Gewoges regsamem / Geschaukel*) (ll. 8490-8491). In other words, Helena has not yet become fully classical in the sense that J.J. Winckelmann (1717-1768) defined it — as *edle Einfalt und stille Größe*, i.e., "noble simplicity and quiet grandeur."[76]

Act III

The last time we saw Faust was in the scene set on the Lower Peneios when he set off with Manto to descend, Orpheus-like,

---

becomes the prime medium of Romantic art, and ranges from the simple allegorical schemes of [Philip Otto] Runge's paintings to complicated symbolic structures, as, for instance, in the tale of Atlantis told in Novalis' [*Heinrich von*] *Ofterdingen*, which is highly abstruse" (Roger Cardinal, *German Romantics in Context* (London: Studio Vista, 1975), pp. 42-43.

[75] Kerényi, *Humanistische Seelenforschung*, p. 144.

[76] Winckelmann, "Thoughts on the Imitation of the Painting and Sculpture of the Greeks" [1755], in H.B. Nisbet, *German Aesthetic and Literary Criticism: Winckelmann, Lessing, Hamann, Herder, Schiller, Goethe* (Cambridge: Cambridge University Press, 1985), pp. 32-54 (p. 42).

into the realm of Persephone to secure Helena's release from the underworld. Presumably he has succeeded, because now in Act III we see Helena — not simply her phantom, as in Act I, but "really" and in person. But what does it mean to talk about the "real" Helena?

Act III was first published independently as a separate drama in 1827 titled *Helena: Classical-Romantic Phantasmagoria, an Interlude to Faust*. So, the text has a status outside of its function in *Faust II*, which is to develop further Goethe's treatment of the traditional Faust legend, according to which Mephistopheles conjures up Helen of Troy to serve as a concubine for Faust. Cyrus Hamlin reads the final stage direction after line 10038 as an indication that Mephisto, in the guise of Phorcyas he has assumed in the Classical Walpurgis Night of Act II (cf. ll. 7951-8033), acts as a sort of daimonic stage manager for the entire interlude, which means that none of it is "real" and we should read the entire Act as a kind of Dream Life Sequence (441). On this account, all the characters who appear in the Act are spirits, including presumably Helena herself, but certainly the Chorus and the attendants of Faust's castle as well as the dwarfs whom Phorcyas commands into action with a clap of her hands in the stage direction after line 8937. Thus the entire sequence has the status of "a theatrical show, a phantasmgoria of the poetic imagination" with a dual function: first, to convince Helena (as, at first, it does) that she is really alive, even though this is a deception; and second, to establish "a literary, poetic, artistic, and theatrical medium [...] within which it is possible for Faust to be united with Helena" (441).

To argue for this position is to argue that reality cannot be achieved within "a literary, poetic, artistic, and theatrical medium," against which one might offer the counterargument that, despite or precisely because of the fact that there may well have been no historical Helen of Troy, her existence within such a medium *is* the "real" one. In other words, the "reality" of Helena lies precisely in her being a mythological rather than a historical figure; in other words, she falls into the category of what the Roman historian Sallustius called "things that *never happened,* but *always are.*"[77] In fact, Hamlin — despite his comments quoted above — himself comes close to this position when he argues that the *Helena* drama (and, *mutatis mutandis,* Act III) is "a mythical-poetic recapitulation or re-creation" of what Goethe himself (in his letter to Sulpiz Boisserée of 22 October 1826) called "a good three thousand years" of the Western cultural tradition, that is, the period from the Sack of Troy in 1250 B.C.E. (according to Herodotus, although other historians give other dates) via the Germanic Middle Ages to the destruction of Missolonghi in 1824, when Byron died from fever (441, cf. 531). As "a theatrical event in symbolic terms," the marriage of Faust and Helena as "the union of classicism and Romanticism" or as the "synthesis of the ancient and the medieval" produces "the self-consuming spirit of modern poetry" (441-442); or, in other words, it is *archetypal.*

What guarantees and what actually brings about the "reality" of Helena across the three parts of Act III — the scene before the palace of Menelaus at Sparta, the inner courtyard of a (medieval) castle, and the final scene set in a shady grove — is Goethe's use of *language.* Language — not so much in the structuralist sense of signifier and signified, which would see Helena as some kind of master-signifier, defined as a signifier that points to itself instead of other signifiers, and by Lacan (in his Seminar III) in terms of a signifier out from which everything "radiates" and around which everything "is organized," or "the point of convergence that enables everything that happens in this discourse to be situated,"[78]

---

[77] See the Roman historian Sallustius in *On the Gods and the World,* §4: "Now these things never happened, but always are. And Mind sees all things at once, but Reason (or Speech) expresses some first and others after. Thus, as the myth is in accord with the Cosmos, we for that reason keep a festival imitating the Cosmos, for how could we attain higher order?" (translated in Gilbert Murray, *Five Stages of Greek Religion,* 3rd edn. (Garden City, NY: Doubleday, 1955), pp. 191-211 [p. 195]).

[78] Jacques Lacan, *The Seminar of Jacques Lacan, Book III, The Psychoses, 1955-*

but rather language as something both conceptual and emotional, both intellectual and physical, both a manifestation of *Sinn* (in the sense of meaning) and *die Sinnen* (in the sense of sensuousness). (Language, in other words, in the sense that it is understood by Ludwig Klages as uncovering an archaic dimension of Being.)[79]

The first section of Act III, "Before the Palace of Menelaus at Sparta," is an imitation of Greek tragedy in both *structural* and *metrical* terms, notably its use of iambic trimeter (a six-stress iambic line commonly used in speeches in Greek tragedy): *Bewúndert víel und víel geschólten, Hélená*. By using the iambic trimeter in his initial draft of *Helena* in 1800, Goethe was (Hamlin notes) the first writer in German to imitate this metrical form, subsequently used by Schiller in his play *Die Braut von Messina* (1803) and by Mörike in his poem discussed above, "Auf eine Lampe" (1846); indeed, Goethe's imitation in the *Helena* of the three parts of the Greek choral ode, consisting of strophe, antistrophe, and epode, is "without precedent in German drama" (241, fn. 1; 242, fn. 7). Despite speaking in perfect metrical form, Helena complains (as we have just seen) about finding herself in a stupor from her journey across the sea (which must also be a journey up from the underworld, thanks to Faust's intervention). She is accompanied by a chorus of captive Trojan women, led by Panthalis, the same name as one of her attendants as found in Pausanias's account of a fifth century B.C.E. painting of the Fall of Troy by Polygnotos. Helena's account of her homecoming and her relationship with Menelaus (who won the hand of Helena in marriage in competition with many other suitors and who, together with his brother Agamemnon, raised a fleet of a thousand ships to go to Troy and secure her return, after she was taken there by Paris) derives from Euripedes's plays

---

1956, ed. Jacques-Alain Miller, trans. Russell Grigg (New York and London: Norton, 1993), p. 268.

[79] See Paul Bishop, "Ludwig Klages and his philosophy of language," *Journal of European Studies*, vol. 50, no. 1 (2020), 17-29.

Orestes and *The Trojan Women*, and her shock and horror — "the stark horror which, since time first origin / Uncoiled from hoar Night's womb" (*das Entsetzen, das, dem Schoß der alten Nacht / Von Urbeginn entsteigend*, trans. Arndt) (ll. 8649-8650) — when she encounters one-eyed, one-toothed Phorcyas recalls the incident in Aeschyleus's *Eumenides* when the Pythian priestess enters the temple at Delphi and is filled with panic at the sight of the Furies.

By staging an exchange between Helena, the ideal of classical Beauty, and Phorcyas, an embodiment of the primordial ugliness of the Phorcyads or Graiae, as well as a dialogue between Phorcyas and members of the Chorus in the classical Greek form of stichomythia (a sequence of single alternating lines or pairs of lines) Goethe is inverting the conventional view of antiquity as espoused by Winckelmann and others, including Goethe himself, that regarded the art and culture of classical Greece as the highest embodiment of the ideal of Beauty (cf. 432-433). And the reality of that ideal is itself put in question when Helena, reminded by Phorcyas of that part of the legend that told of how the real Helena was carried off by Hermes to Egypt and left there to languish while a mere image (*Idol*) of her was taken by Paris to Troy (ll. 8872-8873), is no longer able to distinguish which of those Helenas was the real one, saying: "Myself now what in truth I am, that know I not" (*Selbst jetzo, welche denn ich sei, ich weiß es nicht*) (l. 8875). And it is put even more into question when Helena, reminded again of yet another part of the legend that relates how she and Achilles were, as spirits after their deaths, united in marriage on the island of Leuce, where they lived together and produced a son, Euphorion (ll. 8876-8878), actually faints, sinking into the Semi-Chorus's arms as she swoons, as she responds, "Eidolon I, to him eidolon plighted me!" (*Ich als Idol ihm dem Idol verband ich mich*), adding: "It was a dream! Nay, say not so the words themselves. / I fade away, idolon to myself I grow!" (*Es war ein Traum, so sagen ja die Worte selbst. / Ich schwinde hin und werde selbst mir ein Idol*) (ll. 8880-8881).

Once Helena recovers from her faint and returns to the center stage, Phorcyas tells her (in the trochaic tetrameters used by Euripides in his dramas to signify moments of emotional intensity) that Menelaus is now planning to execute her (and the Chorus) as an act of sacrifice, and claps her hands together to summon a troop of muffled, dwarflike figures to make preparations for the ceremonial beheading of Helena (while the Chorus, by contrast, is apparently going to be put to death by hanging). Their means of escape from this grisly fate comes in the form of the prospect held out to them by Phorcyas of being rescued by Faust and his attendants. As Phorcyas-Mephisto describes Faust, his castle (identified by critics as the medieval Crusader castle at Mistra in the Peloponnese)[80] and its heraldic arms, and the youthful attendants, so a shift is operated between the classical era and that of the medieval German. The sound of trumpets in the distance, conjured up by Phorcyas, startles and alarms the Chorus; consequently Helena, in response to Phorcyas's offer, "Speak thou the last. Say solemnly and clearly — Yes. / Straightway I'll fence thee round with yonder castle" (ll. 9048-9049), affirms her acceptance: "I have bethought me what I may adventure first. / A Cacodaemon [*Ein Widerdämon*] art thou, that I well perceive, / And fear that unto Evil thou the Good wilt turn [*Und fürchte, Gutes wendest du zum Bösen an*].[81] / Yet to the Castle first of all I'll follow thee. / The rest I know" (ll. 9072-9075). As an ode spoken by the Chorus marks the end of the classical section of Act III, and descending fog signals the transition to the medieval German world of the second section — a transition also signaled in Goethe's language and his choice of lyrical metre.

---

[80] For further discussion, see Busch-Zentner, *Faust-Stätten in Hella*, pp. 39-61; and Wilhelm Blum, "Mistra and the Peloponnese in Goethe's *Faust II*," in Hans Schulte, John Noyes, and Pia Kleber (eds), *Goethe's "Faust": Theatre of Modernity* (Cambridge: Cambridge University Press, 2011), pp. 129-137.

[81] Note the contrast to what is said about Mephisto in Part One (see ll. 1335-1136) (see above, pp. 31-32). A cacodaemon ("evil spirit") is the opposite of an agathodaemon.

For while at the beginning of the scene set in the "Inner Courtyard of a Castle" the Chorus and its Leader and Helena speak in loose trimeters, on his first appearance Faust (dressed in medieval knightly court costume and accompanied by a procession of pages and squires) speaks in blank verse, as typically used in Shakespearean and German classical drama alike. For her part, Helena replies in blank verse, adapting the metrical form of her discourse to his. As the Warden of the Tower, Lynceus sings two rhymed ballads, recalling the stanza form of medieval German courtly love poetry, the first of which celebrates the beauty of Helena in a manner entirely in keeping with the traditions of *Minnesang*, while the second offers to her as a tribute the spoils of war that have been accumulated by Germanic tribes in their military conquests. Classical forms have thus given way to medieval German ones, and the birth of another Western form — the rhyme — is enacted in the following exchange between Helena (who invites Faust to join her at her side) and Faust (who willingly accepts and describes himself as "Worshipper, servant, guardian all in one" (l. 9364):

FAUST:
If but our people's speech is pleasing to thee,
O then its song will surely ravish thee,
Content thine ear, thine inmost-seated mind.
Yet were it best to practise it straightway —
Alternate speech will charm it, coax it forth.

HELENA:
Say how I too can speak in such sweet wise!

FAUST:
'Tis easy, so but from the heart it rise.
And when the breast with yearning doth o'erflow,
You look around and ask —

HELENA:

Who shares the glow?

FAUST:

Nor back nor forward in an hour like this
The mind doth look; the present —

HELENA:

Is our bliss.
(ll. 9372-9382)

Thus, Helena has literally been taught not just how to speak German (*die Sprechart unsrer Völker*) but how to speak in rhyming couplets. "Alone the present moment" (*Die Gegenwart allein*) is their "bliss" (*ist unser Glück*) in a preeminently aesthetic sense: The unity of Faust's and Helena's discourse is essentially linguistic, but it is no less "real" for that.[82] And Faust and Helena move from speaking rhyming couplets to becoming a rhyming couple, unified in language as a sign of their mutual erotic attraction. True, one can see their union as king and queen as a representation of the *coniunctio* of Sol and Luna, but it surely goes beyond the specificity of that context and actually embodies in linguistic form a union that transcends space and time, as the following exchange both relates and enacts:

HELENA:
I feel so far away, and yet so near.
Am but too fain to say: Here am I, here!
[*Ich fühle mich so fern und doch so nah
Und sage nur zu gern: Da bin ich! da!*]

---

[82] For further discussion of this stichomythic exchange between Faust and Helena, see Pierre Hadot, "'The Present Alone Is Our Joy': The Meaning of the Present Instant in Goethe and in Ancient Philosophy," *Diogenes*, vol. 34, no. 133 (1986), 60-82.

FAUST:
I scarce can breathe, I tremble, speech is dead;
It is a dream, and space and time are fled.
[*Ich atme kaum, mir zittert, stockt das Wort;*
Es ist ein Traum, verschwunden Tag und Ort.]

HELENA:
O'erlived I seem to be, and yet so new,
Woven in thee and to the unknown true.

FAUST:
Brood not upon the rarest destiny!
Were't but a moment, duty 'tis to be.
[*Dasein ist Pflicht, und wär's ein Augenblick.*]

(ll. 9411-9418)

The merest mention of the word *Augenblick*, recalling the terms of the wager, brings Mephistopheles in the guise of Phorcyas bursting onto the scene. This interrupts the illusion (or is it the reality?) that Faust and Helena have achieved in linguistic form and warns them that her husband Menelaus is approaching. As the sound of signals, explosions from the towers, trumpets and bugles, martial music, and powerful forces on the match fills the air, Faust reverts momentarily to iambic trimeters (ll. 9435-9441), before recovering himself and returning to rhyming couplets (ll. 9442-9481).

In so doing, Goethe moves the theme of military conflict into the foreground, a theme that will become central in Act IV; and the imagery of war and suffering plays an important part later in Jung's *Red Book* too. Faust's speech at this point is an amalgamation of three distinct historical periods: first, the Dorian invasion of the Peloponnese in the period after the Trojan War, coinciding with the shift from preclassical dialects and traditions in southern Greece to those from Classical Greece but also marking a period of cultural and economic breakdown, the entry into the so-called Greek Dark Ages (i.e., from c. 1100 B.C.E. and the end of the Mycenaean palatial civilization to c. 750 B.C.E. and the beginning of the Archaic age); second, the migrations of Germanic tribes across Europe in the early Christian era who overran the ancient world; and third, the Crusader invasions of the Peloponnese in the 13th century (Hamlin, 267, fn. 9). This fusion of historical epochs in the timeless Now of poetry serves as a prelude to a long speech by Faust (ll. 9506-9573), described by Hamlin as Faust's "survey of pastoral" (447).

Now "pastoral," defined as "a fictional imitation of rural life [...] the life of an imaginary Golden Age, in which the loves of shepherds and shepherdesses play a prominent role,"[83] is a tradition that can be traced back to the *Idylls* of Theocritus in the third century B.C.E. and arguably reaches one of its finest expressions in the *Eclogues* of Virgil. In providing a résumé of the European pastoral tradition, Faust also adapts it to the needs of Goethe's drama: Arcadia, the pastoral's vision of harmony with nature, was named after a Greek province the Peloponnese, and Faust refers to the river Eurotas, which flows south from Arcadia to Sparta, the town of which Helena was Queen, and which was the site of Leda's confrontation with Zeus as a swan. The combination of these and other references (such as to Helena's emergence from her egg) illustrate, in Hamlin's words, an "accommodation of a European poetic tradition to the particular thematic situation of Goethe's drama" with an "intricacy and precision" which is "astonishing and entirely unique" (447). Moreover, in so doing, Arcadia itself as the ideal pastoral landscape and setting for the conclusion of Act III is thus "created by *and through* Faust's poetic depiction of it" (449; my italics).

---

[83] J.E. Congleton and T.V.F. Brogan, "Pastoral," in *The New Princeton Enyclopedia of Poetry and Poetics*, ed. Alex Preminger and T.V.F. Brogan (Princeton, NJ: Princeton University Press, 1993), pp. 885-888 (p. 885).

The figure of Pan (l. 9538), the god of wild nature with the hindquarters, legs, and horns of a goat, evoked by Faust when he says, "Pan shields them there, and Life-nymphs there in legions / In the moist cool of bushy clefts dwell free, / And striving yearningly to higher regions / Rears itself, branchwise, crowded tree on tree" (ll. 9538-9541), forms a link back to Act I, in which the Emperor appeared, accompanied by people dressed as fauns and satyrs, as Pan (see ll. 5801-5814), and anticipates the Dionysian chaos of the third section of Act III — another example of the structural principle of interrupted tragedy. In fact, this chaotic disruption occurs on two levels in Act III, being enacted first in the fate that befalls the figure of Euphorion.

Euphorion, whose name means "the abundant" (Εὐφορίων), was, according to legend, born as a son to Achilles and Helen during their posthumous marriage on the Islands of the Blessed and was endowed with a pair of wings. Icarus-like, he tried to fly to heaven but was knocked down with a thunderbolt as a punishment for his hubris by Zeus. (According to Paul Diel, Icarus serves as a symbol of the tragic as a false response to the banality of life.)[84] The early life of Euphorion (in Goethe's modification of this figure as the child of Helena and Faust) is recounted by Phorcyas, including the episode from which Euphorion emerges transformed: From his birth onward, he is used to leaping and springing at will, although his parents warn him not to try and fly; one day, he falls into a mountain crevice, disappears from sight but returns — transformed — as if adorned with flowers, tassels on his forearms, ribbons on his chest, in his hand a golden lyre ("like a little Phoebus"), and a kind of halo around his head.

Within the context of Act III, Euphorion has a fourfold function: first, as a personification of the spirit of poetry, of *heilige Poesie* (l. 9863) — "holy Poesy" (trans. Latham) or "Poesy pure"

---

[84] Paul Diel, *Le Symbolisme dans la mythologie grecque* (Paris: Payot, 1970), pp. 23-44.

(trans. Arndt) (see Goethe's conversation with Eckermann of 20 December 1829); second, as a representation of Lord Byron and the daimonic force with which Goethe associated him (see Goethe's conversation with Eckermann of 5 July 1827 and *Dichtung und Wahrheit*, book 4, chapter 20); and third, as a sort of *transposition d'art*, recalling the Italian Baroque painter Annibale Carracci's painting "The Genius of Fame" (c. 1588), now in the Gemäldegalerie Alte Meister in Dresden, which depicts a naked youth with wings, soaring up into the heavens. And finally, the fate of Euphorion puts into doubt the permanence of Faust's rescue of Helena from beyond the grave and the stability of her presence:

HELENA AND FAUST:
Scarcely called to life, discerning
Scarce the morning's blithesome beam,
From the giddy steeps art yearning
For the fields with woe that teem?
Are then we
Naught to thee?
[*Sind denn wir
Gar nichts dir?*][85]
Is the gracious bond a dream?
[*Ist der holde Bund ein Traum?*]
(ll. 9877-9883)

---

[85] Throughout this second section of the Helena Act, there is repeated play on a motif in a famous but anonymous example of German *Minnesang*, which runs thus:

*Dû bist mîn, ich bin dîn.
des solt dû gewis sîn.
dû bist beslozzen
in mînem herzen,
verlorn ist das sluzzelîn:
dû muost ouch immêr darinne sîn.*

Cf. ll. 9699-9706, 9729-9736, and ll. 9877-9883 (cited here).

Euphorion starts dancing through the Chorus, tracing a winding path and drawing its members away to dance; he picks up a young girl, whom he sets on fire, and she flares up as a flame; he leaps ever higher up the cliffs, until he launches himself upon the air, is carried for a while by his garments but plunges down to the ground, a trail of light from his shining head marking his descent. Lying at the feet of Helena and Faust, his corporeal body vanishes, and his aureole rises like a meteor to the sky, leaving behind only his robe, cloak, and lyre. From the depths, Euphorion's voice can be heard, lamenting: "Me in the gloomy realm / Mother, leave not alone!" (*Laß mich im düstern Reich, / Mutter, mich nicht allein!*) (ll. 9905-9906).

The function of the Chorus switches to performing a funeral dirge and, following the fall and disappearance of Euphorion as an emblem of Poetry, now it is time for Helena as the embodiment of the classical ideal of Beauty to disappear in turn. She speaks these final words (in iambic trimeters) to Faust, before she embraces him and her corporeal substance vanishes, leaving in his arms her robe and her veil (a symbol of poetry for Goethe in his poem *Zueignung* or "Dedication" as well as being associated with the goddess, Isis):[86]

> Woe's me, an ancient adage proves on me its truth,
> That Fortune weds with Beauty never abidingly.
> In sunder rent the bond of life is, as of love,
> And both bewailing anguished I say farewell,
> Upon thy bosom casting me yet once again.
> Receive, Persephoneia, thou the child and me!
>
> (ll. 9939-9944)

Helena's reference to Fortune (*Glück*) is a play on the name of Faust himself (as *faustus* = the favored one), while the sentiment

---

[86] See Pierre Hadot, *The Veil of Isis: An Essay on the History of the Idea of Nature* [2004], trans. Michael Chase (Cambridge, MA, and London: The Belknap Press of Harvard University Press, 2006).

that good fortune and beauty cannot be permanently united is a sentiment borrowed from Calderón's play *The Purgatory of St. Patrick* (*El purgatorio de San Patricio*) of 1628, where Luis says to Polonia, "[…] since creation's hour / Beauty has ever one unvarying dower, / It brings misfortune with it, it is this / Makes beauty rarely live long time with bliss" (Act II, Scene 10; trans. Denis Florence MacCarthy). Phorcyas advises Faust to hold fast to Helena's robe, as a token of what Helena represents: "The Goddess whom thou lostest is it not, / But god-like is't" (*Die Göttin ist's nicht mehr, die du verlorst, / Doch göttlich ist's*) (ll. 9949-9950). As Helena's garments dissolve into clouds, they surround Faust, lift him up, and drift past with him (and we shall not see Faust again until Act IV). Phorcyas gathers up Euphorion's robe, cloak, and lyre, saying: "Enough remains for poets' initiation, / Guild and trade-jealousy to whet, / And are the talents not in my donation, / At least I'll lend the trappings yet" (ll. 9958-9961), or in other words — what remains of "sacred poetry" is sufficient to keep the "business" of poetry ticking over!

Thus, Act III has ended in disaster: Euphorion has plunged to his death and vanished; Helena has disappeared, and her garments have dissolved into clouds; and there is one further transformatory moment to come. For the Chorus now undergoes an astonishing metamorphosis into four groups of elemental nymphs, as another verse form (trochaic tetrameters) asserts itself. The members of the Chorus are transformed into Dryads (tree nymphs), Oreads (mountain nymphs), Naiads (water nymphs), and into the grapes of the vine from which wine will be made; all a parallel to the four elements triumphantly hailed by the participants in the Aegean Sea Festival at the end of Act II. The celebration of the ripening of grapes and the treading of the wine turns into an evocation of four pagan deities: Bacchus (the Roman god of the grape-harvest and ecstasy), Helios (the personification of the sun), Dionysos (the Greek equivalent of Bacchus), and Silenus (a satyr who represents winemaking and drunkenness, and a companion to Dionysos). The evocation of these elemental forces becomes increasingly wild, ecstatic, and orgiastic, a Dionysian revel that brings Act III to a drunken and chaotic conclusion. As the curtain falls, Phorcyas rears up in the proscenium as a gigantic figure, and casts off her mask and veil to reveal herself as Mephistopheles; this gesture itself is said to be in order to "provide in an epilogue such commentary on the play as might be necessary," but this epilogue is left unspoken, and perhaps the gesture itself, underscoring the theatricality of what we have witnessed, is sufficient.

Act IV

Act IV of *Faust* is the part of the drama that has tended to receive the least attention, not simply because it was, in fact, the last section of the work that Goethe actually wrote, but rather because it stands in abrupt contrast to the three preceding acts: the exuberance of the Carnival scene in Act I; the mythological and symbolic richness of the Classical Walpurgis Night in Act II; and the metrical *tour de force* of the Helena scenes in Act III. And yet, if Homunculus's yearning to be united with the sea and Faust's striving to unite with Helena address the erotic side of Faust's desire, Act IV returns us (in the sphere of politics) to another dimension of that desire — the desire for power, as part and parcel of his ambition as he described it in Part One, "That I the mighty inmost tether / May know, that binds the world together" (*Daß ich erkenne, was die Welt / Im Innersten zusammenhält*) (ll. 382-383). And it returns us to the plotline of Faust's dealings with the Emperor, whose *economic* problems he sought to solve in Act I and whose *military* problems he will try to solve in this act.

The opening scene is set on "High Mountains," up onto whose sheer, jagged pinnacles a cloud drifts, then divides, and out from which Faust steps. Just as he was somehow magically transported to the "Charming Landscape" at the opening of Act I, so the cloud formed from Helena's garments following her disappearance has thus transported Faust to these rocky peaks in the Alps. In the biblical Book of Kings, it is recounted how a long drought leaves the countryside arid and all the springs parched, until Elijah the Tishbite gathers the people on Mount Carmel and slays the priests of Baal. Prostrating himself with his face to the earth, Elijah tells his servant, "Go up, and look towards the sea": "And he went up, and looked, and said: There is nothing. And again he said to him: Return seven times. And at the seventh time: Behold a little cloud arose out of the sea like a man's foot" (3 Kings 18: 43-44). And soon a great rain begins to fall ... Later Mount Carmel, a mountain range in the Holy Land on which Christian hermits in the late 12th and early to mid-13th centuries built a monastery dedicated to the Virgin Mary, became a prototype of the kind of landscape in which, in the words of the Letter to the Hebrews, chosen souls "wandering in deserts, in mountains, and in dens, and in caves of the earth" (11:38) were able to find God.[87] These "High Mountains" at the beginning of Act IV look forward to the "Mountain Gorges" at the end of Act V, and provide Faust with what he himself calls "deepest solitude" (l. 10039), from which he contemplates how the cloud that has carried him changes its shape, until it becomes a kind of archetypal form of the feminine:

> Aye, mine eye deceives me not!
> On sun-illumined pillows, gloriously couched,
> A woman-form, gigantic, fashioned like the gods [*ein*
> > *göttergleiches Fraungebild*].
> I see it, like to Juno, Leda, Helen, how
> Majestically lovely in mine eye it floats!

---

[87] Abbot Guéranger, *The Liturgical Year*, vol. 13, *Time After Pentecost: Book* 4, trans. Laurence Shepherd, 4th edn. (Great Falls, MT: St. Bonaventure Publications, 2000), p. 110-113.

> Alas, it is dislimned. Towering formless-wide
> Like far-off snow-capped mountains in the East it hangs,
> And mirrors dazzling transient days' high pregnancy.
>
> (ll. 10047-10054)

Now Goethe was interested in the science of clouds, particularly the work of the English meteorologist Luke Howard (see his essay of 1817, *Wolkengestalt, nach Howard*).[88] The cloud formation that carries Faust back and assumes "a godlike female form" (*ein göttergleiches Fraungebild*) has been identified as a cumulus, while a second cloud that takes shape, described as "an entrancing form, / Like youthful-first, long-unenjoyed, supremest bliss" and identifiable as Gretchen, is a cirrus. In this meteorological or nephological way, the ascent of this cloud — "Drawing away with it the best my soul contains," as Faust says (l. 10066, trans. Arndt) — anticipates the final ascent of Faust himself in the "Mountain Gorges" scene, when his own soul follows the penitent spirit of Gretchen.

This ethereal mood is interrupted, as so often, by the arrival of Mephistopheles, wearing huge seven-league boots which, once he has stepped out of them, hurry off on their own. Finding themselves together on the mountains, Faust and Mephisto return to the debate between Vulcanism and Neptunism that had begun between Anaxagoras and Thales in the Classical Walpurgis Night. When he saw the Swiss Alps in the summer of 1796, Hegel recorded the following response in his diary: "Reason finds in the thought of the permanence of these mountains or in the kind of sublimity that is ascribed to them nothing that impresses it, that demands wonder and admiration. Seeing these dead masses gave me nothing but the monotonous and in time boring idea: this is the way it is

---

[88] For a selection of Goethe's writings on meteorology, see Goethe, *Scientific Studies*, pp. 143-154.

[*es ist so*]."[89] As if in response to this reaction, Mephistopheles expresses a similar idea but in a different way: "Earth bristles still with ponderous foreign masses, / Who shall explain such hurling-energy? / The wit of the philosopher it passes; / There lies the rock, needs must we let it lie" (ll. 10111-10114).

The exchange between Faust and Mephisto in the wake of Faust's response to Mephisto's own Vulcanist views, "'Tis well worth while, as I'm a living creature / To see what views the Devils hold on Nature" (ll. 10122-10123), introduces the theme of getting great things done. "Be Nature what she will — what do I care? / A point of honour 'tis, the Devil was there!" (*'s ist Ehrenpunkt: der Teufel war dabei!*), Mephisto says, adding: "We are the people, we, for great achieving; / Might, tumult, frenzy! Seeing is believing!" (ll. 10124-10127), and it is significant that the desire to do great things (*Großes zu erreichen*) is so clearly indexed to the Devil! For his part, Faust confesses: "A great work did bespeak / My purpose," and he invites Mephisto to guess what this work was.

In a kind of rerun of the story of Christ's temptation in the desert, Mephisto tries to tempt Faust to choose between two different life choices: first, a bourgeois city life; and second, an aristocratic country life.[90] The latter, with its opportunities for seducing women, is scornfully rejected by Faust (with a reference to the dissolute king of Assyria): "Base and modern! Sardanapalus!" (l. 10176) and dismissing Mephisto's jibe that he wants to go to the moon, Faust declares: "This round of earth, methought, / Hath scope for great achieving ever. / Strength do I feel for bold endeavour. / A deed of

---

[89] Hegel, "Auszüge aus dem Tagebuch der Reise in die Berner Oberalpen (25. Juli bis August 1796)", in *Werke*, ed. Eva Moldenhauer und Karl Markus Michel, 20 vols (Frankfurt am Main: Suhrkamp, 1971), vol. 1, *Frühe Schriften*, p. 618.

[90] These two options recapitulate and revise those offered by Mephisto in the "Witch's Kitchen" scene in Part One, where Faust is offered this choice of how to be rejuvenated: either by money or medicine or magic, or by a return to the simple life of agriculture (ll. 2351-2361) — a passage that would attract the attention of Jung in "The Relations between the Ego and the Unconscious" (CW 7 §258) (see Chapter 3).

wonder shall be wrought" (*Ich fühle Kraft zu kühnem Fleiß*) (ll. 10181-10184), a rhetoric reminiscent of the opening "Night" scene of Part One (cf. l. 464). What he really wants (as Faust clarifies in response to Mephisto) is not fame or renown (*Ruhm*), but rather — in another echo of Part One, his translation of the opening of St. John's Gospel (cf. l. 1237) — the deed (*die Tat*)! Faust mocks Mephisto for having no understanding of human ambition, and he expounds his vision of driving back the sea and reclaiming the land that will become his central motivation in Act V:

> Mine eye was drawn towards the vasty ocean.
> It swelled aloft, up to high heaven it vaulted,
> Then sinking, shook its waves [*die Wogen*] in fierce commotion
> And all the width of level shore [*des flachen Ufers Breite*]
> assaulted.
> And that did gall me, e'en as insolence [*der Übermut*]
> Galls the free mind [*den freien Geist*] that prizes every right,
> And through hot blood [*Blut*] wrought up to vehemence
> With a fierce sense of outrage doth excite.
> I thought it chance, mine eyeballs did I strain,
> The billow stood awhile, rolled back again,
> And from the goal so proudly won withdrew.
> The hour is nigh, the sport it will renew.
> [...]
> Then in my mind [*im Geiste*] I fashioned plan on plan: —
> Achieve thyself the exquisite emotion
> To shut out from the shore [*vom Ufer*] the imperious ocean
> [*das herrische Meer*],
> The confines of the moist expanse to straiten
> And back upon itself to thrust it beaten. —
> From step to step the ways and means I've reckoned,
> That is my wish, that do thou dare to second.
> (ll. 10198-10209 and 10227-10233)

As Ulrich Gaier notes, underlying this passage is an analogy between natural elements and the psyche (so that water : shore :: blood : mind); this analogy underpins Faust's twofold goal of establishing mastery (over the psyche) and acquiring possession (of the elemental), so that this passage can be construed as follows: The relation between the sea [*die Wogen*] and the shore [*des flachen Ufers Breite*] is analogous and galls me just as much as the insolence [*der Übermut*] which excites the mind [*den freien Geist*] with a fierce sense of outrage (*Kommentare I*, 983).

For his part, Freud used a similar image in his *New Introductory Lectures on Psycho-Analysis* when he wrote of the "therapeutic efforts of psychoanalysis" that "its intention is, indeed, to strengthen the ego, to make it more independent of the super-ego, to widen its field of perception, and enlarge its organization, so that it can appropriate fresh portions of the id," adding: "Where id was, there ego shall be [*Wo Es war, soll Ich werden*]. It is a work of culture, not unlike the draining of the Zuider Zee."[91] Faust's plan is thus immensely symbolic of the project of civilization, of controlling both external nature (i.e., the environment) and internal nature (here called *Blut*, i.e., drives, instincts, affects, uncontrolled sensuousness and corporeality) (Gaier, 984).[92] With good reason, then, Faust declares, "Me to despair it doth disquiet truly, / This aimless might of elements unruly [*Zwecklose Kraft unbändiger Elemente!*]. / A lofty flight I dare, nor deem it idle / Here would I battle, this I fain would bridle [*Da wagt mein Geist, sich selbst zu überfliegen; / Hier*

---

[91] Freud, *SE*, vol. 22, p. 80.

[92] For further discussion of this aspect of Faustian ambition, see Paul Bishop, "Analytical Psychology and the Dialectic of Enlightenment," in Jon Mills and Daniel Burston (eds), *Critical Theory and Psychoanalysis: From the Frankfurt School to Contemporary Critique* (London and New York: Routledge, 2023), pp. 95-114; and Paul Bishop, "Adorno and Jung, Bloch and Klages: Disorientation and Reorientation of Consciousness in the Totally Administered Society," in *Eranos Yearbook* (forthcoming).

möcht ich kämpfen, dies möcht ich besiegen]" (ll. 10218-10221)!
But if this is Faust's plan, how is he going to execute it?

At this moment, the sound of drums and military music interrupts the scene, the sound of war. Whereas in Act I the Emperor had *economic* problems, in Act IV he has *political* and *military* ones: as his realm falls apart into chaotic anarchy, a Rival Emperor emerges, aiming to reestablish imperial power and supported by the leading clergy, because they fear the loss of Church possessions in these anarchic conditions. Below them, Faust and Mephisto can see the rival troops, in position and ready for what could be the final battle. If "we join them," Mephisto suggests about the Emperor's troops, "their victory is decided," and in reply to Faust's dismissive reaction about the usefulness of any intervention, "It's fraud! Vain magic, sleight of hand," Mephisto retorts: "It's stratagems that win a battle!" (ll. 10298-10301). (And at this point Mephisto mentions in passing that, if successful in defending the Emperor's throne and lands, Faust will be entitled in return to land along the coastline.) These stratagems prove, however, to be typically Mephistophelian: They will involve the primal powers of the mountains themselves, "From primal mountains, primal human force" (*Aus Urgebirgs Urmenschenkraft*), personified by the Three Mighty Men, called in German *Raufebold, Habebald,* and *Haltefest* (translated by Latham as Swashbuckler, Havequick, and Holdfast; and by Arndt as Pugnacious, Rapacious, and Tenacious), alluding — so a stage direction by Goethe tells us —to the biblical figures of the "valiant men of David": Jashobeam (or Ishbaal), Eleazar, and Shammah (2 Samuel 23:8-17).[93] (These three ruffians seem to have little to

---

[93] Jashobeam (or Ishbaal), son of Hachmoni, "brandished his spear over eight hundred men" (or "three hundred men"; 1 Chronicles 11:11); Eleazer, son of Dodo the Ahohite, "cut down the Philistines until his hand was so stiff that he could not let go of the sword"; and Shamma, son of Elah the Hararite, "took his stand in the middle of [a field full of lentils], held it, and cut down the Philistines; and Yahweh brought about a great victory" (2 Samuel 23:8-12, trans. NJB). Ulrich Gaier reads these three figures as the "quintessences of aggression, greed, and avarice (*Kommentar*

do with their biblical counterparts; their function is, as Mephisto suggests, largely "allegorical" [l. 10329].) They descend as a group down the mountain, and the following scene is in the foothills, where the Emperor's tent is being pitched.

While the description of military tactics in this scene may weary some readers, the scene reflects Goethe's interest in military technique, even if there is no particular battle it describes. The Emperor — who says that he's never felt more sovereign than now ("A rival Emperor stands me in good stead. / Now do I feel me Emperor indeed!") (ll. 10407-10488) — has just sent some heralds to challenge the Rival Emperor, when Faust, wearing armor, and the Three Mighty Men enter. Faust presents himself — recalling the earlier theme of magic — as the emissary of the Sabine necromancer of Norcia and offers the use of supernatural force by unleashing the powers of the mountain. The Three Mighty Men are sent into battle to fight for the Emperor, and to support them Mephistopheles also sends in a host of armed men — in reality, empty suits of armor that are daimonically activated. The glittering tips of their spears and the flickering flames on their lances alert the Emperor to the involvement of supernatural forces: "It is not Nature worketh here!", he says, "Meseems too spectral is the light" (ll. 10583 and 10597), while Faust tries to pass off these luminous effects as a case of St. Elmo's fire.

Above the battlefield, an eagle and a griffin, symbols of the Emperor and his Rival, swoop in circles, attacking each other — an omen of the kind found in Homeric epic (see *Iliad*, Book 12, ll. 200-209). While Mephistopheles already claims victory, the Emperor is aware that, in reality, his side is losing badly; but Mephisto takes comfort from the message brought by two ravens, birds associated with Apollo as the god of prophecy and traditional

---

I, 989); Albrecht Schöne draws attention to the name of the son born to Isaiah and the prophetess, "Hasten-to-take-away-the-spoils, make-haste-to-take-away-the-prey" (DRV) or "Speedy-spoil-quick-booty" (NJB) (*Kommentare*, 668).

attributes of the pagan war god, Wotan. Mephisto sends his ravens to unleash elemental forces of water and fire: first, the Undines, or water sprites, who create the illusion of floods of water that push back the Rival Emperor's forces; and second, the dwarf-folk (*das Gezwergvolk*) of the mountains where they work with metal and stone in their smithy, who use summer lightning as illusory fire raining down on the army. Finally, Mephisto uses empty armor as an echo chamber to create an enormous noise, unleashing a "panic," deriving from the shriek associated with the great god Pan, which becomes "strident-harsh and shrill-satanic," presumably defeating the Rival Emperor's army and plunging the scene into warlike tumult from the orchestra that gradually merges into cheerful martial music.

We know that the Emperor has defeated his rival because the final scene of Act IV is set in his tent, where the Three Mighty Men are divvying up the booty. They are interrupted and told to leave by four of the Emperor's bodyguards, who sense there is something *geisterhaft* ("spectral" or "spooky") about the thuggish three. The four-stress trochaic meter of Mephisto's and the Emperor's speeches in the preceding Act (ll. 10640-10663), typical of Spanish Baroque drama, is replaced here by the six-stress iambic line of classical Alexandrines — modern politics, Goethe seems to be suggesting, is a tragedy!

The bodyguards withdraw when the Emperor enters accompanied by four political heavyweights — four princes, whom the Emperor appoints to four posts of state: the Arch-Marshal, the Arch-Chamberlain, the Arch-Steward, and the Arch-Cupbearer (corresponding to the figures of the Quartermaster, the Marshal, the Treasurer, and the Herald of the Carnival in Act I). They are joined by a fifth figure, the Arch-Chancellor, who is also the Archbishop (and whose dual rôle reflects his wish to get as much money for the Church as possible). When the four lay princes withdraw, the Archbishop and the Emperor have a separate conversation. As an act of penance for his collusion with the powers of Satan (*mit*

Satanas im Bunde) (l. 10982), the Emperor agrees to sign a formal "deed of transfer" of land and power to the Church, a kind of latter-day "Donation of Constantine," including a commitment to build an elaborate Gothic cathedral. As an afterthought, the Archbishop also demands the "tithe and rent and bounties" from the piece of coastal land that, earlier in Act IV, the Emperor had granted to Faust (ll. 11035-11038; cf. ll. 10304-10306). Thus, the loot-grabbing, daylight robbery of the thuggish Mighty Men at the beginning of the scene has its equivalent in the highest echelons of society in the form of the Archbishop's demands of the Emperor. More important, a motive for the final Act is established: for the coastline land granted to Faust is, as the Emperor petulantly remarks, "not yet there — it lies beneath the foam!" to which the Archbishop piously responds: "Who patience hath and right, his day will surely come" (*für den kommt auch die Zeit*) (ll. 11039-11040). And in the final Act, Faust's hour — in all senses — will indeed come.

Act V

The fifth and final act of Part Two opens with the archetypal figure of the wanderer — a favorite figure of Goethe's, reflected in his early poem (and a reflection of his separation from Friederike Brion), *Der Wandrer*; the great hymn, *Wandrers Sturmlied*; and the two famous poems, titled *Wandrers Nachtlied* —[94] returning to a part of the open country which he had left many years ago. The figure of the wanderer has a triple significance: If, in the first place, it acts as a cipher for Goethe himself, it also has a second,

---

[94] For further discussion, see R. Ellis Dye, "Goethe's »Der Wandrer«: Portrait of a Modern Man," *Sprachkunst*, vol. 34, no. 1 (2003), 1-23; L.A. Willoughby, "*Wandrers Sturmlied*: A Study in Poetic Vagrancy," in Elizabeth M. Wilkinson and L.A. Willoughby, *Goethe: Poet and Thinker* (London: Arnold, 1962), pp. 35-54; and L.A. Willoughby, "The Image of the 'Wanderer' and the 'Hut' in Goethe's Poetry," *Etudes germaniques*, 6 (1951), 207-219.

Faustian dimension: "Am I not fugitive, the homeless rover, / The man-beast void of goal or bliss" (*Bin ich der Flüchtling nicht? der Unbehauste? / Der Unmensch ohne Zweck und Ruh*) (ll. 3348-3349; trans. Arndt), Faust had cried out in Part One in the "Forest and Cave" scene, describing himself as a kind of "cataract" thundering "from crag to crag" and about to sweep away Gretchen's "little hut" (*Hüttchen*), a powerful symbol of his destructive effect on her "little world." And third, there is an allusion to the tale in Ovid's *Metamorphoses*, in which Jupiter and Mercury appear on the earth in disguise as wanderers, seeking hospitality — which, it turns out, only the poor and humble old couple, Philemon and Baucis, deign to provide (see below). (This episode is a popular one in European literature, exemplified — to take just one example — by Joseph Haydn's one-act puppet-opera of 1773, *Philemon und Baucis, oder Jupiters Reise auf die Erde*, based on a play by the Franco-German writers and translator, Gottlieb Konrad Pfeffel [1736-1809].)[95] In this sense, then, the wanderer *is* a truly archetypal figure: recalling the long, wandering journey of Odysseus and its Neoplatonic reading that suggests that Odysseus's homecoming is an allegory for rediscovering that we are divine …

In this scene, Ovid's tale of Philemon and Baucis is not simply alluded to, its significance is radically changed.[96] Rather than receiving a visit from two deities, they receive a visit from an anonymous wanderer: While the framework around the story of Faust is theological, here we encounter a world that is seemingly

---

[95] For further discussion, see Manfred Beller, *Philemon und Baucis in der europäischen Literatur: Stoffgeschichte und Analyse* (Heidelberg: Winter, 1967).

[96] For further (and insightful) discussion of this episode, see L.J. Rather, "Some Reflections on the Philemon and Baucis Episode in Goethe's *Faust*," *Diogenes*, vol. 7, no. 2 (March 1959), 60-73; and Wolfgang Giegerich, "Hospitality toward the Gods in an Ungodly Age: Philemon — Faust — Jung," *Spring*, 1984, 61-75; reprinted in *The Neurosis of Psychology: Primary Papers Towards a Critical Psychology* [Collected English Papers, vol. 1] (London and New York: Routledge, 2020), pp. 197-218.

without the divine. "Godless" — *gottlos* — is how Baucis later describes Faust, but the absence of the deity can be felt at the beginning of this scene. Together with their visitor, Philemon surveys the new landscape, created by the reclamation of land achieved by installing a series of dikes to push the sea back, and on which a new city has been built. Yet as the three of them sit down to supper, Baucis confesses her misgivings about how this has all been achieved. "Something in their doings yonder / Was not what it ought to be" (*Denn es ging das ganze Wesen / Nicht mit rechten Dingen zu*) (ll. 11113-11114), she says, recalling how strange lights flickered at night and how human lives were lost, suggesting that devilish powers had been involved in the works. "Godless" Faust, she adds, is now keen to acquire the land where their humble cottage stand: "Wicked [*Gottlos*] is he, for he lusteth / For our cottage, for our grove" (*Gottlos ist er, ihn gelüstet / Unsre Hütte, unser Hain*) (ll. 11131-11132). When the meal is over, Philemon and Baucis wander down to their little chapel to pray: "Let us ring and kneel and bending / Pray, and trust the God of old" (l. 11141-11142). Yet how much good will their prayers do them? Does the "God of old" (*dem alten Gott*) still exist in this brave new (Faustian) world?

The next scene is set in the spacious ornamental gardens of a palace, incorporating a large, straight canal. For the first time since the middle of Act IV, we see Faust: He has aged and is now extremely old. (In his conversation with Eckermann of 6 June 1831, Goethe suggested that Faust lives to be a hundred years old).[97] On the watchtower, Lynceus (whom we first encountered in this function in the middle section of the Helena Act) paints a word-picture of an idyllic evening, as the ships come into harbor — a moment of the kind the German Marxist philosopher Ernst Bloch (1885-1977) would call *erfüllter Augenblick*.[98] Yet this fulfilment is *not quite*

---

[97] Eckermann, *Conversations of Goethe*, p. 413.
[98] Ernst Bloch, *Das Prinzip Hoffnung* [1959], 3 vols (Frankfurt am Main: Suhrkamp, 1980), vol. 3, p. 1154.

complete: Starting violently, Faust is incensed by the sound of the bell from the chapel of Philemon and Baucis. It reminds him that his project is *not quite* complete; it is like a thorn in his side, or like a splinter in his mind, driving him mad...

Enter Mephistopheles and the Three Mighty Men from Act IV, who disembark from a splendid galleon, richly laden with all sorts of exotic goods, which they begin to unload. Mephistopheles sinks a hymn of praise to free trade, or to the inseparable trinity of "commerce, war, and piracy" (*Krieg, Handel und Piraterie*) — which might amount to the same thing! He congratulates Faust on his achievement, telling him that he can say, "From thy palace in its grasp / Thine arm the whole wide world shall clasp," that *here* the work began, that *here* the first work-hut stood, that *here* — only to be interrupted by Faust's explosion of fury: "That accurséd *here*! / 'Tis that that doth oppress me sheer" (ll. 11225-1126 and 11233-11234). The tinkling sound of the chapel bell, the aroma of the linden blossom, remind him that even *his* will has limitations, that "Here the all-powerful's free will / Doth break on yonder sandy hill" (ll. 11255-11256). Why not, Mephisto asks, simply remove them? Surely, they should have been colonized (*kolonisieren*) long ago? "Go then and shift them," Faust commands, instructing that Philemon and Baucis be relocated in a little farm he has prepared for them. But the fact that the task will be carried out by the Three Mighty Men, and Mephisto's reference to the biblical story of Naboth's vineyard (see 1 Kings, chapter 21),[99] suggests that the outcome will not be good; while the reference to Naboth reminds us that, as Mephisto cynically observed of Faust's seduction of

---

[99] According to 1 Kings, chapter 21, Naboth of Jezreel owned a vineyard that was close to King Ahab's palace and which Ahab wanted to buy. When Naboth refused to sell, because the land was his ancestral inheritance, Queen Jezebel set up for two witnesses to accuse Naboth (falsely) of cursing God and the king, Naboth was stoned to death outside the city walls, and his corpse was licked by the stray dogs. On hearing of this crime, Elijah the Tishbite pronounced God's sentence, threatening to wipe out the House of Ahab, prompting Ahab to repent.

Gretchen in Part One (*das ist der Lauf der Welt*, and *Sie ist die erste nicht*), Philemon and Baucis will not be the first to be murdered for their property.

And just as we do not see the *actual* seduction of Gretchen, nor do we see the *actual* murder of Philemon and Baucis. Yet we become witnesses to this deed, thanks to the figure of Lynceus, who evokes (in a kind of Neoplatonic way) the perfection of the world:

> To see is my dower,
> To look my employ,
> My charge is the tower,
> The world is my joy.
> My glances afar light,
> My glances light near,
> On sun, moon and star-light,
> On woodland and deer.
> In all the eternal
> Adornment I see,
> Well-pleaséd with all things,
> Well-pleased too with me.
> Ye eye-balls entrancéd,
> Whate'er ye have seen,
> Where'er ye have glanced,
> So fair hath it been!
> [*Es sei, wie es wolle,*
> *Es war doch so schön!*]
> (ll. 11288-11303)

After a pause, the tone (and the versification) changes, and we learn from Lynceus of how the old couple's hut is set on fire, their chapel catches alight, and Philemon and Baucis die from the smoke.

When Mephistopheles returns with the Mighty Three, we get *his* account of the brutal death of Philemon and Baucis — and the visiting wanderer. Faust plays the part of Henry II when his henchman reveal they have murdered Thomas Beckett, affecting innocence: "Exchange I wished, not robbery" (l. 11371), but the Chorus, making its second brief intervention in this scene, intervenes to confirm what one might call the historical lesson from this murderous affair:

> The good old saw is still good sense:
> Be willing slave of violence,
> And art thou bold and steadfast, pelf
> And house and home mayst stake, and self!
>
> (ll. 11374-11377)

Or in other words, might is right! Are these lines an expression of an almost Mephistophelian kind of cynicism on Goethe's part? Or do they offer, spoken as they are by a Chorus, a kind of tragic insight?

Sitting alone on his balcony, it seems to Faust that the stars now shine less brightly and the fire in which Philemon and Baucis have died is receding. Out of the burning ruins of their cottage and its chapel, four shadowy figures emerge — and what is arguably the weirdest scene in the second part of *Faust* begins. This scene is titled "Midnight." At this witching hour, four allegorical figures in the form of four gray hags or crones introduce themselves one by one to Faust: Want (*der Mangel*), Guilt or Debt (*die Schuld*), Care (*die Sorge*), and Need (*die Not*). Of these three, only one is able to enter into Faust's palace: Care, who "through the key-hole slips stealthily in" (l. 11391).[100] (Later, Heidegger designated Care or

---

[100] For further discussion, see Konrad Burdach, "Faust und die Sorge," *Deutsche Vierteljahrsschrift für Literaturwissenschaft und Geistesgeschichte*, 1 (1923), 1-60; and Ellis Dye, "Sorge in Heidegger and in Goethe's *Faust*," *Goethe Yearbook*, vol. 16 (2009), 207-218. For further discussion of Goethe and Heidegger, see Jean Lacoste, "«L'œil clairement ouvert sur la nature»: Heidegger et Goethe," *Littérature*, no. 120

Sorge as a key existential category in *Being and Time* [part 1, chapter 6; and part 2, chapters 1 to 4].)[101] While Want, Guilt, and Need see appearing in the distance a *fifth* allegorical figure, identified as their brother, Death (*der Tod*), Faust notes that he had seen four figures approach, but only three go away: a kind of reduced version of the numerology of seven and eight that we saw earlier in the Cabiri scene. This numerical observation introduces the first of two great confessional monologues that constitute the heart of this scene.

To begin with, Faust realizes that, however much he might have achieved, he has still not yet entirely "fought his way to freedom" (*mich ins Freie gekämpft*). He regrets his use of magic, that Mephistophelian magic that we have seen at work throughout the drama: tricking the students in Auerbach's Cellar; taking Faust to the Witch's Kitchen to be rejuvenated; and producing the box of jewelry with which Faust can begin his seduction of Gretchen in Part One; and, in Part Two, the huge chest of magical gold whose contents Mephistopheles gathers and molds into a giant phallus, and the magical extinguishing of the fire in the Carnival scene; the conjuring up of Paris and Helena for the Emperor's entertainment after Faust's descent to the Mothers; the magical interventions orchestrated by Mephisto's ravens in the battle between the opposing forces of the Emperor and the Rival; and the dubious

---

[Poésie et philosophie] (December 2000), 105-127 (cf. Goethe's remark to Schiller in a letter of 28 June 1787, *der Dichter hat einen heitern Blick über die Natur* [HA Briefe, vol. 2, 281]; R. Ellis Dye, "Goethe's »Faust« and Heidegger: Commonalities," *Sprachkunst: Beiträge zur Literaturwissenschaft*, vol. 41, no. 2 (2010), 171-192; Robert Ellis Dye, "'Unmöglich ist's, drum eben glaubenswert': Paradox in Goethe and Heidegger," *Seminar: A Journal of Germanic Studies*, vol. 50, no. 4 (November 2014), 413-435; Albina Sayapova and Oksana Amurskaya, "Symbolic Interpretation of the Image of Goethe's Faust in the Context of Heidegger's Notions 'The Earth' and 'The Sky,'" *Mediterranean Journal of Social Sciences*, vol. 6, no. 6 (December 2015), 43-49; and Thomas Rendall, "Goethe's *Faust* and Heidegger's Critique of Technology," *ISLE: Interdisciplinary Studies in Literature and Environment*, vol. 22, no. 1 (Winter 2015), 115-131.
[101] See Charles E. Scott, "Care and authenticity" in Bret W. Davis (ed.), *Martin Heidegger: Key Concepts* (Abingdon and New York: Routledge, 2014), pp. 57-68.

powers employed in the dark of night as part of Faust's great land reclamation project. Above all, Faust fears that he has failed ultimately in his attempt to be what, through his association with Mephistopheles, he can probably never be — put simply, to be a human being (*ein Mensch*):

> Not yet into the Open have I won.
> Could I but from my path all magic banish,
> Bid every spell into oblivion vanish,
> And stand mere man before thee, Nature!
>
> (ll. 11403-11407)

Yet, that is what, before his pact with the Devil, Faust was — a human being, before he turned to the dark side (*im Düstern*) and cursed himself and the world (cf. ll. 1583-1606). Now, however, the air is thick with spirits, the reason of daytime is entangled with the nocturnal web of dreams, and the beauty of nature is compromised by a premonitory bird call:

> Then
> 'Twere worth the while to be a man with men.
> Such was I once, the gloom ere I explored,
> And cursed myself, the world, with impious word.
> Now with such glamour doth the air o'erflow
> That how he should avoid it none doth know.
> If one day lit with reason on us beams,
> Night trammels us within a web of dreams.
> From the young fields we turn us home elate,
> A raven croaks! What doth he croak? Ill-fate [*Mißgeschick*]!
> Us Superstition soon and late entwines,
> With happenings, with warnings, and with signs.
>
> (ll. 11408-11417)

In this haunting episode (or episode of haunting), the door creaks, but no one enters; and yet someone stands before him — it is Care. In a scene from which Jung later quotes *in extenso* in his paper "The Relations between the Ego and the Unconscious" (1928; [2]1934), Care describes her ubiquitous presence in human life, incorporating a rhyme on the words *Gestalt* (= form, shape) and *Gewalt* (= force, violence) that we have seen elsewhere in the work:

> Though of ear unheard, the groaning
> Heart is conscious of my moaning;
> In an ever-changing guise [*Gestalt*]
> Cruel power [*Gewalt*] I exercise.
> On the highway, on the billow,
> Cleave I close, a carking fellow;
> Ever found, an unsought guest,
> Ever cursed and aye caressed.
>
> (ll. 11424-11431)

Turning to Faust, she asks him directly: "Hast thou not Care already known?" (l. 11432), eliciting a further confessional monologue, as if this exchange were somehow cathartic or therapeutic for Faust:

> Athwart the world I have but flown,
> Grasped by the hair whatever I did covet,
> Loosed it, had I no pleasure of it,
> Did it elude me, made no moan.
> I did but wish, achieve, and then again
> Did wish, and thus I stormed through life amain,
> First vehemently, with majestic passion,
> But shrewdly now I tread, in heedful fashion.
> The round of earth enough I know, and barred
> Is unto man the prospect yonderward.
> O fool, who thither turns his blinking glances,

> And of his like above the clouds romances!
> Let him stand firm, and round him gaze on earth.
> Not mute the world is to the man of worth.
> What need hath he to range infinitude?
> What he perceives, that may be understood.
> Thus let him journey down his earthly day;
> When spectres haunt him, let him go his way;
> In onward-striding find his bale, his bliss,
> He, that each moment [*Augenblick*] uncontented is.
>
> (ll. 11433-11452)

In this great speech, at the beginning of which he laments that all he has done is to "race through life" (*durch die Welt gerannt*), Faust strikes a tone that can still be felt around a century later when, at the end of Kafka's novel *The Trial*, Josef K. confesses: *Ich wollte immer mit zwanzig Händen in die Welt hineinfahren*, "I always wanted to snatch at the world with twenty hands, and not for a very laudable motive, either."[102] (And in "The Remains of Earlier Temples" in *The Red Book*, Jung will admit: "I did not live, but was driven" — *Ich lebte nicht, sondern war getrieben* [RB, 274].) For his part, Faust confesses to having stormed his way through life;[103] to having been caught up in the cycle of desire, satisfaction, and further desire; to have embraced the power principle (*Macht*); to having been (as he had earlier described himself in the opening "Night" scene of Part One, cf. l. 358) a "fool" (*Tor*); and to having mistakenly placed more emphasis on eternity (*Ewigkeit*) than on

---

[102] Franz Kafka, *The Trial*, chapter 10 (translated Willa and Edwin Muir); in *The Trial; America; The Castle* [...] (London: Secker & Warburg/Octopus, 1976), p. 126.
[103] As Gottfried Diener puts it, "one could consider Faust's entire journey through life — *before* and *after* the "attainment" [*Erlangen*] of Helena — as an uninterrupted, futile or successful, justified or unjustified, intervention — constantly driven by the fateful drive of his insatiable entelechy — in more or less different areas, at whose expense he seeks, while being inherently a rich man, to enrich himself ever further and thereby becomes their debtor" (Diener, *Faust's Weg zu Helena*, p. 50).

the here-and-now, which itself offers plenty of opportunities for any capable individual (*der Tüchtige*). Such an individual, he avers, can continue unperturbed by spirits, finding bliss (*Glück*) and torment (*Qual*) in every stride, even if (or rather *because*) every moment (*Augenblick*) — one of the key words in the wager — remains unsatisfied.

In chilling lines in trochaic meter that have (as Hamlin notes) the effect of a chant or a mystical reverie (476) — analogous, perhaps, to the chants "in the ancient manner" in "The Incantations" in *The Red Book* (RB, 299-304) — Care evokes her spectral omnipresence in human life: Where, in conversation with Wagner in the "Night" scene in Part One, Faust had reflected on how "deep in the heart nests Care [*Sorge*], a guest unbidden. / There doth she work her sorrows hidden" (ll. 643-644), Care now reveals just *how* very deep in the heart she nestles. At the end of their exchange in *this* scene, Faust defiantly asserts that, however difficult it might be to get rid of daimons because the "strict spirit-bond" (*das geistig-strenge Band*) is so strong, he will never recognize *her* power: "And yet, O Care, though stealthy-great it be, / Thy might I'll not acknowledge ever!" (*Doch deine Macht, o Sorge, schleichend groß, / Ich werde sie nicht anerkennen*) (ll. 11493-11494). Yet it is Care who has the last word: turning away and cursing him, she breathes on Faust and, in so doing, blinds him.[104] Yet this blinding, which recalls the moment in the opening scene of Part Two when he is "blinded" by the sun (l. 4702), seems to offer him a new and different kind of vision. Just as the blindness of Homer was said by the Neoplatonists

---

[104] For discussion of this episode, in relation to Goethe's belief that "the ear is dumb, the mouth is deaf; but the eye perceives and speaks. In it the world is mirrored from outside, from inside the individual. The totality of inner and outer is completed [*vollendet*] through the eye" (WA, II. Abteilung, vol. 5/ii, p. 12), see Peter Michelsen, "Fausts Erblindung," *Deutsche Vierteljahrsschrift für Literaturwissenschaft und Geistesgeschichte*, vol. 36, no. 1 (May 1962), 26-35; and, in addition, Alan P. Cottrell, "Faust's Blindness and the Inner Light: Some Questions for the Future," in *Goethe's "Faust": Seven Essays* (Chapel Hill, NC: University of North Carolina Press, 1976), pp. 103-131.

to betoken the turning of his sight inward to the contemplation of things not usually visible,[105] and just as in Sophocles's *Oedipus Rex* the prophet Tiresias, though blind, can see more than Oedipus can, which in turn leads to Oedipus's self-blinding (Hamlin, 325, fn. 5), so now Faust in turn now discovers an inner light: "More deeply-deep Night seemeth to enfold me, / Yet clear the daylight shines within mine heart" (*Allein im Innen leuchtet helles Licht*) (ll. 11499-15000). Thus emboldened, Faust embarks on one final act of construction that will bring his project — his "greatest work" (*das größte Werk*) — to fulfilment:

> I'll hasten to fulfil the plan doth hold me;
> The master's word alone doth weight impart.
> [...]
> To speed the greatest enterprises
> One mind for thousand hands suffices.
>   (ll. 11501-11502 and 11509-11510)

In the following scene, Mephistopheles appears as a supervisor, leading a group of workers: In fact, they are lemures, spirits of the malign dead (figures from classical mythology, probably known to Goethe from a bas-relief in a grave near Cumae on which he wrote an essay).[106]

---

[105] Manly Palmer Hall, *Neoplatonism: Theology for Wanderers in the New Millennium* (Los Angeles, CA: Philosophical Research Society, 2010), p. 113. For further discussion, see Robert Lamberton, *Homer the Theologian: Neoplatonist Allegorical Reading and the Growth of the Epic Tradition* (Berkeley: University of California Press, 1989), pp. 1-43 ("The Divine Homer and the Background of Neoplatonic Allegory"); and Robert Lamberton, "The Neoplatonists and the Spiritualization of Homer," in Robert Lamberton and John J. Keaney (eds.), *Homer's Ancient Readers: The Hermeneutics of Ancient Greek's Earliest Exegetes* (Princeton, NJ: Princeton University Press, 2019), pp. 115-133.

[106] See "A Grave Near Cumae" [1812], in Goethe, *Essays on Art and Literature*, ed. John Gearey, trans. Ellen and Ernest H. von Nardroff [Goethe Edition, vol. 3] (New York: Suhrkamp Publishing, 1986), pp. 28-35.

Groping his way out of the palace, the blinded Faust emerges, to give his instructions to this construction team of spirits — and to offer, in a literal sense, a kind of "vision statement" for his project. Whereas, with his father, the younger Faust had poisoned all his patients (ll. 1050-1055), now he wants to rid the community of a plague-ridden marsh, and open up the space for millions to live in a way that he characteristically describes as *tätig-frei*, i.e., "active and free":

> A marish skirts the mount, whose smell
> Infecteth all the land retrievéd.
> To drain the festering sump as well!
> Then were the last the best-achievéd.
> I open room for millions there, a dwelling
> Not idly sure, but to free toil compelling;
> Green fields and fruitful, men and herds at home
> Upon the earth new-wrested from the foam;
> Straight-settled on the hill-strength, piled on high
> By swarming tribes' intrepid industry.
> Within, a paradise, howe'er so grim
> The flood without may bluster to the brim.
> And as it nibbles to shoot in amain
> Flock one and all to fill the breach again.
>
> (ll. 11559-11572)

In his final words after having been blinded by Care in the previous scene, Faust had spoken about a "bright light" that was "inside" him (*im Innern*); now, this interiority is projected outward, as he envisions how, "within" the new sea walls (*im Innern hier*) there will be "a paradisiacal land" (*ein paradiesisch Land*) that will allow crops and cattle to be farmed. *Mais il faut cultiver notre jardin*, as Voltaire said in *Candide* (1759); but Goethe takes the phrase seriously, as Faust sets out a vision in which "pure activity" (*reine Tätigkeit*) (l. 705) has eminently practical connotations.

This vision leads to Faust's dramatic words just before he dies — words that fulfill (or might not fulfill) the wager:

> My will from this design not swerveth,
> The last resolve of human wit [*der Weisheit letzter Schluß*],
> For liberty, as life, alone deserveth
> He daily that must conquer it.
> Thus childhood, manhood, and grey old age here,
> With peril girt, shall spend their strenuous year.
> Fain would I see such glad turmoil,
> With a free people stand on a free soil.
> To such a moment past me fleeing,
> Tarry, I'd cry, thou art so fair!
> The traces of mine earthly being
> Not countless aeons can outwear.
> Now, in the presage of such lofty bliss,
> The highest moment I enjoy, e'en this.
>
> (ll. 11573-11586)

These words could be described as Faust's last testament: They set out the meaning (*Sinn*) to which he is committed, and the final conclusion that Wisdom (or, as the Gnostics would say, Sophia) can reach. This is his insight: that both freedom (*Freiheit*) and existence (*Leben*) are something that have to be earned, and only someone who reconquers them on a daily basis deserves them both. On the land that Faust has reclaimed from the element of the sea, which still surrounds it, there is an opportunity for an active, fulfilling life: a life that will last the entire lifetime of the individual from youth through to adulthood and then old age. Yet this is not just an individual existence: It is a *collective* one, as Faust imagines an entire community, living as a free people on free land (*Auf freiem Grund mit freiem Volke stehn*).

And now come the words of the wager — sort of. In the second "Study" scene, Faust formulates the wager thus: *If I say to the moment: "But tarry! You're so beautiful!"* then Mephisto will have won and can have his soul. Now Faust says the same, only in a modal subjunctive form: *I might say to the moment: "But tarry! You're so beautiful!"* For he has now, he continues, achieved a kind of permanence, or a kind of immortality: The "traces" of his "earthly days" will not, he boasts, disappear in aions (that is, in Gnostic terms, they stand under the sign of the god of eternity). But has he achieved "high happiness" (*hohes Glück*)? He has, he says, achieved a foretaste or presage of it (*im Vorgefühl*), but this presage is enough for him to enjoy his "highest moment" (*den höchsten Augenblick*). So, has Faust lost the wager? Has Mephistopheles finally won?

Mephistopheles certainly thinks he has, and the words of the Chorus suggest he might be right. Again, let's go back to the wager — there Faust says: *The clock may stop, its hands fall still, / Let my time be over then!*. These details recur in the words of Mephisto and the Chorus in Act V:

MEPHISTOPHELES:
[...]
Time triumphs, lies the graybeard in the sand.
The clock stands still —

CHORUS.
   Stands still! As midnight hushed and dead!
The finger falls.

MEPHISTOPHELES.
   It falls! 'Tis finished!

CHORUS.
'Tis past and over [*vorbei*].

MEPHISTOPHELES.
Past! [*Vorbei!*] a stupid word.

It was late at night that Faust nearly committed suicide, before the sound of the church bells saved him; it was at midnight that Faust was confronted by Care and blinded by her; and now, Faust dies at midnight (and the motif of midnight plays, as we shall see, a central role in Nietzsche's *Zarathustra*). In his cry, "'Tis finished!", Mephisto echoes the words spoken as Christ dies on the Cross, variously translated as "It is consummated" (DRV), "It is finished" (KJV), "It is fulfilled" (NJB) (see John 19:30).

Yet the Chorus, as if recognizing that the message of Goethe's *Faust* is anything other than a Christian one, resists this statement; rather, they say, it is finished (*es ist vorbei*) — a phrase that elicits from Mephisto a snort of disgust. To the very end, Mephisto remains what he is: a cynic (in the modern sense), a scoffer and mocker, and a nihilist. For something to be finished, he retorts, there had to be something there in the first place; and this is what Mephisto, as "the spirit who always says no" (*der Geist, der stets verneint*) (l. 1338), always denies. Something that is finished, he argues, is something that never was, even if it recurs, as if it *were* something. (Here we find another curious anticipation of the Nietzschean doctrine of eternal recurrence!)[107] Rather than get caught up in the dialectic of being and nonbeing, Mephistopheles says that he prefers nothing at all — *das Ewig-Leere*, or eternal emptiness. Yet, it is precisely *this* preference that the final scene of *Faust II* will vigorously contest.

But before that, there is the "Entombment" scene, in which Goethe alludes to the medieval iconography of Christ's entombment (and, it has been argued, in particular to the 14th-century frescoes in

---

[107] As Erich Heller notes: "These are anticipatory echoes of Nietzsche's Eternal Recurrence of a positivistically self-contained world that has no opening into meaning and sense" ("Nietzsche and Goethe," in *The Importance of Nietzsche: Ten Essays* (Chicago and London: Chicago University Press, 1988), pp. 18-38 [p. 31]). Tellingly, this essay was first published in 1952 in a collection entitled *The Disinherited Mind*!

the Campo Santo Cemetery next to the Cathedral in Pisa; attributed to Francesco Traini and Bonamico Buffalmacco around 1340, these depict the Triumph of Death, the Last Judgement, and Hell).[108] Yet this traditional iconography of fat devils with short straight horns, lean devils with long, crooked horns, and the ghastly jaws of Hell,[109] is subverted by a confrontation with another iconography: the iconography of a heavenly "glory" (*aureole*), a heavenly host and angels strewing roses.[110] Out of this confrontation emerges the great plot twist that distinguishes Goethe's *Faust* from all its predecessors:[111] For the angels have come to rescue Faust's immortal essence, in effect stealing it away from Mephistopheles, who is distracted by the erotic excitement of seeing the naked bodies of *putti* or angels that look like small plump boys, such as are familiar from works of the European Rococo.

As humorous (if politically incorrect) as this scene is, it reactivates one of the ideas about the act of Redemption proposed in the first centuries of Christianity by Origen and other Greek Church Fathers, namely: the idea of Satan duped by the Cross. Proposed by such Patristic figures as St. Gregory of Nyssa (c. 335-

---

[108] See Gaier, *Kommentare I*, 1104 and 1122. For images, see "The Frescoes by Buonamico Burlamacco at the Campo Santo of Pisa"; available online HTTP: <https://www.barnum-review.com/portfolio/the-frescoes-by-buonamico-burlamacco-at-the-campo-santo-of-pisa>. See also below, pp. 173 and 217.

[109] Mephisto's words in ll. 11644-111651 echo those spoken by Virgil in Dante's *Divine Comeds* (see *Inferno*, Canto 8, ll. 67-75); cf. Steiner, *Erläuterungen*, vol. 1, p. 243; cf. Emil Sulger-Gebing, *Goethe und Dante: Studien zur vergleichenden Literaturgeschichte* [1907] (Hamburg: Severus Verlag, 2013), p. 94.

[110] According to Steiner, the roses strewn by the angels are "a symbol of spiritual love from above" (*Erläuterungen*, vol. 1, p. 187) (or a symbol of *Geisteswissenschaft* itself [p. 54]).

[111] Much to the consternation of Peter Kreeft: "In *Faust*," he writes, "Goethe told the traditional moral story of Faust, the man who sold his soul to the Devil, from an antitraditional, antimoral point of view." Changing the original tale by 180 degrees, "in *Faust* God and the Devil turn out to be allies, because they both move Faust up the ladder of enlightenment and maturity and away from his earlier moralistic innocence," so that "the whole point and end of the old Faust story is turned into its opposite": "Faust is not damned at all but enlightened," and "he is not punished but rewarded for disobeying the moral law" (*The Platonic Tradition*, p. 103).

395) in his *Great Catechism* (§24),[112] by St. Maximus the Confessor (c. 580-662) in his *Ad Thalassium*, §64 ("On the Prophet Jonah and the Economy of Salvation"),[113] and by St. John Damascene (c. 676-749) in his *An Exact Exposition of the Orthodox Faith*, Book 3, Chapter 27),[114] this thesis interprets the Crucifixion as a kind of

---

[112] "... [I]t was not in the nature of the opposing power to come in contact with the undiluted presence of God, and to undergo His unclouded manifestation, therefore, in order to secure that the ransom in our behalf might be easily accepted by him who required it, the Deity was hidden under the veil of our nature, that so, as with ravenous fish, the hook of the Deity might be gulped down along with the bait of flesh, and thus, life being introduced into the house of death, and light shining in darkness, that which is diametrically opposed to light and life might vanish; for it is not in the nature of darkness to remain when light is present, or of death to exist when life is active" (*Great Catechism*, §24); cf. https://classicalchristianity.com/2011/10/19/the-divine-bait.

[113] "I am a worm and not a man (Ps. 21:7, LXX). He truly became, and was thus called, a worm because He assumed the flesh without being conceived by human seed. For, just as the worm is not born through copulation or sexual procreation, so too our Lord was not born in the flesh through sexual procreation. Moreover, the Lord mounted His flesh on the fish-hook of His divinity as bait for the devil's deceit, so that, as the insatiable serpent, the devil would take His flesh into his mouth (since its nature is easily overcome) and quiver convulsively on the hook of the Lord's divinity, and, by virtue of the sacred flesh of the Logos, completely vomit the Lord's human nature once he swallowed it. As a result, just as the devil formerly baited man with the hope of divinity, and swallowed him, so too the devil himself would be baited precisely with humanity's fleshly garb; and afterward he would vomit man, who had been deceived by the expectation of becoming divine, the devil himself having been deceived by the expectation of becoming human. The transcendence of God's power would then manifest itself through the weakness of our inferior human nature, which would vanquish the strength of its conqueror. As well, it would be shown that it is God Who, by using the flesh as bait, conquers the devil, rather than the devil conquering man by promising him a divine nature" (Ad Thalassium 64: On the Prophet Jonah and the Economy of Salvation); cf. https://classicalchristianity. com/2011/10/19/the-divine-bait.

[114] "Since our Lord Jesus Christ was without sin (for He committed no sin, He Who took away the sin of the world, nor was there any deceit found in His mouth) He was not subject to death, since death came into the world through sin. Rom. 5:12 He dies, therefore, because He took on Himself death on our behalf, and He makes Himself an offering to the Father for our sakes. For we had sinned against Him, and it was meet that He should receive the ransom for us, and that we should thus be delivered from the condemnation. God forbid that the blood of the Lord should have been offered to the tyrant. Wherefore death approaches, and swallowing up the body as a bait is transfixed on the hook of divinity, and after tasting of a sinless and life-giving body, perishes, and brings up again all whom of old he swallowed up. For just as darkness disappears on the introduction of light, so is death repulsed before the assault of life, and brings life to all, but death to the destroyer" (An Exact Exposition of the Orthodox Faith, Bk. 3.27); cf. https://classicalchristianity.com/2011/10/19/the-divine-bait.

divine ruse or trap, expressed in the metaphor of Christ as the bait that the divine fisherman puts on the hook to catch Satan, imagined as a hungry fish. As strange as this idea might seem to us today, its explanatory power was not lost on René Girard, who related it to his own theory of mimetic contagion and declared that "Western theology, in rejecting the idea of Satan tricked by the Cross, has lost a pearl of great price in the sphere of anthropology."[115]

Nevertheless, the morality of this unexpected angelic intervention in *Faust II* has been questioned by some critics, who take the view that, whether or not he has actually won the wager, the pact signed by Faust in blood still provides for Mephistopheles to have power over his soul after death.[116] Yet, Goethe signals in various ways in this scene that he is aiming at something profoundly unorthodox. At one point the Chorus of Angels sings:

> Back to the splendour
> Turn, loving flames now!
> Who himself blames now
> Truth whole shall render.
> He shall unravel
> Trammels of evil,
> In the All-Unity
> Blesséd to be.
> (ll. 11801-11808)

Here the flames of divine love are associated with two actions: first, that those who condemn themselves to damnation (*Die*

---

[115] René Girard, *I Saw Satan Fall Like Lightning* [1999], trans. James G. Williams (Maryknoll, NY: Orbis Books, 2001), pp. 149-150. Girard refers to Jean Daniélou, *Origène* (Paris: La Table Ronde, 1948), pp. 264.269; cf. *Origen*, trans. Walter Mitchell (New York: Sheed and Ward, 1955), pp. 269-275.

[116] For a summary of views about the outcome of the wager, see Schöne, *Kommentare*, 752-754.

sich verdammen) are saved, not by God, but by Truth (*Heile die Wahrheit*); and second, that those who damn themselves redeem themselves from evil (*vom Bösen* [...] *sich erlösen*), a thoroughly Pelagian notion.

Then again, Mephistopheles breaks out in boils, a disease that had afflicted Job — the suffering Job, whose story informs the theological framework as we find it in the "Prologue in Heaven": "Job-like [*Hiobsartig*], boil on boil my skin," Mephisto himself cries (l. 11809). And when Mephisto comforts himself with the thought, "Saved are the noble devil's members!" (*Gerettet sind die edlen Teufelsteile*) (l. 11813), he crudely anticipates one of the most significant lines of the following "Mountain Gorges" scene (cf. ll. 11934-11935). The overall effect of this scene is, however, comic: Mephistopheles has been outwitted, and he wonders to whom he should complain! From his point of view, the whole exercise has been a monumental waste of time, and his lustful distraction has left him empty-handed. So much, then, for the Devil: In the final, concluding scene of Part Two. we discover what happens to Faust's immortal essence — it is a scene that is really out of this world.

Mountain Gorges

Or is it? In his "Epilogue" in *Psychology and Alchemy*, Jung notes that, whenever an archetype constellates itself yet remains unconscious, it acquires possession of an individual and impels the person to play a corresponding role. In the case of *Faust*, for instance, Faust cannot resist intervening in the reenactment of the rape of Helena by trying to replace Paris in Helena's affections (thus bringing the "ghostly masque," the *Fratzengeisterspiel*, to an unexpected end), and such other "births" and rejuvenations as those undergone by the Boy Charioteer and Homunculus are "destroyed by the same greed" (CW 12 §558). Here we find, Jung suggests, the "deeper reason" why the "final rejuvenation" of Faust — his last and ultimate transformation — can only take place "in the post-mortal state, i.e., is projected into the future" (CW 12 §558).[117]

Yet the key point about the final scene of *Faust*, Part Two, titled "Mountain Gorges" and set among forests, cliffs, and wilderness, is that it presents the afterlife or the post-mortal state in terms taken from the Christian iconographical tradition. (As Goethe remarked to Eckermann on 6 June 1831, "the conclusion, where the redeemed soul is carried up, was difficult to manage," adding: "Amid such supersensual matters, about which we scarcely have even an intimation, I might easily have lost myself in the vague, if I had not, by means of sharply-drawn figures, and images from the Christian Church, given my poetical design a desirable form and substance.")[118]

We have already seen this move in the previous scene, and it is possible that the frescoes showing stories about the Desert Fathers or the Thebaid in the Campo Santo in Pisa or Titian's painting of St Jerome in the wilderness were among the visual sources for *this* scene. The major intertext, however, is likely to be a literary rather than a visual one — the mystical ascent of Dante into heaven in the final cantos of the *Paradiso*. In the conclusion to the third book of the *Divine Comedy*, Dante passes upward through ranks of various saints and mystics and attains a mystical vision of the Virgin Mary; similarly, in "Mountain Gorges," Faust (or his immortal essence) passes through ranks of Holy Anchorites and up beyond them to the Mater Glorioso. In turn, the conclusion of Part Two has served as the basis for Mahler's Eighth Symphony, sometimes called the "Symphony of a Thousand" (because of the larger number of performers required to play it!), which draws in its first part on the text of the Latin hymn, *Veni creator spiritus*, and in its second on the closing scene of *Faust* — "Try to imagine the whole universe

---

[117] For an interpretation of the concluding scene, see Max Kommerell, "Die letzte Szene der Faustdichtung. Ein Interpretationsversuch," *Zeitschrift für deutsches Altertum und deutsche Literatur*, vol. 77, nos. 2/3 (1940), 175-188.

[118] Eckermann, *Conversations of Goethe*, p. 414.

beginning to ring and resound," Mahler wrote to his friend Willem Mengelberg on 18 August 1906. "There are no more human voices, only planets and suns revolving in their orbits."

The scene opens with Holy Anchorites scattered up the mountainsides, settled among the clefts in the rocks. The tradition of the anchoritic life has its roots in the hermitic (not the Hermetic!) tradition of the first centuries of the Christian era, beginning in Egypt in the third century with Paul of Thebes, often known as Paul the First Hermit or Paul the Anchorite. The hermitic and anchoritic traditions alike had the aim of turning away from the world, going to live in the wilderness, and absolute dedication to an ascetic life of prayer. (Many of the early Christian hermits went into the Scetes Desert in Egypt and hence are known as the Desert Fathers; one of the most famous was St. Anthony the Great, who inspired thousands to follow his example, so much so that St. Athanasius of Alexandria wrote in his biography of Anthony that "the desert was made a city.")[119] In *The Red Book*, Jung will encounter Ammonius in "The Desert."

The opening lines of this scene are spoken by a Chorus and its Echo, whose twofold dactylic lines emphasize, in a way that would deeply impress Jung in his letter to Bernhard Baur-Celio (1895-1981) of 30 January 1934 (see Chapter 3), the sacred mysteriousness of the setting:

> Billows the forest on,
> Lean them the cliffs thereon,
> Grapple the roots thereon,

---

[119] *Life of Antony*, chapter 14; in Athanasius, *The Life of Antony and the Letter to Marcellinus*, trans. Robert C. Gregg (Mahwah, NJ: Paulist Press, 1980), pp. 42-43: "And so, from then on, there were monasteries in the mountains and the desert was made a city by monks, who left their own people and registered themselves for the citizenship in the heavens." For textual extracts and discussion, see E. Kadloubovsky and G.E.H. Palmer (eds), *Early Fathers from the Philokalia* (London and Boston: Faber and Faber, 1954); and Peter France, *Hermits: The Insights of Solitude* (New York: St. Martin's Press, 1996), chapter 2, "The Desert Fathers," pp. 20-51.

Trunk crowding trunk upon;
Wave gushes after wave,
Shelters the deepest cave;
Softly the lions, dumb-
Friendly about us come,
Honour the holy seat,
Sanctified love-retreat.

(ll. 11844-11853)

The incantatory style of these verses recalls the hymn of the Archangels in the "Prologue in Heaven," the self-description of the Earth Spirit, the angelic and other choruses that announce the Easter tidings, and the spirit chorus in the first "Study" scene, as well as the chorus of spirits accompanying Ariel in the "Charming Landscape" scene and the songs of the Sirens in the "Classical Walpurgis Night." As Hamlin points out, in these opening lines the sense of the dactylic meter is confused by the caesura after the second syllable in many lines, while the last word in each of the first four lines is a direction adverb, i.e., *heran, dran, an, heran.* This repetition creates an incantatory effect and, together with the elemental natural objects (forests, rocks, roots, trunks, waves, caves, and lions) and their various motions (swaying, weighing, entwining, gushing, slinking), creates "a network of dynamic, organic interrelationships [...], evoking a sense [...] of great creating nature as cosmic symbolic power" (486). The lion is, of course, an emblematic animal associated with St. Jerome, as well as being featured as a pair in the Thebaid frescoes in Pisa; it also has a symbolic function in Nietzsche's *Zarathustra* and in Jung's *Red Book.*

We now move through a series of patristic figures, called Pater Ecstaticus, Pater Profundus, Pater Seraphicus, and Doctor Marianus respectively, suggestive of ascending degrees of mystical knowledge of the divine (in the hierarchical sense of Pseudo-

Dionysius the Areopagite). All four figures include in their hymnic discourses the key word of this entire scene: love, or *Liebe*. To begin with, the Pater Ecstaticus recalls the figure of St. Philip Neri (1515-1595) as described by Goethe in his account of his second stay in Rome,[120] although the great Flemish mystic John van Ruysbroeck (1293/1294-1381) was known as the Doctor Divinus Ecstaticus. In his ecstatic condition, he is able to levitate; and, evoking the arrows, lances, bludgeons, even lightnings (!) typical of martyr saints, the Pater Ecstaticus expresses the wish that all that has no value (*das Nichtige*) entirely disappear (*alles verflüchtige*) and the lasting star of "timeless love's core" shine forth.

Next, down in the depths, is the Pater Profundus. This epithet is associated with, among others, St. Bernard of Clairvaux (1090-1153), who appears in Dante's *Paradiso* as a replacement for Beatrice as the poet's guide toward the concluding mystic vision. His hymnic discourse praises how "Almighty Love, unfailing, / Doth fashion all and cherish all" (ll. 11872-11873). Then, from a middle region, the Pater Seraphicus speaks; in the *Paradiso*, Dante describes St Francis of Assisi as being "in his ardour all / Seraphic" (Canto XI, l. 37).[121] Here the Pater Seraphicus relates how a wispy morning cloud floats up, containing a chorus of Blessed Boys — children, that is, who had died unbaptized and immediately after being born, and who, in traditional Catholic theology (until recently revised), were believed to be in the Limbo of Infants.[122]

---

[120] See Johann Wolfgang von Goethe, *Italian Journey*, eds. Thomas P. Saine and Jeffrey L. Sammons, trans. Robert R. Heitner [Goethe Edition, vol. 6] (New York: Suhrkamp Publishers, 1989), pp. 258-260 and 371-380; cf. HA 11, 327-329 and 462-475.

[121] Dante, *Paradise*, trans. Dorothy L. Sayers and Barbara Reynolds (Harmondsworth: Penguin, 1962), p. 150.

[122] See the report of the International Theological Commission, commissioned by Pope John Paul II and authorized for publication in April 2007 by Benedict XVI, entitled "The Hope of Salvation for Infants Who Die without Being Baptised." Available online HHTP: <https://www.vatican.va/roman_curia/congregations/cfaith/cti_documents/rc_con_cfaith_doc_20070419_un-baptised-infants_en.html>. Accessed 25 May 2024.

Pater Seraphicus urges them to continue their *Steigerung*, that is, ascent, reassuring them: "For in ether free, supernal, / This as spirit-food still holdeth, / Revelation of Eternal / Love that unto bliss unfoldeth" (ll. 11922-11925). Finally, the chorus of Blessed Boys is circling around the highest peaks.

And this is significant, because their trajectory is Faust's trajectory. Or, more precisely, the trajectory of his immortal essence (*Unsterbliches*). Originally, Goethe had used the word *Entelechie* ("entelechy"): a notion found in Aristotle as *entelecheia* (ἐντελέχεια), where it is related to *energeia* (ενέργεια), and employed by Goethe in the sense of Leibniz's notion of the indestructible monad.[123] Thus an **entelechy** is a kind of secularized notion of the soul, understood as a dynamic principle that turns what is *potential* into something *actual*.[124] (John Peck has argued persuasively for the importance of Aristotle's "action template" in his *Poetics* and his notion of *entelechy* in his biology and natural history for Jung's theory of

---

[123] See Goethe's conversation about the entelechy with Eckermann on 3 March 1830, where he remarks that "the obstinacy of the individual, and the fact that man shakes off what does not suit him [...] is a proof to me that something of the kind exists," adding: "Leibnitz had similar thoughts about independent beings, and indeed what we term an entelechy he called a monad" (Eckermann, *Conversations of Goethe*, p. 353). Earlier, in a famous conversation with Johann Daniel Falk (1768-1826) after the funeral of Christoph Martin Wieland (1733-1813), Goethe had speculated at some length about the immortality of the soul (see *Characteristics of Goethe: From the German of Falk, von Müller, etc.*, trans. Sarah Austin, vol. 1 (London: Wilson, 1833), pp. 66-86). For further discussion, see Gaier, *Kommentar I*, pp. 720-722; Werner Kohlschmidt, "Faustens »Entelechie« — doch der Doctor Marianus?", *Orbis Litterarum*, 29 (1974), 221-230; and Lauri Seppänen, "Goethe und seine *Entelecheia*," *Neuphilologische Mitteilungen*, vol. 84, no. 1 (1983), 126-131.
[124] See Schöne, *Kommentare*, p. 800; cf. Aristotle's *Metaphysics*, where the notions of potentiality and actuality are introduced in book 8 (Z) and analysed in book 9 (Θ) (vol. 2, pp. 1623-1644 and 1651-1661). On 19 March 1827, Goethe wrote to Zelter: "The entelechical monad must preserve itself in unceasing activity alone"; and on 1 September 1829, he said to Eckermann: "I doubt not of our immortality, for Nature cannot dispense with the entelechy," and adding: "But we are not all in like manner immortal; and he who would manifest himself in future as a great entelechy must be one now" (Eckermann, *Conversations of Goethe*, p. 331).

individuation.[125] In an interview with Jung in 1952, Ximena de Angulo suspected that Jung may have had a prejudice against Aristotle because of the "intellectual aridity and doctrinaire rigidity" of so-called "Aristotelian" thinking in the Church; but, when she pushed him on whether individuation was "what made a tree grow into a tree" and "if it was not the same thing as the Aristotelian entelechy," Jung — after hesitating — conceded it *was* the same thing.)[126] Just as the chorus of Blessed Boys has ascended to the higher peaks, so we now see there, floating in the higher atmosphere, Angels bearing Faust's immortal essence. These Angels now declaim lines which, according to Goethe in his conversation with Eckermann of 6 June 1831, contain the "key to Faust's salvation":

> Freed is the noble scion of
> The Spirit-world from evil.
> »Him can we save that tireless strove
> Ever to higher level.«
> And if Supernal Love did stoop
> To him with predilection,
> Then him shall hail the angelic troop
> With brotherly affection.
>
> (ll. 11934-11941)

---

[125] "The sections of Aristotle's *Poetics* devoted to the structure of action rendered symbolically [...] supplied Jung with his terms. [...] The nugget for Jung in this action template is the pressure or drift in psychic energy, the apparent purposiveness in life processes, which is akin to the finalistic perspective invoked by him for certain dreams, but which typically remains a bane in modern science, and certainly is baneful to theorists of unconscious processes when those processes are tied to the least shred of traditional teleology" (John Peck, "Introduction," in C.G. Jung, *Dream Interpretation Ancient & Modern: Notes from the Seminar Given in 1936-1941*, ed. John Peck, Lorenz Jung, and Maria Meyer-Grass, trans. Ernst Falzeder with Tony Woolfson (Princeton, NJ, and Oxford: Princeton University Press, 2014), pp. xxi-lii [p. xxxiv]).

[126] "Comments on a Doctoral Thesis" [1952], in William McGuire and R.F.C. Hull, *C.G. Jung Speaking: Interviews and Encounters* (Princeton, NJ: Princeton University Press, 1977), pp. 205-218 (p. 211); cited in Peck, "Introduction," in Jung, *Dream Interpretation Ancient & Modern*, p. xxxv.

So, in what sense do these lines contain the key to Faust's salvation? As Goethe himself explained, "In Faust himself there is an activity which becomes constantly higher and purer to the end, and from above there is eternal love coming to his aid. This harmonizes perfectly with our religious views, according to which we cannot obtain heavenly bliss through our own strength alone, but with the assistance of divine grace."[127] Except that's not *quite* what the lines imply.

Earlier, in the "Entombment" scene, we heard the chorus of angels declare that those who condemn themselves to damnation may be saved by the Truth and that they can *redeem themselves* (*sich erlösen*) (ll. 11803-11806); now we are told by another set of angels that Faust, "this noble member / of the spirit world," has been redeemed (*gerettet*) from (the) evil (one), and they declare that whoever strives (*strebend*) and makes an effort (*sich bemüht*) is someone whom they (as angels, and presumably hence as agents of God?) can redeem (*Den können wir erlösen*). This use of *wir* is important, as it implies that the notion of redemption (*Erlösung*) with which Goethe is operating here is less the Christian notion of redemption from the consequence of original sin through the redemptive power of the death of Christ, God become Man, on the Cross, and more a Neoplatonic notion of redemption as a kind of cleansing, stripping-away, or removal (= *Abstreifung, Ablösung*) (see below).[128] Crucially, however, these two lines are placed within quotation marks; marks, not present in Goethe's handwritten manuscript (H[33]) but added in pencil to the final manuscript (H), and hence to be regarded as passively authorized by Goethe.[129] What these quotation marks mean remains unclear, but they can only serve as some kind of distancing device. Yet here, too, the

---

[127] Eckermann, *Conversations of Goethe*, p. 413.
[128] Schöne, *Kommentare*, 801; Gaier, *Kommentar I*, 1143.
[129] Schöne, *Kommentare*, 800-802.

emphasis is on the salvific power of love — on "love from above" (*die Liebe gar / Von oben*).

A group of Younger Angels picks up the song, declaring that the roses they strew to distract Mephistopheles and his devils in the previous scene came from the hands of penitent women, anticipating their imminent appearance in this scene. Then a group of More Perfected Angels offer further insight into the notion of redemption as it is operating here:

> Still doth some earth remain,
> Still doth arrest us.
> 'Tis not all free from stain
> Were it asbestos.
> When spirit-might hath blent
> Closely-consorted
> With Earth's gross element,
> Angels ne'er parted
> Natures knit two in one,
> Near interwoven.
> By Eternal Love alone
> Can they be cloven.
> (ll. 11954-11965)

The perfection of *these* angels is, it seems, greater because of their refusal of *any* earthly remnant, recalling Plotin's conception of the "remainder" (*to loipon*) as something from which the soul must be purified, inasmuch as "the soul is evil when it is thoroughly mixed with the body and shares its experiences" (*Enneads*, "On Virtues," I.2 §3),[130] and it becomes ugly (*aischra*) through this

---

[130] Plotinus, vol. 1, *Porphyry on Plotinus; Ennead I*, trans. A.H. Armstrong (Cambridge, MA, and London: Harvard University Press, 1995), p. 135. On the use of the concept of the "remainder" in relation to Schelling, see Slavoj Žižek, *The Indivisible Remainder: An Essay on Schelling and Related Matters* (London and New York: Verso, 1996).

mixing and union as well as its desire for the body and for the material world (see *Enneads*, "On Beauty," I.6 §5).[131] Here the "remainder" (*Rest*) is applied to those earthly elements from which Faust's entelechy will in the course of its ongoing metamorphosis be freed — a transformative process which will, as we shall see, result in the emergence of a new bodiliness (see below). Such a view corresponds to the doctrine of such Neoplatonists as Plutarch, Plotinus, Porphyry, and Proclus, for whom the "astral body," or *okhēma* (i.e., the "carrier" or "vehicle" of the soul), bears the burden of matter during one's earthy life but is purified of it after death.[132] In the case of these angels, to bear these earthly remainders is a source of toil (*peinlich*), yet this is perhaps not surprising, given that one of Faust's "two souls" was said in Part One to "hold fast with joyous earthly lust / Onto the world of man with organs clinging" (ll. 1114-1115, trans. Arndt). As Gaier suggests, the persistence of Faust's earthly traces in his immortal essence would seem to be unusual for the angels, indicating the remarkable strength of this entelechy, even in the afterlife![133]

"Asbestos," deriving from the ancient Greek ἄσβεστος, i.e., "unquenchable" or "inextinguishable," reflecting its use for wicks that would never burn up or be consumed, emphasizes the earthly element of this ineradicable remainder. For the angels, it is impossible to "separate" the two aspects of this *geeinte Zwienatur*, this "union-of-two-fused-into-one" (l. 11962), recalling those "two souls" within Faust's breast (ll. 1112-1121). This concept should be read as reflecting not so much a dualistic (and, in this sense, un-Goethean) outlook that distinguishes between the mental and the physical (or between *Geist* and matter) as the alchemical

---

[131] Plotinus, vol. 1, pp. 247-249. For further discussion of the "erotic metaphysics" of Plotinus, see Alberto Bertozzi, *Plotinus on Love: An Introduction to his Metaphysics through the Concept of "Eros"* (Leiden and Boston: Brill, 2021).
[132] Gaier, *Kommentar I*, 1145.
[133] Gaier, *Kommentar I*, 1145.

notion, taken up by Goethe in his doctrine of metamorphosis, of purification or *Läuterung*: only love, "eternal love" (*die ewige Liebe*) can cleanse the "pure" substance of the entelechy from its "impure" attachments.[134] The Younger Angels notice that the crowd of Blessed Boys have emerged from the cloud, and are enjoying the "new spring" of the "upper world": Let Faust, they suggest, in his dynamic of *Steigerung* join them! In response, the Blessed Boys welcome into their midst Faust in his "pupal stage" (*Puppenstand*), predicting that he will, butterflylike, emerge from it — "beautiful and great / From sacred life" — as he casts off his flaky husks (*die Flocken*) (ll. 11987-11988).

And so, we come to the fourth of the four patristic hermits in this scene — to Doctor Marianus. The epithet *marianus* is conventionally applied to two theologians: to the Benedictine monk and later Archbishop, Anselm of Canterbury (c. 1033-1109); and to the Scottish Catholic priest and Franciscan friar, Duns Scotus (c. 1265-1308), also known as Doctor Subtilis. In the context of the *Paradiso* (and the great Mariological prayer in Canto XXXIII), Doctor Marianus also evokes the figure of Bernard of Clairvaux. For his part, Jung associates Marianus with a seventh-century alchemist Morienus Romanus, said to have been the teacher of the Umayyad prince, Khālid ibn Yazīd, in turn a reputed alchemist (CW 12 §558; cf. CW 12 §386). In the conclusion to his discussion of the *lapis*-Christ parallel in his lecture on "Religious Ideas in Alchemy," Jung cited (via Michael Maier) the following dictum of Morienus: "Take that which is trodden underfoot in the dunghill, for if thou dost not, thou wilt fall in thine head when thou wouldst climb without steps,"[135] a dictum which he glossed as meaning that "if someone refuses to accept what they have spurned, it will recoil

---

[134] Schöne, *Kommentare*, 802-803.
[135] Maier, *Symbola aureae mensae duodecim nationum* (Frankfurt am Main, 1617), p. 141; cf. Morienus, "Sermo de transmutatione metallorum," in *Artis Auriferae*, 2 vols (Basel, 1593), vol. 2, pp. 7-54 (pp. 35-36).

upon them the moment they want to go higher" (CW 12 §514). Yet is this dictum of Morienus — namely, that the integration of everything that one has spurned is a prerequisite for a successful *Steigerung* — really compatible with the message of the final scene of *Faust*?

For we see Doctor Marianus in the highest, purest cell, indicative of the fact that this figure, a mystical devotee of the Blessed Virgin (and as such a sublime counterpart to Faust in his study at the beginning of Part One), represents the highest attainable level of human perfection (Hamlin, 341, fn. 9). Marianus hymnically declares that "Here is the prospect free, / The soul uplifted" (*Hier ist die Aussicht frei, / Der Geist erhoben*) (ll. 11989-11990), a counterpoint to Faust's cry when walking in the country-side in "Before the City Gate" in Part One, "Here I am Man, am free to be!" (*Hier bin ich Mensch, hier darf ich's sein!*) (l. 940), as he looks up in rapture to the Virgin Mary in glory, "Virgin pure from stain of earth, / Mother honour-throned, / Chosen Queen, and peer by birth / With the Godhead owned!" (ll. 12009-12012). Yet even here, in these exalted heavenly circles, there is still a moment of theological reflection, when Marianus asks:

> Into frailty borne away,
> Hardly to deliver!
> Who lust's chain hath torn away
> Of his own strength ever?
> On the slant and slippery path
> Is the foothold fleeting?
> Whom beguiles not flattering breath,
> Glance and honeyed greeting?
> (ll. 12024-12031)

Even at this highest stage of mystical contemplation, the question of whether we can or cannot redeem ourselves (i.e., of own accord burst the chains of desire) seems unresolved: Are we as human beings constitutionally prone to slip or to be misled? Or to put it another way: Do we as humans have the wherewithal or the capacity to be redeemed?

After (1) the scene has been set by the Chorus, (2) Pater Profundus has described Nature as nourished by love, (3) Pater Seraphicus has recognized and assisted the chorus of Blessed Boys, (4) the Angels have carried Faust's immortal essence into the highest atmosphere, and (5) Doctor Marianus bursts out in ecstatic praise of the Queen of Heaven, two sections are left in this final scene: (6) the intercession of the chorus of Penitent Women; and (7) the final prayer of Doctor Marianus.[136]

In the scene "By the City Wall" in Part One we saw Gretchen turning in prayer to the Mater Dolorosa; now, in the rarefied atmosphere of this iconographical landscape, the Mater Gloriosa — the Blessed Virgin Mary as the Queen of Heaven in all her Dante-esque splendor — floats into view on high. A chorus of three penitent women pray to her, imploring her intercession; they are the Magna Peccatrix (or the great sinful woman, i.e., the woman known from the Gospel of Luke who expresses her penitence by washing Jesus's feet and drying them with her hair; the Mulier Samaritana (or the Samaritan woman, i.e., the woman who gives Jesus water to drink); and Maria Aegyptica (or Mary of Egypt, i.e., an Egyptian saint whose *Vita* was written by St. Sophronius, the Patriarch of Jerusalem, and who is highly venerated in the Coptic and Eastern Orthodox Churches as well as commemorated by Roman Catholics as the patron saint of penitents). These three women are joined by a fourth — a penitent, formerly known as Gretchen, on whose behalf they have been interceding. For her part, Gretchen's prayer to the Virgin, "Ah! bow / Thy gracious brow, / O peerless Thou, / And radiant, on my radiant bliss! / My youth's beloved, / From grief removed, / Returning is" (ll. 12068-12075), echoes her

---

[136] On this sevenfold formal structure, see Gaier, *Kommentar I*, 1126-1133.

earlier petition to the Mater Dolorosa, "Ah, bow / Thy gracious brow, / Mother of Woes, to the woebegone!" (ll. 3587-3589) and expresses her joy at Faust's postmortem return to her. As the chorus of Blessed Boys circles closer, they curiously praise his physical maturity ("Great-limbed already he / Grows, us transcending, / Will requite lavishly / Our careful tending") and suggest that the erstwhile academic professor might now really have something to teach them: "Early removed were we / Forth of Life's chorus; / Us will he teach what he / Hath learned before us" (ll. 12076-12083). And as Gretchen intercedes in turn for Faust, she too evokes his new bodiliness — confirming the principle of Friedrich Christoph Oetinger (1702-1782) that "bodiliness is the end of God's works" (*Leiblichkeit ist das Ende der Werke Gottes*) —[137] in these words:

> Lo, how he bursts with gladsome gesture
> Each old-enswathing bond of earth,
> And radiant from ethereal vesture
> The pristine strength of youth gleams forth.
> Grant me to teach him! Radiant-shining
> Still dazzles him the new-sprung day.
>> (ll. 12088-12093)

Just as Faust was, in the opening scene of Part Two, blinded by the physical sun (ll. 4702-4703) and, earlier in Act V, blinded by Care (l. 11497), so he is here blinded a third time by the refulgent splendor of this (divine) "new day." Gretchen's intercession is successful: Obtaining permission from the Mater Gloriosa to soar upward herself to higher spheres, she does so in order that, thus preceding him, Faust will intuit her presence and follow her. In his final prayer, Doctor Marianus, prostrate in adoration, calls on us all to look up to the "saving glance" — the *Retterblick,* as opposed to Faust's moment or

---

[137] Oetinger, *Biblisches und Emblematisches Wörterbuch* (Stuttgart 1776), p. 407); cited in Gaier, *Kommentar I,* 721, 723, and 1144.

Augenblick — of the Mater Gloriosa. May each of us, he prays, place our "better sense" (*jeder beßre Sinn*) in her service; and he implores her to remain gracious and merciful, hailing her in a fourfold sense as "Virgin, Mother, Queen, / Goddess" (ll. 12102-12103).

And so, we come to the final lines of the scene, the famous Chorus mysticus:

> All things corruptible
> Are but reflection.
> Earth's insufficiency
> Here finds perfection.
> Here the ineffable
> Wrought is with love.
> The Eternal-Womanly
> Draws us above.
> (ll. 12104-12111)[138]

What does this Chorus mean? It is certainly mysterious, if not also mystical. In his interpretive notes in the Norton Critical Edition, Cyrus Hamlin examines over three pages what the Chorus proclaims in these eight lines, statement by statement; and in their commentaries, Gaier and Schöne alike devote five pages to them. Clearly, we cannot do full justice to these lines here, but the following points are perhaps the most important.

To begin with, it declares that all things that pass (*Alles Vergängliche*, in grammatical terms an adjectival noun) are a *Gleichnis* — a likeness, a simile, an analogy, or a parable; all these senses are implied, and the adverb *nur* (i.e., only) should not be read as reducing or devaluing the importance of those transient

---

[138] In his ETH lectures on the history of modern psychology, Jung comments on this "utterly unorthodox and highly original vision at the end of *Faust*, adding: "Those who think Goethe was merely fabulating are completely off the track" (C.G. Jung, *History of Modern Psychology: Lectures Delivered at ETH Zurich, 1933-1934*, ed. Ernst Falzeder, trans. Mark Kyburz, John Peck, and Ernst Falzeder (Princeton, NJ, and Oxford: Princeton University Press, 2019), p. 136).

things, but rather as explaining that this is *precisely* what they are.[139] To put it another way, to see transitory things as a *Gleichnis* is to appreciate their *symbolic* dimension; as Goethe wrote in 1825 in his *Versuch einer Witterungslehre*, "It is not given to us to grasp the truth, which is identical with the divine, directly. We perceive it only in reflection, in example and symbol, in singular and related appearances. It meets us as a kind of life that is incomprehensible to us, and yet we cannot free ourselves from the desire to comprehend it."[140] It is in just this sense that Oetinger wrote, summarizing the mystical thought of Jakob Böhme: "The external world is a principle because it has its own life, born of both inner eternal realities [of darkness and of light], as a revelation of both, a model and likeness [*Gleichnis*] of what is eternal in God; such a model is located in the wisdom of God."[141] As Geier remarks, the full ambivalence of the adverb *nur* comes to the fore, so that while what is transient is reduced to a mere *simile* or *simulacrum*, at the same time as a *Gleichnis* it is a revelation in time of what is eternal in God.[142]

---

[139] See the entry on *nur* in Jacob and Wilhelm Grimm, *Deutsches Wörterbuch*, vol. 13, *N – Quurren* (Munich: Deutscher Taschenbuch Verlag, 1984), cols 998-1008.

[140] Cf. "Excerpt from 'Toward a Theory of Weather,'" in Goethe, *Scientific Studies*, ed. and trans. Douglas Miller, p. 145: "We can never directly see what is true, i.e., identical with what is divine; we look at it only in reflection, in example, in the symbol, in individual and related phenomena. We perceive it as a life beyond our grasp, yet we cannot deny our need to grasp it."

[141] Friedrich Christoph Oetinger, *Swedenborgs irdische und himmlische Philosophe* [= *Sämtliche Schriften*, vol. II.2] [1858], ed. Karl Christian Eberhard Ehmann, re-ed. Erich Beyreuther (Stuttgart: Steinkopf, 1977), p. 249; cited in Gaier, *Kommentare I*, 1159-1160.

[142] Gaier, *Kommentare I*, 1160. According to Rudolf Steiner, Goethe "created from the kind of knowledge possessed by the mystics," and "from this source he derived the capacity for seeing Life — 'things transitory' — as symbols only, as a reflection": "A period of inexhaustible inner development lies between the time (Part I.) when Goethe wrote his words of despair at being so remote from the 'mirror of eternal truth' [cf. l. 615] and the time when he wrote the 'Chorus Mysticus' whose words express the fact that 'things transitory' are to be seen only as 'symbols' of the Eternal" (*Goethe's Standard of the Soul* [*Goethes Geistesart in ihrer Offenbarung durch seinen Faust und durch das Märchen von der Schlange und der Lilie*, 1918], trans. D.S. Osmond (New York: Anthroposophic Press, 1925), p. 15).

And in this line there is a kind of anticipation or preecho of Heidegger: In his discussion in his essay *Sprache und Heimat* ("Language and Homeland") (1960) of works by Johann Peter Hebel (1760-1826), Heidegger explored how, in the poem *Der Sommerband* ("Summer's Evening") and other texts, Hebel presented images of a woman combing her hair and the rays of the sun in a way that suggested some kind of "animistic union."[143] "Who could deny', he wrote, "that here [i.e., in *Das Habermus*], as in *Der Sommerabend*, the sun is being compared with the motherly farmer's wife? Or is it the other way round, and what is essential [*das Wesende*] about the farmer's wife and the mother appears in the great heavenly image of the sun? Is the one really being compared [*verglichen*] with the other at all? Probably the poem is not speaking in a comparison [*in einem Vergleich*], but in a simile [*im Gleichnis*]. *Gleich* means: *gelich* — collected into the same *lich*, into the same shape."[144]

Second, whatever cannot reach its goal because of its internal insufficiency (*das Unzulängliche*)[145] here *does* reach it: It becomes an "event," an *Ereignis* (another term that was to acquire significance in the thought of Heidegger),[146] not least in its etymological sense

---

[143] See Martin Travers, "Trees, Rivers, and Gods: Paganism in the Work of Martin Heidegger," *Journal of European Studies*, vol. 48, no. 2 (2018), 133-143 (p. 140).

[144] Martin Heidegger, *Aus der Erfahrung des Denkens, 1910-1976* [*Gesamtausgabe*, vol. I.13], ed. Hermann Heidegger (Frankfurt am Main: Klostermann, 1983), pp. 155-180 (p. 179).

[145] *Unzulänglich* covers a range of meanings, including "unattainable," "inaccessible," "insufficient"; see Schön, *Kommentare*, 814.

[146] Variously translated as "event," "appropriation," "enowning," and "coming-into-view," Heidegger's notion of *Ereignis* was a key part of his "turn" (*Kehre*) following the publication in 1927 of *Being and Time*, and the concept is elaborated in two works between 1936 and 1942, *Beiträge zur Philosophie (Vom Ereignis)* and *Das Ereignis*. Heidegger's own gloss (given during one of his seminars given in Le Thor) on *Ereignis* as the event of givenness of presence or being, and as "a matter [...]" of understanding that the deepest meaning of being is *letting* [*lassen*]," is entirely apposite in the context of Goethe's Chorus mysticus (see Heidegger, *Four Seminars*, trans. Andrew Mitchell and François Raffoul (Bloomington, IN: Indiana University Press, 2003), p. 59). For further discussion, see Daniela Vallega-Neu, "*Ereignis*: the event of appropriation," in Bret W. Davis (ed.), *Martin Heidegger: Key Concepts* (Abingdon and New York: Routledge, 2014), pp. 140-154, and "*Ereignis*," in

that it "comes into view" (*er-äugnen*).[147] Third, whatever cannot be described in language (or inscribed into language) is here — well, *done* (or "enacted," it "becomes deed," recalling Faust's translation of the word *logos* in the opening of St. John's Gospel "In the beginning was the deed [*die Tat*]" [l. 1237]). What is being presented here in the final scene transcends language; it *happens*, it is not so much "said-and-done" as simply — *done*. Finally, in response to Mephisto's jibe about how he prefers eternal emptiness or *das Ewig-Leere*, the Chorus mysticus asserts that the Eternal-Feminine *draws us on*.

In *Psychological Types* (1921), Jung identified the Eternal-Feminine as the third and final stage of a sequence of figures beginning with Gretchen, then Helena; as such, it was a "primordial image" that recurred more completely in the Gnostic tradition in the idea of the divine harlot as represented by Eve, Helena, Mary, and Sophia-Achamoth (CW 6 §317).[148] Later in this same work, Jung made the bold assertion that, just as in Canto XXXIII of the *Paradiso,* Dante speaks "through the mouth of St. Bernard" as "an indication of the transformation and exaltation of his own being," so "*the same transformation* also happens to Faust" (my emphasis);

François Raffoul and Eric S. Nelson (eds), *The Bloomsbury Companion to Heidegger* (London and New York: Bloomsbury, 2016), pp. 283-289; and Martin Travers, "The Happening of *Ereignis*: The Presence of Greek Ritual in Heidegger's Concept of Enowning," *Seminar: A Journal of Germanic Studies*, vol. 51, no. 1 (February 2015), 1-9; and Thomas Sheehan, "The Turn: All Three of Them," in Raffoul and Nelson (eds), *The Bloomsbury Companion to Heidegger*, pp. 31-38.

[147] See Schöne, *Kommentare*, 815 and 453. For his part, Rudolf Steiner came up with the intriguing suggestion that the choice of the word *Ereignis* rested on a mistake by the scribe who had misunderstood Goethe's Frankfurt accent and written *Ereignis* instead of *Erreichtes* — that is, "what has been attained" — meaning that what had been striven for in the physical world had been attained in the spiritual world (*Erläuterungen*, vol. 1, p. 36; cf. Adalbert Rudolf, "Abgerissene Bemerkungen zu Goethes Faust," *Archiv für das Studium der neueren Sprachen und Litteraturen*, 37. Jahrgang, vol. 70 (1883), pp. 462-473 [p. 473], which suggests reading *Ereignis* as *Erreichnis*).

[148] See CW 15 §211; and CW 16 §361; and letter of 22 March 1939 (L1, 264-266); discussed in Chapter 4 below (pp. 375-381).

arguing that Faust's nature is "altered by repeated figurative deaths (Boy Charioteer, Homunculus, Euphorion)", that is, in line with thesis of interrupted tragedy as a structural principle, Jung proposed that Faust "finally attains the highest goal as Doctor Marianus," and it is in this guise that he, Faust, "utters his prayer to the Virgin Mary" (§378). Now while there is nothing in the text to suggest that we should identify Doctor Marianus with Faust, Jung is surely right to suggest that this final scene should be understood primarily in terms of its upward dynamic. If so, it helps answer the questions raised by Hamlin, namely: Who is meant by "us"? And what does it mean to be "drawn onward"?

Hamlin makes a strong case for reading the entire final Chorus as "a kind of meta-commentary on the drama that is now and here completed" (490). But one could also read the final lines as enacting a remarkable inversion of the Faustian dynamic in the work: In Part One, Faust wants to know "the inmost force / That bonds the very universe" (*was die Welt / Im Innersten zusammenhält*) (ll. 382-383); he feels "emboldened now to venture forth, / To bear the bliss, the sorrow of this earth" (*mich in die Welt zu wagen, / Der Erde Weh, der Erde Glück zu tragen*) (ll. 464-465); he wants to experience "what to all mankind is apportioned [...] in my own self's core" (*was der ganzen Menschheit zugeteilt ist [...] in meinem innern Selbst* (ll. 1770-1771), while in Part Two, he recognizes that "I only sped the whole world through" (*Ich bin nur durch die Welt gerannt*) (l. 11433), yet he still insists, even when blinded by Care, that "I hasten to fulfill my thought's designing" (*Was ich gedacht, ich eil es zu vollbringen*) (l.11501); and he regards it as "Wisdom's last verdict" (*der Wahrheit letzter Schluß*) that "He only earns both freedom and existence / Who must reconquer them each day" (*Nur der verdient sich Freiheit wie das Leben, / Der täglich sie erobern muß*) (ll. 11574-11575; trans. Arndt). In other words, up until now the entire dynamic of Faust has been organized around the concept of *Streben*, striving, pushing, expanding; now he is experiencing an entirely different dynamic, not one of pushing but of allowing oneself to be pulled or drawn — onward and upward.

In this respect, one should recall the conclusions Jung draws in *Symbols and Transformations of Libido* in relation to the story of Job (and, in particular, to the second of the discourses of Yahweh), a key part of the theological framework of *Faust*. For here Jung identifies "the primitive power which Job's Hymn of Creation vindicates, the unconditional and inexorable, the unjust and the superhuman [*Übermenschliche*]" as "truly and rightly attributes of libido" — which, in the words of *Wilhelm Meister*,[149] "leads us into life" and "lets the poor be guilty" — "against which struggle is in vain," which leads Jung to conclude: "Nothing remains for humankind but to work in harmony with this [divine] will" (PU §111). (And he adds that Nietzsche's *Zarathustra* "teaches us this impressively.")

As we have seen in this chapter, it is no exaggeration to describe *Faust* as a text of transformation: Faust himself is transformed into a younger man, then rejuvenated a second time; Mephistopheles changes sex and becomes Phorcyas; Homunculus, seeking to become fully alive, plunges into the sea; to say nothing of the fiery

---

[149] Johann Wolfgang von Goethe, *Wer nie sein Brot mit Tränen ass*:
> *Wer nie die kummervollen Nächte*
> *Auf seinem Bette weinend sass,*
> *Der kennt euch nicht, ihr himmlischen Mächte!*
> *Ihr führt ins Leben uns hinein,*
> *Ihr lasst den Armen schuldig werden,*
> *Dann überlasst ihr ihn der Pein:*
> *Denn alle Schuld rächt sich auf Erden.*"
> "Who never ate his bread in tears,
> Who never throughout sorrowful nights,
> Sat weeping on his bed,
> He knows not you, Heavenly Powers.
> You bring us into life,
> The poor man you let fall into guilt,
> Then leave him to his pain:
> For all guilt is suffered for on earth"
(translated by Richard Stokes in *The Book of Lieder* (London: Faber and Faber, 2005).

fate of Euphorion. Yet the ultimate transformation that is operated in the final scene is this: from *erkennen*, *wagen*, *genießen*, and *durchstürmen*, *vollbringen*, and *erobern*, to being *entführt*, *getragen*, and finally *hinangezogen*. This transformative process in *Faust* is underpinned by two key Goethean principles: polarity (*Polarität*) and enhancement or intensification (*Steigerung*), principles which he once described as the *zwei großen Triebräder der Natur* ("two great driving forces in all nature"), defining the former as a property of matter "insofar as we think of it as material" and as "a state of constant attraction and repulsion," and the latter as a property of matter "insofar as we think of it as spiritual," and as "a state of ever-striving ascent"; moreover, the relation between these two principles is reciprocal.[150] In this concluding scene, as throughout the work as a whole, both these principles are illustrated by, on the one hand, the striving (*strebend*), active (*tätig*), even violent (*Gewalt*) masculinity of Faust, and by, on the other, the gracious (*gnädig*), saving love presented under the likeness (*Gleichnis*) of the feminine — the *Eternal Feminine* (*das Ewig-Weibliche*).[151]

In short, the astonishing conclusion of *Faust II* illustrates one more time the importance of the motif of transformation, enacting a *Steigerung* of transcendence in a way which makes use of the iconography of Catholicism, while yet being entirely compatible with the tradition of Sufi mysticism associated with Hafiz and celebrated by Goethe in his *West-Eastern Divan*, notably in his poem "Higher and Highest" (*Höheres und Höchstes*) in the concluding "Book of Paradise":

---

[150] See Goethe's comments about his aphoristic essay "On Nature" to Chancellor Friedrich von Müller (1779-1849); in Goethe, *Scientific Studies*, ed. and trans. Miller, p. 6.
[151] Schöne, *Kommentare*, 817.

Lighter now I'm penetrating	*Und nun dring ich aller Orten*
Spheres eternal evermore,	*Leichter durch die ewgen Kreise,*
Where God's word is permeating	*Die durchdrungen sind vom Worte*
All revitalising pure.	*Gottes rein-lebendger Weise.*
Ardently impelled ascending	*Ungehemmt mit heißem Triebe*
There's no end, no let nor stay,	*Läßt sich da kein Ende finden,*
Till beholding love unending	*Bis im Anschaun ewger Liebe*
Soaring we dissolve away.	*Wir verschweben, wir verschwinden.*[152]

---

[152] Johann Wolfgang von Goethe, *West-Eastern Divan; West-oestlicher Divan*, trans. J. Whaley (London: Wolff, 1974), pp. 222-223; cf. Schöne, *Kommentare*, 818.

Chapter 3

Goethe's *Faust* in Jung's Works [A]: *Faust* in Jung's Autobiographical and Early Works

In the opening "Night" scene, the aged and frustrated Faust described *his* project thus, "That I the mighty inmost tether / May know, that binds the world together" (*Daß ich erkenne, was die Welt / Im Innersten zusammenhält*) (ll. 382-383); precisely this was Jung's project too, only in an introjected form, that is, rendered internal to the psyche. Jung's life is, then, like a mandala, inasmuch as it turns in its entirety around a central point: or, as he put it: "Everything can be explained from this central point [*aus diesem zentralen Punkt*], and all my works relate to this one theme" (MDR, 232). Given what Jung says elsewhere, one could also paraphrase this as saying: If one wants to understand the project of Analytical Psychology, one has first to understand how it emerges from (and engages with) Goethe's *Faust*.

When did Jung first read Goethe's *Faust*? While we do not know exactly when, it was probably during Jung's years at school; when (according to *Memories, Dreams, Reflections*) Jung's mother said to him "suddenly and without preamble": "You must read Goethe's *Faust* one of these days" (MDR, 78). If this account is to be believed, Jung immediately identified with Goethe's poetic drama, describing it as "pour[ing] [...] like a miraculous balm" into his soul. Why should this work have had such a profound effect? According to *Memories, Dreams, Reflections*, his reading of *Faust* was tied up with the deep crisis of religious belief that Jung underwent during his school years. In part, this crisis can be traced back to those powerful dreams and visions that Jung is said to have experienced as a child: his dream of a giant phallus — a "subterranean god," something "not to be named" — in an underground temple beneath the meadow behind the vicarage at Laufen (MDR, 26-28), as well as his vision of God defecating on the roof of Basel Cathedral (MDR, 56-57). In part, it can be traced back to his witnessing of his father's own collapse of faith, yet failure to come to terms with the consequences of that collapse (MDR, 111-117). And in part, it can be traced back to Jung's curious mixture of embarrassment and pride about his own "legendary kinship with Goethe," reflected in his description of the legend that his grandfather had been an illegitimate son of Goethe as "annoying," together with his persistence in repeating this legend — "with a certain gratified amusement," as Aniela Jaffé notes (MDR, 52). In Wolfram's epic, Parzival asked, *waz ist got*, "What is God?" (§119, l. 17; vol. 1, p. 68, and §332, l.1; vol. 1, p. 188). Jung thought he knew the answer: God alone "was real — annihilating fire and an indescribable grace" (MDR, 74). And Jung thought that Goethe had known this was the answer too.

After all, in the figure of Faust, Goethe had portrayed someone who took the Devil seriously, so seriously as even to conclude a pact with him — a blood pact, no less, with the adversary of God himself who had the power to frustrate God's plan to make a perfect world (MDR, 78). (Here we are reminded of the story of Genesis — as well as the story of Job, to which Goethe alludes in the "Prologue in Heaven"). At the same time, Jung was critical of Faust: He should not have been so one-sided and so easily tricked! He should have been cleverer, more moral! How childish to have been so frivolous as to have gambled away his soul! Far more interesting than Faust, Jung felt, was the figure of the Devil — Mephistopheles himself. Yet the motif of the "cheated devil" at the end of *Faust II* irritated Jung: After all, Mephistopheles had been anything but a stupid devil, and he *had* been cheated of his rightful prize by a bunch of silly little angels! In fact, the "real problem" of the drama, Jung argues, lay with Mephistopheles: His figure made the "deepest impression" on Jung, not least because he was somehow related to "the mystery of the Mothers" (MDR, 78) — the Mothers of whom, as Mephisto says, "Only to speak of them the brain doth swim" (1. 6215; MDR, 101). Even if Mephistopheles and the "great initiation" of the concluding scene remained at this time for Jung "a wonderful and mysterious experience on the fringes" of his "conscious world," the drama as a whole served to confirm for Jung that some people had seen "evil and its universal power" — its "mysterious role in delivering humankind from darkness and suffering" (MDR, 78). To this extent, Goethe became for Jung — in the highest form of praise Jung can extend — nothing less than "a prophet" (MDR, 79).

One of the reasons that Goethe spoke so directly to Jung — in fact, he describes Goethe as his "godfather and authority" (*Pate und Gewährsmann*) — was that *Faust* spoke to the part of Jung that he described as Personality No. 2. (In *Memories, Dreams, Reflections*, Jung tells us that, as a child, he increasingly came to see himself under two aspects: one related to the here-and-now of the contemporary world, which he called Personality No. 1; and one that was open to history, to the past, to the archaic dimension of life, which he called Personality No. 2.) This Personality No. 2 was related to the Middle Ages — those Middle Ages "within" himself which Jung, in *The Red Book*, said that he has to "catch up with," promising (or threatening) his ego that he will carry it "through an utterly medieval Hell" (RB, 457-458) — a Middle Ages personified, in Jung's words, by Faust as the "legacy of a past which had obviously stirred Goethe to the depths" (MDR, 107). In order to convey the depth of his own response, Jung offers a rather surprising comparison: *Faust*, he came to realize as a student, now meant more to him that did his favorite gospel, the Gospel according to John (MDR, 107). Now the Christ presented to us in the Gospel of John (often thought of as the gospel closest to Gnosticism) might have been "strange" to Jung, but the figure of Christ presented by the Synoptics in their gospels (Matthew, Mark, and Luke) was even stranger; whereas Faust was in some sense a "living equivalent" of his own Personality No. 2, and in this respect "the answer which Goethe had given to the question of his times" (MDR, 107). (In a passage omitted from the English translation of *Memories, Dreams, Reflections*, Jung goes on to say that, at this stage, his understanding of *Faust* was still only "provisional," and that he found four aspects of Goethe's drama problematic: the solution of the work in the final scene; the playful underestimation of Mephistopheles; the ruthless arrogance of Faust; and, in particular, the murder of Philemon and Baucis [ETG, 92]. This final point is one to which we shall return.)

In his chapter on Jung's student years, *Faust* serves as the benchmark against which to measure the impact of another great work in the tradition of the German epic of transformation, Nietzsche's *Thus Spoke Zarathustra*. Jung describes his reading of *Zarathustra* as a "tremendous experience," and in this respect comparable to his reading of *Faust*: If Zarathustra had been Nietzsche's Faust (and, in this sense, his No. 2 Personality), now Jung's Personality No. 2 corresponded to Zarathustra (MDR, 123). Yet there was a crucial difference: Although Faust "did not deserve his initiation into the great mysteries" (*die Einweihung in die großen Mysterien*), nevertheless the work concluded with "the greatest initiation at the end" (*die große Einweihung am Schluss*), and in this sense, *Faust* had "opened a door" for Jung (MDR, 78 and 124). By contrast, Nietzsche had spoken carelessly about his *arrheton* (the term for the "unspeakable" in the ancient Greek mystery cults); had "fallen into the mystery' — *das Mysterium*, the same term used by Jung in his *Red Book* — "and into the unspeakable [*das Nichtzusagende*]"; and so *Zarathustra* had "slammed a door shut" for Jung (MDR, 123-124).

Thus, Jung's autobiographical reminiscences as recorded in *Memories, Dreams, Reflections,* confirm the significance for him of Goethe's *Faust* as a schoolchild and as a student. (Now the original protocols for *Memories, Dreams, Reflections* have been published, it is interesting to see how they confirm this point.)[1] Another indicator of this importance is that one of Jung's most telling remarks about *Faust* is made in the context of his account in the chapter "Confrontation with the Unconscious" of how *The Black Books* and *The Red Book* came to be written. On this account, on the night of 12 November 1913, Jung began to record a series of fantasies in notebooks bound in dark leather that he subsequently elaborated and transferred to a large folio manuscript bound in red leather, where he embellished them with illustrations. Jung conceived of this work, which he apostrophized as the "book of my most difficult experiments" (BB 2, 171), as an exercise in "go[ing] down cleansed into [the soul's] depths" and in "persist[ing] in divine astonishment" (*verharren in göttlicher Fassungslosigkeit*) (BB 2, 171).

As Jung himself observes (and as his critics and detractors would agree), it was "ironic" that he, a psychiatrist, should have encountered at "almost every step" of this experiment "the same psychic material which is the stuff of psychosis and is found in the insane" (MDR, 213). Yet for all the "immediacy of this experience" (BB 2, 171), Jung also came to understand that "this world of unconscious images" is also "the matrix of a mythopœic fantasy, which has disappeared from our rational age" (MDR, 213) — and is also the source of the tradition of which Wolfram's *Parzival*, Goethe's *Faust*, and Nietzsche's *Zarathustra* are part. As if echoing the words of the Lord in *Faust I*, *Es irrt der Mensch, so lang er strebt*, "Whilst still man strives, still must he stray" (l. 317), Jung describes the "uncertain path that leads into the depths of the unconscious" as "a path of error [*Irrtum*], ambiguity,

---

[1] See C.G. Jung and Aniela Jaffé, *Jung's Life and Work: Interviews for "Memories, Dreams, Reflections" with Aniela Jaffé*, ed. Sonu Shamdasani with Thomas Fischer, trans. Heather McCartney and John Peck (Princeton, NJ, and Oxford: Princeton University Press, 2025).

and misunderstanding," and embarking on this path as "a risky experiment or a questionable adventure" (an *Abenteuer* or, as Wolfram would say, an *aventiure*). In fact, at this point Jung cites these lines from *Faust I*, *Vermesse dich, die Pforten aufzureißen*, / *Vor denen jeder gern vorüberschleicht*, "Yes, let me dare those gates to fling asunder / Which every man would fain go slinking by!" (ll. 710-711), referring to Faust's words when, in the opening "Night" scene, he is in despair and contemplating suicide. What Jung is surely saying here is that *The Red Book* was a matter of life and death, but he is doing so in a way that is mediated by Goethe's *Faust*, and by implication *this* work is a matter of life and death as well.

Jung goes on to insist that *Faust II* itself is *"more than* a literary exercise" (MDR, 213; my emphasis), which is something that so few literary critics seem prepared to concede. Indeed, it is not only "more than a literary exercise," for Jung it is "a link in the *aurea catena* [i.e., the golden chain],"[2] or the Western tradition of alchemy or Hermetic philosophy — a chain that leads from the beginnings of philosophical alchemy and Gnosticism down to Nietzsche's *Zarathustra*, and which is said to be "mostly unpopular, ambiguous, and dangerous" — because it is "a voyage of discovery to the other pole of the world" (MDR, 213-214). In so writing, Jung is not only placing himself in what Peter Kingsley has described as an "unbroken lineage linking and connecting the ancient Gnostics

---

[2] On the "golden chain" or *aurea catena*, see Pierre Lévêque, *Aurea catena Homeri: Une étude sur l'allégorie grecque* (Paris: Les Belles Lettres, 1959). For his part, Jung also refers to this chain in CW 12 §148, n. 24 and in CW 14 §344. In his letter to Rudolf Bernoulli of 5 October 1944, Jung notes that the *aurea catena* of which Hermeticism speaks "does not run through schools and conscious tradition but through the unconscious" and that Hermeticism is "not something you choose, it is destiny" (L1, 351). As Peter Kingsley observes, this image of the golden chain was transmitted from classical Greek antiquity into medieval Western alchemy *and* into the Sufi tradition — "where, as the *silsilat adh-dhahab*, it came to play a crucial role for the Naqshbandi Sufi lineage in particular" (Peter Kingsley, *Catafalque: Carl Jung and the End of Humanity*, 2 vols (London: Catafalque Press, 2018), vol. 2, p. 586).

to our modern world: often hidden, sometimes persecuted, always to some degree or other submerged,"[3] but also highlighting the epochal significance within this tradition of such works as Goethe's *Faust* and Nietzsche's *Zarathustra* as well.

In the following chapter, suggestively (and alchemistically) titled "The Work," Jung elaborates on this reading of *Faust*: one which sees it, not as slavishly reproducing the different stages of the alchemical opus, but as emerging from the same tradition as philosophical alchemy. In this sense, Jung can regard his *own* work of alchemy as a sign of his "inner relation" to Goethe (MDR, 232). For Goethe's "secret" is said to be that he was "gripped" (*ergriffen*) by "the process of archetypal transformation [*Wandlung*] which runs through the centuries" (MDR, 209-210). Consequently, he regarded *Faust* as his *opus magnum* or *divinum*, describing it (some 70 or so times between in his diary entries for 11 February 1826 and for 22 July 1831) as his *Hauptgeschäft* (or "main business"),[4] and living within the framework of this drama. Jung emphasizes how one notices "in an impressive way" that there was "a living substance alive and active within him, a suprapersonal process, the great dream of the *mundus archetypus*" (MDR, 232), alluding to an idea that can be traced back to Gerhard Dorn (c. 1530-1584) in his *Physica Hermetis Trismegisti*: namely, that in the beginning God created *one* world, or *unus mundus* (CW 14 §659-§663).[5]

---

[3] Kingsley, *Catafalque*, vol. 1, p. 187.
[4] For a full list of passages, see the "Dokumente zur Entstehungsgeschichte" on the Faust Edition website, available online HTTP: <https://www.faustedition.net/archive_testimonies>. Accessed 25 May 2024.
[5] See Gerhard Dorn, "Physica Hermetis Trismegisti," in *Theatrum Chemicum*, vol. 1, ed. Lazarus Zetzner (Oberursel: Lazarus Zetzner, 1602): "In a way not unlike that in which God in the beginning created one world by meditation alone, so likewise he created one world, from which all things came into being by adaptation" (pp. 362-363); "Also, as there is only one God and not many, so he willed at first in his mind to create from nothing one world, and then to bring it about that all things which he created should be contained in it, that God in all things might be one" (p. 368); and "Beneath this spiritual and corporeal binarius lieth hid a third thing, which is the bond of holy matrimony. This same is the medium enduring until now in all

This idea which Dorn first proposed, that is, that behind the multiplicity of things lies a primordial unity, and which became Goethe's great dream, was the one and the same dream by which Jung, too, was gripped (*ergriffen*). From his 11th year (that is, the year when he first read *Faust*?) Jung began a project that permeated and held together his life through "one work and one goal," namely — to "penetrate into the secret of the personality" (*in das Geheimnis der Persönlichkeit einzudringen*) (MDR, 232). If an early visual-cum-textual part of this project was the experiment in *The Black Books* that led to *The Red Book*, then a later and external part of it was the architectural experiment of the Tower that Jung constructed in Bollingen. (That these two aspects are reciprocally related can be seen if one reads the section in the chapter "The Magician" in *Liber Secundus* about the construction, aided by the Cabiri, of a tower.)

The Tower was built in various stages, and it includes various sculptures and inscriptions; one could write a study about Jung's tower, and some have done just this.[6] Jung describes the Tower as a "place of maturation," resembling "a maternal womb, or a maternal shape [*Gestalt*]" in which Jung became — in Nietzschean terms (and the subtitle of *Ecce Homo*) — who he really was (*wie man wird, was man ist*). It is as if, in the form of his Tower, Jung was somehow being "reborn in stone": The Tower represents "the realization of something previously intuited," it is "a representation of individuation"; in a striking phrase, the Tower is "a memorial

---

things, partaking of both their extremes, without which it cannot be at all, nor they without this medium be what they are, one thing out of three" (p. 371). For further discussion of Dorn, see Frank Geiner, "Dorn," in Wouter J. Hanegraaff et al. (eds), *Dictionary of Gnosis & Western Esotericism* (Leiden and Boston: Brill, 2006), pp. 320-321; and Zoë Van Cauwenberg, *Illustrious Providence and the Supernatural Art: A Renaissance Alchemist and his Pursuit of Salvation*, MA thesis, University of Gent, 2016-2017.

[6] See Chapter 5, "Carl Gustav Jung: The Tower of the Psyche," in Theodore Ziolkowski, *The View from the Tower: Origins of an Antimodernist Image* (Princeton, NJ: Princeton University Press, 1988), pp. 131-148, and David Rosen, *The Tao of Jung: The Way of Integrity* (New York: Viking Arkana, 1996).

aere perennius" (MDR, 252), alluding to one of the representative writers of the age of Augustus, the Roman lyric poet called Quintus Horatius Flaccus (65-27 B.C.E.), known as Horace, one of whose *Odes* (Book 3, §30) opens with these lines about the monument that he as a poet has left:

> *Exegi monumenum aere perennius*
> *Regalique situ pyramidum altius,*
> *Qupd non imber edax, non Aquilo impotens*
> *Possit diruere aut innumerabilis*
> *Annorum series et fuga temporum.*

> I have finished a monument more lasting than bronze,
> more lofty than the regal structure of the pyramids,
> one which neither corroding rain nor the ungovernable
> North Wind
> can ever destroy, nor the countless
> series of the years, nor the flight of time.[7]

Thus, Horace concluded the first three books of his *Carmina* with the hope that he had secured immortal renown as the man who had spun the "Aeolian song" of Sappho and Alcaeus into Latin poetry. Nietzsche liked this phrase, *aere perennius*, that is, more lasting than bronze or brass,[8] so much that, in the chapter of *Twilight of the Idols* titled "What I Owe to the Ancients," he had borrowed it and applied it to himself, declaring: "In my writings, up to my Zarathustra, a very strenuous ambition to attain the *Roman* style, the '*aere perennius*' in style will be recognised" (§1).

---

[7] Horace, *Odes and Epodes*, ed. and trans. Niall Rudd (Cambridge, MA: Harvard University Press, 2004), pp. 216-217.

[8] Cf. *Daybreak* §71, titled "The Christian revenge on Rome." For further discussion of this phrase in the context of Nietzsche's encomium of Imperial Rome, see Paul Bishop, *Nietzsche's "The Anti-Christ": A Critical Introduction and Guide* (Edinburgh: Edinburgh University Press, 2022), pp. 33-34 and 171-175.

Over the gate to his Tower, Jung carved the following inscription, *Philemonis Sacrum — Fausti Poenitentia* ("Philemon's shrine — Faust's repentance"). (Originally this inscription was placed over the gate to the original tower; as the building expanded over time, however, it was removed and placed over the entrance to the second tower on the site.)[9] But what does it mean? In part, we find the answer to this in *Memories, Dreams, Reflections* in the chapter on the Tower, where Jung refers to his earlier discussion of his sense of a split in his personality; of his sense that, as Faust says to Wagner in "Before the Gate," "Two souls, alas! within my breast abide" (l. 1112). In so saying, Faust had analyzed the problem but had not explained the cause of the dichotomy; nevertheless, this insight seemed to apply directly to Jung (MDR, 261). But not *just* to Jung — for Goethe's "strange heroic myth" is said to have applied on a collective level as well, inasmuch as it "prophetically predicted the fate of the Germans" (MDR, 261). *Because* it was collective, Jung also felt *personally* implicated (even though he was Swiss rather than German), and so when Faust, as a result of his "hybris and inflation," brought about the murder of Philemon and Baucis, Jung himself felt "guilty" — as if he, too, had "been involved in the past with the murder of the old couple" (MDR, 261). Jung himself describes this as a "strange idea" (*diese sonderbare Idee*), but it was an idea that "terrified" (*erschreckte*) him, and that had a practical consequence: for Jung believed it was now *his* responsibility to "atone for this guilt" or to "prevent its recurrence" (MDR, 261). In a way this idea is even stranger: After all, what would it mean to atone for a crime committed against two fictional characters?

Jung himself seems to have sensed this strangeness, for he refers to his "false conclusion" — a conclusion that nevertheless gives him the opportunity to repeat the "annoying legend" about his grandfather having been an illegitimate child of Goethe's!

---

[9] See Jaffé's note in MDR, 262-263.

Nowadays we might see Jung's claims in terms of a contribution to *psychogénéalogie*, that is, the thesis that what our ancestors experienced can influence us, and that our anxieties, weakness, and illnesses are not a consequence of what we have done but of what our ancestors did. (For a moment, Jung himself toys with the possibility of karma, even if he rejects the idea of reincarnation.) Instead, Jung proposes a twofold explanation: First, thanks to the notion of the unconscious, he can gain a "psychological" understanding of his reactions; but second, as evidence for the fact that "the future is unconsciously prepared long in advance and therefore can be predicted by clairvoyants long before it happens" (MDR, 262). When on 18 January 1871, Wilhelm I of Prussia was proclaimed Kaiser Wilhelm in the Hall of Mirrors in the Palace of Versailles, Jacob Burckhardt is said to have declared, "This is the doom of Germany" (*Das ist der Untergang Deutschlands*)! Looking back at his youth (that is, around 1893), Jung saw himself as having been "unconsciously caught up" in "this spirit of the age" (*Zeitgeist*) — the "spirit of this age" which is, at the opening of *The Red Book*, contrasted to the "spirit of the depths" (RB, 119-120). This spirit is said to have been symbolized by the "archetypes" of Wagner, knocking at the door; and by Nietzsche's "Dionysian experience" (or, more accurately, his experience of Wotan). And the hubris of the Wilhelmine era, Jung argues, alienated the rest of Europe from Germany and "prepared the way for the catastrophe of 1914," that is, the First World War (MDR, 262).

After being placed in Jung's personal and Germany's political context, Goethe's *Faust* now acquires a third level of significance that one could describe as metaphysical: On the one hand, it had "struck a chord" in him and "pierced" him "through" in a way that he could not but understand as "personal," thus echoing Goethe's own words in *Dichtung und Wahrheit* (Part Two, Book 10) about the puppet play through which he had come to know the figure and story of Faust — "The biography of the former had seized my inmost heart. The figure of a rough, well-meaning self-helper, in a wild anarchical time, awakened my deepest sympathy. The significant puppet-show fable of the latter resounded and vibrated many-toned within me. I had also wandered about in all sorts of science, and had early enough been led to see its vanity. I had, moreover, tried all sorts of ways in real life, and had always returned more unsatisfied and troubled. Now, these things, as well as many others, I carried about with me, and delighted myself with them during my solitary hours, but without writing any thing down."[10] (At the same time, the image of being "pierced through" recalls *Parzival* and Sigune's explanation of its hero's name:

> "Thou art *Parzival*," she cried,
> And thy name it shall mean "*to pierce thro'*," for thy
> mother's faithful heart
> With furrow of grief was riven when she from her lord must
> part [...]."
> (§140, ll. 16-20; vol. 1, p. 79)

And in *The Red Book*, Jung warns the mother who "gives birth to [...] a wounded and pain-stricken God" that a sword will "pierce her soul" (RB, 309; cf. Luke 2:35), tells his soul that she is "piercing" him with "unbearable tension" (RB, 382); and, after identifying with Odin, who was pierced by a spear and hung from Yggdrasil, cries out to the "mute son of the earth" to which his soul gives birth, "Off with you, you pierce me with paralyzing force!" [RB, 443 and 448].)

On the other hand, from Jung's point of view, *Faust* also touched on a fundamental problem: namely, the "problem of the opposites of good and evil, of spirit and matter, of light and

---

[10] Goethe, *Autobiography of Johann Wolfgang von Goethe (Dichtung und Wahrheit)*, trans. John Oxenford (New York: Horizon Press, 1969), vol. 2, book 10, p. 20.

darkness" (MDR, 262). These opposites were personified in the figures of Faust, the "inept and clueless philosopher," and his "uncanny shadow," that is, Mephistopheles, who — despite his "negating nature" (cf. *Ich bin der Geist, der stets verneint* [l. 1338]) — represents the "true spirit of life [*Lebensgeist*]" as opposed to the "desiccated scholar, who just escapes suicide" (cf. *die Pforten* [...], *Vor denen jeder gern vorüberschleicht* [ll. 710-711]) (MDR, 262). At the same time, Jung gives us the greatest possible insight into himself (as well as paying the greatest possible compliment to Goethe's work) when he declares that, in *Faust*, he found that his own "inner contradictions" appeared "in dramatised form" (*dramatisiert*), and that Goethe had provided him with a template for his own conflicts *and their solutions* (MDR, 262). The division into two between Faust and Mephisto came together into a single person — in other words, in Jung himself! (No wonder, then, that the more we read Goethe, the more we understand Jung.)

Jung goes on to make an important structural point about the work, seeing it as governed by a series of moments of peripeteia (cf. περιπέτεια, meaning a "sudden change" or "reversal of fortune"). (In his *Poetics*, Aristotle defines peripeteia as "a change by which the action veers round to its opposite, subject always to our rule of probability or necessity," adding that "the finest form of Discovery is one attended by Peripeteia, like that which goes with the Discovery in Oedipus" [*Poetics*, 1452a].)[11] "All the peripeties of the drama," Jung explains, seemed to relate to him and evoked a response: sometimes approval, other times disagreement. In other words, Jung did not just read *Faust*: He lived *Faust*. No moment of resolution (*Lösung*) was a matter of indifference, and the work as a whole as well as in its parts elicited a response from him. In fact, Jung decides to place his own project entirely under the sign of *Faust*, claiming

---

[11] Aristotle, *On the Art of Poetry*, trans. Ingram Bywater (Oxford: Clarendon Press, 1920), §11 (pp. 46-48).

that later he deliberately chose to link his work to what Faust had ignored: "respect for the eternal human rights, recognition of the ancient, and the continuity of culture and intellectual history" (*die Respektierung der ewigen Menschenrechte, die Anerkennung des Alten und die Kontinuität der Kultur und der Geistesgeschichte*) (MDR, 262).

We said that we could find part of the answer to the meaning of the strange inscription, *Philemonis Sacrum – Fausti Poenitentia* ("Philemon's shrine — Faust's repentance"), in these comments in *Memories, Dreams, Reflections*. Another part can be found in a letter he wrote to Paul Schmitt (1900-1953), the Swiss publisher and journalist, dated 5 January 1942. Unfortunately, we do not have the earlier letter that Schmitt wrote to Jung, because he refers to the "welcome news" from Schmitt that "the pebbles ejected by the volcano on whose edge" Jung was sitting had "landed somewhere" and caused "an echo" (L1, 309).[12] And Jung says that Schmitt has "hit the mark absolutely" and that "all of a sudden and with terror" it has become clear to him that he (i.e., Jung) has "taken over *Faust as my heritage*, and moreover as the advocate and avenger of Philemon and Baucis" (L1, 309). Unlike Faust "the superman," Philemon and Baucis (as we see them in *Faust II*) are "the hosts of the gods in a ruthless and godforsaken age" (L1, 309). While this is a "personal matter" between Jung and Goethe, his ancestor (*proavus*), it is also a *political* one: Jung declares — and one must remember that he is writing this in 1942 — that it is "unavoidable to give an *answer* to Faust," and that this answer takes two forms. For one, Jung writes that we must "continue to bear the terrible German problem that is devastating Europe"; for another, we must "pull down into our world some of the Faustian happenings in the Beyond, for instance the benign activity of Pater Profundus" (L1,

---

[12] On the image of the volcano crater in Jung, see Kingsley, *Catafalque*, pp. 197, 204-205, 270-271, 294, 584, 614, and 782 (discussed further in Volume 4 in this series).

310), a figure identified by some critics as Bernard of Clairvaux, whose hymn in the concluding scene of *Faust II* includes the lines, "E'en so Almighty Love, unfailing, / Doth fashion all and cherish all" (ll. 11872-11873). He then asks a very good question, expressing his curiosity — "I would give the earth to know," he says — as to whether Goethe himself knew why he called the two old people Philemon and Baucis (L1, 310). And he attempts a kind of philological explanation, speculating that Faust "sinned from the beginning against these first parents (φιλία and Baubo)", i.e. φιλία or *philía* as the highest form of love (as opposed to *storgē* [στοργή], *agápē* [ἀγάπη], and *érōs* [ἔρως]), and Βαυβώ, the goddess of mirth and sexual bawdiness, who lifted her skirts to Demeter and revealed her private parts, and thus the personification of the lowest form of love.[13] Thus Faust's "sin," Jung hints, lies in having rejected love in *all* its forms, from *philía* to *érōs* (or from Helena to Gretchen). Is this a credible explanation? Perhaps Jung is right when he says that

---

[13] Old Baubo is referred to in the Walpurgis Night scene of *Faust*, Part One (ll. 3962-3967) (see Chapter 1 above, p. 51) as well as in Nietzsche's *The Gay Science* (GS Preface §4). In his *Protreptikos* Clement of Alexandria relates the following about Baubo: "[...] Demeter, wandering through Eleusis, which is a part of Attica, in search of her daughter the Maiden, becomes exhausted and sits down at a well in deep distress. This display of grief is forbidden, up to the present day, to those who are initiated, lest the worshippers should seem to imitate the goddess in her sorrow. [...] Baubo, having received Demeter as a guest, offers her a draught of wine and meal. She declines to take it, being unwilling to drink on account of her mourning. Baubo is deeply hurt, thinking she has been slighted, and thereupon uncovers her secret parts and exhibits them to the goddess. Demeter is pleased at the sight, and now at last receives the draught, — delighted with the spectacle! These are the secret mysteries of the Athenians! These are also the subjects of Orpheus' poems. I will quote you the very lines of Orpheus, in order that you may have the originator of the mysteries as witness of their shamelessness: "This said, she drew aside her robes, and showed / A sight of shame; child Iacchus was there, / And laughing, plunged his hand below her breasts. / Then smiled the goddess, in her heart she smiled, / And drank the draught from out the glancing cup" (*Exhortation to the Greeks*, Chapter 2; in *The Exhortation to the Greeks; The Rich Man's Salvation; and the Fragment of an Address entitled To the Newly Baptized*, trans. G.W. Butterworth (Cambridge, MA, and London: Harvard University Press; Heinemann, 1960), pp. 1-263 [pp. 41-43]). For further discussion, see Monika Gsell, *Die Bedeutung der Baubo: Kulturgeschichtliche Studien zur Repräsentation des weiblichen Genitales* (Frankfurt am Main: Stroemfeld Verlag, 2001).

one must have "one foot in the grave [...] before one understands this secret" (L1, 310).

And yet there is another question one must ask. There is only one Baucis, that is, the female character in the Greek legend of how Zeus and Hermes (or Jupiter and Mercury) visited the earth and could only find hospitality from an old couple; a tale told by Ovid in his *Metamorphoses* that served Goethe as a source for Act V of *Faust II*. But which Philemon are we talking about? For Philemon is a surprisingly common name:

- Philemon, an Athenian poet and playwright of the Attic New Comedy (c. 300 B.C.E.)
- Philemon the Younger, a Attic comedy writer of the third century B.C.E.
- Philemon, another Attic comedy writer of the second century B.C.E.
- Philemon, an Attic lexicographer of around 300 B.C.E.
- Philemon, an ancient Greek geographer of the first century C.E.
- Philemon, an Atticist and grammarian of around c. 200 C.E.
- and Philemon, a Latin grammarian of the first half of the third century C.E.[14]

not forgetting:

- Philemon, the recipient of St. Paul's Epistle to Philemon in the New Testament.

And there is:

- Philemon, the husband of Baucis, in Ovid's tale of the perils of inhospitality and the benefits of offering hospitality (*xenia*).

---

[14] Tim Junk, Heinz-Günther Nesselrath, Stephanos Matthaios, Hans Armin Gärtner, Gregor Damschen, and Paolo Gatti, [entries titled] "Philemon," in Hubert Cancik and Helmuth Schneider, Christine F. Salazar, Manfred Landfester, and Francis G. Gentry (eds), *Brill's New Pauly Online* (2006). Available online HTTP <http://dx.doi.org/10.1163/1574-9347_bnp_e919770>. Consulted online 24 June 2021.

But of course, there is also:

- Philemon, the fantasy figure who arose out of the Elijah figure in Jung's *Red Book*.

This Philemon is described by Jung as "a pagan" who brought with him "an Egypto-Gnostic-Hellenistic atmosphere, a really Gnostic hue" (cited BB 1, 34; cf. MDR, 207).

In *Memories, Dreams, Reflections*, Jung recollects the first epiphany of Philemon in a dream: Against a blue sky and the blue water of the sea, a winged being in the shape of an old man with the horns of a bull suddenly appeared from the right. He had the wings of a kingfisher and, in his hand, a bunch of four keys, one of which was held as if it were about to open a lock (MDR, 207). In *The Red Book*, the first appearance of Philemon is less dramatic but far more suggestive. At the end of the chapter titled "The Way of the Cross" in *Liber Secundus*, Jung decides to go off to "a far country, where a great magician lived," of whose reputation Jung had heard (RB, 395). And at the beginning of the next chapter, "The Magician," Jung discovers "after a long search" where ΦΙΛΗΜΩΝ the magician lives with his wife, ΒΑΥΚΙΣ — in a small house in the country with, at the front, a large bed of tulips. (Why tulips? Perhaps because tulips often symbolize love and affection; or because the tulip appears on a number of the Major Arcana cards of Oswald Wirth's deck of Tarot cards, including the Magician; or because, in Goethe's story, Philemon's house has to be destroyed to make way for Faust's land reclamation scheme, similar to land drainage schemes in the Netherlands, and (in the words of the song) tulips come "from Amsterdam"…?)

In *The Red Book*, ΦΙΛΗΜΩΝ cuts a frail figure: The watering can shakes in his hand when he goes to water the tulips, he can still murmur a few spells in exchange for cash-in-hand, but it is uncertain if he really understands their meaning, and his desire and creative drive have expired. He is, like the Magician in Nietzsche's *Zarathustra*, "retired from service" (*außer Dienst*; or here: *vom*

Geschäft zurückgezogen). In a way, he is like an even more decrepit version of Faust; except that he is enjoying "his well-earned rest" and, of course, that he is living with his wife. As ΦΙΛΗΜΩΝ and ΒΑΥΚΙΣ water their bed of tulips and "tell each other about the flowers that have newly appeared," so their days "fade into a pale, wavering mixture of light and dark, little frightened of the darkness of what is to come" (RB, 396).

So, there are really three Philemons:

- Jung's Philemon, a retired magician; based on the figure of
- Goethe's Philemon, the old man living with Baucis whom Faust murders; based on the figure of
- Ovid's Philemon, the hospitable husband of the equally hospitable Baucis in *Metamorphoses*.

Except that Goethe's Philemon has really nothing to do with the legendary figure who offers hospitality to the gods, as Goethe told Eckermann on 6 June 1831: "My Philemon and Baucis [...] have nothing to do with that renowned ancient couple, and the tradition connected with them. I gave this couple the names merely to elevate the characters. The persons and relations are similar, and hence the use of the names has a good effect."[15] As Jung observed in his letter to Alice Raphael of 7 June 1955, we can read this response as "a typical Goethean answer to Eckermann!" — typical, that is, inasmuch as it shows us Goethe "trying to conceal his vestiges."[16] And Jung hinted at any etymological interpretation of the name Philemon as derived from Φιλημα, i.e. "kiss" (see below, pp. 213-214).

Trying to disentangle the relation between these various Philemon-figures is essential to understanding Jung's mysterious

---

[15] Johann Peter Eckermann, *Conversations of Goethe*, ed. J.K. Moorhead, trans. John Oxenford [1830] (New York: Da Capo Press, 1998), p. 413.
[16] See Jung's letter to Alice of Raphael of 7 June 1955 (published in Sonu Shamdasani, "Who is Jung's Philemon? An Unpublished Letter to Alice Raphael," *Jung History*, vol. 2, no. 2 (Fall 2007), 5-7).

inscription in his Tower at Bollingen. In a letter of 2 January 1928 to Count Hermann von Keyserling (1880-1946), Jung told his correspondent how he had been "compelled to respect Nietzsche's *amor fati*" until he had "had his fill of it" (L1, 49). Given the date of this letter, that is, in the same year as Jung received from Richard Wilhelm a copy of *The Secret of the Golden Flower*, became interested in alchemy, and ceased working on *The Red Book*, it seems possible to read this reference to *amor fati* as an allusion to Jung's engagement in *The Red Book* with the "fate" or "necessity" of the archetypal world. At this point, Jung told Keyserling, he began his work on the Tower at Bollingen and carved the inscription, *Philemonis Sacrum — Fausti Poenitentia*, and "dis-identified" (*»des-identifizierte«*) himself from god (*von dem lieben Gott*): It was, he added, a "certainly very unholy act [*unheilige Handlungsweise*]" but one that he had never regretted (L1, 49). This description of the process undertaken or undergone by Jung in *The Red Book* as "dis-identification" is (as we shall see in Volume 4 in this series) a useful one for understanding Jung's ambitions in that work.

Then again, writing over a decade later after his letter to Schmitt, Jung referred in a letter of 7 June 1955 to Goethe's remarks to Eckermann about Philemon and Baucis. (His correspondent on this occasion was none other than Alice Raphael, herself a translator of *Faust* and the author of *Goethe and the Philosophers' Stone*.) Jung described these comments as "a typically Goethean answer!", an attempt on Goethe's part to "conceal his vestiges" (whatever that is supposed to mean). For his part, Jung gestures toward an etymological explanation of the episode: on the one hand, "*Philemon* (Φιλημα = kiss), the loving one, the simple old loving couple, close to the earth and aware of the gods," and thus "the complete opposite to" — on the other hand — "the Superman Faust, the product of the devil." And then Jung makes a personal confession, telling Raphael about a "hidden inscription" in his Tower at Bollingen, *Philemonis*

Sacrum — *Fausti Poenitentia*, and he offers two crucial clues as to its meaning. First, he recounts how, when he encountered the archetype of the Wise Old Man, he "called himself *Philemon*"; in other words, Jung's Philemon appropriates his name from Goethe's Philemon, who in turn appropriates his name from Ovid's (even though he has "nothing to do" with one of "renowned ancient couple"). And second, in comparison with a range of alchemical couples — Zosimos and his female student Theosebeia, Nicolas Flamel (1330-1418) and his wife, Perenelle Flamel (1320-1397), Thomas South and his daughter Mary Anne Atwood (née South) (1817-1910), and ultimately the pair of Sol and Luna in the *Mutus Liber*) — Jung suggests that Philemon and Baucis can be understood in an alchemical sense as representing "the *artifex* or *vir sapiens* and the *soror mystica*" (or, in autobiographical terms, Jung himself and Toni Wolff) (cited in RB, 396).[17]

The meaning of the inscription, *Philemonis Sacrum – Fausti Poenitentia* ("Philemon's shrine — Faust's repentance"), is thus remarkably complicated, involving as it does the dual (or even triple) significance of Philemon: as (1) the archetypal figure encountered by Jung and represented in *The Red Book*; and (2) the legendary figure depicted by Goethe; but (3) borrowed in terms of name (although not in terms of substance) from Ovid. So much for the figure to whom the Tower as a shrine is dedicated; who is the repentant Faust? Given all the remarks that Jung makes about identifying with Faust (both in a personal and in a collective sense, that is, as identifying with the Germans), could one reasonably conclude that the figure who is repentant is surely Jung himself — Jung as the *artifex* or *vir sapiens*?

In his *Catafalque* (2018), Peter Kingsley attributes a central significance to this "hidden inscription" in the Tower at Bollingen. For Kingsley, it reveals the true nature of Jung's project and, indeed,

---

[17] Cf. CW 14 §181, fn. 317; cf. Shamdasani, "Who Is Jung's Philemon?", pp. 5-7.

his status. In relation to the function of the Tower as "a sacred place for his inner teacher," Kingsley notes how Jung himself associated the notion of the shrine or sanctuary with the notion of secrecy in his letter to Bernhard Baur-Celio (1895-1981) of 30 January 1934. Now Baur-Celio, a teacher of French and Italian in Küsnacht, had asked Jung whether he possessed any "secret knowledge" not contained in his writings (L1, 140, fn). He received the intriguing response that Jung had had "experiences which are, so to speak, 'ineffable,' 'secret' because they can never be told properly and because nobody can understand them"; indeed, Jung was not even sure if he had understood them himself (L1, 140-141)! He went to describe these experiences as "dangerous," "catastrophic," and "taboo-ed": dangerous, because 99% of people would declare Jung to be mad if they heard such things; catastrophic, because the prejudices caused by telling them might block the way to "a living and wondrous secret" (*zu einem lebendig-wunderbaren Geheimnis*) for other people; and "taboo-ed," because they are an ἄδυτον (*adyton*, that is, something "not to be entered," an "innermost sanctuary or shrine," often an area where the cult image of the deity was kept), protectively surrounded by δεισιδαιμονία (*deisidaimonía*, i.e., "fearing or reverencing the divine") — the latter being correctly described by Goethe in the conclusion to *Faust II* in the words of the Chorus and Echo:

Shelters the deepest cave;	*Höhle, die tiefste, schützt.*
Softly the lions, dumb-	*Löwen, sie schleichen stumm-*
Friendly about us come,	*Freundlich um uns herum,*
Honour the holy seat,	*Ehren geweihten Ort*
Sanctified love-retreat.	*Heiligen Liebeshort.*

(ll. 11847-11853)

These lines of two-stress dactyls require, Cyrus Hamlin has suggested, "particularly close attention" (485). The assignment of these lines to Chorus and Echo is especially "cryptic," he notes, comparing them to the hymn of the Archangels in the "Prologue in Heaven," the self-presentation of the Earth Spirit, and the spirit chorus that holds Faust in hypnotic fascination in the first Study Scene in Part One; and to the chorus of nature spirits that accompanies Ariel in the opening "Charming Landscape" scene and the songs of the Sirens in the "Classical Walpurgis Night" in Part Two (485). In them, Hamlin suggests, Goethe "give[s] voice to nature itself" — "powers of the spirit express the activity that gives them identity in a language that perfectly fuses sign and signified" (485). Both the rhythm and the syntax of these lines defy translation: in the original, each of the first three lines (not included in the passage quoted above), a single bisyllabic noun, referencing a natural object, is followed by a phrase constructed from an appositional pronoun and a predicate (defining the activity of the named object) (485). In his translation, Latham replaces the opening noun with a verb but captures the parallel structure in these three lines, thus: *Waldung, sie schwankt heran* ("Billows the forest one"), / *Steine, sie lasten dran* ("Lean them the cliffs thereon"), / *Wurzeln, sie klammen an / Stamm dicht an Stamm hinan* ("Grapple the roots thereon, / Trunk crowding trunk open") (ll. 11844-11847). In this way, the sense of the dactylic meter disappears, as the caesura after the second syllable breaks the rhythm of the line (485).

In the remaining lines of the passage (which *are* quoted above by Jung), the pattern of bisyllabic nouns continues: *Woge* ("wave"), *Höhle* ("cave"), and *Löwen* ("lions), although the appositional pronoun (*sie*, i.e., "they") now occurs only in the case of the lions. Where in the first four lines we find adverbs based on –*an* and designating directionality of some kind, i.e., *heran, dran, an, hinan*, now we find more varied, active verbs, i.e., *spritzen* ("gush up") and *schützen* ("shelter"), and the lions are metrically foregrounded further by the "bold" enjambment of double-adverbial construction, viz., *stumm- / Freundlich* (rendered by Latham as "dumb- / Friendly") (486). Furthermore, the statement about the lions introduces a different directional adverb, *herum* (or "around"), adding a prepositional phrase and the first-person plural pronoun (*um uns*, or "around us"). In this way, the reader becomes included in this plurality: a plurality of lions, to be sure, and perhaps also the plurality of *Pater* figures in the concluding scene of *Faust II*. The concluding couplet, in which the verb *ehren* ("to honor") has a double accusative as its direct object, i.e., *geweihten Ort / Heiligen Liebesort* ("the holy seat, / Sanctified love-retreat"), appears directed to these lions, and constitutes a "remarkable formulation of blessing, consecration, and love"; in Hamlin's estimation, this Chorus and Echo is "just as remarkable — indeed, astonishing — a poetic achievement as the concluding Chorus Mysticus," yet it "has not received much attention from critics" (486). Nevertheless, it did not, it seems, escape the attention of Jung: Yet again, we see how Jung turns to Goethe to express something that it is of the utmost significance to him — applying a secular text to something that is sacred, and thereby sacralizing Goethe's text in turn.

(In his commentary, Albert G. Latham suggests another possible visual intertext for the lines, "Softly the lions, dumb- / Friendly about us come," again from a fresco in the Campo Santo of Pisa: namely, the *Anchorites in the Thebaïa*, with its depiction of huge cliffs on the banks of the Nile, to which trees cling with their roots, while hermits sit in huts and caves, some lions dig a grave for a dead anchorite, and other lion guard the abodes of the hermits (406-407).[18] And Goethe's collection of engravings included one representing St. Jerome in the Wilderness, with his signature lion. As a biblical source informing these two works, Latham suggests the famous prophecy of Isaiah about the coming judgment, in which "the wolf and the lamb shall feed together, the lion and the ox shall eat straw" [Isaiah 65:24].)

---

[18] For images, see "The Frescoes by Buonamico Burlamacco at the Campo Santo of Pisa"; available online HTTP: <https://www.barnum-review.com/portfolio/the-frescoes-by-buonamico-burlamacco-at-the-campo-santo-of-pisa>. See above, pp. 169 and 173.

Further on in his letter to Baur-Celio, Jung asked whether "anyone can say 'credo' when he stands *amidst* his experience, πιστεύων ὁράματι δεινῷ (i.e., *pistévon orámati deinó*, i.e., *in faith trusting the terrifying apparition*),[19] when he knows just how superfluous 'belief' is, when he more than just 'knows,' when the experience has even pressed him to the wall?" (L1, 141). (In Greek mythology, Deino [δεινῷ] — meaning "dread," or "eddy," "whirlpool" — is one of the Graeae or Phorcydes, hideous sea-hags who were the daughters of the sea-deities Ceto and Phorcys and who shared one eye and one tooth among them; as we know from Mephisto's transformation into Phorcyas in *Faust II*.) Jung's insistence on this experiential dimension is underlined when he goes on to say that the so-called investigation of the unconscious — by which he here means Analytical Psychology — has "discovered the age-old, timeless *way of initiation*," compared with which Freudian psychoanalysis is merely an apotropaic exercise in defending oneself against the "long road" (*lange Straße*), or expressed in terms of the Grail legend — "only a 'knight' dares 'la queste' and the 'aventiure'" (L1, 141).

However grateful the world may be to Freud for his "bastard of a science," Jung believes that "nothing is submerged for ever" (*nichts ist endgültig versunken*),[20] adding that this is "the terrifying discovery everyone makes who has opened that portal" (*das ist die erscheckende Entdeckung eines jeden, der jene Tür geöffnet hat*) — echoing the phrase "Now let me dare to open wide the gate / Past which men's steps have never flinching trod" (*Vermesse dich,*

---

[19] Translated in the German edition of the *Briefe* as "gläubig der erschreckenden Erscheinung vertrauend."

[20] As William Faulkner remarked, "The past is never dead. It's not even past," and this insight informs the remarkable opening paragraph of *Transformations and Symbols of the Libido* (PU §1) (cited below). For discussion of the notion of psychological archaeology, see Paul Bishop, "Digging Jung: Analytical Psychology and Philosophical Archaeology," *History of European Ideas*, vol. 48, no. 7 (2022), 960-979.

die Pforten aufzureißen / Vor denen jeder gern vorüberschleicht)
(ll. 710-711) associated in *Memories, Dreams, Reflections* with
the experiences behind *The Red Book* (MDR, 213). For Jung, it is
not just his *credo* but the "greatest and most incisive experience"
of his life that there is a door, "a highly inconspicuous side-door
on an unsuspicious-looking and easily-overlooked footpath" (*jene
Tür, eine höchst unscheinbare Seitenpforte, auf einen zunächst
unverdächtigen und leicht übersehbaren schmalen Fußpfad*) (L1,
141). This path is "narrow and indistinct [*schmal und undeutlich*]
because only a few have set foot on it," and this path leads to
"the secret of transformation and renewal" (*zum Geheimnis der
Wandlung und Erneuerung*) (L1, 141).

At this point in his letter, Jung pivots away from *Faust*
(and the Chorus and Echo) and from the Grail legend (and its
conceptions of *la queste* and *aventiure*), and toward the Gospel of
Matthew (cited in the Vulgate). The passage in question contains
the famous doctrine of the two ways — to which Goethe alludes in
the "Prelude in the Theater" in Part One (l. 52) — and a warning
about false prophets (Matthew 7:13-15). Here Jung highlights how
the narrow gate and the hard road lead *to life*, that *only a few find
it*, and that the false prophets are *underneath ravening wolves* (L1,
142). Hence, Jung concludes, his preference for saying *scio* ("I
know"), not *credo* ("I believe") — thus anticipating his famous
response to John Freeman in his BBC interview of October 1959,
"I don't need to believe, I know" — because, he adds, he does not
want to "act mysterious [*geheimnisvoll*]." For it would *look* as if he
were acting mysterious, if he were to speak of "a real, living secret
[*einem wirklichen, lebendigen Geheimnis*]," for "one *is* mysterious
[*geheimnisvoll*] if one speaks of a *real* secret [*einem **wirklichen**
Geheimnis*]" (L1, 142).

In this letter to Baur-Celio, we find one of the governing
tropes of *Memories, Dreams, Reflections* and one of Jung's favorite

topics — the notion of the secret.[21] Peter Kingsley draws attention to the way the Latin word *sacrum* itself had strong connotations of something "secret."[22] As Lizette Andrews Fisher points out, the Grail legend is "immediately connected" with the idea of the "secret"; specifically, the "secret" supposedly confided by Christ to Joseph of Arimathea in prison as recounted by Joseph de Borron in *Joseph d'Arimathie* (or the *Metrical Joseph*), as well as in the *Prose Joseph*, in the *Prose Perceval*, and in *La Queste del Saint Graal*.[23] (In so arguing, Fisher takes issue with Jessie Weston's interpretation that opposes the identification of the "secret" of the Grail with that of the Eucharist.) In a sense, the secret that is uncovered by Jung's inscription (and indeed, on Kingsley's account, by Jung's work as a whole) is what — in the chapter of *The Red Book* which follows Jung's descent into Hell and is called "The Sacrificial Murder" — is described as "humankind's complicity in the act of evil" (RB, 323). (This is the conclusion from the shocking episode at the beginning of this chapter, in which the soul of a dead child demands that Jung eat part of the liver from the corpse. Performing this anthropophagic deed is a way of recognizing this complicity — and "bear[ing] witness to this recognition by eating from the bloody sacrificial flesh" [RB, 323].)

Expressed in this way, "complicity in evil" sounds quite abstract, if somewhat disturbing, but in his memorandum to the UNESCO in 1948 Jung explained it in a much more down-to-earth way. "In view of the actual condition of the world," he argued, any intelligent person will admit that there is "something utterly

---

[21] For a definition of what Bertrand Vergely has called the "dialectic of the secret," see the extract from his talk given at I.D.E.E. PSY in Paris on 5 September 2012, quoted in Paul Bishop, *Reading Goethe At Midlife: Ancient Wisdom, German Classicism & Jung*, 2nd edn. (Asheville, NC: Chiron, 2020), pp. xxvi-xxvii.

[22] Kingsley, *Catafalque*, vol. 2, p. 583.

[23] L.A. Fisher, *The Mystic Vision in the Grail Legend and in the "Divine Comedy"* (New York: Columbia University Press, 1917), pp. 63-65; cited in Kingsley, *Catafalque*, vol. 2, p. 583.

wrong with our attitude," yet this statement "rarely ever includes the individual in question" (CW 18 §1396)! It is "a very long step," he shrewdly observed, "from this conviction" — namely, that one's own attitude is "surely right and only needs confirmation and support, but no change" — "to the conclusion: the world is wrong and therefore I am wrong too" (§1396). And even then, Jung acknowledged, "to pronounce such words is easy," but to feel their truth in the marrow of one's bones is "a very different matter" (§1396). Given the constant virtue-signaling of today's social media, one might feel that Jung had a point; and Kingsley indexes this sense of evil to today's "ruthless search for improvement" and the way it turns all of us into "vicious innovators" and "vicious developers." In a way, we have *all* become Faust.

And we *are* all like Faust, inasmuch as (in the words of the chapter in *The Red Book* called "Nox secunda") we are "a blinded and deluded race" that lives "only on the surface, only in the present, and think[s] only of tomorrow" (RB, 346). This is an exact description of Goethe's Faust, who wants only to live in the present — and, in his wager, specifically undertakes never to want the present to turn into eternity ("When to the moment fleeting past me, / Tarry! I cry, so fair thou art! / Then into fetters mayst thou cast me, / Then let come doom, with all my heart! / Then toll the death-bell, do not linger, / Then be thy bondage o'er and done, / Let the clock stop, let fall the finger, / Let Time for me be past and gone!" [ll. 1699-17067]); Faust, who in the opening scene of Part Two is blinded by the sunlight (l. 4703-4704) and at the end is literally blinded by Sorge (Care), who tells him, "Men commonly are blind their whole life through, / Blind be thou, Faustus, in life's ending!" (ll. 11497-11498). In Jung's words in *The Red Book*, we "treat the past brutally, because we do not receive the dead" (RB, 346); we are only interested in work that brings "visible success," and above all we "want to be paid" (RB, 346). This is Goethe's Faust who, in his *Lebensrückschau* in Act V, confesses: "Athwart the world I have but flown, / [...] I did but wish, achieve, and then again / Did wish, and thus I stormed through life amain" (ll. 11433 and 11437-11439).

Instead, in his *Red Book* Jung proposes an explicitly anti-Faustian program. We must not, he says, "fail to hear the dead"; and this involves a "necessary but hidden and strange work [*ein notwendiges, aber verborgenes und seltsames Werk*] — a major work [*ein Hauptwerk*] — which you must do in secret [*im Geheimen*], for the sake of the dead" (RB, 346). The "necessity of life" forces us to prefer "tangible fruits" and makes it seem "insane" to undertake "a hidden work" that performs "no visible service to humankind" (RB, 346). But it is, he adds, precisely those "who have been led astray by the surface of the world" who suffer from "the tempting and misleading influence of the dead" (RB, 346). One should note that Jung's project is not entirely lacking a pragmatic aspect: for the dead demand "the work of atonement" (*das Sühnwerk*) from anyone who cannot attain a "visible field [*Acker*] and vineyard [*Weinberg*]," he says (echoing Mephisto's cynical advice for rejuvenation without recourse to money or medicine or magic, "Betake thee to the field with speed, / Turn up the clods, and dig out ditches; / [...] Live with the brutes as brute, and think not shame to dung / Thyself the field [*Acker*] thou reapest" (ll. 2353-2354 and 2358-2859), and his even more cynical observation to the audience about what is going to happen to Philemon and Baucis, "Here haps but what hath happed of yore, / For Naboth's vineyard [*Weinberg*] was before" (ll. 11286-11287), referring to the biblical story in the First Book of Kings, Chapter 21.) Unless this "work of atonement" is fulfilled, the individual's path to "external work" (*zu[m] äußeren Werke*) is blocked, for "the dead do not leave him" (*die Toten lassen ihn nicht*) (RB, 346).

In other words, the relation between inner and outer is reciprocal: In order that the dead "let him go" (*ihn entlassen*), the individual must "go inside himself and quietly do what they ask and accomplish what is secret [*das Geheime*]," and Jung advises us "Don't look forward so much, but look back and into yourself, so that you don't fail to hear the dead" (RB, 346). After all, Jung apostrophizes toward the end of "Nox secunda," "what the ancients did for the dead!" (RB, 347). He pours scorn on those who believe they can absolve themselves from "the care of the dead" because "what is dead is past" and because they do not believe in the immortality of the soul. Simply because one believes that immortality is possible, Jung provocatively asks, does this mean that the dead do not exist? Attacking the "word idols" (*Wortgötzen*), Jung asserts that "the dead produce effects" (*die Toten wirken*) and this is enough (RB, 347). And he insists that there can be "no explaining away" (*kein Wegerklären*) in the inner world, just as little one could "explain away the sea in the outer world" (RB, 347) — although what exactly it would mean to "explain away" the sea is unclear.[24] Jung calls on the reader finally to understand what the real purpose of all such "explaining away" is: It is to "seek protection" — protection, as the *Draft* puts it, "against chaos" (RB, 347).

In this conceptual schema, there is a dialectical relationship between the two terms of Jung's hidden inscription, consisting of (a) Philemon's shrine, and (b) Faust's repentance. On the one hand, Philemon (as the archetypal figure encountered by Jung and represented in *The Red Book*) functions as a teacher or guru, teaching Jung the extent to which he is like Faust and a representative of the godforsaken ruthlessness of the age, suffering from hubris and inflation, and steeped in violence, murder, and evil. In this sense,

---

[24] Is there an allusion here to the story of how St. Augustine, walking along the shore of the Mediterranean and pondering the mystery of the Trinity, came across a young boy carrying a bucket of water from the sea and pouring it into a hole in the sand? When asked what he was doing, the boy explained he was pouring the sea into the hole in the sand. When Augustine laughed and said that this could not be done, because the sea is so vast and the hole is so small, the boy replied that it was the same with Augustine and the Trinity — the mystery of the Trinity being so large and Augustine's mind so small. And after saying this, the boy disappeared.

the shrine or sanctuary of Philemon enables Jung to repent from being Faust. On the other, Jung assumes the task of repentance and accepting or receiving the dead, recognizing our "complicity in evil," and atoning for the murder of Philemon (as the legendary figure depicted by Goethe, which stands *mutatis mutandis* for all the crimes of the 20th century). In this sense, Jung's repentance turns the Tower into a shrine to Philemon.

Both senses are linked to the feminine in various ways: through the figure of Baucis; through the reference to φιλία ("high" love) and Baubo ("low" love); and through Faust's relation in Goethe's drama to four different forms of the feminine (personified by Gretchen, Helena, Mary, and the Mater Gloriosa). Curiously, however, Jung fails to mention that the final scene of *Faust II* does contain a figure of repentance, but it is not Faust. Described as UNA POENITENTIUM (formerly known as Gretchen), who is "nestling nearer," this figure sings:

> Ah! bow
> Thy gracious brow,
> O peerless Thou,
> And radiant, on my radiant bliss!
> My youth's beloved,
> From grief removed,
> Returning is.
>   (ll. 12069-12075)

The opening lines of this hymnlike intervention, *Neige, neige*, recall Gretchen's prayer in *Faust I* in front of the image of the Mater Dolorosa (the "sorrowful mother") (ll. 3587-3619), which begins, *Ach neige, / Du Schmerzenzreiche*. These lines raise all sorts of questions: Why should Gretchen be penitent when she was surely more sinned against than sinning? But this raises an even bigger question about Jung's apparent elision of Goethe's Philemon and his own Philemon — as well as his categorical elision of the literary and the historical, of the murder of a pair of legendary or fictional characters and "the great conflagration of German cities, where all the simple people burned to death" (as he put it in his letter to Alice Raphael) — or indeed (and unmentioned by Jung in this context, as elsewhere) the Holocaust. In turn, this elision is part of another elision in Jung's writings between the First World War and the Second: between, on the one hand, the crowning of Kaiser Wilhelm I at Versailles, Jacob Burckhardt's cry — *Das ist der Untergang Deutschlands*, the archetypes of Wagner knocking at the door, and Nietzsche's Dionysian experience, that is, the disaster of 1914 (MDR, 262); and, on the other, the reawakening of Wotan that Jung associates in his seminar on *Zarathustra*, in his "Wotan" essay (1936), and in his essay "After the Catastrophe" (1945), with the catastrophe(s) of 1939 to 1945. And in all of this, the one repentant figure explicitly referred to as such in Goethe's *Faust* is never once mentioned.

"Nox secundus" could not be clearer in its emphasis on the need for a "hidden and strange work" which must be performed in secret "for the sake of the dead" — a "work of atonement" (RB, 346). Elsewhere in *Memories, Dreams, Reflections*, Jung formulates his "suprapersonal life-task" somewhat differently, claiming it is "the meaning" (*der Sinn*) of his existence that life has posed him a question; or that conversely *he* is a question that is addressed to the world — a question, moreover, to which Jung himself must supply the answer, or else resign himself to the answer provided by the world (MDR, 350)! Could it be a question, he wonders, which had preoccupied his ancestors, those paternal ancestors with whom he felt such "fateful links" when working on three stone tablets bearing their names which he placed in the courtyard to his Tower (MDR, 259-260) — a question which they had been unable to answer (MDR, 350)? In turn, these give rise to further questions which touch directly and indirectly on the theme under discussion here:

- Could this question be the reason why Jung is "impressed" by the fact that the conclusion to *Faust* contains no solution?
- Or why he is impressed by the problem on which Nietzsche came to grief: the Dionysian experience that appears to have escaped Christianity?
- Could it be that the restless Wotan-Hermes of his Alemannic and Frankish ancestors is posing these challenging questions?
- Or could it be that Richard Wilhelm was right when he jokingly remarked that in a previous life Jung had been a rebellious Chinese man who was having to discover his Eastern soul in Europe as a punishment? (MDR, 321)

Now whatever the answers to these questions, Jung sees himself as caught up in something that could be described as the life of his ancestors, or as karma, or as "an impersonal archetype that is keeping the world on tenterhooks" and has gripped (*ergriffen*) Jung in particular: the centuries-old development of the divine triad and its confrontation with the feminine principle, or the still unanswered Gnostic question about the origin of evil, or the incompleteness of the Christian image of God (MDR, 350). In other words, is Jung ultimately grappling with Parzival's question, *waz ist got*, "What is God?" (§119, l. 17; vol. 1, p. 68, and §332, l.1; vol. 1, p. 188)?

The Role of Goethe's *Faust* in Jung's Works

A passage from *Transformations and Symbols of the Libido* (Part 2, Chapter 7) offers a good example of Jung's method of argumentation in his writings in general. For here he compares the psychological concept of the libido to the Hindu notion of *tapas*, which — following the German Indologist and professor of philosophy Paul Deussen (1845-1919) — he translates as to be one's own source of heat and which he compares to the Stoic notion of creative, primal warmth (PU §597-§598). In order to illustrate this point — part and parcel of his attempt to develop his own (anti-Freudian) redefinition of the concept of libido — Jung constellates a passage from the *Rigveda* with a text by Goethe. As an expression of the Hindu assumption that "creation results from introversion in general," Jung cites these lines from the *Nāsadīya Sūkta*, also known as the Hymn of Creation, in the *Rigveda* (10:129):[25]

> What was hidden in the shell.
> Was born through the power of fiery torments,
> From this first arose love,
> As the germ of knowledge,
> The wise found the roots of existence in non-existence,
> By investigating the heart's impulses. (cited PU §598)

After the paradoxical opening of the poem, which states that "in the beginning" there was "neither Being nor Not-Being" (RV, §3 and §1), the text describes in §3 how being unfolds, and how "whatever was, that one [...] was generated by the power of heat" (or *tapas*, i.e., heat in the sense of inner energy) (RV, §3). In §4, "desire" (or *kāma*) is described as being the "first seed of mind," hailing "wise seers" (or *kavayas*) as those who, "searching within their hearts, found the bond of Being in Not-Being" (RV, §4). [26]

On Jung's account, this "philosophical view" of the world as an "emanation of libido" is also expressed by Goethe when, in his poem "Ultimatum," he writes:

---

[25] Of this hymn (10:129), Wendy Doniger has written: "This short hymn, though linguistically simple [...] is conceptually extremely provocative and has, indeed, provoked hundreds of complex commentaries among Indian theologians and Western scholars. In many ways, it is meant to puzzle and challenge, to raise unanswerable questions, to pile up paradoxes" (*The Rig Veda*, ed. and trans. Wendy Doniger (Harmondsworth: Penguin, 1981), p. 125).

[26] For an alternative translation, see *Hindu Scriptures*, ed. and trans. R.C. Zaehner (New York: Knopf, 1992), pp. 13-14.

> You follow a false trail;
> Do not think that we are not serious;
> Is not the kernel of nature
> In the hearts of men?
>
> (cited PU §599)[27]

(In the course of his lectures on the psychology of yoga and meditation given in 1938 at the ETH, Jung returns to this comparison, a fact which points to a remarkable continuity of thought and approach over a quarter of a decade or so.)[28] If the *Rigveda* and Goethe are right, and the world itself is an "emanation of the libido," then this insight must be accepted in an epistemological as well as a psychological sense, which means that "the function of reality [*die Realitätsfunktion*] is a drive-function [*Triebfunktion*] with the character of biological adaptation [*biologischen Anpassung*]" (PU §599). What does the term *Realitätsfunktion* mean? To understand this term *Realitätsfunktion*, we need to look back to Jung's earlier argument when he introduces it.

In Part 2, Chapter 2, Jung sets out — over and against Freud's sexual conception of libido — his own "genetic theory" of the libido as "psychic energy" (PU §221-§222). Drawing on a model that he would use elsewhere,[29] Jung wrote that "the original sexual character of these biological institutions became lost in their organic fixation and functional independence":

---

[27] See Goethe, *Werke*, ed. Erich Trunz [HA, vol. 1] (Hamburg: Wegner, 1960), p. 306.

[28] For further discussion, see C.G. Jung, *Psychology of Yoga and Meditation: Lectures Delivered at the ETH Zurich, 1938-1940*, ed. Martin Liebscher, trans. Heather McCartney and John Peck (Princeton, NJ, and Oxford: Princeton University Press, 2020), p. 9.

[29] For example, see his account of the indigenous Australian tribe of the Watschandies (PU §245).

Even if there can be no doubt about the sexual origin of music, still it would be a poor, unaesthetic generalization if one were to include music in the category of sexuality. A similar nomenclature would then lead us to classify the cathedral of Cologne as mineralogy because it is built of stones.[30] It can be a surprise only to those to whom the history of evolution is unknown to find out how few things there really are in human life which cannot be reduced in the last analysis to the propagation-drive [*Propagationstrieb*]; it includes very nearly everything, I think, which is beloved and dear to us. (PU §223)

The point here is that Jung is less interested in reducing everything (as, he argues, Freud did) to sexuality than in showing how, while "countless complicated functions to which today must be denied any sexual character" were "originally pure derivations from the general propagation-drive [*Propagationstrieb*]," they have evolved away from or *beyond* sexuality (PU §223). Significantly, an important role in establishing this argument accrues to the aesthetic, for "the first artistic drives [*Kunsttriebe*][31] in animals [are] used in

---

[30] Jung uses this argument in his lecture "On Psychological Understanding" (1914), published as a supplement to the second edition of *The Content of the Psychoses* (1908; ²1914), when he writes: "Anyone who understands *Faust* "objectively," from the causal standpoint, is — to take a drastic example — like someone who tries to understand a Gothic cathedral under its historical, technical, and finally its mineralogical aspect. But where is the *meaning* [*der Sinn*] of the marvellous edifice? Where is the answer to that all-important question: what goal of redemption did the human being of the Gothic period seek in his work, and how have we to understand his work subjectively, in and through ourselves" (CW 3 §396). This choice of the Gothic style as a point of comparison may well have been suggested by Goethe's reflections on Strasbourg cathedral in *Dichtung und Wahrheit* or in his essay "On German Architecture" (1772), published in *Concerning German Art and Manner* (1773), edited by J.G. Herder.
[31] Compare with Nietzsche's description in *The Birth of Tragedy* (§1) of Apollo and Dionysos as *Kunsttriebe*.

the service of the propagation-drive, and limited to the breeding season" (PU §223) — but later become drives in their own right.

Jung pursues a dual strategy of embedding his work within the German philosophical tradition, as well as revising and repurposing key concepts in psychoanalysis. Thus, on the one hand, Jung identifies his concept of libido with Schopenhauer's conception of the will; on the other, he redefines Sándor Ferenczi's concept of "introjection" (which the Hungarian psychoanalyst had defined as taking the outer world into the inner world)[32] as a "placing of psychological perceptions into the object" (PU §223). Jung identifies this conception of introjection with a "voluntaristic" formulation of the Freudian pleasure-principle (*Lustprinzip*), while his "voluntaristic" conception of the reality-principle (*Realiätsprinzip*) is said to equate to what Jung calls *Realitätskorrektur* (i.e., a correction of reality) or to what the German-Swiss philosopher Richard Avenarius (1843-1896) in *The Human Conception of the World* (1891) somewhat complicatedly calls *empiriokritische Prinzipialkoordination* (PU §223).[33] (Wisely, perhaps, Beatrice M. Hinkle does not translate this term, which literally means "empirio-critical coordination of principles"!) On Jung's account, introjection gives rise to the concept of power (*Kraftbegriff*), and he recalls a remark made by Galileo about this concept of power having its origin in the subjective perception of one's own muscular power (PU §223).

In addition to aligning himself with a strand of the German philosophical position (primarily Schopenhauer and Nietzsche)

---

[32] See Sándor Ferenczi, "Introjektion und Übertragung," *Jahrbuch für psycho-analytische und psychopathologische Forschungen*, 1 (1909), 422-457 (p. 422).

[33] See Richard Avenarius, *Der menschliche Weltbegriff* (Lepizig: Reisland, 1891), p. 25. Put succinctly, empirio-criticism is a term for the claim put forward by Avenarius and Ernst Mach that all we can know is our sensations and that knowledge should be confined to pure experience; see Nicholas Bunnin and Jiyuan Yu, *The Blackwell Dictionary of Western Philosophy* (Malden, MA, and Oxford: Blackwell, 2004), p. 208.

and redefining psychoanalytic concepts, Jung uses a third strategy: identifying mythological parallels. So in addition to equating his conception of the libido with Schopenhauer's concept of the Will, Jung refers to the "cosmogonic meaning" of Eros in Plato (presumably, in the *Symposium*) and in Hesiod (in his *Theogeny*); to the Orphic figure of Phanes or the "shining one" as the first created, the "father of Eros"; to Priapus; and to the bisexual god of love similar to Dionysos Lysios, whose sanctuary was in Thebes, as well as to Plotinus and the Neoplatonic conception of the world-soul as the energy of the intellect (PU §223). After a brief excursus into Neoplatonism, Jung concludes that "this fragment of the history of philosophy [...] shows the significance of the endopsychic" — or as we might now say, "intrapsychic" — "perception of the libido and its symbols for human thought" (PU §225).

All in all, these few key paragraphs in *Transformations and Symbols of the Libido* reveal just how extensive is Jung's use of an astonishingly wide variety of intellectual, cultural, and literary sources in expounding his argument. Of those many sources, two in particular stand out — Goethe's *Faust* (as we are exploring in this volume) and Nietzsche's *Zarathustra* (as we shall see in the next). In addition to *using* Goethe's *Faust* as an argumentational and presentation resource (as we shall see, *Faust* plays a key role at critical junctures in *Transformations and Symbols of Libido*), Jung is also *taking a Goethean stand* in relation to the question of what constitutes reality. "People always talk of the study of the ancients," Goethe told Eckermann on 29 January 1826, adding: "but what does that mean, except that it says, turn your attention to the real world, and try to express it [*richte dich auf die wirkliche Welt und suche sie auszusprechen*] — for that is what the ancients did."[34] For, contrary to what many of his critics and opponents say, Jung is very much

---

[34] Johann Peter Eckermann, *Conversations of Goethe*, ed. J.K. Moorehead, trans. John Oxenford [1930] (New York: Da Capo Press, 1998), p. 126.

concerned with the question of reality. On his account, "sexual primal libido" has evolved to develop "derivatives" (*Abspaltungen*) in which the functions are maintained by "a special differentiated libido," which has correspondingly become "desexualized" (*desexualisiert*). Thus, the developmental process (of evolution) has led to "an increasing transformation [*zunehmende Aufzehrung*] of the primal libido [*Urlibido*]" — that is, a libido which only produced such "products of generation" (*Fortpflanzungsprodukte*) as eggs, seeds, and sperm — into the "secondary functions" of allurement (or attraction of the opposite sex) and of protecting the young. This shift, Jung argues, involves "a very different and very complicated reality to reality [*Verhältnis zur Wirklichkeit*], a true function of reality [*Wirklichkeitsfunktion*], which, functionally inseparable, is bound up with the needs of procreation, that is, the altered mode of propagation carries with it as a correlate a correspondingly heightened adaptation to reality" (PU §227).

Eine entsprechend erhöhte Wirklichkeitsanpassung — stripped of its jargon, what Jung is saying here in dry, technical (psychoanalytic) terms is the same as what, in a far more dramatic and (literally) colourful way, he explores (and experiences) in *The Red Book*. The question that Jung poses here is also the $6 million question of transformation: How does one adapt oneself to a *higher reality*? In Wolfram's *Parzival*, this higher reality is symbolized by the Grail; in Goethe's *Faust*, it is symbolized by Faust's journey through *die kleine Welt, und dann die große*, and finally the ascent into the afterlife of the "Mountain Gorges"; in Nietzsche's *Zarathustra*, it is symbolized by coming to terms with a godless world, by willing the thought of eternal recurrence, and by thus becoming an *Übermensch*; and in *The Red Book*, it is symbolized by giving birth to one's god — by opening the egg so that the god can leave it, "healed" and "his figure [...] transformed," and so that when Jung thinks he has caught the mighty one and holds him in his cupped hands, he is "the sun itself" (RB, 319 and 308).

Goethe's *Faust* in *Transformations and Symbols of (Faustian) Libido*

Jung's great signature work of 1911-1912, *Transformations and Symbols of the Libido*, opens with a sweeping (if somewhat backhanded) tribute to Freud's intellectual originality by noting the centrality in psychoanalysis of the Oedipus Complex: "Anyone who can read Freud's *Interpretation of Dreams* without scientific rebellion at the newness and apparently unjustified daring of its analytical presentation, and without moral indignation at the astonishing nudity of the dream interpretation, and who can allow this unusual array of facts to influence his mind calmly and without prejudice," he writes, "will surely be deeply impressed at that place where Freud calls to mind the fact that an individual psychological conflict, namely, the incest fantasy, is the essential root of that powerful ancient dramatic material, the Oedipus legend" (PU §1). In an arresting passage, Jung goes on to evoke the power of the archaic — or, in other words, the power of the past in the present —[35] to impress itself upon us even in the midst of our workaday lives:

> The impression made by this simple reference may be likened to that wholly peculiar feeling which arises in us if, for example, in the noise and tumult of a modern street we should come across an ancient relic — the Corinthian capital of a walled-in column, or a fragment of inscription. Just a moment ago we were given over to the noisy ephemeral life of the present, when something very far away and strange appears to us, which turns our attention to things of another order; a glimpse away from the incoherent multiplicity of the present to a higher coherence in history. (PU §1)

---

[35] For further discussion, see Paul Bishop (ed.), *The Archaic: The Past in the Present* (London and New York: Routledge, 2012), especially pp. 3-54.

In other words, Freud's reference to the Oedipus legend makes the same impression on us as the sight of a monument of antiquity does: Whereas before we had been "still engaged with the confusing impressions of the variability of the individual soul, suddenly there is opened a revelation of the simple greatness of the Oedipus tragedy — that never extinguished light of the Greek theatre" (PU §1).

As well as transporting us back to the distant past, however, Jung wants to situate his argument in the pages that follow in the context of the very contemporary debate in the tradition of psychoanalysis, referring to works by Franz Riklin (1878-1938), Karl Abraham (1877-1925), Otto Rank (1844-1939), Alphonse Maeder (1882-1971), Ernest Jones (1879-1958), and Herbert Silberer (1882-1923), all of whom were, in one way or another, chipping away at precisely the Oedipal edifice of the sexual theory of the libido that Jung had, in his opening paragraph, ostensibly been praising. And Jung himself was now about to join the ranks of Freud's critics; and in a footnote at the end of Chapter 2, Jung cites the view of the great Swiss historian Jacob Burckhardt (1818-1897) to the effect that "every Greek of the classical era carried in himself a fragment of the Oedipus, just as every German carries a fragment of Faust" (PU §56).[36] This statement reveals Jung's methodological strategy in *Transformations and Symbols of the Libido*: namely, to use Goethe's *Faust* in a way that is as central to his argument as

---

[36] In a footnote, Jung invites us to consider Burckhardt's letter to Albert Brenner of 11 November 1855: "I have absolutely nothing stored away for the special interpretation of Faust. You are well provided with commentaries of all sorts. Hark! let us at once take the whole foolish pack back to the reading-room from whence they have come. What you are destined to find in Faust, that you will find by intuition. Faust is nothing else than pure and legitimate myth, a great primitive conception, so to speak, in which everyone can divine in his own way his own nature and destiny. Allow me to make a comparison: What would the ancient Greeks have said had a commentator interposed himself between them and the Oedipus legend? There was a chord of the Oedipus legend in every Greek which longed to be touched directly and respond in its own way. And thus it is with the German nation and Faust" (PU §56; see Hans Brenner-Eglinger, "Briefe Jakob Burckhardts an Albert Brenner," *Basler Jahrbuch 1901*, 87-110 [p. 92]).

Oedipus had been to Freud's. (And so indeed, as we shall see, is this the case.)

This deep, structural affinity between *Faust* and *Transformations and Symbols of the Libido* represents the nugget of truth in the legend that Jung was somehow related to Goethe. Jung even tried to persuade Freud of the validity of this legend: in his letter to Freud of 18 January 1911, he wrote: "My paper" — i.e., what would become *Transformations and Symbols of the Libido*? — "grows and grows. After seeing a performance of *Faust* yesterday, including bits of Part II" — i.e., a performance at the Schauspielhaus Zürich, also known as the "Pfauenbühne" (or Peacock Stage), in which the famous Austrian actor Alexander Moissi played the role of Faust — "I feel more confident of its value," adding: "As the whole thing sprang into life before my eyes, all kinds of thoughts came to me, and I felt sure that my respected great-grandfather would have given my work his placet, the more willingly as he would have noted with a smile that the great-grandchild has continued and even extended that ancestral line of thought."[37]

On the surface, however, Jung's argument in *Transformations and Symbols of the Libido* is constructed around the fantasies of Miss Frank Miller, an American woman whom Jung had never met but whose writings he had come across in the work of Théodore Flournoy (1854-1920) and whose fantasies Jung presented as an object for "an extended commentary on a practical analysis of the prodromal stages of schizophrenia" (CW 5, p. xxv). It was, in other words, a case study. Yet in the background (that is, in the footnotes) and sometimes even in the foreground lies Goethe's great poetic

---

[37] *The Freud/Jung Letters: The Correspondence Between Sigmund Freud and C.G. Jung*, edited by William McGuire, trans. Ralph Manheim and R.F.C. Hull (Cambridge, MA: Harvard University Press, 1988), pp. 384-385. For Freud's eye-twinkling way of playing along, see his letters to Jung of 9 March 1909 and 22 January 1911 (pp. 210-211 and 388); in the latter, Freud tells Jung, "If you speak to your little great-grandfather in the near future, tell him I have long taken an interest in his Mignon and that he is quite a master of concealment" (p. 388).

drama, shaping and guiding the argument. In turn, Miss Miller's fantasies and Goethe's *Faust* shared a cultural backdrop, namely the biblical Book of Job, the masterpiece of Jewish wisdom literature. (After all, the story of Job informs the "Prologue in Heaven" in *Faust I* and its central motivating idea of the divine wager.) As Miss Miller's own references to Job, Milton's *Paradise Lost* (1667), and Edmond Rostand's *Cyrano de Bergerac* (1897) suggest (PU §92 and §101), her fantasies offer material which illustrates "the indirect course of the libido as truly a way of sorrow," just as when "humankind, after the sinful fall, had the burden of the earthly life to bear, or like the tortures of Job, who suffered under the power of Satan and of God, and who himself, without suspecting it, became a plaything of the superhuman forces which we no longer consider as metaphysical, but as metapsychological" — and *Faust* also offers us "the same exhibition of God's wager" (PU §106):

> Mephistopheles:
> What will you bet? There's still a chance to gain him
> If unto me full leave you give
> Gently upon my road to train him! [*Faust I*, ll. 312-314]

> Satan:
> But put forth thine hand now, and touch all that he hath, and he will curse thee to thy face. — [Job 1:11]

As Jung notes, however, there is one, all-important difference between the Book of Job and *Faust*: Whereas in the biblical book the conflict between the two great tendencies is presented as being one between Good and Evil, in Goethe's drama the conflict is a "decidedly erotic one," that is, a battle between sublimation and Eros, which casts the Devil in the fitting role of the "erotic tempter" (PU §107). By contrast, this erotic dimension is "missing" in Job, and indeed he does not even seem to be aware of "the conflict within his own soul" and is therefore continuously disputing the arguments of his friends who are trying to convince him of the evil in his own heart (PU §107). In this respect, Jung suggests, Faust is actually superior to Job; he is "considerably more honorable" than Job, inasmuch as he "openly admits to the divisions within his soul" (PU §107).

Further on, Miss Miller's poem "The Moth to the Sun" is placed in an explicitly Goethean context when Jung claims that its idea of "a small ephemeral being, something like the day-fly, which, in lamentable contrast to the eternity of the stars, longs for an imperishable daylight,"[38] reminds us of Faust:

> Mark how, beneath the evening sunlight's glow
> The green-embosomed houses glitter;
> The glow retreats, done is the day of toil,
> It yonder hastes, new fields of life exploring;
> Ah, that no wing can lift me from the soil
> Upon its track to follow, follow soaring!
> Then would I see eternal Evening gild
> The silent world beneath me glowing.
> [...]
> Yet, finally, the weary god is sinking;
> The new-born impulse fires my mind, —
> I hasten on, his beams eternal drinking,
> The day before me and the night behind.
> Above me heaven unfurled, the floor of waves beneath
> me, —

---

[38] Was Schopenhauer thinking of this passage when, in his chapter "On Death and Its Relation to the Indestructibility of Our Inner Nature" in the second volume of *The World as Will and Representation*, he wrote: "Whether the fly buzzying around me goes to sleep in the evening and buzzes again in the following morning, or whether it dies in the evening and in the spring another fly buzzes which has emerged from its egg, this in itself is the same thing" (Schopenhauer, *The World as Will and Representation*, trans. E.F.J Payne, 2 vols (New York: Dover, 1966), vol. 2, p. 478).

> A glorious dream! though now the glories fade.
> Alas! the wings that lift the mind no aid
> Of wings to lift the body can bequeath me.
>
> (ll. 1070-1077 and 1084-1091; PU §133)

Not long after this speech to Wagner in the scene "Before the Gate," Faust sees "the black dog roving there through cornfields and stubble" (l. 1147), the dog who will turn out to be the Devil — "the tempter, in whose hellish fires Faust has singed his wings" (PU §134). For while Faust believed himself to be giving his great yearning for beauty to the sun and to the earth, he "went astray" (*verließ er sich selbst*) —[39] and fell into the hands of the Evil One:

> "Yes, resolute to reach some brighter distance,
> On earth's fair sun I turn my back."
>
> (ll. 708-709; PU §134)

In these lines Jung reads a "true recognition of the state of affairs," but in Faust's personal dilemma Jung also sees a wider cultural problematic. Just as Satan is said to be able to disguise himself as an angel of light and, in the first to fourth centuries C.E., the Mithraic religion offered "threatening competition" to Christianity (right up to and including Julian the Apostate's unsuccessful attempt to reinstate paganism in the place of Christianity), so a shift in humankind's relationship to nature took place in the time when the medieval story of Faust was set. For, on Jung's account, "the honoring of the beauty of nature led the Christian of the Middle Ages to pagan thoughts which lay in an antagonistic relation to his conscious religion" (PU §135).

---

[39] See Petrarch, *The Ascent of Mount Ventoux*, citing St Augustine, *Confessions*, Book 10, Chapter 8; in turn cited in Jacob Burckhardt, *Die Kultur der Renaissance in Italien*, Abschnitt 4, "Die Entdeckung der Welt und des Menschen."

In a powerful paragraph, Jung sets out in impassioned prose how "the longing of Faust became his ruin": This dilemma is not just Faust's but that of modernity as a whole (and, as we know from *Memories, Dreams Reflections*, it was Jung's own dilemma too):

> The *longing for the Beyond* had brought as a consequence a loathing for life, and he stood on the brink of self-destruction. The *longing for the beauty of this world* led him anew to ruin, into doubt and pain, even to Marguerite's tragic death. His mistake was that he followed after both worlds with no check to the driving-force of his libido, like a man of violent passion. Faust portrays once more the popular-psychological [*völkerpsychologischen*] conflict of the beginning of the Christian era, but what is noteworthy, in a reversed order. (PU §136)

Parallels to this dilemma, Jung suggests, can be found in the case of Alypius of Thagaste, as related in his *Confessions* by St. Augustine (PU §122, fn. 29).

In Book 6, Chapters 7 and 8, Augustine recounts how the young Alypius was taken by friends to watch violent Roman games in the amphitheater in Rome. Initially, he resisted and kept his eyes shut, but eventually he was enticed by the sounds to succumb and open his eyes. Now Alypius finds himself, to his horror, actually enjoying the cruel and bloody spectacle, returning to the amphitheater and even inviting others to join him. Had we been living in the age of antiquity, Jung ponders, it is likely that we would have seen how its culture was inevitably going to collapse, since humanity itself rejected it; and he points to Virgil's famous fourth *Eclogue* as evidence of a widespread longing for redemption (PU §137). The general expansion of Christianity brought in its wake, however, a turning to asceticism in the form of monasticism and the anchoritic life — something that would bring "a new misfortune" to many (PU §138).

Whereas many of the early Christians sought new life in asceticism, Faust does the exact reverse, rejecting the ascetic ideal as death. Instead, Faust "struggles for freedom" and "wins life," but at the same time "giving himself over to the Evil One" and thereby becoming the "bringer of death to her whom he loves most, Marguerite" (PU §139). In the end, however, he "tears himself away from pain and sacrifices his life in unceasing useful work, through which he saves many lives" in the form of his land reclamation scheme:

> Below the hills, a marshy plain
> Infects what I so long have been retrieving:
> This stagnant pool likewise to drain
> Were now my latest and my best achieving.
> To many millions following let me furnish soil.
>
> *(Faust II*, ll. 11559-11563)

In Jung's view, "the analogy [*Analogie*] of this expression" with an earlier passage in Part One — where Faust, in conversation with Wagner, talks about his involvement with his father's (unsuccessful) alchemical endeavors in a way that hints at Faust's own "double mission as saviour and destroyer" — is striking:

> WAGNER:
> With what a feeling, thou great man, must thou
> Receive the people's honest veneration!
>
> FAUST:
> Thus we, our hellish boluses compounding,
> Among these vales and hills surrounding.
> Worse than the pestilence, have passed.
> Thousands were done to death from poison of my giving;

And I must hear, by all the living,
The shameless murderers praised at last!
(ll. 1011-1012 and 1050-1055; PU §139)

A parallel to just such a "double role" can, Jung suggests, also be found in the famous passage in the Gospel of Matthew where Christ says, "I came not to send peace, but a sword" (Matthew 10:34; PU §140). Is Faust, then, a kind of Christ figure?

Hence the iconic significance of the figure of Faust: For Jung, he "clothes in words a problem of modern humankind which has been turning in restless slumber since the Renaissance, just as was done by the drama of Oedipus for the Hellenic sphere of culture" (see above), and Jung formulates this problem as follows: *What is the way out between the Scylla of renunciation of the world and the Charybdis of the acceptance of the world* (PU §141)? Nowhere in Goethe's play is this dilemma more powerfully expressed than in Faust's dramatic suicide monologue in the "Night" scene:

"Out on the open ocean speeds my dreaming!
The glassy flood before my feet is gleaming,
A new day beckons to a newer shore!

A fiery chariot, borne on buoyant pinions,
Sweeps near me now; I soon shall ready be
To pierce the ether's high, unknown dominions,
To reach new spheres of pure activity!
This godlike rapture, this supreme existence
Do I, but now a worm, deserve to track?
Yes, resolute to reach some brighter distance;
On Earth's fair sun I turn my back!"
(ll. 699-709; PU §143, fn. 9)[40]

---

[40] These lines echo the so-called Merkabah mysticism (i.e., "Chariot" mysticism) based on such visions as those of Ezekiel (chapters 1, 8, and 10), Isaiah (chapter

which is echoed in these despairing words in the scene "Before the Gate":

> Ah, that no wing can lift me from the soil,
> Upon its track to follow, follow soaring!
> Then would I see eternal Evening gild
> The silent world beneath me glowing.
> [...]
> And now before mine eyes expands the ocean,
> With all its bays, in shining sleep!
> [...]
> The newborn impulse fires my mind,
> I hasten on, his beams eternal drinking."
> (ll. 1074-1077 & 1083-1084 & 1084-1086; PU §143, fn. 9)

We find "the same longing and the same sun," Jung argues, in the case of Miss Miller's poem "The Song of the Moth," in which, just as in *Faust*, the focus turns "from the realms of the religious world [...] towards the sun of this world," mingled with a sense of something very different and represented by the moth which has fluttered so long around the light that it has burned its wings (PU §143).

Given the overall thrust of Jung's argumentation in *Transformations and Symbols of the Libido* and his thesis that "the primitive symbolism of light gradually developed, with the increasing depth of the vision, into the idea of the sun-hero, the 'well-beloved'" (PU §180), it should come as no surprise that one of the reasons why Jung is so interested in *Faust* is because of

---

6), and Daniel (chapter 2), or other accounts of ascents to the heavenly palaces and the vision of the Throne of God. For discussion of the complementary notion of descent, see Guy G. Stroumsa, *Hidden Wisdom: Esoteric Traditions and the Roots of Christian Mysticism*, 2nd edn. (Leiden and Boston: Brill, 2005), chapter 10, "Mystical Descents," pp. 169-183.

this work's solar symbolism. At the same time, it is worth noting that Jung does not simply shoehorn Goethe's *Faust* into his own arguments but is as always alert to nuances and subtle differences. Thus, he remarks in a footnote that the "development of the sun symbol in *Faust* does not go so far as an anthropomorphic vision," but "stops in the suicide scene at the chariot of Helios" (cf. "A fiery chariot, borne on buoyant pinions, / Sweeps near me now") (ll. 702-703). As he further notes, the motif of the fiery chariot that comes to retrieve the dying or departing hero can be found in the story of Mithras and in a legend about St. Francis, as well as in the story of the ascension of Elijah.[41] Over and above the significance within the context of Jung's argument here of parallels between Faust's flight over the sea and that of Mithras — as well as those between ancient Christian pictorial representations of the ascension of Elijah and Mithraic representations of the horses of the sun-chariot rushing upward to heaven, leaving the solid earth behind, and pursuing their course over Oceanus, a water god, who lies at their feet — is the significance of the figure of the biblical prophet Elijah himself, who will play a major role in Jung's own fantasies in *The Red Book* (see Volume 4).

Further on, Jung considers the etymological links between speech and light in support of the Hindu metapsychology which "conceives speech and fire as emanations of the inner light from which we know that it is the libido" (PU §257). After producing numerous etymological examples of language roots that unite the meanings of "to desire," "to play," "to radiate," and "to sound' (PU

---

[41] See 2 Kings 2:1-13. Ezekiel's account of the chariot in his vision (1:4-26) is an important source of the school of early Jewish mysticism known as Merkabah or Merkavah mysticism, (i.e., Chariot mysticism). For further discussion, see Gershom G. Scholem, *Jewish Gnosticism, Merkabah Mysticism, and Talmudic Tradition* (New York: Jewish Theological Seminary of America, 1960). Jordan B. Peterson chooses to open his study of the Pentateuch and the Book of Jonah with the story of Elijah (*We Who Wrestle with God: Perceptions of the Divine* (London: Allen Lane, 2024), pp. xv-xxxi).

§262), Jung suggests that precisely this idea can be found in the notion of the music of the spheres as reflected in two passages from Goethe's *Faust*, one from the "Prologue in Heaven":

> The sun orb sings in emulation,
> 'Mid brother-spheres, his ancient round:
> His path predestined through Creation,
> He ends with step of thunder sound.
>
> (ll. 243-246; PU §266)

and the other from the opening scene in Act I of *Faust*, Part Two:

> Hearken! Hark! the hours careering!
> Sounding loud to spirit-hearing,
> See the new-born Day appearing!
> Rocky portals jarring shatter,
> Phœbus' wheels in rolling clatter,
> With a crash the Light draws near!
> Pealing rays and trumpet-blazes,
> Eye is blinded, ear amazes;
> The Unheard can no one hear!
> Slip within each blossom-bell,
> Deeper, deeper, there to dwell, —
> In the rocks, beneath the leaf!
> If it strikes you, you are deaf.
>
> (ll. 4666-4679; PU §266)

— passages which are supplemented by a quotation from Heinrich Heine's poem "A star is falling slowly" (*Es fällt ein Stern herunter*) from his *Buch der Lieder*, by a reference to the poetic drama in blank verse by Gerhart Hauptmann (1862-1946) called *The Sunken Bell* (*Die versunkene Glocke*) (1896) (discussed by Jung in his seminars on Nietzsche's *Zarathustra*), and by some lines from Friedrich Hölderlin's poem "Sunset" (*Sonnenuntergang*) (PU §267).[42]

Yet as well as solar symbolism, *Transformations and Symbols of the Libido* explores the significance of phallic symbolism: such as the "Tom-Thumb" figure found in the Katha-Upanishad (section 4, §12–§13), whose meaning can, as Jung says, "easily be divined" (PU §206).[43] For "the phallus is this hero dwarf, who performs great deeds; he, this ugly god in unassuming form, who is the great doer of wonders, since he is the visible expression of the creative strength incarnate in humankind" (PU §206). This "extraordinary contrast" is also evinced in another example of the phallic symbol of the libido in the Mothers Scene in *Faust II*:

MEPHISTOPHELES:
I'll praise thee ere we separate: I see
Thou knowest the devil thoroughly:
Here take this key.

FAUST:
That little thing!

MEPHISTOPHELES:
Take hold of it, not undervaluing!

FAUST:
It glows, it shines, increases in my hand!

MEPHISTOPHELES:
How much it is worth, thou soon shalt understand,
The key will scent the true place from all others!

---

[42] Friedrich Hölderlin, *Poems & Fragments*, trans. Michael Hamburger, 3rd edn. (London: Anvil Press Poetry, 1994), pp. 46-47.
[43] See *Hindu Scriptures*, ed. and trans. Zaehner, p. 224.

Follow it down! — 'twill lead thee to the Mothers!
(ll. 6257-6264; PU §206)

Jung links this "marvellous tool, a phallic symbol of the libido," which the Devil puts into Faust's hand in Part Two with the earlier scene in Part One when the Devil, initially in the form of the black dog that had accompanied Faust back to his study, introduces himself in these words (PU §207):

"Part of that power, not understood.
Which always wills the bad and always creates the good."
(ll. 1335-1336; PU §207)

For Jung, it seems as if the entirety of *Faust* could be described as an adventure in the libido! He links this power back to the action of Part One where Faust, united to this "power" (*Kraft*), succeeds in "accomplishing his real life task, at first through evil adventure" and then in Part Two "for the benefit of humanity," arguing that "without what is 'Evil' there is no creative power" (PU §208). Here, in the "mysterious" Mothers Scene where "the poet unveils the last mystery of the creative power to those of understanding," Faust has need of Mephisto's phallic magic wand, in whose strength he initially has no confidence, in order to perform "the greatest of wonders, namely, the conjuring-up of Paris and Helen" (PU §208).

Yet phallic symbolism extends beyond the way "this small, insignificant instrument" enables Faust to "attain the divine power of working miracles," for the phallic symbol of the libido can also be found in the figures of the Cabiri, those "mysterious chthonic gods" to whom great miraculous power was ascribed and associated with the cult of Hephaestus, while their cult at Samothrace, about which F.W.J. Schelling (1775-1854) had written, was associated with that of the ithyphallic Hermes which had, according to Herodotus, been brought to Attica by the Pelasgians.[44] On the one hand, Jung links these figures with the magic phallic wand of the Mothers Scene ("The key will scent the true place from all others! / Follow it down! — 'twill lead thee to the Mothers!") (ll. 6263-6264) but, on the other, he recognizes them as significant mythological figures in their own right — as the "first wise men, the teachers of Orpheus, and discovered the Ephesian magic formulas and *musical rhythms*" (PU §209). With their characteristic "ugliness and deformity" we meet the Cabiri in the Aegean Festival scene of *Faust II* — and in the episode where the tower is constructed in Jung's *Red Book*.[45]

Together with the detail of the magic key, the Mothers Scene includes the description of the glowing tripod (l. 6283), which Jung associates with a mystic interpretation of the biblical story of the three men in the fiery furnace in the Book of Daniel (as found in an old German incunabulum of 1471 known as the *Biblia pauperum*). (In a later footnote, he also associates the tripod with the significance that is said to accrue to the altar as signifying the uterus in the alchemical text *The Visions of Zosimos* [PU §317, fn. 78; cf. §233-§234, §493 and §598].)[46] Accordingly, he reads the glowing furnace as a "mother symbol, where the children are produced"

---

[44] See Herodotus, *Histories*, Book 2, §51, and Book 3, §37; in *The Landmark Herodotus: The Histories*, ed. Robert B. Strassler (London: Quercus, 2008), pp. 141 and 224.

[45] The juglike, squat, and deformed appearance of the Cabiri is borne out by their somewhat alarming depiction in a drawing by Rudolf Steiner in 1918 (see Rudolf Steiner, *Geisteswissenschaftliche Erläuterungen zu Goethes «Faust»*, 2 vols. (Dornach: Rudolf Steiner Verlag, 1982), vol. 2, plate opposite p. 208). For Steiner, "the old conceptions of the Cabiri were really the secret of humankind's becoming [*das Menschenwerde-Geheimnis*]," representing how "in a way the spiritual correlate of being born as a human should be seen in the spiritual world" (pp. 202-203). Intriguingly, in the light of Jung's later numerological approach to the Cabiri (see Chapter 4, pp. 331 and 336), Steiner noted that "among the various names given to the Cabiri are those where one Cabir is called Axieros, the second Axiokersos and the third Axiokersa, Kadmilos the fourth," but that "there was a vague feeling that there was a fifth, a sixth, and a seventh" (p. 202).

[46] This work continued to fascinate Jung; see his Eranos lecture of 1937, published as "The Visions of Zosimos" (CW 13 §85-§144).

(PU §274). At the end of Part Two, Chapter Four, Jung assimilates the figure of Ahasver (the Wandering Jew) to that of Faust (PU §302), and he summarizes his core thesis so far. On Jung's account, many of the mythological heroes (Gilgamesh, Dionysos, Hercules, Christ, Mithras, etc.) are wanderers because wandering itself is "a representation of longing [*Sehnsucht*]" or of "the ever-restless desire which nowhere finds its object, for it is seeking, unknown to itself, the lost mother" (PU §317). By the same token, these heroes also represent the sun as it, too, wanders (in the solar pattern), thus justifying the conclusion that *the myth of the hero is a solar myth*.

Translated into his own psychological terms, "the myth of the hero [...] is [...] the myth of our own suffering unconscious, which has an unquenchable longing for all the deepest sources of our own being, for the body of the mother, and through it for communion with infinite life in the countless forms of existence," at which point Jung turns yet again to "the words of the Master who has divined the deepest roots of Faustian longing," quoting *in extenso* from the Mothers Scene (PU §317):

"Unwilling, I reveal a loftier mystery. —
In solitude are throned the Goddesses,
No Space around them, Place and Time still less:
Only to speak of them embarrasses.
They are THE MOTHERS! [...]

"[...] Goddesses unknown to ye,
The Mortals, — named by us unwillingly.
Delve in the deepest depths must thou to reach them:
'Tis thine own fault that we for help beseech them."

"Where is the way?"

"No way! To the Unreachable,
Ne'er to be trodden! A way to the Unbeseechable,
Never to be besought! Art thou prepared?
There are no locks, no latches to be lifted!
Through endless solitudes shalt thou be drifted!
Hast thou through solitudes and deserts dared?

[…]

"And hadst thou swum to farthest verge of ocean
And there the boundless space beheld,
Still hadst thou seen wave after wave in motion,
Even though impending doom thy fear compelled.[47]
Thou hadst seen something — in the beryl dim
Of peace-lulled seas, the sportive dolphins swim;
Hadst seen the flying clouds, sun, moon and star;
Nought shalt thou see in endless Void afar —
Not hear thy footstep fall, nor meet
A stable spot to rest thy feet.

[…]

"Here, take this key! […]
The Key will scent the true place from all others;
Follow it down! 'Twill lead thee to the Mothers.

[…]

---

[47] Is Mephisto here echoing the Book of Baruch, where the prophet asks, "Who hath gone up into heaven, and taken her [i.e., wisdom], and brought her down from the clouds? Who hath passed over the sea, and found her, and brought her preferably to chosen gold? There is none that is able to know her ways, nor that can search out her paths" (Baruch 3: 29-31)?

"Descend then! I could also say: Ascend!
'Twere all the same. Escape from the Created
To shapeless forms in liberated spaces!
Enjoy what long ere this was dissipated!
There whirls the press, like clouds on clouds unfolding;
Then with stretched arm swing high the key thou'rt holding!

[…]

"At last a blazing tripod, tells thee this.
That there the utterly deepest bottom is.
Its light to thee will then the Mothers show,
Some in their seats, the others stand or go,
At their own will: Formation, Transformation,
The Eternal Mind's eternal recreation.
Forms of all Creatures, — there are floating free.
They'll see thee not! for only wraiths they see.
So pluck up heart, — the danger then is great.
Go to the tripod ere thou hesitate,
And touch it with the key."
(ll. 6212-6216 & 6218-6227 & 6239-6248 & 6259 & 6263-
6264 & 6275-6280 & 6283-6293; PU §317)

Jung's identification of his own project with Goethe's *Faust* could not be clearer (although the fact that recalcitrant Germanists will probably insist on asking whether this means it is justified is another question altogether).

In addition to the emphasis on the solar imagery of light and fire, Jung touches in Part Two, Chapter Five, on the maternal significance of water (and hence the sea as the symbol of birth), quoting in this connection the words spoken by the spirit summoned up by Faust in the opening "Night" scene of Part One:

"In the flood of life, in the torrent of deeds,
I toss up and down,
I am blown to and fro!
Cradle and grave,
An eternal sea;
A changing web,
A glowing life."
                    (ll. 501-507) (PU §334)

In this context, the "primitive libido symbolism" of Mephisto's magic, phallic key acquires fresh significance as "it grows, it shines, increases" in Faust's hand (l. 6261) (PU §335). Another aspect of the symbolism of water and the related symbol of trees is illustrated by the way in which, in the biblical Book of Revelation, the unconscious psychology of religious yearning (*Sehnsucht*) is revealed as the longing for the mother (PU §340). In this yearning for the mother, the religious believer is yearning for there to be "no more sins, no repression, no disharmony with one's self, no guilt, no fear of death and no pain of separation more" (PU §341), and this "radiant, mystical harmony" found at the end of the Book of Revelation with its promise that "there shall be no more curse" (PU §340) is something that Jung regards as having been "caught again 2,000 years later and expressed poetically in the last prayer of Dr. Marianus" in the climactic conclusion to *Faust II* (PU §341):

"Penitents, look up, elate,
Where she beams salvation;
Gratefully to blessed fate
Grow, in recreation!
Be our souls, as they have been,
Dedicate to thee!
Virgin Holy, Mother, Queen,
Goddess, gracious be!"
                    (ll. 12096-12103; PU §341)

The poetical expression of this "radiant, mystical harmony" in precisely such a work as Goethe's *Faust* and its "beauty and greatness of feeling" inevitably prompts the question as to whether it is not too narrow to regard the "primary tendency compensated by religion" as "incestuous" (PU §342). (One might recall Jung's earlier strictures in *Transformations and Symbols of the Libido* and elsewhere about including music in the category of sexuality as being like classifying the cathedral of Cologne as mineralogy [PU §223].) Here Jung concedes the validity of the point, but he responds by presenting his argument in an importantly more nuanced way as follows:

- [A]: The sun myth proves that the fundamental basis of "incestuous" desire does not aim at cohabitation, but at the special thought of becoming a child again, of turning back to the parent's protection, of coming into the mother once more in order to be born again,
- but actual incest itself stands in the path to this goal, that is, the necessity of in some way again gaining entrance into the mother's womb.
- [B]: One of the simplest ways to be born again would be to impregnate the mother and to reproduce one's self identically,
- but here the incest prohibition interferes,
- and therefore, myths of the sun or rebirth all offer possible proposals as to how incest can be evaded.
- [C]: A very simple method of avoidance of incest is to transform the mother into another being or to rejuvenate her after birth has occurred, to have her disappear again or have her change back;
- therefore, it is not incestuous cohabitation itself which is desired, but the rebirth, which can now be attained most readily through cohabitation.

In the parlance of public service broadcasting, other ways of evading incest are available, and Jung is at pains to emphasize how the "resistance to the incest prohibition makes the phantasy inventive" (for instance, by attempting to impregnate the mother by means of a magic fertility charm). While such attempts "remain in the stage of mythical phantasies," they have triggered a process; and this use of fantasy to create fantastic possibilities gradually produces paths (*Bahnen*) in which the libido, taking an active part, can flow off. And thus, Jung concludes, "*the libido becomes spiritualized in an imperceptible manner*" (PU §342). In this way, the very power which, in *Faust I*, describes itself as "always wish[ing] evil" (ll. 1335-1336) is nevertheless able to create a "spiritual life" (and, to complete the Goethean allusion, to "create the good").

Noting the remarkable (but etymologically accidental) sound resemblance of of *mar*, *mère* with *meer* = sea and Latin *mare* = sea, Jung speculates whether this similarity could actually point back to the "the great primitive idea of the mother" — that mother who, in Jung's words, "first meant to us our individual world and afterwards became the symbol of all worlds" (PU §381). After all, as Goethe says of the Faustian Mothers, "They are encircled by images of all creatures" (l. 6289), and in the Christian tradition, the Mother of God is united with water in a medieval hymn to the Blessed Virgin, beginning "Ave Maris Stella" (PU §382).

In the context of the visions of Miss Miller and, in particular, one vision of a "purple bay," Jung is prompted to consider the etymological significance of "bay" (*der Bucht*, *la baie*, etc.), ingeniously linking (a) the Catalonian *badia* from *badar* = "to open," the French *bayer* = "to have one's mouth open, to gape"; (b) the German *Meerbusen* = "bay or gulf," the Latin *sinus*; and (c) "golf" or "gulf," related to French *gouffre* = "abyss" (PU §420). He argues that "golf" is derived from κόλπος, which means "bosom" and "womb," "mother-womb," and also "vagina"; the fold of a dress or pocket; a deep valley between high mountains (PU §420).

(Had they ever discovered this passage, Gilles Deleuze or Jacques Derrida might have been delighted to see so many examples of this concept of the fold or *le pli*!)[48] And we can see where this is all leading, as Jung confirms that these examples indicate which "primordial representations" (*Urvorstellungen*) underpin them (PU §420). Yet he also claims that they make intelligible Goethe's choice of words when, in the scene "Before the Gate," Faust wishes to follow the sun with winged desire in order in the everlasting day "to drink its eternal light" (l. 1806):

> "The mountain chain with all its gorges deep,
> Would then no more impede my godlike motion;
> And now before mine eyes expands the ocean,
> With all its bays, in shining sleep!"
>
> (ll. 1080-1083; PU §420)

In this respect this passage represents not just a return to his earlier argument in Part One about the solar aspect of Faust's desire as expressed in the scene "Before the Gate," but also a reaffirmation of Jung's own core thesis that Faust's desire, "like that of every hero," inclines "towards the mysteries of rebirth, of immortality; therefore, his course leads to the sea, and down into the monstrous jaws of death, the horror and narrowness of which at the same time signify the new day" (PU §421):

> "Out on the open ocean speeds my dreaming!
> The glassy flood before my feet is gleaming,
> A new day beckons to a newer shore!

---

[48] See Gilles Deleuze, *Le pli: Leibniz et le baroque* (Paris: Editions de Minuit, 1988), trans. Tom Conley as *The Fold: Leibniz and the Baroque* (Minneapolis, MN: University of Minnesota Press, 1993); and Jacques Derrida, *La Double Séance* (Paris: Tel Quel, 1971), trans. Barbara Johnson as "The Double Session," in *Dissemination* (Chicago: University of Chicago Press, 1981), pp. 173-286.

A fiery chariot borne on buoyant pinions,
Sweeps near me now! I soon shall ready be
To pierce the ether's high, unknown dominions,
To reach new spheres of pure activity!
This godlike rapture, this supreme existence ...

[....]

"Yes, let me dare those gates to fling asunder.
Which every man would fain go slinking by!
'Tis time, through deeds this word of truth to thunder;
That with the height of God's Man's dignity may vie!
Nor from that gloomy gulf to shrink affrighted.
Where fancy doth herself to self-born pangs compel, —
To struggle toward that pass benighted,
Around whose narrow mouth flame all the fires of Hell: —
To take this step with cheerful resolution,
Though Nothingness should be the certain swift
conclusion!"
(ll. 699-706 & 710-719; PU §421)

After this highly articulate and literary text, it is all the more poignant
that Jung concludes his argumentation at this point by observing
that the entire series of Miss Miller's visions is completed by a
confusion of sounds, resembling something along the lines of "wa-
ma, wa-ma" (PU §422). Does all of Jung's learning and erudition,
does Goethe's intricate aesthetic versification, does everything we
say or do amount to no more than a hypersophisticated (but in this
sense, distorted) version of the familiar cry: ma-ma...?

Having so prominently anchored his central argumentation
around the figure of Faust in previous chapters, in the final three
chapters of Part 2 of *Transformations and Symbols of the Libido*
the echoes of Goethe's *Faust* become more muted as the emphasis

is increasingly placed on the late poems of Nietzsche (see Volume 3). Thus Jung now takes it for granted that he has established how the Mothers Scene in *Faust* shows "*the willed introversion of a creative spirit [Geist]*" and that it demonstrates the dynamic by which that spirit or mind, "retreating before its own problem and inwardly collecting its forces, dips at least for a moment into the source of life [*Lebensquelle*], in order to wrest a little more strength from the mother for the completion of its work" (PU §469). Then again, in his discussion of the dual mother role, Jung examines the motif that "wherever the fertilizing god steps, there is fruitfulness" and the associated symbolic meaning of treading (as in treading grapes), referring to the mythological examples of Caeneus, one of the Lapithae, who "splits the earth with outstretched foot" (cf. Pindar, fragment 167),[49] and to Amphiaraus, the great prophet and hero of Argos, who sinks into the earth that Zeus has opened up with a stroke of lightning (cf. Pindar, *Nemean Ode* 10, ll. 7-9),[50] as well as to Faust, who is instructed by Mephistopheles to gain access to the Mothers as follows, "Stamp and descend, stamping thou'lt rise again" (l. 6304) (PU §489). (Jung's explanation of this motif in terms of the regression of the libido to the presexual stage is that this preparatory act of treading is a substitute either for the coitus fantasy or for the fantasy of reentrance into the mother's womb [PU §490].)

Another aspect of the treading or stamping motif is in the context of the heroes in sun-devouring myths struggling in the jaws of a monster (PU §490; cf. §549). Defending himself against being bitten or crushed, an action which for some reason Jung associates with Mephisto's advice to Faust, "There whirls the press, like clouds on clouds unfolding, / Then with stretched arm swing high the key thou'rt holding!" (ll. 6279-6280), the hero sometimes arrives at the interior of the "whale-dragon" where he cuts off the vital organ

---

[49] *The Odes of Pindar, including the Principal Fragments*, trans. John Sandys (London; New York: Heinemann; Putnam, 1927), pp. 603-605.
[50] *Odes of Pindar*, trans. Sandys, p. 415.

or lights a fire in its belly and destroys it, "secretly creating in the womb of death life, the rising sun" (PU §549). With the assistance of a bird, the hero attains again the light of day and, in the context the bird, is said to represent "the re-ascent of the sun, the yearning of the libido, *the rebirth of the phoenix*" (PU §549; my emphasis). (As we saw in Volume 1, Chapter 2, both Nietzsche and Jung have recourse to the idea of the power of the phoenix, and we shall return to the phoenix as the archetypal bird of transformation in Volume 3.)

In a related motif that belongs to the dual mother role, Jung discusses how, as symbolically represented in the case of Siegfried and Fafner in Wagner's *Ring*, "the mother possesses the libido of the son [...] and jealously [..] guard[s] it" or, in psychological terms, "the positive transference [*Übertragung*] succeeds only through the release of the libido from the mother-imago or the incestuous object in general" (PU §578). Only through a "mighty struggle, the whole struggle of adaptation," Jung emphasizes with great conviction, "can one gain one's libido, the incomparable treasure" (PU §578), and he turns for confirmation of the principle to — where else? — Goethe's *Faust*:

> And yet my weal in torpor seek I not.
> The thrill of awe is still mankind's best lot,
> And though the world not lets him feel it cheaply,
> Yet awe-struck, the stupendous feels he deeply.

> [*Doch im Erstarren such ich nicht mein Heil,*
> *Das Schaudern ist der Menschheit bestes Teil;*
> *Wie auch die Welt ihm das Gefühl verteure,*
> *Ergriffen, fühlt er tief das Ungeheure.*]
> (ll. 6271-6274)[51]

---

[51] For Pierre Hadot's view of the immense significance of these lines, see *La Philosophie comme manière de vivre: Entretiens* (Paris: Albin Michel, 2001), p. 172; and *Philosophy as a Way of Life: Spiritual Exercises from Socrates to Foucault*, ed.

On the subterranean level of his text, that is to say in his footnotes, Jung echoes these sentiments expressed by Faust. Discussing the mysteries of Hecate, the spectral goddess of night and phantoms whose cult flourished in Rome toward the end of the fourth century, Jung noted that, among such other symbols as the whip, the snake, the dagger, and the torch, another is the key, echoing the Mothers Scene (PU §587, fn. 81). In fact, as Hecate *prothyraia* (προθυραία) and hence as the guardian of Hades and a psychopompic divinity, the key belongs to her (as it does to Janus, St. Peter, and Aion) (§587). The Temenos of Gaia, a temple to the earth mother in ancient Athens with its abyss and well, recalls the gates of life and death, "past which everyone gladly creeps" (*an denen jeder gern vorüberschleicht*) (l. 711) — gates which Faust (in his suicide monologue) would like to tear open, and which Jung (in *Memories, Dreams, Reflections*) associates with the "uncertain path that leads into the depths of the unconscious" (MDR, 213).

Toward the end of *Transformations and Symbols of the Libido*, however, a shift takes place, and the figure of Friedrich Hölderlin (1770-1843) emerges as the major literary voice through which Jung expresses his project. Consequently, Jung's references even to Goethe's *Faust* become subordinated to the Hölderlinian voice.[52] These quotations from Hölderlin's poems "To the Rose," "Hyperion's Song of Fate" (*Hyperions Schicksalslied*), "Humanity," "To Nature," "Palinode," "Empedocles," "Obituary"

Arnold I. Davidson, trans. Michael Chase (Oxford and Malden, MA: Blackwell, 1995), p. 115.

[52] For further discussion, see Paul Bishop, "On Reading Jung in German: Jung's Significance for *Germanistik*," in Jean Kirsch and Murray Stein (eds.), *How and Why We Still Read Jung: Personal and Professional Reflections* (London and New York: Routledge, 2013), pp. 66-85. For an account of Hölderlin's role in creating the "myth of absence," see Jason Ā. Josephson-Storm, *The Myth of Disenchantment: Magic, Modernity, and the Birth of the Human Sciences* (Chicago and London: University of Chicago Press, 2017), Chapter 3, "The Myth of Absence" (esp. pp. 86-89); and, for a recent biographical account, see Giorgio Agamben, *Hölderlin's Madness: Chronicle of a Dwelling Life, 1806-1843*, trans. Alta L. Price (London: Seagull Books, 2023).

(*Wohl geh' ich täglich* ...), and "Achilles" are said by Jung to "describe more plainly than could be depicted with meagre words" a key psychological dynamic: namely, "the persistent arrest and the constantly growing estrangement from life, the gradual deep immersion into the maternal abyss of the individual being" (PU §650). After these "songs of retrogressive longing," Jung then turns his attention to Hölderlin's late, great work, the "apocalyptic song" of "Patmos" (1808), whose arresting opening lines

Near is the God
And hard to comprehend.
But where Danger threatens
The Rescuer appears

[*Nah ist*
Und schwer zu fassen der Gott.
Wo aber Gefahr ist, wächst
Das Rettende auch]

are said express that the libido has "now sunk to the lowest depths," to where (in the words of the Mothers Scene) "the danger is great" (l. 6291).[53] Boldly assimilating Hölderlin to Goethe, Jung argues that where "danger threatens" (*wo ... Gefahr ist*) or "the danger is great" (*die Gefahr ist groß*), there "the god is near" (*Nah ist ... der Gott*) and the human being may "find the inner sun, his own sun-like and self-renewing nature, hidden in the maternal womb like the sun in the night-time" (PU §652). This Goethean-cum-Hölderlinian dynamic is also precisely the transformational dynamic which we shall see in full play in Jung's *Red Book*.

In fact, in the final chapter of *Liber Primus* in *The Red Book*, Jung sees a "new god, a child, who subdued daimons in his hand,"

---

[53] Hölderlin, *Poems & Fragments*, trans. Hamburger, pp. 482-483.

continuing in the *Draft* version, "I saw that a new god had come to be out of Christ the Lord, a young Hercules" (RB, 204). In the Parzival scene in "Nox quarta" in *Liber Secundus*, Parzival enters, wearing "the lionskin of Hercules [on] his shoulders" and holding "the club in his hand" (RB, 364; see Volume 4), and in *Transformations and Symbols of the Libido* Jung notes that "Hercules' club is made from the wood of the maternal olive tree," just as "Faust's key also knows the Mothers" (*Auch Fausts Schlüssel kennt die Mütter*), indicating how "the libido springs from the mother, and with this weapon alone can the individual overcome death" (PU §658).

The depiction in Hölderlin's "Patmos" of "the passage from Asia through Patmos to the Christian mysteries" is, Jung insists, "apparently a superficial connection, but in reality a very ingenious train of thought," inasmuch as it presents the "entrance into death and the land beyond as a self-sacrifice of the hero, for the attainment of immortality" (PU §660). "At this time," Jung avers, "when the sun has set, when love is apparently dead, the individual awaits in mysterious joy the renewal of all life," as powerfully expressed in Hölderlin's magnificent lines:

> [...] and Joy it was
> From now on
> To live in the loving night and see
> The eyes of innocence hold the unchanging
> Depths of all wisdom.
>
> (cited in PU §660)

Thus the message of Hölderlin's "Patmos" is also the message of Goethe's *Faust*; and, as we shall see, it will also be the message of Jung's *Red Book* — namely, that "in the depths dwells wisdom, the wisdom of the mother," and that "uniting oneself with it is to give us an intuitive sense of deeper things, of the deposits of primordial times whose strata have been preserved by the spirit [*der Geist*]"

(PU §661). The crucial difference between Hölderlin's "Patmos" and Goethe's *Faust* is this: that Hölderlin, "in his diseased ecstasy, feels once more the greatness of what is seen, but he is less concerned to bring up to the light of day what he had found in the depths," even if he is nevertheless ready to embark on his own Empedoclean journey into the volcano:

> *And it is not an evil, if a few*
> *Are lost and never found,* and if the speech
> Conceals the living sound,
> Because each godly work resembles ours;
> And yet the Highest does not plan it all —
> Though the pit bears iron,
> And glowing lava Aetna,
> *Would I had the power*
> *To build an image and see the Spirit [den Geist]* —
> *See it as it was!*[54]
>
> (PU §661; Jung's italics)

Although the poetic voice allows "one hope to glimmer through," expressed in "scanty words" — the image of awakening the dead, the "sign" (of the father) in the thundering sky, and the cry that "Christ for still lives" (PU §662), Hölderlin's poem "die[s] away" in a "painful lament" (PU §663). Alluding to Hölderlin's final years in a state of insanity, Jung declares that this insight — namely, that "the individual must sacrifice the retrogressive longing (the incestuous libido), before the 'heavenly ones' [*die Himmlischen*]

---

[54] Whether consciously or unconsciously, Jung changes this line by writing *Zu schaun, wie er gewesen, den Geist*, whereas the line runs *Zu schaun, wie er gewesen, den Christ*. In the fragments of the later version, however, Hölderlin does write, "Therefore he sent them / The Spirit" (*Drum sandt er ihnen / Den Geist*) (Hölderlin, *Poems & Fragments*, trans. Hamburger, pp. 506-507). For an extensive commentary on this difficult and complex poem, see Hölderlin, *Sämtliche Gedichte*, ed. Jochen Schmidt (Frankfurt am Main: Deutscher Klassiker Verlag, 2005), pp. 969-1013.

tear away the sacrifice, and at the same time the entire libido" — was one that "came too late to the poet" (PU 664).

In this respect, then, Hölderlin "differs" from Faust (PU §661), who descends to the Mothers and yet who *does* return, in order to conjure up those emblems of the ancient past, Paris and Helena. This is why it is Goethe's *Faust* that offers Jung a template for his argument in *Transformations and Symbols of the Libido*, not Hölderlin, but the references to "Patmos," and the allusion to the legend in which Gilgamesh, bringing back the magic herb from the land of the West, is robbed of this prize by the daimonic serpent, sound a note of caution about just how dangerous Jung's own descent to the primordial Mothers as undertaken in *The Red Book* might prove to be.

Goethe's *Faust* in *Psychological Types*

In *Transformations and Symbols of the Libido*, Jung opposes Hölderlin's supposed failure in "Patmos" to Goethe's *Faust*, hailed as a success; but after Jung's experiences in creating *The Red Book* — that is, after 1913 to 1921 — a new note of scepticism comes into his account of *Faust*, reflected in how he uses this work in his writings on typology and in two early programmatic essays. (We shall, for the remainder of this chapter, examine these texts in turn, examining his writings on alchemy in Chapter 4).

In his chapter in *Psychological Types* (1921) on the type problem in classical and medieval thought, Jung directly addresses the question of the relation between intellect and feeling, reflected in the status of science in general and psychology in particular. The aim of psychology, Jung argues, is to "grasp the processes of feeling, sensation, and phantasy in abstract intellectual form" (CW 6 §84). In so doing, scientific psychology "establishes the rights" of the abstract, intellectual standpoint but is unable to validate the claims of "other quite possible psychological points of view" (§84).

Now in *The Black Books* and *The Red Book*, Jung had reflected time and again on the status of science, or *Wissenschaft*. Here, in *Psychological Types* Jung moots the possibility of another kind of science and another kind of psychology: a psychology which, although "no longer science," is nevertheless a "psychological activity of a creative nature," a psychology in which "prior place" is given to "creative phantasy" — or even to "*life* itself" (§84).

As Jung goes on to argue, whenever we "approach the actual business of living from the side of the intellect and science," we immediately run up against "barriers that shut us out from other, equally real provinces of life" (CW 6 §85), and he turns for an example to *Faust*. When Faust declares, "Feeling is everything" (*Gefühl ist alles*) (l. 3456), he articulates — over and above the immediate context of his discussion with Gretchen about religion — a view that is the "antithesis of the intellect" (or the excessively intellectual life he had been leading as an academic), and so he "goes to the other extreme" (§85). What Faust does *not* achieve — neither in Part One nor even (as Jung argues elsewhere) in Part Two — is "that totality of life and his own psyche in which feeling and thinking are united in a third and higher principle" (§85). This higher third is conceived by Jung as "either a practical goal or the creative fantasy that creates a goal," for the "goal of totality" cannot be reached by science, which is an "end in itself," nor by feeling, which "lacks the visionary power of thought" (§85). Instead, Jung proposes that the relation between intellect and feeling should be a *dialectical one*: Each must lend itself "as an auxiliary" to the other, yet so great is the "opposition" between them that "a bridge" is required — a bridge that we can find, already given to us, in "creative phantasy" (§85). Not "born" of intellect or feeling, this bridge is rather "the mother" of both — and it is said by Jung to be "pregnant" with "the child" — "that final goal which unites the opposites" (§85).[55]

Further on in this work, Jung becomes positively hymnic in his praise of creative phantasy, declaring that "every good idea and all creative work are the offspring of the imagination [*Imagination*], and have their source in [...] infantile phantasy [*infantile Phantasie*]," so that "not the artist alone, but all creative individuals whatsoever, owe all that is greatest in their lives to phantasy [*Phantasie*]" (CW 6 §93). Now, the "dynamic principle" of phantasy is *play*, which is also a "characteristic of the child" and, as such, apparently inconsistent with the "principle of serious work." And yet without "this playing with phantasy," Jung insists, "no creative work has ever yet come to birth" (§93). In this image of the child at play as a symbol of creativity, it is hard not to hear an echo of Nietzsche's *Zarathustra* and its description of the transformations of the spirit as camel, then a lion, and finally a child: "Innocence is the child, and forgetfulness, a new beginning, a game, a self-rolling wheel, a first movement, a holy Yea" (Z I 1). And "in the true man," the old woman tells Zarathustra, "there is a child hidden: it wanteth to play. Up then, ye women, and discover the child in man!" (Z I 18).

In Chapter 5 on the type problem in poetry, Jung considers two particular opposites that he sees set out in Carl Spitteler's *Prometheus and Epimetheus* (1881), those opposites of the attitudes of introversion and extraversion that Jung has derived in the preceding chapter from Furneaux Jordan's *Character as Seen in Body and Parentage* (1896). In Jung's view, Spitteler's great allegorical prose epic presents us, not so much with an opposition between the two Titans, Prometheus (the "forethinker") as the introvert and Epimetheus (the "afterthinker," or the man of action)

---

[55] The motif of pregnancy is a common one in Platonic thought and constitutes the starting point of "philosophical midwifery"; see Pierre Grimes and Regina L. Uliana, *Philosophical Midwifery: A New Paradigm for Understanding Human Problems* (Costa Mesa, CA: Hyparxis Press, 1998).

as the extravert, as with the "struggle between the introverted and extraverted lines of development *in one and the same individual*" (§276; my emphasis). In one section, Jung compares Spitteler's conception of Prometheus with this figure as we find it in Goethe, noting that Spitteler's identification of Prometheus with the introverted attitude is not the only way of interpreting this figure.[56]

In fact, in Goethe's works we find *two* versions of Prometheus (and, if we include his early poem of 1773, *three*).[57] First, in the unfinished dramatic fragment of 1773, Prometheus is presented as "the defiant, self-sufficient, godlike, god-disdaining creator and artist" (CW 6 §289). In his relation to Minerva as his soul, this Goethean Prometheus is said to be similar to Spitteler's (§289). In other respects, however, Goethe's Prometheus is judged to be very different from Spitteler's: Whereas the former "creates and works outwards into the world," in the case of the latter "everything goes inwards and vanishes in the darknesses of the soul's depths" (§294). The second version of Prometheus can be found in Goethe's dramatic festival play "Pandora" (written between November 1807 and June 1808 at the request of Leo von Seckendorff and Joseph Ludwig Stoll, and published in fragmentary form in the first two issues of the journal *Prometheus* in 1807 and 1808 but never completed).

---

[56] According to Jung, in Plato's *Protagoras* the bestower of vital powers on the beings that the gods have created out of fire and water is not Prometheus, but Epimetheus (320-321a). On this account, Prometheus is a "crafty and inventive genius" (CW 6 §289).

[57] On the figure of Prometheus in the writings of Goethe, see "Prometheus" (1773), in Johann Wolfgang von Goethe, *Selected Poems*, ed. Christopher Middleton [Goethe Edition, vol. 1] (Boston: Suhrkamp/Insel, 1982), pp. 26-31; and *Selected Poems*, trans. John Whaley (London: Dent, 1998), pp. 18-21. For further discussion, see Walter F. Otto (1874-1958) on "Goethe und Prometheus" in his *Mythos und Welt*, ed. Kurt von Fritz (Stuttgart: Klett, 1962), pp. 83-95; and Gottfried Diener, *Pandora – Zu Goethes Metaphorik: Entstehung, Epoche, Interpretation des Festspiels* (Bad Homburg: Gehlen, 1968).

Now in the Prometheus myth as told by Hesiod, an important role is played by the enigmatic figure of Pandora. In Hesiod's *Theogony* (ll. 560-612), Zeus decides to punish humankind for having received the stolen gift of fire from Prometheus by giving them another gift to compensate. He orders Hephaestus to mold from the earth the very first woman, a "beautiful evil" (l. 585) whose descendants would subsequently torment the human race — Pandora, whom Athena clothes in a splendid silvery gown, an embroidered veil, and an ornate crown of silver. In the version of the myth given in Hesiod's *Works and Days* (ll. 60-105), Pandora is created by Hephaestus, but this time more gods are involved in her completion (ll. 63-82), including the choice of her name. In addition to her deceitful nature, Pandora brings with her a jar or box containing "countless plagues," and Prometheus warns Epimetheus: Do not accept any more gifts from Zeus! As a result of scattering the contents of her jar, the earth and sea are "full of evils" (l. 101); and the only item that did not escape and remained in the jar was *elpis,* or Hope.

Within the context of Spitteler's version of the myth, Jung interprets Pandora and her gift, a precious jewel to ease the sufferings of humankind, as an "unconscious mirror-image that *symbolizes* the real work of the soul of Prometheus" and as signifying a "*God-redeemer*, a renewal of the sun" (CW 6 §297). (On this account, Spitteler's work sounds like a version of the transformational dynamic at work in Jung's *Red Book*, inasmuch as "the sickness of God expresses his longing for rebirth, and to this end his whole life force flows back into the center of the self, into the depths of the unconscious, out of which life is born anew" [§297; cf. CW 6 §301].)

In Goethe's "Pandora" the situation differs from the earlier "Prometheus Fragment" in a significant respect, or so Jung argues, namely, inasmuch as it conveys a "far more complex portrait" of Epimetheus than the fragment does (CW 6 §303). In this later work, Prometheus has become the extraverted man of action and Epimetheus the brooding introvert (§306); but the relation of Prometheus with the soul, or the unconscious feminine principle, is said to be "missing" (§306). (Elsewhere in his discussion of *Faust*, this problematic or deficient relation to the feminine turns out to be crucial.)

In *Psychological Types*, Jung's discussion of Goethe's "Prometheus Fragment" and "Pandora" in relation to Spitteler's *Prometheus and Epimetheus* takes place in the context of an overarching account of European intellectual history, beginning (in Chapter 1) with the problem of types in the history of classical and medieval thought and continuing (in Chapter 2) with Schiller's ideas on the type problem in his *Letters on the Aesthetic Education of Humankind* (1795) and *On Naïve and Sentimental Poetry* (1796). In Schiller's *Letters*, Jung discerns an attempt to solve the "problem of uniting the differentiated with the undifferentiated function" (or in other words, uniting consciousness and the unconscious) — a solution which, in Spitteler's work, takes the symbolic form of Pandora's gift of the jewel (CW 6 §301). In Goethe's "Pandora" and in its symbolic figures of Prometheus and Epimetheus, the problem that Schiller had "sought to master philosophically and aesthetically" in his *Letters* is now "clothed in the garment of a classical myth" (§314). In this respect, Jung argued, the work was typical for its time.

For at the turn of the 18th century, Jung explains, the classical spirit was "felt to contain a compensatory value" and found expression as Philhellenism in aesthetics, philosophy, morals, and politics (CW 6 §314).[58] "Glorified," he says, as *freedom, naïveté, beauty*, etc., it was really the "paganism of antiquity" that met the

---

[58] For further discussion, see Humphry Trevelyan, *Goethe & the Greeks* [1942] (New York: Octagon, 1972); and Damian Valdez, *German Philhellenism: The Pathos of the Historical Imagination from Winckelmann to Goethe* (New York: Palgrave Macmillan, 2014).

"yearnings of that age," springing from a "feeling of imperfection, of spiritual barbarism, of moral servitude, of drabness" and arising from a "one-sided evaluation of everything Greek, and from the consequent fact that the psychological dissociation between the differentiated and the undifferentiated functions became painfully evident" (§314). Yet this attempt at a "regressive Renaissance" had been, Jung claims, "still-born," inasmuch as the "classical solution would no longer work" — as reflected in the fate of Goethe's "Prometheus Fragment" and "Pandora" (§315), or Goethe's failure to complete them. Because the "intervening centuries of Christianity with their profound spiritual upheavals could not be undone," this *penchant* for antiquity "gradually petered out in medievalism" (and it seems that as a problem it remains unresolved, if *The Red Book* is anything to go by, for in it Jung declares: "I must catch up with a piece of the Middle Ages — within myself. We have only finished the Middle Ages of — others" [RB, 457].) As evidence of this medievalizing tendency, Jung points to Goethe's *Faust*, where this problem is said to have been "seized by the horns" (§315). But how? And why?

To begin with, because in the "Prologue in Heaven" the "divine wager between good and evil" is actually accepted. Later on, Faust (a kind of medieval Prometheus) "enters the lists" with Mephistopheles (a kind of medieval Epimetheus) and "makes a pact with him" (CW 6 §315). And here, Jung significantly adds, the problem becomes "so sharply focused that one can see that *Faust and Mephisto are the same person*" (§315; my emphasis). Whereas, in "Pandora," the principle of Epimetheus is represented as thinking everything backward and reducing everything to the primordial chaos of "*gestaltenmischender Möglichkeit*" (l. 12), in *Faust* this principle acquires in the shape of the Devil the more radical form of an evil power that opposes everything living with its "cold devilish fist" (l. 1381) and would like to try to force "the light" back into the "maternal darkness," whence it was born (cf. ll. 1351-1352). In fact, Jung adds, Mephistopheles displays a "true Epimethean thinking" — a thinking in terms of "nothing but," thereby reducing everything living to primordial nothingness (§315). What was Epimetheus's naïve passion for his brother's beloved, Pandora, turns into Mephistopheles's devilish designs on the soul of Faust, while Prometheus's shrewd foresight in rejecting the divine Pandora is "expiated" (*gesühnt*) by the tragedy of the Gretchen episode and the belated fulfillment of Faust's yearning for Helena as well as by his endless ascent to the Mothers Above (in the famous lines, *Das ewig Weibliche / Zieht uns hinan*; ll. 12110-12111).

This Promethean defiance of the accepted gods becomes embodied, Jung argues, in the figure of the medieval magician (CW 6 §316) — that is to say, in the figure of Faust himself! To the extent that he preserves in himself a "piece of primitive paganism," the magician possesses a nature that is untouched by Christian division of the human being into two parts, one valuable and one depraved (cf. §314). Instead, the magician can gain access to the unconscious that is still pagan, where the opposites still lie side by side in their state of original naïveté and which is beyond any sinfulness but, if integrated into conscious life, is apt to beget evil with the same original and therefore daimonic energy as it begets good (cf. *Ein Teil von jener Kraft, / Die stets das Böse will und stets das Gute schafft* [ll. 1335-1336]). This figure is as much a bringer of ruin as well as a savior (and, in this regard, Jung recalls the scene when Faust goes for a walk on Easter morning in the company of Wagner and tells him how his father's potions poisoned the population); and therefore this figure is preeminently suited to becoming a "symbolic bearer of an attempt at unification" (§316).

In addition, the medieval magician exemplifies the dialectical relationship between paganism and Christianity: (1) The classical naïveté is laid aside as impossible, and the Christian atmosphere pervades everything as a result of intense experience; (2) the pagan element drives the magician into Christian self-denial and tearing oneself apart, for his yearning for salvation is so strong it makes use of every means; (3) but now the Christian attempt at a solution fails, and it turns out that the possibility of redemption lies precisely in the yearning for salvation and in its stubborn persistence of the pagan element, as the anti-Christian symbol reveals the possibility of an acceptance of evil (CW 6 §316). On this point Jung is insistent: He argues that Goethe had intuitively understood precisely this problem "with all the clarity one could wish for" (§316). In Jung's view, it says a good deal about Goethe that his other, more superficial attempts at a solution in the "Prometheus Fragment," in *Pandora*, and in his poem *The Mysteries* (*Die Geheimnisse*) all remained uncompleted. (*Die Geheimnisse* is described by Jung as a Rosicrucian compromise involving a syncretism of Dionysian joy with Christian self-sacrifice!)[59]

And now Jung makes a highly original argumentational move. For Faust's redemption, he says, *began at his death*, and "his life retained the character of Promethean divinity until it fell away only with *his death, that is, with his rebirth*" (§317; my emphasis). In psychological terms, he adds, this means that "the Faustian attitude must come to an end in order for the unity of the individual to be

---

[59] A few pages earlier Jung describes the poem *Die Geheimnisse* (i.e., *The Mysteries*) as a "Rosicrucian solution" to the problem of the differentiated and undifferentiated functions, i.e., consciousness and the unconscious: that is to say, an attempt at "the union of Dionysos and Christ, rose and cross" (CW 6 §314, fn.). Jung is, however, skeptical about this success of this endeavor, remarking: "The poem leaves one cold. One cannot pour new wine into old bottles" (§314, fn). Inspired by J.G. Herder's *Ideas for a Philosophy of the History of Humankind* (1784-1781) and following C.M. Wieland's *Oberon* (1780; 1796) in its choice of *ottava rima*, this project to write a religious epic remains a fragment; in conversation with Sulpiz Boisserée on 3 August 1815, Goethe admitted his plan had been too ambitious (*zu groß angefangen*). For the only available translation of this unfinished poem, see Rudolf Steiner's lecture delivered on 25 December 1907 in Cologne and published as *The Mysteries: A Poem for Christmas and Easter by J.W. von Goethe* (Great Barrington: SteinerBooks, 2014), translated by Marianne H. Luedeking from *Die Geheimnisse: Ein Weihnachts- und Ostergedicht von Goethe* (Dornach: Philosophisch-Anthroposophischer Verlag am Goetheanum, 1931).

achieved"; or, to put it another way, the figure that first appeared as Gretchen and then, on a higher level, became Helena, is finally elevated as the Mater Gloriosa. Jung reserves discussion of this "ambiguous symbol" for another occasion, but he notes that what is being constellated here is a "primordial image" (*urtümliches Bild*) that was a major preoccupation of Gnosticism: namely, the idea of the divine harlot represented by Eve, Helena, Mary, and Sophia-Achamoth (§317).[60]

Further on in this chapter on "The Type Problem in Poetry," Jung discusses the psychological phenomenon of personification, understood as a dissociation between the ego and a particular complex (CW 6 §344). The figure of Faust, he goes on, offers a good "literary example" of what happens when people become "too deeply immersed in one of their psychic functions and have differentiated it into their sole conscious means of adaptation" (§344). So, what does happen at the beginning of the tragedy? The "other components" of Faust's personality take shape and approach him, first as the black dog (or "poodle"), and then as Mephistopheles. Now although there are clear associations between Mephistopheles and sexuality, Jung rejects the reading that Mephistopheles is no more than a split-off complex representing "repressed sexuality" (§345). For Jung, Mephistopheles is much more than mere sexuality: He is also *power* (*Macht*), in the sense that he is the entirety of Faust's life *aside* from thinking and researching (and, if he were an academic today, doing administration). As the very success of the pact with the Devil is said to make abundantly clear, "what undreamed-of possibilities unfold out of the rejuvenated Faust!" (§345). So, on Jung's account, Faust has identified with one function (i.e., thinking) and become split off (i.e., as Mephistopheles) from his personality as a whole,

---

[60] See CW 15 §211; and CW 16 §361; and letter of 22 March 1939 (L1, 264-266) (see Chapter 4 below, p. 369, fn. 74).

while later the thinker in the form of Wagner also gets split off from Faust (§345).

In his discussion in Chapter 2 of Schiller's *Letters on the Aesthetic Education of Humankind* (1795), Jung points out that nowhere in them does Schiller express any views about the kind of techniques that might induce the "aesthetic mood." Nevertheless, Jung draws attention to the passage at the conclusion of Letter 15, where Schiller uses the statue of the Juno Ludovisi as an illustration of how, for the Greeks, "both the material constraint of natural laws and the spiritual constraint of moral laws were resolved in their higher concept of Necessity, which embraced both worlds at once," arguing that "it was only out of the perfect union of those two necessities that for them true Freedom could proceed," and adding that "it is not Grace, nor is it yet Dignity, which speaks to us from the superb countenance of a Juno Ludovisi; it is neither the one nor the other because it is both at once" (Letter 15, §9).[61] (The Juno Ludovisi is the massive marble head of the goddess Juno (or Hera), which survives from an acrolithic statue dating back to first-century C.E. Rome.) This cultural reference, Jung argues, illustrates how, for Schiller, the state of "aesthetic devotion" (*ästhetische Andacht*) consists in a complete surrender to and empathy (*Einfühlung*) for the object of contemplation (§200).

While Jung misses from this state of devotion the characteristics of lacking any content or determinant, he suggests on the basis of this passage — and Schiller's following remark that "[w]hile the woman-god demands our veneration, the god-like woman kindles our love; but even as we abandon ourselves in ecstasy to her heavenly grace, her celestial self-sufficiency makes us recoil in terror" (Letter 15, §9) — that the "idea of devotion [*Andacht*] was at the forefront of Schiller's mind" (§200), implying

---

[61] Friedrich Schiller, *On the Aesthetic Education of Man*, ed. and trans. Elizabeth M. Wilkinson and L.A. Willoughby, 2nd edn. (Oxford: Clarendon Press, 1982), p. 109.

that Schiller's problem is not so much aesthetic as religious. This move prompts Jung to consider what is happening in the "empty state of consciousness or the unconscious condition" which arises as a result of the "sinking of the libido into the unconscious" (CW 6 §187).

In fact, this sinking of the libido into the unconscious *is* what Jung understands by "devotion," or *Andacht*, and it leads to a reactivation of childhood complexes: childhood reminiscences, and especially one's relations to one's parents, become alive again (§201). The phantasies produced by this reactivation are the occasion for the emergence of father and mother divinities, as well as for the awakening of childhood religious relations to God and the corresponding childlike feelings. In this respect, however, Jung makes a crucial distinction between his own position and Freud's: where Freud explains the activation of symbols of the parents rather than images of the actual parents in terms of the repression of the parental imago as a result of resistance to incest, Jung goes one step further and, while not entirely disagreeing with Freud, argues that this "symbolic substitution" acquires an "extraordinary significance" (§201). On Jung's account, this "symbolization in the God-image" represents an "immense progress beyond the concretism, the sensuousness of reminiscence," inasmuch as "through the acceptance of the 'symbol' as a real symbol" — *das Annehmen des «Symbols» als eines wirklichen Symbols* — the regression "turns into a progression," whereas if "the so-called symbol were merely interpreted as a *sign* for the actual parents" — *als ein Zeichen für die wirklichen Eltern* — "and thus stripped of its independent character, it would remain a regression" (§201).

In a footnote at this point, Jung refers us back to his earlier argument in *Transformations and Symbols of the Libido* (see PU §180 and §329-§333), but he goes on to synthesize that argument, his discussion of Schiller, and above all his understanding of Goethe's *Faust* in the following remarkable passage, which also casts important light on what had been happening in the creation of *The Red Book*:

> Humanity came to its gods by accepting the reality of the symbol, that is, it came to the *reality of thought*, which has made man lord of the earth. Devotion, as Schiller correctly conceived it, is a regressive movement of libido towards the primordial, a diving down into the source of the first beginnings. Out of this there rises, as an image of the incipient progressive movement, the symbol, which is a condensation of all the operative unconscious factors — "living form" [*«lebende Gestalt»*] as Schiller says,[62] and a God-image, as history proves. It is therefore no accident that he should seize on a divine image, the Juno Ludovici, as a paradigm. Goethe makes the divine images of Paris and Helen float up from the tripod of the Mothers —[63] on the one hand the rejuvenated pair, on the other the symbol of a process of inner union, which is precisely what Faust passionately craves for himself as the supreme inner atonement [*Versöhnung*]. This is clearly shown in the ensuing scene as also from the further course of the drama. As we can see from the example of Faust, the vision of the symbol is a pointer to the onward course of life, beckoning the libido towards a

---

[62] For Schiller's definition of *lebende Gestalt*, see *Letters on the Aesthetic Education*, Letter 15, where he explains that the object of the "sense-drive" (*Sinntrieb*) is life (*Leben*), while the object of the "form-drive" (*Formtrieb*) is form (*Gestalt*), so the object of the ludic drive (*Spieltrieb*) is "living form" (*lebende Gestalt*) — "a concept serving to designate all the aesthetic qualities of phenomena and, in a word, what in the widest sense of the term we call *beauty* [*Schönheit*]" (§2; pp. 100-101).

[63] A clear reference to the scene in the "Baronial Hall" where Faust conjures up Paris and Helena for the Emperor, before intervening and bringing the scene to an explosive conclusion.

still distant goal — but a goal that henceforth will burn
unquenchably within him, so that his life, kindled as by
a flame, moves steadily towards the far-off beacon. This
is the specific life-promoting significance of the symbol,
and such, too, is the meaning and value of religious
symbols. I am speaking, of course, not of symbols that
are dead and stiffened by dogma, but of living symbols
that rise up from the creative unconscious of the living
individual. (CW 6 §202)

Jung warns us that the "immense significance" of such symbols can
be denied only by those who are ignorant of "world history" (*die
Weltgeschichte*) and that precisely such a denial of the "significance
of symbols" is characteristic of the "spirit of our time" (*der Geist
unserer Zeit*) (CW 6 §203) — a figure familiar to readers of *The Red
Book* (RB, 119-123). The "symbol-formation" (*Symbolbildung*)
which arises from the state of "devotion" (*Andacht*) is described by
Jung as one of those "religious collective phenomena" that are not
dependent on "individual aptitude" (§204) — a remark that throws
light on the suggestion that there is a dimension of collective
significance to *The Red Book*. Rather, the "relation to the symbol"
is a "general function" — it is, he says, the "*transcendent function*"
(*transzendente Funktion*) (§205). As contemporary examples of
this function, Jung cites two novels by the Austrian novelist Gustav
Meyrink (1868-1932), *The Golem* (serialized 1913-1914; published
1915) and *The Green Face* (1916). In these (and other works that
Jung categorizes as "belletristic") these phantasies are not observed
and represented in their "pure" state but have undergone an
"aesthetic" elaboration — is this, one wonders, a description that
might also apply to *The Red Book*?

At the opening of Chapter 3 on Nietzsche's concepts of the
Apollonian and the Dionysian, Jung notes that the problem of the
opposites that had been "discerned" and "partially worked out" by

Schiller in his *Letters on the Aesthetic Education of Humankind* and *On the Naïve and the Sentimental in Poetry* had been "taken up again" in a "new and original way" by Nietzsche in *The Birth of Tragedy* (1871). While this early work is "more closely related" to Schopenhauer and to Goethe than to Schiller, Jung notes, it nevertheless shares (or, at least, appears to do so) the aestheticism and Hellenism of Schillerian thinking, at the same time as sharing a certain pessimism and the notion of deliverance with Schopenhauer, to say nothing of "unlimited points of contact" with Goethe's *Faust* (CW 6 §223). In passages such as these, Jung clearly signals the extent to which he sees himself as part of a continuous tradition in German literature and thought, which in these studies we have narrowed down to a focus on Wolfram's *Parzival*, Goethe's *Faust*, Nietzsche's *Zarathustra*, and Jung's *Red Book*.

In his conclusion to Chapter 5 on the type problem in poetry, Jung points to a common feature (as he sees it) of Goethe's *Faust*, Wagner's *Parsifal*, the philosophy of Schopenhauer, and even Nietzsche's *Zarathustra* and finally Spitteler's *Prometheus and Epimetheus* — namely, that the solution to the problem of the opposites is *religious* (CW 6 §324). What does it mean to say that a problem and its solution are religious? For Jung, it means that, psychologically, they are "very significant, of especial value, concerning the whole individual, and thus also the unconscious" — identified here by Jung with the realm of the gods, the world beyond, and so on. In the case of Spitteler, the religious background becomes so intense that the religious problem itself, while gaining "in mythological richness, in archaisms, and thus in a prospective [i.e., forward-looking] symbolism," nevertheless loses "depth" (§320).

The stylistic critique that Jung applies to Spitteler, especially his description of its style as "luxuriance" or "profusion" (*Wucherung*) could surely, one feels, be equally applied to Jung's own *Red Book*: as a work, it is "difficult to access" because "the abstruse, grotesque, and tasteless element that is always attached to mythological profusion hinders our empathy [*Einfühlung*], isolates as a result the meaning of the work, and lends the whole thing a somewhat unpleasant whiff of that originality that can only be successfully distinguished elsewhere from psychic abnormality thanks to an anxiously careful adjustment" (§320). Yet, however "tiresome and unpalatable" this mythological profusion may be, it nevertheless has the singular advantage of allowing the symbol to "unfold, albeit in such an unconscious way that the conscious wit of the poet is at a loss about how to help express its meaning but struggles solely and exclusively to support the mythological profusion and its plastic elaboration" (§324). Again, we might feel entitled to ask: Is this Spitteler that Jung is talking about — or *The Red Book*?

In this stylistic respect, Jung adds, Spitteler's *Prometheus and Epimetheus* differs from Goethe's *Faust* and Nietzsche's *Zarathustra*, in that in both of these works the "conscious participation of the author in the meaning of the symbol" was much greater, as a consequence of which the mythological profusion in *Faust* and the intellectual profusion in *Zarathustra* were correspondingly "cut back [*zurückgedrängt*] to the advantage of the striven-for solution" (§324). So, the result is described by Jung in explicitly *aesthetic* terms: *Faust* and *Zarathustra* are judged to be "much *more beautiful*" than Spitteler's *Prometheus*, although the latter is said to be "*truer* as a relatively faithful depiction of the actual processes in the collective unconscious" (§324). Thus, while *Faust* and *Zarathustra* turn out to be of great help in "the individual coming-to-terms with the problem in question," Spitteler's *Prometheus* can give the reader — thanks to its "mythological profusions that are supported with all available means" — a "more general knowledge of the problem and its collective manner of appearance" (§322). Moreover, *Prometheus* turns out to have an additional function as a prolegomenon to Spitteler's later work, his great verse epic *Olympian Spring* (1900-1905): Spitteler's "rehearsal of unconscious religious contents" is said to hint at the "*symbol of God's renewal*," which is "extensively treated" in his *Olympian Spring* (§322). And what Jung then goes on to say about this symbol, which is said to appear to be "intimately bound up with the opposites in types and functions and obviously has the significance of attempting a solution in the form of a renewal of the general attitude, which is expressed in the language of the unconscious as a renewal of God," could surely also apply, *mutatis mutandis,* to *The Red Book*:

> The renewal of God is a familiar primordial image [*urtümliches Bild*] that one can find as it were everywhere; let me just mention the entire complex of the dying and resurgent God and all its earlier stages down to the charging of fetishes and tjurungas with magical power. This image expresses how the attitude has changed and thereby a new energic potential has arisen, a new possibility of the manifestation of life, a new fecundity. This latter analogy [*Analogie*] explains the amply demonstrated connection of the renewal of the God with the phenomena of the seasons of the year and of growth. One is naturally inclined to extrapolate from these analogies [*Analogien*] to seasonal, vegetational, astral, or lunar myths. In so doing, one entirely forgets that, like anything psychic, a myth cannot be solely determined by an external event. Anything psychic comes with its own inner conditions, so that one would be just as entitled to assert that a myth is purely psychological and uses the data of meteorological or astronomical occurrences merely as expressive materials. The arbitrariness and absurdity of many primitive mythical statements makes this version of explanation often appear more accurate than any other. (CW 6 §325)

In his section on the uniting symbol as the principle of dynamic regulation, Jung describes the division of the psyche in Taoism into a *shen* (or *hawn*) soul and a *kwei* (or *p'o*) soul as a great "psychological truth," and he compares this conception with the well-known passage from *Faust*, Part One (CW 6 §368):

> Two souls, alas! within my breast abide,
>
> The one to quit the other ever burning.
>
> *This*, in a lusty passion of delight,
>
> Cleaves to the world with organs tightly-clinging;
>
> Fain from the dust would *that* its strenuous flight
>
> To realms of loftier sires be winging.
>
> (ll. 1112-1117)

For Jung, this passage speaks to what he calls the existence of two "mutually antagonistic tendences," both of which strive to "drag the individual into extreme attitudes and to entangle them in the world [*in die Welt*], whether its spiritual or its material aspect," thereby creating a dissociation in the individual (*mit sich selber zu entzweien*) (§369).

This sense of radical fissure is, as we have seen, often associated by Jung with Faust: for instance, when in *Transformation and Symbols of the Libido* he writes, "What is to be the way out between the Scylla of renunciation of the world and the Charybdis of the acceptance of the world?" (PU §141), or when in *Symbols of Transformation* (1952) he quotes Faust's remark to Wagner, "You are conscious only of the single urge" (l. 1110), and reflects: "Whoever loves the earth and its glory, and forgets the 'dark realm,' or confuses the two (which is mostly what happens), has spirit [*den «Geist»*] for an enemy; and whoever flees from the earth and falls into the 'eternal arms' has life [*das Leben*] for an enemy" (CW 5 §615).[64]

In his section on the relativity of the symbol in Chapter 5, Jung offers some further remarks on the "medieval background" of *Faust*. The special significance of this background, he argues, lies in the fact that "there actually was a medieval element that stood at the cradle of modern individualism" (CW 6 §376). For modern individualism began, or so Jung explains, with the worship of women (or *Frauendienst*, a notion in the tradition of courtly love), as a consequence of which "the soul of the man became considerably strengthened as a psychological factor" (§376). This is so, Jung declares, because the worship of woman really meant the worship of the soul (*Seelendienst*).

Further consideration of this point leads Jung to discuss Dante's *Divine Comedy*, especially Canto XXXIII of the *Paradiso* (see §377), in which the fact that Dante speaks here through the mouth of St. Bernard is seen by Jung as an "indication of the transformation [*Umgestaltung*] and exaltation [*Erhöhung*] of his own being" (§378). Corresponding to Dante's transformation as a "spiritual knight" is, of course, the transformation of the figure of his lady, Beatrice: Her image is exalted (*erhöht*) into the "otherworldly, mystical figure of the Mother of God — a figure that has detached itself from the object and turned into the personification of a purely psychological affair, namely those unconscious contents whose personification I have termed the soul [*Seele*]" (§377).

---

[64] In this passage, Jung mixes allusions to German classical and biblical texts: the "dark realm" echoes the words of Oreste to Iphigenia in *Iphigenia in Tauris*, Act 3, Scene 1, "Thee let me counsel / To view too fondly neither sun nor stars. / Come, follow to the gloomy realms below!" (ll. 1232-34) (cf. the title of Max Seiling, *Goethe als Okkultist: Komme, folge mir ins dunkle Reich hinab!* (Berlin: J. Baum, 1919), while "eternal arms" echoes the words of Moses in his blessing to the tribes of Israel, "There is no other God like the God of the rightest: he that is mounted upon the heaven is thy helper. By his magnificence the clouds run hither and thither. His dwelling is above, and underneath are the everlasting arms" (Deuteronomy 33: 26-27).

Jung is quick to spot the parallel between Dante's transformation (*Verwandlung*) and Faust's, both across the tragedy as a whole and in its climactic final scene (which is, of course, modeled on Dante's *Paradiso*). On this account, the entire complex drama of *Faust* can be reduced to Faust's ascent from Gretchen to Helena, and then from Helena to the Mother of God: and "as he repeatedly changes his nature through figurative deaths, he attains his highest goal as Doctor Marianus" (§378). It is in the form of the mysterious Doctor Marianus that Faust utters this prayer to the Virgin Mother:

> Thou that reignest as Thy due,
> Lady, of Thy pleasure,
> Let me Thine arcana view
> In the vaulted azure!
> Sanction what man's breast doth move,
> Reverent and tender,
> And with holy bliss of love
> Nigher Thee doth render.
>
> All invincible we grow
> When august Thou willest,
> Tempered straightway is the glow
> If our hearts Thou stillest,
> Virgin pure from stain of earth,
> Mother honour-thronéd,
> Chosen Queen, and peer by birth
> With the Godhead ownéd!
>
> [...]
>
> Tender penitents, your eyes
> Lift where looks salvation.

> Gratefully to bliss arise
> Through regeneration.
> Each best power, Thy service in,
> Prove it efficacious.
> Ever, Virgin, Mother, Queen,
> Goddess, be Thou gracious!
> (ll. 11997-12012 & 12096-12103)

And then there is — tellingly — the legend of the Grail; and, according to Jung, there exist significant psychological relations between the worship of woman (*Frauendienst*) and the legend of the Grail that he regards as being so "peculiarly characteristic" of the early Middle Ages (§401). One of the greatest versions of the Grail legend was, of course, Wolfram von Eschenbach's *Parzival*; and, thanks to Richard Wagner, whose *Parsifal* was in part a revival of Wolfram's *Parzival*, we can see how the vitality of the symbol of the Grail is even today still not exhausted, "even if our age and our psychology constantly strive for its dissolution," he adds (§401).

As we saw above, Jung's concept of the symbol draws, at least in part, on Schiller's conception of "living form" (*lebende Gestalt*) and, in his definition of the symbol in the "Definitions" section of *Psychological Types*, he insists on the vitality of the symbol as the "living symbol" (*das lebendige Symbol*) (see CW 6 §899-§901). At the same time, Jung hints at its Goethean dimension, too.[65] Explaining how the "symbolic attitude" is "a view of the world which *assigns meaning* to events […] and attaches to this meaning a greater value than to bare facts," Jung contrasts this view of things to another "which lays the accent on sheer facts and subordinates

---

[65] For further discussion, see Paul Bishop, "Das Goethe'sche Symbol als Instrument der morphologischen Wandlung in Philosophie und Psychologie: Cassirer, Jung und Klages," in Jonas Maatsch (ed.), *Morphologie und Moderne: Goethes »anschauliches Denken« in den Geistes- und Kulturwissenschaften seit 1800* (Berlin and Boston: de Gruyter, 2014), pp. 157-175.

meaning to them" (§819). (In the language of *The Red Book*, we might call this the contrast between the "spirit of the depths" and the "spirit of this age"). For according to this second view of things, which we might call the "factual attitude," there can be *no symbols whatsoever*, inasmuch as symbolism is said to "depend exclusively on the mode of observation" (*die Symbolik beruht ausschließlich auf der Art der Betrachtung*) (§819).[66]

Even for this attitude, however, symbols do in some sense exist. Consider, for example, the case of Apis or some other bullheaded god, such as one might find in the British Museum or the Metropolitan Museum of Art: surely even the most hard-core "factualist" will conjecture that there must be some kind of hidden meaning. True, one can explain a bullheaded god as simply a depiction of a man's torso with a bull's head on it, but — "this explanation can hardly compete with the symbolic explanation, because the symbolism is too arresting to be overlooked" (§819). In other words, a symbol can have merely historical or philosophical significance, or it can arouse intellectual or aesthetic interest; but it can also be a *living* symbol, and in this case, it is "the best and highest expression for something divined [*Geahntes*] but not yet known [*noch nicht Gewußtes*] to the observer" (§819). Such symbols, Jung says, "compel our unconscious participation" and exercise "a life-giving and life-enhancing effect," of a kind that is expressed when Faust, turning in the "Night" scene from the sign of the macrocosm to the sign of the Earth Spirit (*Erdgeist*) cries out, "How differently this new sign works upon me!" (l. 460). Strangely enough, the word used here is *Zeichen,* or sign; and this is strange, because at the beginning of this definition Jung insists

---

[66] In the terms used by Kenneth Sylvan Guthrie (1871-1940) in *The Song of Mysticism* (1904), there is but one fundamental question: "Which is the Truth — the Symbol, or the Fact?" (see *The Song of Mysticism, Being an Attempt to Solve the Problem: "Which is most Reliable, Facts or Interpretation, Science or Mysticism?"* (Medford, MA: Prophet Publishing House, 1904), p. 1).

on the distinction between the *symbol* (and the symbolic) and the sign (and the semiotic) (§814). So, why does Jung choose to quote this line? Leaving aside the difficult question of the possible Hermetic or magical sources of this figure,[67] I think there are two reasons: first, because of the use of the verb *wirken*, recalling Jung's core dictum that *wirklich ist, was wirkt*;[68] and second, because the contrast between the sign of the macrocosm, which leaves Faust cold, and the sign of the Earth Spirit, which excites his interest, mirrors the contrast between the spirit of this age and the spirit of the (earthly, historical, psychological) depths as one finds it in *The Red Book*. Without rehearsing here in greater detail the specifics of Jung's doctrine of the symbol, we might nevertheless note that it is "neither *rational* nor *irrational*," that it appeals "just as strongly to *thinking* as to *feeling*" and "stimulates *sensation* as much as *intuition*" (§823), that it is essentially "compensatory" (§825), and that it initiates the process of the "transcendent function" (§828). Finally, Jung notes that "hints at the process of symbol-formation" can be found in the "sparse reports of the initiation periods of religion founders," citing as examples (in no particular order, it seems) the struggles between Jesus and Satan, Buddha and Mara, Luther and the Devil, Zwingli and his previous worldly life, or

---

[67] Both the sign of the macrocosm and the sign of the Earth Spirit echo Hermetic and Cabbalistic traditions (in the case of the former, Georg von Wellings *Opus mago-cabbalisticum* [1735] or Robert Fludd's *Utriusque cosmi Maioris scilicet et Minoris, metaphysica, physica atque technica historiae* [*The metaphysical, physical and technical history of the two worlds, namely the greater and the lesser*] [1619]); while in a sketch made by Goethe for a production of *Faust* in 1812 the Earth Spirit looks very much like Apollo or Jupiter/Zeus). Ulrich Gaier suggests that Faust's words in ll. 430-446 suggest that Faust misunderstands how to interpret the sign of the macrocosm: instead of concentrating on the Macrocosm itself, he focuses on its effects on him, and instead of contemplating the divine with religious devotion and ecstatic reverence, he seems himself to be a god (l. 439), weakening the sign's magic effect and thereby condemning his experiment to failure (Gaier 120). If, on one level, Faust wants to "perceive the inner force / That bonds the very universe" (ll. 382-383), on another level he thinks it's all about *him*.

[68] For just two of the many occasions when Jung uses this phrase, see "The Aims of Psychotherapy" (CW 16 §95 and §111).

indeed the "regeneration of Faust through the contract with the Devil" — while in Nietzsche's *Zarathustra,* we are said to find an excellent example of the "suppressed antithesis" in the figure of the Ugliest Man (§829).

Faust in CW 7 and its *Two Essays*

One of Jung's earliest programmatic statements is called "The Psychology of the Unconscious" (1917; [3]1926; [5]1943), an essay that emerged from his revision in 1916 of a paper which had originally appeared in Rascher's *Jahrbuch* for 1912 under the title *Neue Bahnen der Psychologie*. The background to this revision was inevitably the First World War, among whose "psychological accompaniments" Jung listed the "incredible brutalization of common judgments, the mutual slanderings, the unprecedented fury of destruction, the unheard-of lying, and the inability of humans to call a halt to the bloody daimon" (CW 7 p. 4) — but also his anticipation of that War in the visions that led to *The Red Book* (see Shamdasani in RB, 27-30).

In Jung's words, the Great War had drawn attention to the "problem of the chaotic unconscious which slumbers uneasily beneath the ordered world of consciousness," revealing to civilized humankind that we are, in fact, "still barbarians," and showing "what an iron scourge lies in store for us if ever again we should be tempted to make our neighbour responsible for our own evil qualities" (CW 7 p. 4). On the basis that the psychology of the individual is reflected in the psychology of the nation and that what each individual does is also done by the nation (and vice versa), Jung argues that "only a change in the attitude of the individual can initiate a change in the psychology of the nation" (p. 4). This is an important principle because it reveals the *ethical* dimension to *The Red Book*; and it suggests that the project of Analytical Psychology is, in its essence, *inherently political* — for the "great problems of humankind were never yet solved by general laws, but only through regeneration of the attitudes of individuals" (p. 4). Thus, self-reflection is, even or especially in a "catastrophic epoch," the "absolutely necessary and only right thing" because "whoever reflects on themselves is bound to strike upon the frontiers of the unconscious" — which "contains what above all else we need to know" (p. 4).

In this essay, Jung stages a confrontation between the Eros theory (or Freudian psychoanalysis) and the point of view of the will to power (initially theorized by Nietzsche and turned into a therapeutic approach by Alfred Adler [1870-1937]). Nietzsche's theory of the will to power poses a challenge to Freudian psychoanalysis: Is the "poodle's kernel" (*des Pudels Kern*) really Eros, or might it be the power of the ego (CW 7 §42)? In Jung's eyes, *both* interpretations are valid, because "the will-to-power is surely just as mighty a daimon as Eros, and just as old and original" (§42). Each principle was, however, a blind spot in the thinker who proposed the alternative: Nietzsche, for example, dismissed Wagner, arguing that "everything about him is false. What is genuine is hidden or decorated. He is an actor, in every good and bad sense of the word" (see KSA, vol. 11, 26[22], 154), but Jung believed that he did so simply because Wagner "embodied that other elemental urge" which Nietzsche "overlooked" and on which Freudian psychoanalysis is built, that is, Eros. Then again, Freud recognized the urge to power but reduced it to a mere "ego-instinct," relegating it to a "rather pokey little corner" in his psychology (§43).

Instead, Jung embraces a position that could be described as a Goethean one, inasmuch as he constructs it with reference to *Faust*. "In reality," he argues, "human nature bears the burden of a terrible and unending conflict between the principle of the ego" (that is, the will to power) "and the principle of instinct" (that is, Eros), but in a particular way that radically reconceives both these principles: "the ego all barriers and restraint, instinct limitless, and both principles of equal might" (§43). In a sense, Jung adds, we may count ourselves happy if, as Faust tells Wagner, "One only passion is thy bosom's guide" (l. 1110), and it is "prudent" to guard against ever knowing the other. But — if we *do* learn to "know the other," then the game is over: for then we "enter upon the Faustian conflict" (§43). This conflict is, Jung suggests, embodied and embedded in the two parts of *Faust*: In its first part, he says, Goethe has "shown us what it means to accept instinct," and in the case of Faust himself the instinct is principally but by no means solely erotic — the *Gretchentragödie*; while in its second part, he adds, Goethe shows us "what it means to accept the ego and its weird unconscious world," reflected in the Classical Walpurgis Night, the episode of Philemon and Baucis, and the mystical concluding scene (§43).[69] Accepting both instinct and ego is something from which we may shrink, and there is a real risk that, if we "discover that the 'other' in us is indeed 'another,'" that is, "a real individual, who actually thinks, does, feels, and desires all the things that are despicable and odious," then we can demonize and reject this part of ourselves — or, as Jung more colourfully puts it, "declare war on the bogeyman" (§43). In this way, we may save ourselves from "the Faustian catastrophe, before which our courage and our strength might well fail us," but this is not the entire answer, for "the whole individual knows that our bitterest foe (or even a whole host of enemies) does not equal that one worst adversary, the 'other self' who dwells in our bosom" (§43). To put it another way, as Jung

---

[69] In this passage, Jung appears to be echoing Goethe's own words in his conversation with Eckermann of 17 February 1831, where he says of *Faust*: "The first part is almost entirely subjective; it proceeded entirely from a perplexed impassioned individual, and his semi-darkness is probably highly pleasing to [hu]mankind. But in the second part there is scarcely anything of the subjective; here is seen a higher, broader, clearer, more passionless world, and he who has not looked about him and had some experience will not know what to make of it" (Eckermann, *Conversations of Goethe*, pp. 384-385).

himself does in his chapter on the synthetic or constructive method, we have to *come to terms with the unconscious.*

This process of coming-to-terms with the unconscious is described by Jung as a "process" (*ein Prozeß*) or as "suffering or a labour" (*ein Erleiden oder eine Arbeit*) (CW 7 §121) — and whenever Jung says things like this, we should remember the context of *The Red Book*. It could also be called, he says, the "transcendent function," spanning the real and the "imaginary" (as its mathematical equivalent with the same name implies ...) or the rational and the irrational (§121). Jung describes it as a "natural process," as a "manifestation of the energy that springs from the tension of opposites," and — again, one thinks of *The Red Book*! — as a "sequence of fantasy-occurrences which spontaneously appear in dreams and visions" (§121). Tellingly, Jung adds that the same process can be found in the initial stages of some forms of schizophrenia ... As literary examples of this process, Jung turns to Gérard de Nerval's semi-autobiographical novella *Aurélia ou le Rêve et la Vie* (1855),[70] as well as to Goethe's *Faust*, Part Two (§121).

Further literary examples underpin Jung's claim that the "magic daimon" endowed with mysterious powers is one of the archetypes met with the projection of unconscious collective contents: Gustav Meyrink's *Der Golem* (1915); the Tibetan wizard who unleashes world war in Meyrink's *Fledermäuse* (1916); the Magician in Nietzsche's *Zarathustra*; and, in Goethe's *Faust*, the actual hero himself (CW 7 §153). In the case of *The Red Book*, the magician figure is, of course, ΦΙΛΗΜΩΝ, whom Jung first meets in his small house in the country (fronted by a large bed of tulips), where he lives with his wife ΒΑΥΚΙΣ, in chapter 21 of *Liber Secundus* (RB, 395).

---

[70] For further discussion, see C.G. Jung, *On Psychological and Visionary Art: Notes from C.G. Jung's Lecture on Gérard de Nerval's "Aurélia,"* ed. Craig E. Stephenson (Princeton, NJ, and Oxford: Princeton University Press, 2015).

Another example of an early programmatic work is "The Relations between the Ego and the Unconscious" (1928; ²1934), originally a lecture given in French (and published in 1916 as "La Structure de l'inconscient") which Jung subsequently revised and expanded. In his preface to the second edition, Jung described this work as "the expression of a long-standing endeavour to grasp and [...] depict the strange character and course of the *drame intérieur*, the transformation process of the unconscious psyche" (CW 7 p. 121). In this respect, one would not be wrong in reading it as an attempt on Jung's part to understand and to formulate in scientific terms what he had gone through in his work on *The Red Book*. As Jung puts it at the beginning of Part 1, Chapter 2, "the process of assimilating the unconscious yields some very remarkable phenomena" (§221).

Jung notes how Adler used the term "godlikeness" or "god-almightiness" (i.e., *Gottähnlichkeit*) to characterize certain basic features of neurotic power psychology and its drive for *Geltung* (CW 7 §224) (see, for example, Adler's *Praxis und Theorie der Individualpsychologie* [1920]). For his part, Jung identifies the same idea in Goethe's *Faust* in the third scene set in Faust's study where, in a passage satirizing academic life, Mephistopheles — dressed in Faust's academic gown — talks to a student. As a commentary on Genesis 3:5, which he has just asked the student read out in Latin, ERITIS SICUT DEUS, SCIENTES BONUM ET MALUM, Mephistopheles concludes the scene with the following reflection:

> Follow the ancient saw, and follow the snake, my cousin;
> God's image as thou art, thou'lt rue the way thou hast
> chosen!
> (ll. 2048-2049; cf. CW 7 §450)

"Godlikeness" (*Gottähnlichkeit*), Jung adds, refers to "knowledge [*das Wisssen*], the knowledge [*die Erkenntnis*] of good and evil," and in the "analysis and conscious realization of good and evil" he sees an opportunity — but also a danger. For, on the one hand, they can engender "a certain superior tolerance" which may "look very wise and superior" but, on the other, this tolerance brings "all sorts of consequences in its train" (CW 7 §224). The "deeper understanding, [...] the juxtaposition of what was before separated, [...] and the apparent overcoming of the moral conflict" can all give rise to a "feeling of superiority that may well express itself in the form of 'godlikeness'" (§224).

Yet as Jung puts it, with a nod and a wink in the direction of Nietzsche, "not everyone will feel themselves a superman [*ein Gefühl des Übermenschentums*], holding in their hands the scales of good and evil" (CW 7 §224)! Instead, the individual might feel — and one suspects that this is true of Jung himself — "not in the least a Hercules at the parting of the ways,"[71] but rather a "rudderless ship buffeted between Scylla and Charybdis," or (using one of his favorite images from Goethe) like a "helpless object caught between hammer and anvil" (§224).[72] (Discussing in his *Zarathustra* seminar the passage where Nietzsche's Zarathustra declares, "Ye know only the sparks of the spirit: but ye do not see the anvil [*Amboss*] which it is, and the cruelty of its hammer [*Hammer*]!" (Z II 8), Jung latches onto the imagery of hammer and anvil, relating it to the problem of opposites: "Now, these are typical pairs of opposites: the anvil is the Yin part and the hammer is the Yang, the active part, and there must be something in between, but he carefully omits to say what it is. It is [hu]man[kind]. Between the hammer and the anvil is always

---

[71] For further discussion of this motif, see Erwin Panofsky, *Hercules am Scheidewege und andere antike Bildstoffe in der neueren Kunst* (Leipzig and Berlin: Teubner, 1930; reprinted Berlin: Geb. Mann Verlag, 1997).

[72] For the Goethean source of this image, see these lines from "Gesellige Lieder, Ein Anderes": "You must ascend or decline, / You must conquer and rule, / Or serve and lose, / Suffer or triumph, / Be the anvil or the hammer" (*Du mußt steigen oder sinken / Du mußt herrschen und gewinnen, / Oder dienen und verlieren, / Leiden oder triumphieren, / Amboß oder Hammer sein*).

a human being" (276-277). On this occasion, Jung emphasizes the conflictual aspect of *Geist*, saying "You see, it is a terrible conflict" [277].)

Here in "The Relations between the Ego and the Unconscious," too, Jung talks about being "caught up in perhaps the greatest and most ancient of human conflicts, experiencing the throes of eternal principles in collision"; and, in terms redolent of *The Red Book*, he adds: "Well he might feel himself like a Prometheus chained to the Caucasus" — in *The Red Book*, Jung discusses how "the powers of [his] depths are predetermination and pleasure," defining "predetermination or forethinking" as "Prometheus who, without determined thoughts, brings the chaotic to form and definition, who digs the channels and hold the object before pleasure," and pleasure as "the force that desires and destroys forms without form and definition" (RB, 179) — "or as one crucified" (CW 7 §224). In the final chapter of *Liber Primus* in *The Red Book,* Jung "see[s] the cross and Christ on it in his last hour and torment," he is "held fast and [he] spread[s] [his] arms wide," and "with outstretched arms like someone crucified, [his] body taut and horribly entwined by the serpent" (RB, 197), while in the penultimate chapter of *Liber Secundus,* Jung "see[s] the black serpent, as it wound itself upward around the wood of the cross" and "crept into the body of the crucified and emerged again transformed from his mouth" (RB, 388). As Jung puts it in "Nox quarta," after participating in the Good Friday service as Parzival, "this is the Good Friday when we complete the Christ in us and we descend to Hell ourselves [...] the Good Friday on which we moan and cry to will the completion of Christ" (RB, 370).

Feeling oneself to be Prometheus or to be Christ would be "a 'godlikeness' in suffering," he concludes in his essay of 1928 (CW 7 §224). (In an aside, Jung concedes that the term "godlikeness" is "certainly not a scientific concept," and he admits that "not [...] every reader will immediately grasp the peculiar state of mind implied by 'godlikeness,'" suggesting that the term belongs "too exclusively" to the sphere of *belles-lettres* (§224): Does this mean that we should read *The Red Book* as a work of literature ...?)

In Part 1, Chapter 4, Jung returns to the point he had made in his 1916 revision of *Neue Bahnen der Psychologie* published as "The Psychology of the Unconscious" (1917) about Freud's "infantile eroticism" and Adler's "power drive," arguing that, "regardless of the clash of opinions," these two theoretical forces "are *one and the same thing*" (§256; my emphasis). How so? Because in both cases, Jung argues, what is coming to light in the transference is "a fragment of uncontrolled, and at first uncontrollable, primordial instinct," as the "archaic fantasy-forms that gradually reach the surface of consciousness" are said to confirm (§256).

And Jung returns to his point made in "The Psychology of the Unconscious' about how, in *Faust I*, Goethe shows us "what it means to accept instinct" and, in *Faust II*, "what it means to accept the ego and its weird unconscious world" (CW 7 §43), and he now expands on it, constellating several passages from Part Two, then Part One. The experience of a "collapse of the conscious attitude," when one feels "delivered up, disoriented, like a rudderless ship" — here is that image again! — "that is abandoned to the moods of the elements" (§254), can nevertheless, Jung argues, reveal something "extraordinarily important" — namely, the existence of an "unconscious self-regulation" (§257). To a Freudian, that is, to someone who can only see things in terms of infantilism, the response is likely to be, "It was all nonsense, of course. I am a crazy visionary! The best thing would be to bury the unconscious or throw it overboard with all its works" (§257). In this case, the individual will have recourse to the regressive restoration of the persona and become "smaller, more limited, more rationalistic" than before (§257). What is the alternative? Jung describes it as "freedom" (*Freiheit*) — that freedom which, in the second of the three transformations, Zarathustra's lion wants to create for itself

(*Freiheit sich schaffen*, "to create freedom for itself" [Z I 1]), and which here Jung describes as a freedom that, paradoxically, begins by recognizing the restrictions it has hitherto accepted. And he illustrates this solution with a quotation from Act V of *Faust II*.

Now in the "Midnight" scene of Act V, the aged Faust is alone in his palace — alone, that is, apart from the figures of the Four Gray Women who have appeared, called Want, Debt, Care, and Need. Three of them (Want, Debt, and Need) have left again, but one remains — the figure of Care. Faced with Care, Faust renounces his transcendent strivings and condemns his own folly in always wanting more:

> The round of earth enough I know, and barred
> Is unto man the prospect yonderward.
> O fool, who thither turns his blinking glances,
> And of his like above the clouds romances!
> Let him stand firm, and round him gaze on earth.
> Not mute the world is to the man of worth.
> What need hath he to range infinitude?
> What he perceives, that may be understood.
> Thus let him journey down his earthly day;
> When spectres haunt him, let him go his way [...].
> (ll. 11441-11450)
> [In onward-striding find his bale, his bliss,
> He, that each moment uncontented is.]
> [ll. 11451-11452; cf. CW 7 §475]

Yet Jung rejects this renunciation of Faustian striving: This would be a perfect solution, he says, if only one could "shake off the unconscious so completely as to deprive it of its energy and render it inactive" (CW 7 §258). Instead, he continues, experience shows that the unconscious can be deprived of its energy "only in part," for because it is the "source of the libido from which the psychic elements flow," it remains "continually active" (§258). It is, therefore, nothing more than a "delusion" or an "illusion" if one thinks that, "by some sort of magical theory or method," the unconscious could be "finally drained of libido" and thus "eliminated" (§258).

What breaks this delusion or illusion is a moment symbolized by Faust's earlier monologue in this scene, when he expresses regret for the path his life has taken and, in particular, that he has had recourse to magic:

> Now with such glamour doth the air overflow
> That how he should avoid it none doth know.
> If one day lit with reason on us beams,
> Night trammels us within a web of dreams.
> From the young fields we turn us home elate,
> A raven croaks! What doth he croak? Ill-fate!
> Us Superstition soon and late entwines,
> With happenings, with warnings, and with signs.
> Thus are we overawed, we stand alone.
> The door doth creak, and yet doth enter none!
> (ll. 11410-11419)

[Is any here?

CARE:

The question asketh *aye!*

FAUST:
And thou, who art thou then?

CARE:

Lo, here am I!

FAUST:
Withdraw thyself!

CARE:

Here may I fitly dwell.

FAUST (*first wrathful, then softened, to himself*):
Have thou a care and speak no magic spell!]
(ll. 11420-11423; cf. CW 7 §476)

Implicitly Jung reads this passage as expressing a manifestation of the unconscious, for he remarks that "no one [...] can strip the unconscious of its effective power" and that, at best, we merely deceive ourselves (CW 7 §258). Here Jung cites the words spoken by Care, attributing them, so it seems, to the very unconscious itself:

> Though of ear unheard, the groaning
> Heart is conscious of my moaning;
> In an ever-changing guise
> Cruel power I exercise.
>
> (ll. 11424-11427)

There is, Jung asserts, only one thing that is effective against the unconscious, and that is "hard outer Necessity" (*eine äußere unzweifelhafte Not*), but he immediately goes on to add that "those with rather more knowledge of the unconscious" — and, after *The Red Book*, we know that this includes Jung himself — "will see behind the outer Necessity the same face which once gazed at them from within" (CW 7 §258). So it seems that inner and outer are interchangeable,[73] as Jung says that "an inner Necessity can change into an outer one," relating this insight into what happens when outer Necessity is real to the (partly satirical) advice offered by

---

[73] Compare with Goethe's short poem entitled "Epirrhema":
You must, when contemplating nature, *Müsset im Naturbetrachten*
Attend to this, in each and every feature: *Immer eins wie alles achten;*
There's nought aside ansd nought within, *Nichts ist drinnen, nichts ist draußen:*
For she is inside out and outside in. *Denn was innen, das ist außen.*
Thus will you grasp, with no delay, *So ergreifet ohne Säumnis*
The holy secret, clear as day. *Heilig öffentlich Geheimnis.*
(Goethe, *Selected Poems*, ed. Middleton, pp. 158-159; trans. Middleton).

Mephistopheles in the Witch's Kitchen scene in Part One to Faust, who is fed up after the tumultuous scene in Auerbach's Cellar with the "madness of magic" (*das tolle Zauberwesen*, l. 2337):

> [...] Good! No money doth it need,
> No leeches' aid nor aid of witches.
> Betake thee to the field with speed,
> Turn up the clods, and dig out ditches;
> Move ever in a narrow round
> Content, and tug not at thy tether;
> With frugal fare keep body and soul together;
> Live with the brutes as brute, and think not shame to dung
> Thyself the field thou reapest. [...]
>
> (ll. 2351-2359)

From these half-serious, half-satirical words Jung extrapolates a doctrine of the "simple life" — a life which, he says, "cannot to be faked" (CW 7 §258). And surely Jung is right. Poverty, dependence on circumstances, lack of social opportunity: These matters cannot be faked, and equally nor can what one might call a lack of psychological opportunity. That is to say, if we are driven to the "simple life" by the necessity of our own nature, we will inevitably pass over the "problem of our soul," for we shall "lack the capacity to grasp it" (§258). But, once we do have this capacity — once we "see the Faustian problem," so to speak — then "the escape into the 'simple life' is closed for ever" (§258). Here the figure of Faust thus serves as an emblem of existential crisis: a crisis of transformation that Jung experienced, and sought to resolve, through writing *The Red Book*.

As Jung puts it in a later chapter of this essay, what *Faust* (and one of its sources, the Book of Job) depicts as the "wager with God" is the "tragic counterplay between inside and outside" — or in Jung's favorite, Goethe-inspired image, the ego standing between the "demands coming from without and from within" as "between hammer and anvil" (*wie zwischen Hammer und Amboß*) — which represents "the energetics of the life process, the polar tension that is necessary for self-regulation" (CW 7 §311). Whatever the "opposing forces" may be, their "fundamental meaning and desire" is the "life of the individual," and it is around this "centre of balance" that they always "fluctuate" (§311). Precisely because they are reciprocally related, these forces "unite in a mediatory meaning," a meaning which is "born" out of — and is therefore "intuited" by — the individual. We all have a strong feeling of what "should be" — and what "could be," and it is when we depart from this divination — like Faust — that we fall into "error, aberration, illness" (§311). Like Faust ...

In Part Two, Chapter 4, Jung turns to a discussion of a figure he calls the "mana-personality," describing this "dominant" (or "archetype") of the collective unconscious as a "hero, chief, magician, medicine-man, saint, ruler of humankind and spirits, the friend of God" (CW 7 §377). This figure arises when, in Jungian terms, the ego has integrated the anima — a dynamic underpinning much of the psychological action of *The Red Book*. (Jung notes that the figure of the magician has its feminine equivalent: a figure he describes as a "sublime, matriarchal figure, the Great Mother, the All-Merciful, who understands everything, forgives everything, always acts for the best [...]" (§379). Integrating the anima and constellating the archetype of the magician is said to be a dangerous process for it can give rise to inflation, if it turns out that the ego's attempt to integrate or appropriate the anima leads to its subordination to this powerful father-imago. In such a case the individual becomes "a superman [*Übermensch*], superior to all powers, a demi-god [*ein Halbgott*] at the very least," someone who echoes Christ's words in the Gospel of John, "I and the Father are one" (John 10:30) — a "mighty avowal in all its awful ambiguity" —, or in the words of Goethe's *Die Geheimnisse*:

From the power that binds all creatures none is free
Except the one who wins self-mastery!

[*»Von der Gewalt, die alle Wesen bindet,*
Befreit der Mensch sich, der sich überwindet.«]

(ll. 191-192)

(... *der sich überwindet* — Nietzsche will remember this line when, in *Zarathustra*, he calls us as human beings to overcome ourselves: "I teach you the Superman," Zarathustra will announce, adding: "Man is something that is to be surpassed [*überwunden*]. What have ye done to surpass [*überwinden*] man?" [Z Prologue §3].) In this intra-psychic sruggle, the figure of the magician can only take possession of the ego, because the ego seeks victory over the anima; and this advance on the part of the ego is followed by a reciprocal advance from the unconscious — an advance described by Jung once again in terms of the figure of Care from the "Midnight" scene in Act V of *Faust*, Part Two:

In an ever-changing guise
Cruel power I exercise.

[*In verwandelter Gestalt*
Üb ich grimmiger Gewalt.]

(ll. 11426-11427)

The only way to bring this possession of the ego by the magician figure to an end is for the ego to renounce its claim to superiority. So is this (despite what Jung had said above) in fact a psychological restatement of the Goethean doctrine of renunciation?

Thus, there are two aspects to the mana-personality: On the one hand, it is a "being of superior wisdom" (*ein überlegen Wissender*) while, on the other, it is a "being of superior will" (*ein überlegen*

Wollender) (CW 7 §396). If we can make conscious the contents that underlie this personality, we might come to recognize that we have "learned more" and now "want more" than others, and we might even recognize a certain "uncomfortable kinship with the gods" — a kinship that is said to have propelled Angelus Silesius (c. 1624-1677), the German mystic and religious poet who was the author of the *Cherubinischer Wandersmann* ("The Cherubinic Pilgrim"), back from his "super-Protestantism" (*Überprotestantismus*), past the "precarious halfway house of the Lutherans," back to "the nethermost womb of the dark Mother" (§396).[74] And Angelus Silesius is not the only example of this trajectory, for the problems with which he wrestled were, Jung claims, exactly the same as those with which Christ and, after him, Paul also wrestled. And as other (and chronologically closer) examples, Jung cites Meister Eckhart, Goethe's *Faust*, and Nietzsche's *Zarathustra*. In the form of the idea of mastery (*Beherrschungsgedanke*), and specifically through, in the case *Faust*, "the figure of the magician and ruthless man-of-will who enters into a pact with the Devil," and, in the case of *Zarathustra*, "the masterful man and supreme sage who knows neither God nor Devil," both Goethe and Nietzsche are said to have worked through this very same problem — and to have brought it closer to us (§397). As we can see in *The Red Book* (and as we shall explore in Volume 4 of this series), the way in which Goethe and Nietzsche had worked through this problem brought it alarmingly close to Jung himself.

After considering the use of Goethe's *Faust* in Jung's groundbreaking work *Transformations and Symbols of the Libido*, in his writings on typology, and on his early programmatic essays, let us now turn in the final chapter of this study to Jung's writings on alchemy — works which can be as daunting as they are ultimately

---

[74] See Angelus Silesius, *The Cherubinic Wanderer*, ed. Josef Schmidt, trans. Maria Shrady (New York and Mahwah, NJ: Paulist Press, 1986).

illuminating. And yet, inasmuch as they can be read as engaging with themes and issues found in *The Red Book*, these three volumes — *Psychology and Alchemy* (CW 12), *Alchemical Studies* (CW 13), and Jung's late, great magnus opus in the form of *Mysterium Coniunctionis* (CW 14) — can throw considerable light on the epic of transformation on which Jung, like his illustrious predecessors in the form of Wolfram von Eschenbach, Johann Wolfgang Goethe, and Friedrich Nietzsche, was also embarked.

Chapter 4

Goethe's *Faust* in Jung's Works [B]: *Faust* in Jung's Later Works of the Thirties, Forties, and Fifties

As well as in Jung's two major monographs of 1911-1912 (*Transformations and Symbols of the Libido*) and 1921 (*Psychological Types*) and in his theoretical essays from the early decades of the 20th century, Goethe's *Faust* continued to play a significant role in the unfolding development of Jung's thought. This is especially true of his increasing interest in alchemy, which came to replace his work on *The Red Book*, which was effectively concluded in 1930 — two years, that is, after Richard Wilhelm (1873-1930) had sent Jung a copy of his translation of an ancient Chinese alchemical text, *T'ai I Chin Hua Tsung Chih* (or the *Secret of the Golden Flower*). Jung agreed to write a psychological commentary on the work for its publication in late 1929, and in it, he warned of the dangers, as he saw them, that faced the West. Linking Wolfram's *Parzival* and Goethe's *Faust*, he declared that "the Amfortas wound and the Faustian split in the Germanic individual are still not healed" because "his unconscious is still loaded with contents that must first be made conscious before he can be free of them" (CW 13 §70). This comment neatly encapsulates the intellectual-historical context for the project of Analytical Psychology, and summarizes its two main aims — to bring what is in the unconscious into consciousness, and to do so in order to be liberated (and, in this sense, transformed).

Aside from the two major studies published in *Psychology and Alchemy*, Jung devoted a number of other, shorter works to alchemy, and these are collected in Volume 13 of the *Collected*

Works, appropriately titled *Alchemical Studies*. These provide further evidence of Jung's discussion of *Faust* and support the argument that, when Jung says that *Faust* is an "alchemical drama from beginning to end" (CW 12 §85), he means this in the particular sense that he gave to alchemy (see below). But not all his work was focused on alchemy, as his essay of 1930, "Psychology and Literature," shows. This essay provides an aesthetic context to his writings on alchemy and their relation to his understanding of Goethe's *Faust*, not least because of its introduction of the categorical distinction between the psychological and the visionary modes of creation.

In 1929 or thereabouts, Jung received an invitation from Emil Ermatinger (1873-1953), formerly a professor of Germanic philology at ETH Zurich and later a professor at the University of Zurich, to give a lecture on psychology and literature, which was subsequently published in volume entitled *Philosophie der Literaturwissenschaft* (1930). By way of introduction to his lecture, Jung offered a brief account of the rapid development of psychology as an academic subject, conceded its limitations as a discipline, and offered some "points of view by which a psychological approach to poetry might be oriented in a general way" (CW 15, pp. 84-85). In fact, notwithstanding Jung's uncharacteristic modesty, his paper offered nothing less than an aesthetics *in nuce* of Analytical Psychology. At the same time, it contained some clarificatory remarks about the significance, as Jung saw it, of both Parts One and Two of Goethe's *Faust*. Part of the significance of this lecture lies in the way it eschews any alchemical terminology; this is Jung speaking as an academic, not as an alchemist. Yet it also contains some of the most striking descriptions of the psychological dynamic informing Goethe's *Faust* and Nietzsche's *Zarathustra* (and, by implication, *The Red Book*).

For Jung, it is a *sine qua non* that the human psyche is the "womb of all the arts and sciences," hence the task of the psychologist is a dual one: first, to explain the "psychological structure" of the work of art; and second, to reveal the "factors that make a person artistically creative" (CW 15 §133). While the object of study of the former is the concrete work of art itself, a product that is "apparently intentional and consciously shaped," yet is, in fact, a "product of complicated psychic activities," the object of study of the latter is the creative human individual "as a unique personality" (§134). And while both objects of study are "intimately related and even interdependent," neither of them can satisfactorily explain the other. As an example, Jung gives the following case: True, we know about Goethe's relation to his mother (in a famous poem, he claimed that he had inherited from her *die Frohnatur / Und Lust zu fabulieren*),[1] and we can see how this throws some light on Faust's exclamation, "The Mothers, the Mothers, how eerily it sounds" (*Die Mütter! Mütter! —'s klingt so wunderlich!*) (l. 6217). Yet, however deeply the traces of this relationship left in his work allow us to sense its importance for Goethe the man, we cannot see how the attachment to his mother could "produce the *Faust* drama itself" (§134). (Similarly, Jung adds, Wagner's tendency to transvestism — that is, his apparent *penchant* for satin or silk underwear — does not tell us anything about *The Ring of the Nibelungen*, even though he tantalizingly posits the possibility of a "secret connection" between the heroism of the Nibelungen and a "certain psychological effeminacy" on Wagner's part.) In short, an artist's psychological personality may explain many aspects of his or her work — but not the "work itself" (§133). The relationship between psychology and aesthetics is thus reciprocal, but one can never replace or invalidate the other (§135).

---

[1] Translated by Michael Hamburger as "cheerful spirit, / Her love of telling stories" (Johann Wolfgang von Goethe, *Selected Poems*, ed. Christopher Middleton [Goethe Edition, vol. 1] (Boston: Suhrkamp/Insel, 1982), p. 197) and by John Whaley as "my sunny heart / And fancy for a fable" (*Selected Poems*, trans. John Whaley (London: Dent, 1998), p. 119).

Yet, Jung insists on a fundamental difference in the ways psychologists and critics approach a work of art, particularly in the case of literature. In this case, the psychological value of a work may well be in inverse proportion to its literary value: Popular culture or junk literature, in which category Jung places works by Pierre Benoît, Rider Haggard, Arthur Conan Doyle, or even Melville's *Moby Dick*, can — as "literary products of dubious merit" — offer more to the psychologist than works of greater literary sophistication, such as the so-called psychological novel. (Although Jung does not give an example at this point, one might surmise he is thinking of such works as Madame de La Fayette's *The Princess of Cleves*, Stendhal's *The Red and the Black*, or Dostoevsky's *The Brothers Karamazov* or *Crime and Punishment*.)

To illustrate this psychological principle further, however, Jung turns to Goethe's *Faust*. While the "love-tragedy" of Gretchen in Part One is so "self-explanatory" that there is "nothing the psychologist can add to it that has not already been said in better words by the poet," Part Two by contrast "cries out for interpretation" — here the "prodigious richness" of its imaginative material outstrips even the poet's power of expression, so that "nothing explains itself any more and every line only makes the reader's need of an interpretation more apparent" (CW 15 §138). This dichotomy between Part One and Part Two provides the basis for a wider, overarching categorical distinction made by Jung in this essay. This is the distinction between the *psychological* mode of artistic creation and the *visionary* mode.

On Jung's account, the psychological mode works with material drawn from conscious life — with "crucial experiences, powerful emotions, suffering, passion, the stuff of human fate in general" (§139). In other words, the psychological mode is exemplified by *Faust*, Part One: We do not *need* a psychologist to explain why Faust fell in love with Gretchen or why Gretchen was driven to murder her child. (Jung states this with much confidence, although I am not so sure whether today this is necessarily true.) By contrast, the visionary mode is something wholly *other*, and for an entire paragraph, Jung struggles to describe it: It is "something strange," a "primordial experience," it "arises from timeless depths," it is a "revelation," a "vision of beauty": "Is it a vision of other worlds, or of the darknesses of the spirit, or of the primal beginnings of the human psyche?" Jung asks rhetorically, and answers: "We cannot say it is any or none of these" (§141). But what Jung *can* say is that it is exemplified — along with the *Shepherd of Hermas*, Dante's *Divine Comedy*, Nietzsche's "Dionysian experience," Wagner's *The Ring of the Nibelung*, *Tristan and Isolde*, and *Parsifal*, Spitteler's *Olympian Spring*, Blake's painting and poetry, the *Hypnerotomachia* of Francesco Colonna, Hoffmann's *Der goldne Topf*, and Jakob Böhme's "poetic-philosophic stammerings" — by *Faust*, Part Two, and by these famous lines from the Mothers scene: "Formation, transformation, / Eternal Mind's eternal recreation" (*Gestaltung, Umgestaltung, / Des ewigen Sinnes ewige Unterhaltung*) (ll. 6287-6288). (Later, Jung goes on to say that the creative process has a "feminine quality" and that creative work "arises from unconscious depths — we might truly say from the realm of the Mothers" (§159). In this sense, then, the visionary work of art is the *true* work of art.)

Now, according to the Freudian interpretation of art, some sort of "highly personal experiences must lie behind all this phantasmagoric darkness" (CW 15 §144), or in other words, art is a kind of compensation.[2] While, on one level, Jung rejects the reductionism of this approach, on another level he accepts it, albeit by widening his definition of art for, on his account, the (visionary) work of art stands in a compensatory relationship *to the age* in which it is produced. On this account, it is less important to investigate

[2] For further discussion of Freud on art, see Peter Gay (ed.), *The Freud Reader* (London: Vintage, 1995), Part 5, "Psychoanalysis in Culture" (pp. 427-541); and Peregrine Horden (ed.), *Freud and the Humanities* (London: Duckworth, 1985).

the possibility that *Faust* was compensatory to Goethe's conscious attitude and more important to ask: "In what relation does it stand to the conscious outlook of his time, and can this relation also be regarded as compensatory?" (§153). On this account, great poetry "draws its strength from the life of humankind," and its meaning transcends any and all personal factors: In it, the collective unconscious becomes a "living experience" and "is brought to bear on the conscious outlook of an age" — as a creative act, it is an "event" which is of importance "for a whole epoch" (§153). In this respect, a work of art may be justly described as a "message to generations of human beings," and *Faust* is an example of just such a work that "touches something in the soul of every German" (to paraphrase Jacob Burckhardt's remark in his letter to Albert Brenner) (§153).

Later on, Jung makes the point in this way: "it is not Goethe that creates *Faust*, but *Faust* that creates Goethe," because *Faust* is not just a work of literature, it is a *symbol* — it is "an expression for something profound alive in the soul of every German, which Goethe helped to bring to birth" (CW 15 §159). Thus *Faust* is, like Nietzsche's *Zarathustra*, a "primordial image" (*ein großes, urtümliches Bild*), to use Burckhardt's words (see Chapter 3, p. 234); and in a footnote Jung recalls Eckermann's "strange dream" related to Goethe on 21 December 1828, in which Faust and Mephistopheles fall out of the sky to the earth like a double meteor.[3] In this dream, Mephistopheles appears gentlemanlike and

---

[3] "Last night I had a strange dream, which I related to Goethe this evening, and which he thought very pleasant. I imagined myself in a foreign town, in a broad street, towards the south-east, where I stood with a crowd of men, and watched the heavens, which appeared covered with a light mist and shone with the brightest yellow. Every one was full of expectation as to what would happen, when two fiery points appeared, which, like meteor stones, fell to the ground before us with a crash, not far from the spot where we were standing. We hastened to see what had fallen, and behold! there stood before me Faust and Mephistopheles. I was both delighted and astonished, and joining them as acquaintance, walked along with them in cheerful conversation, turning the next corner of a street" (*Conversations of Goethe with Eckermann and Soret*, trans. John Oxenford, 2 vols. (London: Smith, Elder, 1850), vol. 2, pp. 116-117). For further discussion of the significance of dreams for

without malice, sporting "two elegant horns which sprouted from his
youthful forehead, and turned sideways, just as a beautiful growth
of hair raises itself, and then turns to each side" — and is, Jung
notes, reminiscent of Mercurius, a detail which Jung holds to be
"in full accord with the alchemical nature of Goethe's masterpiece"
(§159, fn. 19).

Although Jung suggests that it is "dangerous" to speak
of one's own times because "what is at stake is too vast to be
comprehended," there can surely be little doubt that he believed
his own *Red Book* would have fallen into this category of visionary
art. And Jung goes on to place Goethe's *Faust* into a short historical
survey of such works:

- Francesco Colonna's *Hypnerotomachia Poliphili* (*The
  Dream of Poliphilus* or *Poliphilo's Strife of Love in a Dream*),
  described by Linda Fierz-David as "the symbol of the living
  process of growth which had been set going, obscurely and
  incomprehensibly, in the men of his time and had made of
  the Renaissance the beginning of a new era"[4]

- Goethe's *Faust* and its picture of the "megalomania that
  threatens the Faustian man," as well as its attempts to
  "redeem the inhumanity of this figure by uniting him with
  the Eternal Feminine, the maternal Sophia"

- Nietzsche's proclamation of the "death of God" and his
  announcement of the birth of the *Übermensch* who, in turn,
  is doomed to destruction

- And finally, Carl Spitteler's transformation of the waxing
  and waning of the gods into a "myth of the seasons" in his
  Prometheus and Epimetheus (§154).

Goethe and Eckermann, see Avital Ronell, *Dictations: On Haunted Writing* (Lincoln
and London: University of Nebraska Press, 1993).

[4] Francesco Colonna, *The Dream of Poliphilo*, ed. Linda Fierz-David, trans. Mary
Hottinger (Princeton, NJ: Princeton University Press, 1950), p. 27. For a more recent
translation of this work, see *Hypnerotomachia Poliphili: The Strife of Love in a
Dream*, trans. Joscelyn Godwin (London: Thames & Hudson, 1999).

Each of these poets, Jung declares, "speaks with the voice of thousands and tens of thousands, foretelling changes in the conscious outlook of his time" (CW 15 §154) — and who can say that Jung did not regard his own *Red Book* as the most recent work in this historical series? The visionary mode of creation is closely related to Jung's approach to interpreting alchemical writings, beginning with "The Visions of Zosimos," originally given as a lecture to the Eranos Conference in 1937.

In this lecture, Jung discussed a work by Zosimos of Panopolis, a Greco-Egyptian alchemist and Gnostic who lived at the end of the third and beginning of the fourth centuries C.E. At one point in his lecture, Jung pauses to explain why he is so interested in the "abstruse symbolism of alchemy" (CW 13 §117). It is because, in it, he believes we can hear a "distant echo" of a kind of thinking which, "under the censorship of the Church," was "doomed to destruction" (§117). In this respect, then, alchemy belongs *to the past*. At the same time, however, Jung also detects in alchemy a "groping towards the future, a premonition of the time when the projection would be taken back into the human individual, from whom it had arisen in the first place" (§117). In fact, Jung believed, some alchemists themselves had begun to realize that "only a thin wall separated them from psychological self-awareness" (§120). In this respect, alchemy belongs to the *future* — and maybe to our own present.

While Johannes Valentinus Andreae (1586-1654), writing under the guise of Christian Rosenkreutz — supposedly the founder of the Rosicrucian Order (Order of the Rose Cross) and the author of *The Chymical Wedding of Christian Rosenkreutz* (1616) — was still on the alchemical side of the dividing line, with his *Faust*, Goethe had emerged on the other — inasmuch as he could describe the "psychological problem which arises when the inner individual, or greater personality that had lain hidden in the homunculus, emerges into the light of consciousness and confronts the erstwhile ego, the animal individual" (CW 13 §120). On some level, Jung speculates, Faust must have had "inklings of the metallic coldness" of Mephistopheles who, on his first appearance (at the end of the scene "Before the Gate") had first "circled round him in the shape of a dog" — suggesting, Jung adds, the "uroboros motif" (§120). (In what sense a literary character could be said to have "inklings" of any kind remains unclear.) On Jung's account, Faust used Mephistopheles "as a familiar spirit" and, in the end, "got rid of him by means of the motif of the cheated devil" (§120). Intriguingly, however, Jung adds that Faust nevertheless wanted to claim "the credit for the fame Mephistopheles brought him as well as for the power to work magic," an observation that Jung does not work out fully (but which could be read as an allusion to Faust's relationship to the Emperor in Act I and in Act IV in Part Two). All in all, Goethe's solution is judged by Jung to have been "still medieval," while nevertheless reflecting "a psychic attitude that could get on without the protection of the Church" (§120). (In his papers in *Psychology and Alchemy*, Jung would emphasize the break with the alchemical tradition ushered in by Goethe's *Faust*, rather than its continuity with its medieval sources.)

Here lies, then, an important distinction between Johannes Valentinus Andreae aka Christian Rosenkreutz and Goethe: Whereas the former had been "wise enough" to "stay outside the magic circle" and to live "within the confines of tradition," the latter — although, in part, "still medieval" — had been "more modern," and consequentially "more incautious" (CW 13 §120). This lack of caution on Goethe's part is said to reflect itself in his inability to understand "how dreadful was the Walpurgisnacht of the mind," against which Christian dogma "offered protection" — and this, despite the fact that "his own masterpiece spread out this underworld before his eyes in two versions," that is, the Walpurgis Night of Part One and the Classical Walpurgis Night of Part Two. And then, Jung makes a very telling comment: "An extraordinary number of things," he says, "can happen to a poet without having serious consequences [which] appeared with a vengeance only a hundred years later" (§120). The dating is imprecise (and obviously meant to be so): but, given that *Urfaust* was written between 1772 and 1775, *Faust: A Fragment* was published in 1790, *Faust I* was published in 1808, and *Faust II* was published (posthumously) in 1832, the time frame of a hundred years later would clearly fit within Jung's own lifetime and the geopolitical events that occurred during it — including the First World War and the events leading up to the outbreak of the Second.[5] In fact, his work on *The Red Book* sits right in the middle of the time period from 1875 (the year of Jung's birth) to 1932 (a few years before Jung's seminal lectures on alchemy at Eranos). This emphasis on cultural continuity across time is a hallmark of Jung's thinking, so it is not surprising that he uses one of his favorite images when he concludes that "the psychology of the unconscious has to reckon with long periods of time like this," because it is concerned "less with the ephemeral personality than with age-old processes" — processes compared with which the individual is "no more than the passing blossom and fruit of **the rhizome** underground" (§120).[6]

---

[5] In *Goethe and the Power of Rhythm: A Biographical Essay* [2002] (Ghent, NY: Adonis Press, 2010), John Michael Barnes proposes that a rhythm of 18.6 years underlies Goethe's biography, and that the repeated periods of crisis and renewal in his creative development correspond with those "pulsing life" of nature — the cyclical movements of the earth and the moon. Could Goethe's life and works thus uncover a more general developmental law?

[6] For further discussion of the motif of the rhizome, see James Olney, *The Rhizome and the Flower: The Perennial Philosophy — Yeats and Jung* (Berkeley: University of California Press, 1980); and Mark Gartler, entry on "Rhizome" (*The Chicago School of Media Theory*), available online HTTP: https://csmt.uchicago.edu/glossary2004/rhizome.htm. In critical theory, the notion of the rhizome as non-hierarchical, heterogeneous, multiplicitous, and a-centered is associated mainly with the thought of Gilles Deleuze (1925-1995) and Félix Guattari (1930-1992); see *A Thousand Plateaus: Capitalism and Schizophrenia*, trans. Brian Massumi (Minneapolis, MN: University of Minnesota Press, 1987). For discussion of Jung's influence on Deleuze, see Christian Kerslake, *Deleuze and the Unconscious* (London and New York: Continuum, 2007).

1941 was the 400th anniversary of the death of Philippus
Aureolus Theophrastus Bombastus von Hohenheim, a Swiss
physician and alchemist usually (and more simply) known as
Paracelsus, a name that is thought to be derived from the Greek
word *para* (meaning "by") and the Latin *celsus* (meaning "high"),
either the equivalent of his German surname of "Hohenheim," i.e.,
"at home on high,"[7] or meaning that he "surpassed Celsus," the great
Roman encyclopedist known for his extant work on the subject of
medicine, *De Medecina*. To commemorate this anniversary, which
was not without its political implications,[8] a number of events were
held, including two in which Jung — now in his mid-60s —was
involved: one a lecture given to the Swiss Society for the History of
Medicine and the Natural Sciences titled "Paracelsus the Physician,"

---

[7] Udo Benzenhöfer, *Studien zum Frühwerk des Paracelsus im Bereich Medizin
und Naturkunde* (Munich: Klemm & Oelschläger, 2005), pp. 110-111. For further
discussion, see Franz Hartmann, *The Life and the Doctrines of [...] Paracelsus*
[1887] (New York: Lovell, 1891); and Walter Pagel, *Paracelsus: An Introduction
to Philosophical Medicine in the Era of the Renaissance*, 2nd edn (Basel: Karger,
1982); and Udo Benzenhöfer and Urs Leo Gantenbein, "Paracelsus," and Bruce T.
Moran, "Paracelsianism," in Wouter J. Hanegraaff et al. (eds), *Dictionary of Gnosis
& Western Esotericism* (Leiden and Boston: Brill, 2006), pp. 922-931 and 915-922.
For extracts from his writings, see Jolande Jacobi (ed.), *Paracelsus: Selected Writings*
[1951], trans. Norbert Guterman (Princeton, NJ: Princeton University Press, 1979);
and Nicholas Goodrick-Clarke (ed.), *Paracelsus: Essential Readings* (Berkeley, CA:
North Atlantic Books, 1999).

[8] For further discussion, see Sheila Johnson, "Ideological Ambiguity in G.W. Pabst's
'Paracelsus' (1943)," *Monatshefte*, vol. 83, no. 2 (Summer, 1991), 104-126; and
Hartmut Rudolph, "Zum Paracelsusbild im Nationalsozialismus, vornehmlich bei
Erwin Metzke," in Helmut Koopmann and Frank Baron (eds), *Die Wiederkehr der
Renaissance im 19. und 20. Jahrhundert – The Revival of the Renaissance in the
Nineteenth and Twentieth Centuries* (Münster: mentis, 2013), pp. 115-135. Between
1917 and 1925, the Austrian right-wing novelist Erwin Guido Kolbenheyer (1878-
1962) wrote a trilogy of novels about Paracelsus (*Die Kindheit des Paracelsus*, 1917;
Das Gestirn des Paracelsus, 1921; and *Das dritte Reich des Paracelsus*, 1925); in
1941, the Paracelsus-Gesellschaft was founded in Salzburg with the Nazi Health
Minister Leonardop Coni as its first president; and in 1942, the Austrian director
G.W. Pabst made the film *Paracelsus*, presenting the physician and alchemist as
a representative of "German medicine" and as an ancestor of National Socialist
medical thinking.

and another a lecture to the Society for Natural Research in Basel entitled "Paracelsus as a Spiritual Phenomenon." (Confusingly, the first of these lectures is included in *Collected Works*, Volume 15, while the second is included in *Collected Works*, Volume 13, as if it were unclear to the editors whether Jung's view of Paracelsus relates to *The Spirit in Man, Art, and Literature* or to *Alchemical Studies*.) At the outset of this second lecture, Jung illustrated the "powerful influence" exerted by Paracelsus on "all subsequent generations" with reference to the fact that "it is no secret that Goethe, as is evident from the second part of *Faust*, still felt the impact of the powerful spirit of Paracelsus" (CW 13 §145).[9]

While most critics suggest that, in later life, Goethe moved away from alchemy, Jung argues the precise opposite, claiming that the "impressions he gained in his Leipzig days continued to engross him even in old age," and actually "formed the matrix for *Faust*" (CW 13 §159). In explanation of this remark, Jung recounts further how alchemy, far from being opposed to science, was itself "*the dawn of the scientific age*" (§163) — an age which arose from Wolfram von Eschenbach's *Parzival* as well as from the Renaissance.[10] As a consequence of the rise of science, the

---

[9] For further discussion of Goethe and Paracelsus, see Agnes Bartscherer, *Paracelsus, Paracelsisten und Goethes "Faust": Eine Quellenstudie* (Dortmund: F.W. Ruhfus, 1911); Karl Sudhoff, "Paracelsus und Goethe," *Die medizinische Welt*, 6 (1932), 1409-1412; Amadeo Murase, "The Homunculus and the Paracelsian *Liber de imaginibus*," *Ambix*, vol. 67, no. 1 (February 2020), 47-61; Sepp Domandl, "Goethe als Paracelsuskenner: Zwei neue Belege," *Jahrhuch des Wiener Goethe-Vereins*, 80 (1976), 41-48; and H.C. Binswanger and K.R. Smith, "Paracelsus and Goethe: Founding Fathers of Environmental Health," *Bulletin of the World Health Organization*, vol. 78, no. 9 (2000), 1162-1164. Not surprisingly, the constellation of Paracelsus and Goethe caught the attention of the anthroposophist Rudolf Steiner, reflected in his lectures entitled "Von Paracelsus zu Goethe," given in Munich on 19 November 1911 and in Winterthur on 13 January 1912 (see Rudolf Steiner, *Goethe und die Gegenwart: Fünfunddreißig Vorträge in verschiedenen Städten 1889-1912*, ed. by Monika Philippi (Basel: Rudolf Steiner Verlag, 2017), pp. 491-510 and 511-539).

[10] For further discussion, see Tatsuhiro Nakajima, "Psychology of the 12th Century Renaissance in Wolfram von Eschenbach's *Parzival*," *Studia Hermetica Journal*, vol. 8, no. 1 ("Hermetism and the Underworld") (2018), 23-40.

daimon of the scientific spirit, as Jung put it, compelled nature and its forces into the service of humankind as never before: a development reflected for Jung in two iconic texts, Goethe's *Faust* and Nietzsche's *Zarathustra*. "Out of the spirit of alchemy," Jung declares, Goethe created the figure of the "superman" Faust; and, in turn, out of this figure of the *Übermensch*, Nietzsche's Zarathustra was able (a) to declare that God was dead, and (b) to announce the will to give birth to the *Übermensch* out of one's own sense of power (or, as Zarathustra puts it, "to create a god for yourself out of your seven devils" [Z I 17].) Here, in Jung's view, lie the "true roots" of the "secular, psychic preparatory processes" leading to "those factors that are at work in the world today," a world that has been conquered by science — but at the expense of the psyche itself, Jung suggests (§163). Without going into the same detail that he does in *Psychology and Alchemy* (and without mentioning his own compositional work on his *Red Book*), Jung wonders how many (or how few) people nowadays could even imagine what "coming to terms with the unconscious" might mean; he fears there would be "only too few" (§210).

Yet, Jung brings this "coming-to-terms with the unconscious" (and, *mutatis mutandis*, his own *Red Book*) into proximity with Goethe's *Faust* by suggesting that Part Two of this work presents "only incidentally and in doubtful degree an aesthetic problem, but primarily and in far greater degree a human one" (CW 13 §210). Here lies the huge bone of contention between academic approaches to Goethe's *Faust* and the kinds of reading proposed by Jung, Steiner, and others. For academic critics, Goethe's *Faust II* is essentially an aesthetic exercise, symbolized within the work by the figure of Helena, the emblem *par excellence* of the beauty of antiquity (and the beauty of antiquity): conjured up from the dead by Faust in Act I and actually presented as speaking in iambic trimeters in Act

III.[11] Yet for such readers as Jung or Steiner, Goethe's *Faust* — while obviously an aesthetic creation — is preeminently a work of immense *human* (existential, psychological, and dare one say it, spiritual?) import. It is this aspect of the work that Goethe himself designated as *inkommensurabel*.[12]

Jung links *Faust*, Part Two, back to Goethe's preoccupation in his young years, describing it as an "alchemical encounter with the unconscious," and equating it in Paracelsian (or Boehmian) terms with the *labor Sophiae*, that is, the "labour of Sophia" or "working for wisdom."[13] There is a twofold aspect to this "labour": on one hand, it is an "endeavour to understand the archetypal world of the psyche," while on the other, it is a "struggle against the sanity-threatening danger of fascination by the measureless

---

[11] For discussion of the metrical aspects of *Faust*, see Anthony Phelan, "Deconstructing Classicism: Goethe's *Helena* and the Need to Rhyme," in Richard Sheppard (ed.), *New Ways in Germanistik* (Oxford: Berg, 1990), pp. 192-210. For a contrasting view, see "Poetry as Symbolic Form," in R. H. Stephenson, *Studies in Weimar Classicism: Writing as Symbolic Form* (Berne: Lang, 2010), pp. 197-239 (p. 232).

[12] On two separate occasions, Goethe says: "But *Faust* is really something quite incommensurable and all attempts to make it accord with reason are in vain. Also one has to remember that the very first part proceeded from a rather dark condition in the individual. But the very darkness attracts people and they tire themselves out on it, as on all insoluble problems" (3 January 1830); and: "What is important with all such compositions is merely that the individual parts be clear and significant, while it always remains incommensurable as a whole and for this very reason, like an insoluble problem, it attracts people to repeated contemplation of it" (13 February 379) (Johann Peter Eckermann, *Conversations of Goethe*, ed. J.K. Moorhead, trans. John Oxenford [1830] (New York: Da Capo Press, 1998), pp. 341 and 379).

[13] "Ruland's *Lexicon Alchemiae* of 1612 defined the "work of Sophia" in the same sense as Boehme: *Labor Sophiae, id est, paradisus, alter mundus*" (Andrew Weeks, *Boehme: An Intellectual Biography of the Seventeenth-Century Philosopher and Mystic* (Albany, NY: State University of New York Press, 1991), p. 122); and: "A more sublime aspect of the female principle in creation is the *labor sophiae*, defined as 'the other paradise of this world, in which no disease grows, no disease remains, no poisonous creature dwells or enters ...' [...]. '[The long life] lies solely *in labore sophiae*, in which the *operationes elementorum* occur in the fullness of their powers ...' [...]. The elements can only approach the divine female principle Sophia in this heightened labor in which their powers achieve the fullest activation" (Andrew Weeks, *Paracelsus: Speculative Theory and the Crisis of the Early Reformation* (Albany, NY: State University of New York Press, 1991), p. 127).

heights and depths and paradoxes of psychic truth" (CW 13 §210). This labor can be described as reaching the limits of the "denser, concretistic mind of the daytime" or, expressed in Paracelsian-cum-Goethean terms, as entering a place inaccessible to the "Cendurini" (Paracelsus) or "men of crasser temperament" (*homines crassorium ingeniorum*) (Dorn), for there is no way "to the unexplorable / Aye unexplored [...] to the unimplorable, / Aye unimplored!" (*Ins Unbetretene, / Nicht zu Betretende* [...] *ans Unerbetene, / Nicht zu Erbittende*) (ll. 6222-6224), a place where "the Aquaster [i.e., the spirit of water akin to matter] does not break in" (*neque hunc locum infringet aquaster*), as Paracelsus puts it (§210).[14] And it can also be described in (Jungian) psychological terms — as the confrontation of the human mind with "its own origins, with the archetype," or of "finite consciousness with preconditions," or the "mortal ego with itself eternal self: the Anthropos, purusha, atman," and so on (§210).

In this respect, Goethe's *Faust* and Jung's *Red Book* are very much aligned in their methodology and their goal: Both are in search of what Jung (in "The Relations Between the Ego and the Unconscious") called "this 'something' [which] is strange to us and yet so near, wholly ourselves and yet unknowable, a virtual centre of so mysterious a constitution that it can claim anything — kinship with beasts and gods, with crystals and with stars — [...]," a centre that he terms *the self* but which could equally, he adds, be called "the 'God within us'" (CW 7 §398-399). Or to put it another way, both are in search of an experience which Jung (in "Paracelsus as a Spiritual Phenomenon") describes as follows: "Akin and alienated

---

[14] The realm thus so described is, of course, the realm of the Mothers, and in this context it is interesting to note a possible Paracelsian source in addition to the usual Plutarchan one; see: "The elements are frequently equated to '**mothers**' (mütter, *matres*, or *matrices*) of the entities created out of them. There are 'vier matres elementorum' [...]. In contrast to the more active and dynamic *tria prima* or *arcana*, the four elements are '4 müter' [...]" (Paracelsus (Theophrastus Bombastus von Hohenheim, 1493-1541), *Essential Theoretical Writings*, ed. and trans. Andrew Weeks (Leiden and Boston: Brill, 2008), p. 116).

at one and the same time, [the individual ego] recognizes and yet does not recognize its unknown brother, who intangibly yet really approaches it" (CW 13 §210). Or to use another set of Paracelsian terms, both involve the encounter with "the true man [who] is the star in us,"[15] the *homo maximus,*[16] Adech (a name derived from Adam),[17] or Archeus (§168).[18] In fact, Paracelsus talks about "that difficult Adech" (*difficilis ille Adech*) or "that great Adech" (*maximus ille Adech*),[19] a difficulty which is then said by Jung to lie in the fact

---

[15] See *Astronomia magna*, in Paracelsus, *Sämtliche Werke*, 1. Abteilung, *Medizinische, naturwissenschaftliche und philosophische Schriften*, ed. Karl Sudhoff and Wilhelm Matthiessen, 14 vols. (Munich and Berlin: Oldenbourg, 1929), vol. 12, pp. 1-444 (p. 55).

[16] See Paracelsus, *Das Buch Paragranum*, ed. Franz Strunz (Leipzig: Diederichs, 1903), pp. 45 and 59.

[17] See Paracelsus, *De Vita Longa*, ed. Gerhard Dorn (Frankfurt am Main, 1583), pp. 169-170. According to Franz Hartmann (1838-1912), Adech can be defined as "the inner (spiritual) man; the lord of thought and imagination, forming subjectively all things in his mind, which the exterior (material) man may objectively reproduce. Either of the two acts according to his nature, the invisible in an invisible, and the visible one in a visible manner, but both act correspondingly. The outer man may act what the inner man thinks, but thinking is acting in the sphere of thought, and the products of thought are transcendentally substantial, even if they are not thrown into objectivity on the material plane. The inner man is and does what he desires and thinks. Whether or not his good or evil thoughts and intentions find expression on the material plane is of less importance to his own spiritual development than to others who may be affected by his acts, but less by his thoughts" (*Life and Doctrines of Paracelsus*, p. 37). For further discussion, see "Controversial Paracelsian Doctrines — Sources and Protoscientific Significance," in Walter Pagel, *The Smiling Spleen: Paracelsianism in Storm and Stress* (Basel: Karger, 1984), pp. 97-142.

[18] See Paracelsus, "Von den dreyen ersten essentiis," in Paracelsus, *Bücher und Schrifften, des Edlen, Hochgelehrten und Bewehrten Philosophi und Medici, Philippi Theophrasti Bombast von Hohenheim, Paracelsi genannt*, ed. by Johannes Huser, 10 vols. (Basel: Waldkirch, 1589-1591), vol. 1, pp. 323-326: "He is therefore similar to man and consists of the four elements and is an Archeus and is composed of four parts; say, then, he is the great Cosmos" (p. 325). Jung aligns this fourfold aspect of the Primordial Man with the fourfold deity of Gnosticism (equating "God is four" with the *Barbelo*). According to Frantz Hartmann, Archeus can be defined as "the formative power of Nature, which divides the elements and forms them into organic parts. It is the principle of life; the power which contains the essence of life and character of everything" (*Life and Doctrines of Paracelsus*, p. 40).

[19] Cf. CW 13 §209 and §214; citing Paracelsus, *De Vita longa*, Book 5, Chapter 5 (in *Sämtliche Werke*, vol. 3, pp. 249-292 [p. 94]).

that "the more [the ego] is bound and confused in time and space,
the more it will feel the other as 'that difficult Adech' who crosses
its intentions, gives an unexpected twist to its fate, and sets what it
fears as its task" (§210). Indeed, in the final chapter of his treatise
De vita longa, Paracelsus says that if he were to count himself
"among the Scaiolae [i.e., lovers of wisdom] in the manner of the
Necrolii [i.e., adepts], this would be something that [...] should be
undertaken, but it is hindered by that great Adech, who redirects
our intentions but not the work."[20]

For assistance in understanding this passage — which even
Jung himself describes as "dark"! — we can turn to a later section
of "Paracelsus as a Spiritual Phenomenon." Here, Jung devotes
himself to a discussion of the figure of Melusina, a water-nixie,
usually depicted as a woman whose lower half is a serpent or a fish.
(The textual basis of Jung's discussion here is Book 5, Chapter 5,
of Paracelsus's *Die vita longa*, and Gerard Dorn's commentary on
this work [cited *in extenso* in CW 13 §214].)[21] Jung ponders, only
then to dismiss, the possibility that this figure, described by Dorn
as *apparentum in mente visionem* or "appearing in the mind," is a
projection onto a real woman, insisting that a kind of "hyperreality"
(*einen hohen Wirklichkeitsgrad*) attends on Paracelsus's Melusina
as it does in the case of Lady Polia in Francesco Colonna's
Hypnerotomachia Poliphili (translated as *The Dream of Poliphilus*)
(1499) — far more so, Jung adds, than in the case of Beatrice in
Dante's *Paradiso*, but not as much as Helena in *Faust II* (§215). For

---

[20] Paracelsus, *De vita longa*, ed. Dorn, pp. 174-175 (cited in CW 13 §211).
[21] The figure of Melusina attracted the interest of Goethe as well: see his literary
fairytale *Die neue Melusine*, published as part of his last great prose work, *Wilhelm
Meisters Wanderjahre* (1821/1829). For further discussion, see C.A.H. Russ,
"Introduction," in Goethe, *Three Tales* (Oxford: Oxford University Press, 1964),
pp. 7-41; and Renata Schellenberg, "Goethe and *Die neue Melusine*: A Critical
Reinterpretation," in Misty Urban, Deva Kemmis, and Melissa Ridley Elmes (eds.),
Melusine's Footprint: Tracing the Legacy of a Medieval Myth (Leiden and Boston:
Brill, 2017), pp. 303-323. For further discussion, see pp. 367-368 below.

Jung, the mysterious, yet alluring figure of Melusina is "certainly not an allegorical unreality or a mere metaphor, but has her particular psychic reality in the sense of an eerie appearance which, by its nature, is on the one hand a psychically determined vision, but on the other — thanks to the soul's capacity for imaginative realization, the so-called Ares — is a distinct, objective entity" (§216). Or as he puts it in a short, pithy summary, Melusina is "a dream that temporarily becomes reality" (§216). In other words, in Jungian terms Melusina is an anima figure (§216).

For Paracelsus, Melusina's appearance arises from the intervention of those Scaiolae or the "driving spiritual forces emanating from the *homo maximus*" which the alchemical opus serves and whose goal is to "raise the human being to the sphere of the Anthropos" (CW 13 §220). On this account, the philosophical alchemist's goal of "higher self-development," Paracelsus's production of the *homo maior*, and what Jung calls "individuation" are simply different ways of saying the same thing. In all cases, the beginning of the opus or *Individuationsprozess* is the same: loneliness, *Einsamkeit*; in his entry in the fifth of his *Black Books* for 18 March 1914, Jung writes: "A number of times I read in Nietzsche the expression 'ultimate solitude.' This is the phrase that stands before me" (BB5, 203). This absolute solitude, together with the alchemist's preoccupation with the "endlessly obscure work," serves to activate the unconscious, stirring the imagination (*imaginatio*) into action and bringing into appearance things that had previously not been there. In the form of these "fantasy images" (*Phantasiebilder*) the unconscious itself becomes visible (*anschaulich*) and tangible (*erfahrbar*), just as Melusina emerges from the watery realm and assumes human form (§220). (Or, one might add, just as Mephistopheles becomes present to Faust, or Elijah and Salome become figures in *The Red Book* with whom Jung can converse.)

In the case of *Faust I*, Faust's desperation leads him directly
into the arms of Gretchen, the form in which Melusina would
most likely have remained, if there had not been the catastrophe
that drives Faust deeper still into magic (*die Magie*): As it were,
Melusina "changes into" Helena! Even then, however, she does not
remain the same, for "all attempts at concretization shatter — like the
retort of Homunculus against the throne of Galatea" (CW 13 §220).
Instead, another power takes over, namely "that difficult Adech"
(*difficilis ille Adech*) who (in the words of Dorm's commentary)
"at the end [...] changes himself" (§220). As the "greater man," he
"hinders our purpose," and Faust himself has to undergo a radical
change after his death, becoming like one of the "Blessed Young
Boys" (*selige Knaben*) — or "one to whom," as Jung puts it, "the
true world will only be shown when all desirousness has fallen
away" (§221). (Oh, "miserable mortals, to whom Nature has denied
her first and best treasure, the *lumen naturae*!", as Paracelsus cries.)

This "inner man," Adech, guides with his Scaiolae the
intention of the adept and enables him to see those (fantasy)
"images" from which he could nevertheless draw false conclusions
(CW 13 §221); similarly, Melusina's acts are said to be "deceptive
fantasy images," in which "supreme sense" and "pernicious
nonsense" are mixed, but from which the wise individual will learn
to extract and distill the "precious drops of the *liquor Sophiae*" in
his soul (§222). Jung draws attention to Paracelsus's emphasis on a
"discriminative process" or a "critical judgment" — one which can,
so to speak, separate the wheat from the chaff. (Far from being the
proponent of irrationalism that he is sometimes accused of being,
here Jung is both explicit and emphatic about the need for critical
judgment!) And now Jung formulates an important principle: "It
requires no art," he says, "to become foolish [*närrisch*]; but to
extract wisdom [*Weisheit*] from folly [*Narrheit*], therein lies the
whole art [*die ganze Kunst*]," for "folly [*Narrheit*] is the mother of
the wise, but cleverness [*Klugkeit*] never" (§222). Goethe himself

says something similar when, in a short essay of 1820 titled "Doubt and Resignation" (*Bedenken und Ergebung*), he articulates his own version of this existential response to the epistemological gap: "Here we encounter the very difficulty, which is not always made clear and conscious, namely that there appears to be a certain gap fixed between idea and experience, which all our powers vainly try to overcome," he wrote, adding: "Nonetheless our whole endeavour consists in trying to overcome this hiatus with reason, understanding, imagination, faith, feeling, illusion and, when all else fails, with folly [*mit Albernheit*]".[22]

In relation to the famous *Schlußszene* with which *Faust II* concludes, in a footnote in "Paracelsus as a Spiritual Phenomenon" Jung drew attention to the analogies between Doctor Marianus's prayer to the Mater Gloriosa at the end of *Faust* and the prayer to Isis at the end of Apuleius's *Metamorphosis* or *The Golden Ass* (CW 13 §228, fn. 19).[23] (In Apuleius's novel, the redemption of its hero, Lucius, who has been transformed into an ass, begins when he eats a crown of roses from the hand of one of the priests of Isis. In return, Lucius is initiated into the mysteries of Isis, beginning with the Navigium Isidis that initiates him into the priesthood of the mother goddess, the equivalent of the Mater Gloriosa.) Jung presents these parallels in tabular form:

---

[22] See Goethe, *Scientific Studies*, ed. and trans. Douglas Miller [Goethe Edition, vol. 8] (New York: Suhrkamp, 1988), pp. 33-34 (translated here by R.H. Stephenson).
[23] For further discussion of Lucius's prayer in book 11 of *Metamorphoses*, see Friedemann Drews, "A Platonic Reading of the Isis Book," in W.H. Keulen and Ulrike Egelhaaf-Gaiser (eds), *Apuleius Madaurensis Metamorphoses, Book XI, The Isis Book: Text, Introduction and Commentary* (Leiden: Brill, 2015), pp. 517-528; and Marie-Louise von Franz, *The Golden Ass of Apuleius: The Liberation of the Feminine in Man* (Boston and London: Shambhala, 1992), pp. 187-210.

Tender penitents, your eyes

Lift where looks salvation.

Gratefully to bliss arise

Through regeneration.

Each best power, Thy service in,

Prove it efficacious.

Ever, Virgin, Mother, Queen,

Goddess, be Thou gracious !

O holy and blessed dame, the perpetuall comfort of humane kind, who by thy bounty and grace nourishest all the world, and hearest a great affection to the adversities of the miserable, as a loving mother thou takest no rest, neither art thou idle at any time in giving thy benefits, and succoring all men, as well on land as sea; thou art she that puttest away all stormes and dangers from man's life by thy right hand, whereby likewise thou restrainest the fatall dispositions, appeasest the great tempests of fortune and keepest backe the course of the stars: the gods supernall doe honour thee: the gods infernall have thee in reverence: thou environest all the world, thou givest light to the Sunne, thou governest the world, thou treadest downe the power of hell: By thy meane the times returne, the Planets rejoyce, the Elements serve: at thy commandment the winds do blow, the clouds increase, the seeds prosper, and the fruits prevaile, the birds of the aire, the beasts of the hill, the serpents of the den, and the fishes of the sea, do tremble at thy majesty, but my spirit is not able to give thee sufficient praise, my patrimonie is unable to satisfie thy sacrifice, my voice hath no power to utter that which I thinke, no if I had a thousand mouths and so many tongues: Howbeit as a good religious person, and according to my estate, I will alwaies keepe thee in remembrance and close thee within my breast.

Now by presenting these texts in parallel, Jung implies that their relationship is purely one of analogy. (As far as I know, the possibility of this parallel has never been pursued further.) [24] Of course, given that Apuleius's work has itself always been an important textual source for knowledge of the ancient mysteries, both in the 18th century and in our present day,[25] the relation may well be one of literary borrowing rather than simply analogy! Nevertheless, the apparent textual parallels support the idea of cultural continuity across the centuries, a key tenet of Jungian thought; and illustrates one more time the broad cultural-historical landscape in which Jung always sought to situate Goethe's *Faust*.

In two lectures given at the Eranos Conference in 1942 that were subsequently published together under the title "The Spirit Mercurius" (1943; [2]1948), Jung explored a number of themes that prove to be of considerable relevance to his reading of Goethe's *Faust* and to his creation of *The Red Book* alike — notably, the significance of the figure of Christ and its relation (thanks to the law of compensation) to the figure of Mercurius. In this regard, Jung highlighted how, in *Faust*, Part One, the compensatory figure is not — as one might have expected, given its author's

---

[24] It has been suggested that the ass's head of the figure of the Empusa in the Classical Walpurgis Night (ll. 7744-7747) and the verses, "And ye, fair cousins, though so tender, / So languishing, all doubts engender. / Behind your cheeks' alluring roses / I fear there lurk, too, metamorphoses" (ll. 7756-7759), represent a recollection of Apuleius's *Metamorphoses* (Horst Rüdiger, "Curiositas und Magie: Apuleius und Lucius als literarische Archetypen der Faust-Gestalt," in Harri Meier and Hans Sckommodau (eds.), *Wort und Text: Festschrift für Fritz Schalk* (Frankfurt am Main: Klostermann, 1963), pp. 57-82). According to Hans Ruppert's guide to the *Goethe Bibliothek* (nos. 1359 and 1427), Goethe did not own a copy of the *Metamorphoses*, but his library did contain the *Apologia* (see G. Sandy, "Knowledge and Curiosity in Apuleius' *Metamorphoses*," *Latomus*, vol. 31, no. 1 (January-March 1972), 179-183 [p. 181]), and Horst Rüdiger suggests that Goethe may well have known the *Metamorphoses* in translation.

[25] See "Apuleius: Die Mysterien der Isis erobern die griechisch-römische Welt," in Jan Assmann and Florian Ebeling, *Ägyptische Mysterien: Reisen in die Unterwelt in Aufklärung und Romantik: Eine kommentierte Anthologie* (Munich: Beck, 2011), pp. 29-47 (p. 29).

"classical predilections" — the "wily messenger of the gods," that
is, Mercurius, but is instead, as the very name *Mephistopheles*
suggests,[26] "a *familiaris* risen from the cesspits of medieval magic,"
a fact which is said to prove the "ingrained Christian character of
Goethe's consciousness" (CW 13 §295). To the Christian mentality,
Jung argues, the "dark antagonist" is always the Devil, a figure to
which Mercurius is very close, yet not identical (§295). For, despite
all his ambiguity and duplicity, Mercurius "scorns to carry on
opposition at all costs" and "keep[s] outside the split" since, as an
"ancient pagan god," he possesses a "natural undividedness" which
is "impervious to logical and moral contradictions," and "gives
him invulnerability and incorruptibility" (§295). And these are the
qualities we need to "heal the split in ourselves," and significantly,
the split in Faust is never entirely healed in *this* life, only in the
afterlife (as Jung also argues in his "Epilogue" to *Psychology and
Alchemy*, to which we shall now turn).

Faust in *Psychology and Alchemy*

Psychology and Alchemy, Volume 12 in the *Collected Works*,
brings together two major studies which grew out of material
originally presented as lectures at Eranos conferences in 1935 and
1936, "Individual Dream Symbolism in Relation to Alchemy" and
"Religious Ideas in Alchemy." For inclusion in this volume, Jung
added a substantial "Introduction to the Religious and Psychological
Problems of Alchemy," as well as a short, but highly significant
"Epilogue," in which Goethe's *Faust* features prominently.

In "Individual Dream Symbolism in Relation to Alchemy,"
Jung boldly remarks that "*Faust* is an alchemical drama from

---

[26] According to Albert Martins's Latin dictionary, the name *Mephistophiles* derives
from the Latin *mephitis* (i.e., noxious exhalation of the earth) which, combined with
the ancient Greek φίλος (*phílos*, i.e., "friend," "beloved," "loving"), would mean
"someone who loves foul smells"!

beginning to end" (CW 12 §85). This remark looks like an invitation to read *Faust* in terms of the process of alchemy, as several critics have done.[27] Yet I would argue that Jung's point is, however, as usual more subtle. For he goes on to say that *Faust* is an alchemical drama — "although the educated person of today has only the haziest notion of this" (§85). Might it be that Jung's argument is really less about *Faust* as an alchemical text and more about correcting our lack of education or *Bildung*? Could it be that the project of Analytical Psychology — "respect for the eternal rights of humankind, recognition of 'the ancient,' and the continuity of culture and historical history" (MDR, 262) — is not simply "consciously linked" to what Faust had "pass over," but directly indexed to our knowledge and understanding of Goethe's *Faust*?

Now the context of this remark by Jung about *Faust* as an "alchemical drama" is an analysis of a series of 59 dreams (concluding with the so-called "great vision" of the World Clock) out of a thousand or so dreams experienced by one of Jung's clients. (Although Jung preserves the dreamer's anonymity, we now know the dreamer in question was the theoretical physicist Wolfgang Pauli [1900-1958].)[28] Central to Jung's interpretation here is the

---

[27] See the monograph-length studies by Edinger, Gerber-Münch, and Wilkerson (listed in the "Jungian/alchemical readings of *Faust* (in chronological order)" above). For an early reading of *Faust* in Jungian-alchemical terms see Gustav F. Hartlaub, "Goethe als Alchemist," *Euphorion*, 48 (1954), 19-40. For a critique of this approach, see Harold Jantz, "Goethe, Faust, Alchemy, and Jung," *The German Quarterly*, vol. 35, no. 2 (March 1962), 129-141. In Jantz's view, "the *Faust* as Goethe wrote it obviously cannot be construed into an alchemical parable": "Before that can be done, drastic revisions of the text, action, and sequence have to be undertaken. — But then, it is no longer Goethe's *Faust*. Only Carl Jung's *Faust* is alchemical, Goethe's *Faust* is something else entirely" (135).

[28] See C.G. Jung and Wolfgang Pauli, *Atom and Archetype: The Pauli/Jung Letters, 1932-1958*, ed. C.A. Meier, trans. David Roscoe (Princeton, NJ, and Oxford: Princeton University Press, 2001), p. 10. After his lecture at Eranos in 1935, in 1944 Jung reworked this material into *Psychology and Alchemy*, but in 1936 and 1937 Jung gave a series of lectures, first in Bailey Island, Maine, and then in New York, in which he explored further the personal aspects of Pauli's dreams; see C.G. Jung, *Dream Symbols of the Individuation Process: Notes of C.G. Jung's Seminars on*

principle that dreams such as these form "a coherent series," in the course of which "the meaning gradually unfolds more or less of its own accord" (CW 12 §50). And *"the series,"* Jung argues, *"is the context which the dreamer himself supplies,"* going on to compare the practice of dream interpretation to the analysis of literary texts, for it is "as if not one text but many lay before us, throwing light from all sides on the unknown terms," so that "a reading of all the texts is sufficient to elucidate the difficult passages in each individual one" (§50): an excellent hermeneutic principle!

In the 13th dream of the initial series of 22 dreams, the figure of the father cries out anxiously, "That is the seventh!" (CW 12 §82). On Jung's account, this anxious father is the "representative of the traditional spirit" and a "psychic component of the dreamer himself" (§83-§84). Correspondingly, this "seventh," Jung suggests, means "not only a sort of culmination but something rather ominous as well" (§84). Via the fairy tale of Tom Thumb and the Ogre, Jung discovers (or, as his critics would say, invents) a link to what E.A. Wallace Budge in his translation of the Pyramid inscriptions call a *paut neteru* or a "company of the gods,"[29] depicted by Pseudo-Thomas Aquinas in the 16th-century manuscript "De alchimia" as the seven gods of the planets (or six planets united in the seventh, Mercury) or by Mylius in *Philosophia reformata* (1622) as the seven gods of the planets in Hades.

Here Jung urges us not to get caught up in the precise numerological significance of the number seven itself. He points out that, even if a company of gods is described as "nine," it often proves to be not nine at all but 10 or even more, and he cites the French Egyptologist Gaston Maspero (1846-1916) as explaining that the first or last members of a series can be added to, or doubled,

---

Wolfgang Pauli's Dreams, ed. Suzanne Gieser (Princeton, NJ, and Oxford: Princeton University Press, 2019).

[29] E.A. Wallis Budge, *The Gods of the Egyptians, or Studies in Egyptian Mythology*, 2 vols. (London: Methuen, 1904), vol. 1, p. 87.

without injury to the number nine (§84).[30] What matters, Jung is suggesting, is not *how many* gods are said to be in any given *paut,* or company, but what *happens* to the gods themselves over time. After all, he says, in the "post-classical age," when the Greco-Roman or Babylonian gods in the classical *paut* became "degraded to daimons and retired partly to the distant stars and partly to the metals inside the earth," the very nature of those gods themselves steps into the foreground; and the nature of the most important of those gods, Hermes or Mercurius, now becomes clear.

It turns out that this god possesses a "double nature," being a "chthonic god of revelation" as well as the "spirit of quicksilver" (that is, the chemical element with the symbol **Hg** and the atomic number 80), and as a result he was represented — as in the depiction of Mercurius as a homunculus in the alchemical vessel or the "philosopher's egg" in the *Mutus liber* in 1702 — as a hermaphrodite (CW 12 §84). These images serve to represent the dual nature of Mercurius: as the planet Mercury, he is closest to the sun, and so related to gold; as quicksilver, he dissolves gold. Hence the dual depiction of Mercurius in the Middle Ages: on the one hand, as a ministering or helpful spirit, a πάρεδρος (*páredros*) or *familiaris*; and, on the other, as a *servus* or *cervus fugitivus*, or an elusive, deceptive goblin, or even the Devil. In the hierarchy of alchemy, Mercurius is the lowest, the *prima materia* ("base matter"), but also the highest, the *lapis philosophorum* (the philosopher's stone). As Hermes psychopompos, he is the alchemist's guide, but also their tempter; he is their good fortune — but also their ruin.

Jung's point here is that the so-called "black art" of alchemy is, far from being remote, of the utmost relevance to the interpretation of dreams (and to much else as well). As himself an educated man, Jung surmises, his client *must* have read *Faust*

---

[30] Gaston Camille Charles Maspero, *Études de mythologie et d'archéologie égyptiennes*, 7 vols. (Paris: E. Leroux, 1893-1916), vol. 2, p. 245.

— an assumption that may have been valid in Jung's time but not
necessarily so today — and Goethe's work is said to illustrate
the principle that "our consciousness is far from understanding
everything, but the unconscious keeps an eye on the 'age-old, sacred
things,' however strange they may be, and reminds us of them at
a suitable opportunity" (§85). The expression "age-old, sacred"
(*uralt heil'gen*) is probably taken from a poem by the Austrian
poet Robert Hamerling (1830-1889) who, as Rudolf Steiner puts
it, links "grey primordial time with the immediate present."[31] And
this is precisely Jung's point. Could it be, Jung wondered, that his
dreamer-client had been as much affected by *Faust* as Goethe had
been affected by Paracelsus when, in his Leipzig days, he studied
the works of this Swiss physician and alchemist with Fräulein von
Klettenberg (1723-1774) —[32] or, indeed, as much as Jung himself
had also been affected by *Faust* (see Chapter 3 above)?

Hence it is symbolism in general, rather than the specific
numerical symbolism, that is at stake here, inasmuch as the
"mysterious equivalence" of seven and eight had apparently "sunk
deep" into the dreamer-client's soul, "without his conscious mind

---

[31] See Rudolf Steiner, "Ein vergessenes Streben nach Geisteswissenschaft innerhalb
der deutschen Gedankenentwickelung" (Berlin, 25 February 1916), in *Aus dem
mitteleuropäischen Geistesleben: Fünfzehn öffentliche Vorträge gehalten zwischen
dem 2. Dezember 1915 und dem 15. April 1916 im Architektenhaus zu Berlin* [GA
065] (Dornach: Rudolf Steiner Verlag, 2000), pp. 407-457.

[32] See *Dichtung und Wahrheit*, Part Two, Book 8. As Gero von Wilpert notes, Goethe's
engagement with Paracelsus during a period of convalescence in 1769 followed his
reading — at the instigation of Susanne von Klettenberg (1723-1774) — of the *Opus
mago-cabbalisticum* by Georg von Welling (1655-1727), and one should add that it
accompanied his reading of writings by the 15th-century alchemist Basilius Valentinus,
Jan Baptist van Helmont (1580-1644), the founder of "pneumatic chemistry," and
George Starkey (1628-1665), who wrote under the pseudonym Eirenaeus Philalethes.
Certain Paracelsian motifs, such as the doctrine of microcosm and macrocosm, the
four elementary spirits, the Earth Spirit (*Erdgeist*), and the figure of the homunculus
in the retort, not to mention the father's medical campaign against the plague, seem to
have influenced — not without a certain irony in their usage — Goethe's *Faust* (Gero
von Wilpert, *Goethe-Lexikon* (Stuttgart: Kröner, 1998), p. 807).

ever unravelling the mystery" (CW 12 §85).[33] This argument is substantiated with reference to the next dream, the 14th, in which the dreamer is in America, looking for an employee "with a pointed beard" (§86). Jung uses this dream as a springboard for some rather broad-brush *Kulturkritik*. America, he says, is a land of "practical, straightforward thinking," a country which is "uncontaminated by our European sophistication": in effect, the intellect itself is kept "as an employee" (§87). But what happens to the intellect when it is thus kept? This *lèse-majesté* has consequences, Jung suggests, which are symbolized by the man with a pointed beard: He is said to represent "our time-honoured Mephisto whom Faust 'employed' and who" — and here Goethe departs, of course, from the traditional legend — "was not permitted to triumph over him in the end," despite the fact that Faust had "dared to descend into the dark chaos of the historical psyche and steep himself in the ever-changing, seamy side of life that rose up out of that bubbling cauldron" (§87).

On this reading, Mephistopheles or the man with the pointed beard represents the astrological (or alchemical) Mercurius, with the attributes of "versatility of mind" as well the "inventive gift and scientific leanings" — qualities that emphasize his ambivalence, the ambivalence of an "obliging, if somewhat dangerous spirit," or a real *familiaris* (CW 12 §88). In this dream, it is not simply the case that the intellect is shown to have been "degraded from the supreme position," "put in second place," and "branded as daimonic," for, in fact, it had never been anything *other* than daimonic — only the dreamer had not recognized how he had come to be "possessed" by the intellect as the "tacitly recognized supreme power." Now, however, that he can examine this function more closely as the

---

[33] Of course, there is numerical symbolism in *Faust*: see CW 12 §84 and §204, on the missing eighth!

"uncontested dominant of his psychic life," he might well exclaim
with Faust, "So that's what was inside the poodle!" (§88).

According to Jung, the negative aspect of any given function
can only be perceived when, as in this dream, it is objectified or
personified and becomes a separate entity. As is suggested by the
first of Eugène Delacroix's 17 illustrations for a French translation
of Goethe's *Faust*, Part One, by Albert Stapfer (published in
Paris in 1828), which depicts Mephistopheles in the scene from
the "Prologue in Heaven," flying above the nocturnal city skyline
and commenting on his recent interview with the Lord, "I like
to see the Old Man now and then, / and take good care to keep
on speaking terms" (ll. 350-351), Mephistopheles is both aerial
spirit *and* ungodly intellect; and, as the "diabolical aspect of every
psychic function that has broken loose from the hierarchy of the
total psyche," he now enjoys "independence and absolute power"
(CW 12 §88). As a confirmation of this reading, Jung recalls that,
in one of the "Parabolae" contained in the second volume of a
three-volume series with the subtitle "Ein güldener Tractat vom
philosophischen Steine" (1625) included in the second volume
of a book titled *Geheime Figuren der Rosenkreuzer aus dem
16ten und 17ten Jahrhundert* (1785-1790) (a work analyzed by
Herbert Silberer [1882-1923] in his *Problems of Mysticism and its
Symbolism* [1914]), the narrator comes to a meadow with a circle
of fruit-bearing trees and finds himself in the midst of a company of
old, gray-bearded men, including a young man with a black pointed
beard — a figure about whom Silberer is uncertain, conjecturing
that he might be death or the Devil.[34]

This curious figure recurs in the 22nd dream in the series,
in which a large ape-man threatens to attack the dreamer with a
club until the man with the pointed beard appears and stares at the

---

[34] See Herbert Silberer, *Problems of Mysticism and Its Symbolism* [1914], trans.
Smith Ely Jelliffe (New York: Moffat, Yard, 1917), pp. 2 and 63.

aggressor until he is spellbound, and a voice says, "Everything must be ruled by the light" (CW 12 §117). In his commentary on this dream, Jung wonders: "Who knows how much Faust owed his imperturbable curiosity, as he gazed on the spooks and bogeys of the classical *Walpurgisnacht*, to the helpful presence of Mephisto and his matter-of-fact point of view!" (§119). If only, Jung added wistfully, more people could remember the "scientific or philosophical reflections of the much-abused intellect" (§119)! While the intellect, Jung concludes (referring again to the earlier discussed drawing by Delacroix), may be the Devil, the Devil is — in the words of *Faust I* — "the strange son of chaos" (*Des Chaos wunderlicher Sohn*) (l. 1384, cf. l. 8028), who can be trusted, as Jung mysteriously says, "to deal effectively with his mother" — perhaps an allusion to the "maternal night" (*Mutter Nacht*) that is in a state of permanent struggle with the light (cf. l. 1351).

In the second part of his study, Jung focuses on the symbolism of the mandala and discusses a second series of dreams by his dream-client that refer specifically to the mandala. In the 31st dream of this second (mandala) series, the dreamer-client sees a round table on which there is standing a glass filled with some kind of gelatinous substance (CW 12 §241). On Jung's interpretation, the glass in the dream corresponds in alchemical terms to the *unum vas* (or "unique glass") and its contents to the "living, semi-organic mixture from which the body of the *lapis*, endowed with spirit and life, will emerge" (§243). Analogously, Jung identified in *Faust* three figures that correspond to the *lapis*, each of which is said to "burst into flames" (or, more precisely, to undergo some kind of dispersal): in Part Two, Act I, the Boy Charioteer who returns to his rural background; at the end of Act II, Homunculus, who merges with the sea at the feet of Galatea; and in Act III, Euphorion, who aspires to fly but falls to his death, a trail of light following him from his shining head (§243). The fate of all three, Jung says, symbolizes "a dissolution of the 'centre' into its unconscious

elements" (*Auflösung der "Mitte" ins Unbewußte*); one might,
then, call Jung an alchemical deconstructionist!

As discussed in Chapter 2 above, the Classical Walpurgis
Night in Act II of Part Two concludes with the Aegean Festival,
a scene rich in dense imagery that attracted the attention of
Karl Kerényi.[35] In "Individual Dream Symbolism in Relation
to Alchemy," Jung focuses on a particular part of this scene, the
epiphany of the mysterious figures of the Cabiri. The context for
these remarks is his discussion of the 22nd of this second series of
dreams, and Jung picks up on the numerological point made earlier
in his discussion of the Seventh in the thirteenth dream of the first
series. Jung interprets this new dream (with its detail of a lift going
to the third or fourth floor, then to the seventh or eighth) as an
expression of the "tendency to re-establish a state of wholeness"
and as an engagement with the "problem of the fourth function"
(CW 12 §201-§202). In Jungian terms, wholeness involves the use
of all four functions — thinking, feeling, sensation, and intuition
— but this dream, Jung suggests, expresses a certain hesitation
"before the last step to wholeness" (§203). And it is at this point
that Jung broadens his discussion to include *Faust II* and a number
of numerological motifs.[36]

The Cabiri Scene of Goethe's *Faust*, Part Two, belongs to
that part of the "Classical Walpurgis Night" in Act II set in the
"rocky inlets of the Aegean Sea," in which the Sirens, the Nereids,
and the Tritons introduce the equally mythical figures of the Cabiri,
raising as they do so various numerological questions about them.

---

[35] Karl Kerényi, *Das Ägäische Fest: Die Meergötterszene in Goethes Faust II*
(Amsterdam and Leipzig: Pantheon, 1941); 3rd edition as *Das Ägäische Fest:
Erläuterungen zur Szene "Felsbuchten des Ägäischen Meers" in Goethes Faust
II* (Wiesbaden: Limes Verlag, 1950); and in *Humanistische Seelenforschung*
(Darmstadt: Wissenschaftliche Buchgesellschaft, 1966), pp. 116-149.
[36] For Jung's discussion of the problem of the Three and the Four, found on his
account in alchemy, Tantric Yoga, and *Faust II*, in his lectures given in 1936 and 1937
on Bailey Island and in New York, see Jung, *Dream Symbols of the Individuation
Process*, ed. Gieser, pp. 197-198, 251-257 and 273-275.

Hitherto the Cabiri have been usually seen in the light of two earlier discussions of them on which Goethe drew, namely: Friedrich Creuzer's *Symbolik und Mythologie der alten Völker* (1810-1823) and FW.J. Schelling's *The Deities of Samothrace* (1815). Since the publication of *The Red Book*, however, it is impossible to overlook the specific significance these diminutive figures had for Jung in relation to the construction (described in *Liber Secundus* and the chapter titled "The Magician") of Jung's Tower. Their special significance is underscored by the fact that the dialogue between Jung's "I" and the Cabiri is not found in *Black Book 4*, but it *is* in the *Handwritten Draft*, which has led Sonu Shamdasani to surmise that it may have been written separately, prior to the summer of 1915 (RB, 425, fn. 310). What, however, is the function of these strange figures for Goethe in *Faust*, Part Two? And what is their numerological significance?

On the level of narrative action, the Cabiri — in the form of mysterious, silent idols — are carried by a procession of Nereids and Tritons, held in the gigantic tortoise shell of Chelone (a nymph transformed by Hermes into a sea tortoise), to the festival in honor of Neptune, the god of the sea (and the Roman counterpart to the Greek god, Poseidon). Even if Goethe once described Schelling's *On the Divinities of Samothrace* (*Über die Gottheiten von Samothrake*) as a "going-off on the wrong dark, poetic, philosophical, clerical track,"[37] the function of these passages is, as Albrecht Schöne notes, by no means purely satirical, for it is precisely Schelling who supplies Goethe with crucial details about these figures, especially their hungry yearning (cf. *Sehnsuchtsvolle Hungerleider*; ll. 8204-8205). Schelling explains that the name of one of the Cabiri, Axieros, means

---

[37] See Goethe's letter to Meyer of 25 August 1819. Schelling's treatise is cited here from Robert F. Brown (ed.), *Schelling's Treatise on "The Deities of Samothrace": A Translation and an Interpretation* (Missoula, MT: Scholars Press, 1974); and F.W.J. Schelling, *Ueber die Gottheiten von Samothrace* (Stuttgart and Tübingen: Cotta, 1815).

in the Phoenician dialect "'hunger,' 'poverty,' and in consequence 'yearning,' 'seeking'" (*den Hunger, die Armuth, und was daraus folgt, das Schmachten, die Sucht*) (18; 11). He notes that, of the diverse fragments of the Phoenician cosmogony that have been preserved, one of them "locates time above all the gods, which time itself has no number because it is the common context and bearer of all numbers; next to it, however, and therefore as the first number, it mentions the wistful longing [*die schmachtende Sehnsucht*]" (19; 15). Indeed, Schelling argues that "the representation of longing as the beginning, as first ground of creation, was indigenous to Phoenician cosmogony" (*die Vorstellung der Sehnsucht als Anfangs, als ersten Grundes zur Schöpfung* (20; 16), and on the evidence of a text by Pliny he extends this principle to the cult at Samothrace (20). Identifying another of the Cabiri, Axiokersa, with Persephone or Ceres, Schelling claims that Ceres, "as [the pining for reality, as] the hunger for being which we recognize as the most inward aspect of all [longing-filled] nature" (*der Hunger nach Wesen, den wir noch als das Innerste der ganzen Natur erkennen*), is "the moving power through whose ceaseless attraction everything, as if by magic, is brought from the primal indeterminateness to actuality or formation" (20; 17).[38] Or as the Nereids and Tritons in *Faust II* describe them:

> Far horizons they beseech,
> Peerless, distance-cherishers,
> Ever-famished perishers
> For the out-of-reach.
>   (ll. 8202-8205)

According to Schelling, the "holy, revered" teaching of the Cabiri was "the representation of insoluble life itself as it progresses in a sequence of levels from the lowest to the highest" (*Darstellung des*

---

[38] For further discussion, see Schöne, *Kommentare*, p. 567.

unauflöslichen, in einer Folge von Steigerungen vom Tiefsten in's Höchste, forschreitenden Lebens) (29; 39), a doctrine which, for Gottfried Diener, is "indeed the meaning of the Classical Walpurgis Night, the secret of the Aegean Festival, indeed the core of the entire Faust work" (514). Yet while these Proteus-like Samothracian deities thus appear in the context of this cultic festival essentially as embodiments of "Faustian" desire (Schöne, *Kommentare*, 567-568), Jung focuses instead on the numerological aspects of this scene — on what he calls "the problem of three and four, seven and eight" (CW 12 §209).[39]

According to Jung, this problem was "a great puzzle to alchemy," and he traces it back historically to texts ascribed to the anonymous seventh-century author Christianos (CW 12 §209). In a treatise titled "The Production of the 'Mysterious Water'" in Berthelot's *Alchimistes grecs* (vol. 3, pp. 388-390), we read how "the Hebrew prophetess cried without restraint, 'One becomes two, two becomes three, and out of the third comes the One as the fourth'" (*De là vient que la prophétesse hébraïque s'est écriée sans réticence: «Un devient deux, et deux deviennent trois, et au moyen du troisème, le quatrième accomplit l'unité; ainsi deux ne font plus qu'un»*). In a footnote, Berthelot identifies this saying as the axiom of Mary the Jewess, interpreting it as meaning that "the transmutation is achieved by the successive combination of 3 or 4 metal bodies, initially distinct, but identical at the end of the operation." This figure is identified elsewhere in alchemical literature as the third-century alchemist Maria Prophetissa,[40]

---

[39] For further discussion, see Diener, *Fausts Weg zu Helena*, pp. 495 and 513. Diener cites Strabo's *Geography* (Book 10, Chapter 3) as another historical source on which, in their turn, Benjamin Hederich (1675-1748), Creuzer, and Schelling drew (513). Noting Goethe's mockery of the exaggerated numerological speculations of the Romantic symbolic thinkers, Diener nevertheless emphasizes how it is organically integrated into the hymnic style of the scene as a whole (514).

[40] For further discussion of this significant figure for Jung, see Raphael Patai, *The Jewish Alchemists: A History and Source Book* (Princeton, NJ: Princeton University

possibly known also to Goethe,[41] and Jung notes how "the almost
bestial ἐχραύγαξεν" — which he translates as "shriek" (*schreien*)
and Marcellin Berthelot as *s'est écriée sans reticence* — points
most likely to an "ecstatic condition" (§209, fn. 75). (Is there, Jung
wonders, a link between this Maria, variously known as Maria
Prophetissa, Mary the Jewess, sister of Moses, or Mary the Copt,
and the Maria of Gnostic tradition, that is, with Mariamne or the
Mary Magdalene of the *Pistis Sophia*?)

In another text, "Consilium coniugii" in the *Ars chemica*
(1566), the "philosophical man" is said to consist of the "four
natures of the stone," three of which are earthy or in the earth, but
the fourth nature is "the water of the stone, namely the viscous gold
which is called red gum and with which the three earthy natures are
tinted" (cited in CW 12 §209). This critical fourth nature is said to
be duplex, that is, masculine and feminine, and at the same time
"the one and only *aqua mercurialis*" (§209). On Jung's reading,
this fourth nature leads straight to the "Anthropos idea" or the
notion of human wholeness — the conception of a single being who
existed before humankind and at the same time represents its goal
(§210). As Jung puts it (thinking of the illustration in the "Ripley
Scrowle" of the three manifestations of the Anthropos during his
transformation as body, soul, and spirit), "the one joins the three as
the fourth and thus produces the synthesis of the four in a unity"
(§210). So much for the solution for the problem of three and four:
On this account, the three is in some sense always yearning to

---

Press, 1995), Chapter 5, "Maria the Jewess" (pp. 60-80), and Chapter 6, "Zosimus
on Maria the Jewess" (pp. 81-91); and Lucia Raggetti, "Maria the Alchemist and
Her Famous Heated Bath in the Arabo-Islamic Tradition," and Matteo Martelli,
"Maria's Practica in Early Modern Alchemy," in Francesca Antonelli, Antonella
Romano, and Paolo Savoia (eds), *Gendered Touch: Women, Men, and Knowledge-
making in Early Modern Europe* (Leiden and Boston: Brill, 2022), pp. 21-39 and pp.
40-65.
[41] Diener, *Fausts Weg zu Helena*, p. 515; cf. *Farbenlehre: Historischer Teil*,
"Alchimisten" (Goethe, *Naturwissenschaftliche Schriften*, ed. Paul Stapf [*Werke*, vol.
8] (Berlin, Darmstadt, Vienna: Deutsche Buch-Gemeinschaft, 1967), p. 326).

become the four, a quaternity which signifies a unity at a higher level.[42]

The structure of the problem of seven and eight is similar, even if this motif occurs less frequently. In Paracelsus's *Ein ander Erklärung der gantzen Astronomey* (apparently known to Goethe),[43] we read, "One is powerful, / Six are subjects, the Eighth is also powerful,"[44] and Jung adds that this Eighth is somewhat more powerful than the first (cited in §210). Exactly this situation of the "One" as the king and the "Six" as his servants is depicted in the *Pretiosa margarita novella* (or *Precious New Pearl*) of the late medieval alchemist Petrus Bonus of Ferrara as King Sol and the six planets or metallic homunculi. In this text, however, the eighth does not appear, and Jung surmises that it is, in fact, an invention of Paracelsus. Because the Eighth is "[more] powerful" than the first, surely the crown is bestowed on him? According to Jung, the motif of the Eighth recurs in *Faust II* in the figure of the eighth who dwells on Olympus — a "direct reference," Jung claims, to the Paracelsan text, insofar as this work describes the "astrology of Olympus" (that is, the structure of the *corpus astrale*).[45]

On this account, the feminine figures of the "resplendent mermaids," that is, the Nereids (accompanied by the Tritons), represent the sea and the waves of the unconscious (§203). In the form of the giant shield of Chelone they bring a "form severe" (*ein*

---

[42] For further discussion of the motif of the Third and the Fourth, see Paul Bishop, *Reading Plato through Jung: Why must the Third become the Fourth?* (Cham: Palgrave Macmillan, 2022), 127-133.

[43] See Bartscherer, *Paracelsus, Paracelsisten und Goethes "Faust,"* p. 206. The original German of Jung's text refers in a footnote to Goethe's *Dichtung und Wahrheit*, but *Dichtung und Wahrheit* does not specifically mention this work by Paracelsus; for a general reference to Paracelsus, see Part Two, Book 8.

[44] Cited by Jung from Paracelsus, *Sämtliche Werke*, ed. Karl Sudhoff and Wilhelm Matthiessen, vol. 12, pp. 447ff; here from Paracelsus, *Opera*, ed. Huser, vol. 10, p. 451. This text continues: "And is the same as the first / And is more than the first in numerous points" (*und ist gleich dem ersten / und ist mehr dann das erst in ettlichen Puncten*).

[45] Paracelsus, *Opera*, ed. Huser, vol. 1, p. 530.

streng Gebilde), the adjective "severe" reminding us (or so Jung
says) of "'severe' architectural or geometrical forms which illustrate
a definite idea without any romantic (feeling-toned) trimmings"
(§203). This form "gleams" (*entglänzt*) from the shell of a tortoise,
an animal which, "primitive and cold-blooded like the snake," is
said to symbolize the "instinctual side of the unconscious" (§203).
This form (*Gebilde*) is declared by Jung to be "somehow identical"
with the Cabiri, those "unseen, creative dwarf-gods, hooded and
cloaked manikins" (§203).

Jung highlights the essentially ambivalent function of the
Cabiri, who are, on the one hand, "kept hidden in the dark *cista*"
(that is, a box or basket, originally made of wicker to hold fruits
and vegetables, used for mystical purposes in sacred rites), and, on
the other, "appear on the seashore as little figures about a foot high,
where, as kinsmen of the unconscious, they protect navigation, i.e.,
the venture into darkness and uncertainty" (§203). For this second
reason, Jung associates the Cabiri with the Dactyls, a mythical race
of male spirit-beings associated in turn with the cult of the Great
Mother, credited with metalworking skills and healing powers;
Jung describes them as "the gods of invention, small and apparently
insignificant like the impulses of the unconscious but endowed
with the same mighty power" (§203). In his *History of the Roman
Empire* (Book 5, Chapter, §5-§10), Herodian of Antioch tells us how
Emperor Elagabalus worshipped the Phoenician god Elagabalus
(El-Gabir or Cabiri, i.e., Kronos, "the great, the mighty one"),
and Jung reminds us of this etymology (§203).[46] This procedure
is typical of Jung, tracking simultaneously the parallels between

---

[46] See William Galloway, *Dissertations on the Philosophy of Creation and the First
Ten Chapters of Genesis allegorized in Mythology* (Edinburgh, London: Gemmell;
Hamilton, Adams, 1885), p. 85. According to Galloway, "the Dioskuri or Cabiri, or
Corybantes or Samothracians: — These are all of them names of the same gods"
(ibid.). Available online HTTP: https://archive.org/stream/cu31924031786894/
cu31924031786894_djvu.txt.

clinical material, archaic myth, Romantic philosophy, and literary text. (Jung tends to leave out explicit mention of the third of these elements, that is, Romantic philosophy, and so his argumentation often appears more arbitrary than in fact it really is.)

Next Jung quotes the exchange between the Nereids and Tritons and the Sirens, focusing on the problem of the three and the four:

> NEREIDS AND TRITONS:
> Three have followed where we led,
> But the fourth refused to call;
> He the rightful seer, he said,
> His to think for one and all.
> SIRENS:
> A god may count it sport
> To set a god at naught.
> Honour the grace they bring,
> And fear their threatening.
> (ll. 8186-8193; CW 12 §203)

According to Jung, it is typical of Goethe's "feeling-toned" nature that the fourth function is thinking, or in other words, the fourth Cabiri is the thinker (§204). Recalling the famous line, "Feeling is all" (*Gefühl ist alles*), from the scene in "Martha's Garden" where Faust and Gretchen discuss religion (l. 3456), Jung argues that, if feeling is the supreme principle, then thinking comes to play a less favorable role, to be submerged, and finally to disappear. On his account, this development is portrayed in *Faust I*, and Goethe served as his own model. In such a case, thinking becomes the fourth (or "taboo") function, and through its contamination with the unconscious it acquires the grotesque form of the Cabiri; for, as chthonic gods, the Cabiri are correspondingly misshapen. ("I call them pot-bellied freaks of common clay," says Homunculus [ll.

8219-8220].) Thus, the Cabiri stand "in grotesque contrast" to the heavenly gods, poking fun at them. ("The Devil," as Luther once said, "is the ape of God" [*Der Teufel ist der Affe Gottes*].)

This structure returns in the form of the problem of seven and eight, for the Nereids and the Tritons go on to sing:

> Seven there should really be.
> SIRENS:
> Where, then, stay the other three?
> NEREIDS AND TRITONS:
> That we know not. You had best
> On Olympus make your quest.
> There an eighth may yet be sought
> Though none other gave him thought.
> Well inclined to us in grace,
> Not all perfect yet their race.
> Beings there beyond compare,
> Yearning, unexplainable,
> Press with hunger's pang to share
> In the unattainable.
> (ll. 8194-8205; CW 12 §204)

Here the problem of the Fourth recurs in the problem of the Eighth: We are told there are "really" (*eigentlich*) seven Cabiri but, although the Sirens confusedly (and confusingly) ask about the other three, the Nereids and Tritons insist on the eighth. Whereas the previous emphasis was on the Cabiri's "lowly origin in the dark," in these lines they are relocated to Olympus, the home of the 12 gods in Greek mythology. Because they are "eternally striving" — that central Faustian motif! — "from the depths to the heights," the Cabiri are always to be found "both below *and* above" (CW 12 §205). In an analogous way, the "severe image" (*strenges Gebilde*) is said to represent "an unconscious content that struggles towards the light," and for this reason Jung identifies it with what elsewhere he calls the "treasure hard to attain."[47]

Jung finds confirmation of this reading in the following lines of the Sirens:

SIRENS:
Fame is dimmed of ancient time,
Honour droops in men of old;
Though they have the Fleece of Gold,
Ye have the Cabiri.
(ll. 8212-8216; CW 12 §205)

Now in Greek mythology, the Golden Fleece is a symbol of divine authority, the coveted goal of the adventure on which Jason and his crew of Argonauts embark at the behest of King Pelias (or, as Jung puts it, "the perilous quest that is one of the synonyms for attaining the unattainable") (§206). A few lines on, the philosopher Thales declares, "That is indeed what men most week on earth; / 'Tis rust alone that gives the coin its worth!" (ll. 8223-8224). Jung interprets this paradoxical remark as a kind of "alchemical quip," expressing the insight that there is "no light without shadow and no psychic wholeness without imperfection" (§208). In order to round itself out (*Vollendung*), Jung says, life calls not for "perfection" (*Vollkommenheit*) but for "completeness" (*Vollständigkeit*), and hence there is always a need for the "thorn in the flesh": For without the "suffering of defects" there can be no "progress" — and no "ascent" (§206). Thus, between them, the Cabiri and the Golden Fleece represent the transformative powers of the unconscious.

In a beautiful riff on a passage from the *Rosarium philosophorum* (see *Artis Auriferae*, vol. 2, p. 220), Jung describes

---

[47] See Jung, CW 12 §155, §205, §222, §438, §442-§446 and §448; cf. *Symbols of Transformation*, CW 5 §393, §450, §510, §569 and §659.

the unconscious as "the fly in the ointment" — as "the skeleton in the cupboard, the painful lie given to all idealistic pronouncements, the earthliness that clings to our human nature and sadly clouds the crystal clarity we long for" (CW 12 §207). In the alchemical view, however, rust is, like verdigris, the "metal's sickness," but at the same time "this leprosy is the *vera prima materia*, the basis for the preparation of the philosophical gold" (§207). Linking this excursus on *Faust II* back to the clinical material of his client's dream, Jung identifies the red-haired man in the 22nd dream (in the second series) with the man with the pointed beard in the 14th dream (of the first series), and both of them with the "shrewd Mephisto, who magically changes the scene because he is concerned with something that Faust himself never saw": namely, the "severe image" (*"strenges Gebilde"*), which means the supreme treasure, that is, "something immortal" (*das "Unsterbliche"*) (§211). And so, Jung swiftly moves in a footnote to the concluding scene of Goethe's *Faust II*, in which the angels, after cheating the Devil of it, bear Faust's "immortal part" (*"Unsterbliches"*) to heaven. (In the words of the original draft, Faust's immortal part is called his "entelechy" [*Entelechie*].) This is a point to which Jung returns in his "Epilogue" to *Psychology and Alchemy*, written in 1944 (see below).

Jung's analysis in "Individual Dream Symbolism in Relation to Alchemy" of these two sequences of dreams concludes with his analysis of a vision he describes as the great vision of the World Clock, discussed in greater detail in *Psychology and Religion* (CW 11 §112-§125).[48] This vision or dream falls into the category of the so-called "big dream" or "great dream," exemplified by one reported to Jung himself by Patrick Evans in 1956 (see L1, 325-327); that

---

[48] In "Nox Tertia," the "strokes of the World Clock" sound 12 o'clock midday — "the twelfth hour is complete," "and now silence enters," and "everything is rigid and deathly still" (RB, 351). This moment corresponds to the motif of the Great Noontide in Nietzsche's *Zarathustra* (I 22 §3; III 5; III 10; IV 20), which ushers in the decisive moment of transformation (Z III 15; Z IV 19): "O Man, take heed! What saith deep midnight's voice indeed?".

is to say, a dream whose significance extends beyond the dreamer and involves a collective significance as well. At the beginning of his analysis, Jung suggests that this vision of the World Clock may have the same function as the "severe image" (*strenges Gebilde*) carried by the Nereids and the Tritons in the form of the giant shield of Chelone (namely, of expressing "the most sublime harmony," as the dreamer-client himself put it); consequently, the four children or four little men with pendulums in the vision would correspond to the Cabiri. In the course of Jung's discussion, the references and parallels proliferate to an alarming degree (the Kabbalah, astrology, Gnosticism, etc.), but the most extensive parallel uncovered by Jung is a work titled *Le Pèlerinage de l'Âme* by the French Cistercian monk Guillaume de Deguileville (1295-c. 1358) (the second of a trilogy whose other titles are *Le Pèlerinage de la Vie Humaine* and *Le Pèlerinage de Jesucrist*).[49] The last canto of this second *Pèlerinage* consists of a vision, written independently of Dante, of Paradise as consisting of seven large spheres containing seven smaller spheres (§315).

Amid the most intricate theological and zodiacal symbolism, Guillaume asks for — and receives! — an explanation of the Trinity. An angel answers in terms of three principal colors (green, red, and gold), but Jung, mindful as always of the so-called "dilemma of Three and Four" (to which, in his view, the opening of the *Timaeus* dialogue alludes when Socrates asks, "One, two, three — but where, my dear Timaeus, is the fourth of those guests of yesterday who were to entertain me today?" [17a]),[50] repeats the question and asks, "Three there are, but where is the fourth?" — in other words, why is the colour blue missing (CW 12 §320)?

---

[49] For further discussion of these works, see Marco Nievergelt and Stephanie A. Viereck Gibbs Kamath (eds.), *The Pèlerinage Allegories of Guillaume de Deguileville: Tradition, Authority and Influence* (Woodbridge and Rochester, NY: Boydell and Brewer, 2013).

[50] For further discussion, see Bishop, *Reading Plato through Jung*, pp. 17-50.

On Jung's account, what Guillaume's vision omits or *excludes* (namely, the element of the feminine) is *included* in Dante's great final vision in *Paradise* — as well as in the final scene of *Faust*, Part Two. Here the figure of Doctor Marianus prays (in words that Jung attributes to Faust himself), "Supreme Mistress of the world! / Let me behold your secret / In the outstretched azure canopy of heaven" (ll. 11997-12000). Thus, his dreamer-client's vision of the World Clock, the "severe image" of the Aegean Festival, the vision of Paradise in Guillaume's *Le Pèlerinage de l'Âme*, and the concluding scene of *Faust II* are, in Jungian terms, all examples of mandalas, that is, a representation of integrated wholeness. For Jung, this is the epochal significance of *Faust*: that it integrates what, by and large, our Western culture has tended to occlude — the feminine, the darkness, the earth — in its vision of wholeness, and it does so in a very explicit way through its conclusion with the Chorus mysticus's address to the Mater Gloriosa.

This development, Jung argues, had already been anticipated by Guillaume prior to his lesson on the Trinity when, in his vision of paradise as spheres within spheres, he sees, sitting next to the King on his throne, the Queen on a throne made of earth-brown crystal (CW 12 §315) — for, as Jung asks, "what is heaven without Mother Earth? And how can we reach fulfilment if the Queen does not intercede for our black souls?" (§322). If only "by the subtlest of suggestions," he adds, this Queen shows that she "understands the darkness," because she has taken "her throne — the earth itself — to heaven with her" and, by "add[ing] the missing blue to the gold, red, and green," she thus "completes the harmonious whole" (§322). (This episode finds its counterpart in Jung's *Red Book*, in the episode described in a marginal note in the Calligraphic Volume as a "Visio," when "the throne of God ascends into empty space, followed by the Holy Trinity, all of Heaven, and finally Satan himself," even though Satan resists (RB, 420), and (in *Black Book 4*) Jung has to "pull him out by the hands," as Satan "crawls out of a dark hole with horns and tail" [BB4, 241].) At the same time, however, Jung's interpretation of Guillaume's vision sounds a note of caution. For what Faust's (or Marianus's) words also teach us is that, because of the intervention or involvement of time and space in the here-and-now that constitutes reality, this wholeness can only ever be realized "for a moment only — the moment that Faust was seeking all his life" (§321).

This sense of a certain cautious hesitation about what *Faust* can teach us returns in the "Epilogue" to *Psychology and Alchemy*, where Jung turns for the last time in this work to *Faust II* — and to the scene in Act I when Faust conjures up Paris and Helena. Here Jung rehearses his argument that alchemy had "reached its final summit, and with it the historical turning-point," in Goethe's *Faust*, itself "steeped in alchemical forms of thought from beginning to end" (CW 12 §558).[51] The choice of expression here should give us pause for thought: Jung does *not* say here (as he had done earlier) that *Faust* actually *is* an alchemical drama, but rather that it is saturated with alchemical ways of thinking (*mit alchemistischen Gedankengängen durchtränkt*). As a work, *Faust* reflects what Jung

---

[51] In Chapter 6 of "Religious Ideas in Alchemy," entitled "Alchemical Symbolism in the History of Religion," Jung defines the unconscious as the "matrix of symbols" and chooses as a paradigm the symbol of the unicorn. He undertakes to investigate this symbol as an example of how the symbolism of Mercurius becomes intermingled with the traditions of pagan Gnosticism and of the Church (CW 12 §518). Jung's analysis encompasses the unicorn in alchemy; in ecclesiastical allegory; in Gnosticism; in those great religious texts of ancient India, the Vedas; the creation myth of Zoroastrianism, the Bundahishn; in the Jewish tradition in the Talmud and various examples of midrash; and in Chinese traditions, before turning to the symbol of the unicorn cup, in the context of which he discusses Wolfram's *Parzival* (see Volume 1 in this series, Chapter 2, pp. 167-169). These assorted unicorn symbolisms, Jung argues, provide us with but a sample of what he calls the "extremely intricate and tangled connections" between pagan and natural philosophy, Gnosticism, alchemy, and ecclesiastical tradition: connections which, in turn, exercised a "deep and lasting influence on the world of medieval alchemy" — and beyond. For Jung's attempt to uncover "just how far alchemy was a religious-philosophical or 'mystical' movement" goes so far as to suggest that the alchemical tradition may well have "reached its peak" in Goethe's "religious *Weltanschauung*, as this is presented for us in *Faust*" (§554).

sees as the epochal change from the classical age of alchemy (from antiquity to the mid-17th century) to the modern age of chemistry and technology — and all its attendant problems, including the hypertrophy of collective life, and the response in the form of neurotic individualism (§557).

So, what is really going on in Goethe's *Faust* can be most clearly seen, Jung suggests, in the scene set in the "Hall of Chivalry" (with its "dim illumination"). "To the medieval alchemist," Jung confidently asserts, this episode would have represented "the mysterious *coniunctio* of Sol and Luna in the retort"; by contrast, however, the modern individual, who is "disguised in the figure of Faust," *recognizes the projection* and, "assuming the place of Paris and Sol, takes possession" — or at least attempts to — "of Helena or Luna," that is, our own "inner, feminine counterpart" (CW 12 §558). In other words, the "objective process of the union" has become the "subjective experience of the 'artifex,' that is, the alchemist," so that instead of *watching the drama*, we *become one of the actors* (§558). And so, Faust *intervenes* in what he is watching.

This intervention, says Jung, has the disadvantage of compromising "the goal of the entire process," which is the "production of the incorruptible substance" (§558). As a consequence, the fruit of Faust and Helena's union — the *filius philosophorum*, who is supposed to be imperishable and "incombustible" — represented in Act III by Euphorion, ends up disappearing in flames (CW 12 §558). And because Faust cannot resist usurping the role of Paris in Helena's affections, such other "births" and rejuvenations as the Boy Charioteer and Homunculus are also destroyed as a result of his "greed." As an emblem of the modern individual, Faust simply *cannot leave well alone*, and he interferes in the alchemical process, producing disaster. And as a consequence, the final rejuvenation of Faust himself has to be projected into the future (see below).

For, by identifying with Paris, Faust manages to bring the *coniunctio* back "from its projected state into the sphere of personal psychological experience and thus into consciousness" (CW 12 §559).[52] For Jung, this is a "crucial step," inasmuch as it finally solves the "the alchemical riddle" — but what *is* the "riddle" of alchemy? (At the beginning of this "Epilogue," Jung explains that this riddle revolves in turn around the question of what the alchemical *lapis* actually is, a question that can only be answered when we know what was the "unconscious content" that the alchemists were projecting (§555). According to Jung, Analytical Psychology finds itself in a unique position to answer this question because it teaches that "so long as a content remains in the projected state it is inaccessible," and this is why the alchemists have revealed to us "so little of the alchemical secret" (§555). From the symbolical material, however, Jung believes he can show that alchemy is closely related to the process of individuation [§555].)

Translated back into the terms of *Faust*, Goethe's work can be said to reveal the "secret" of personal *transformation*, and Faust's identification with Paris thus represents "the redemption [*Erlösung*] of a previously unconscious part of the personality" (§559). Yet this in turn creates a problem. For in Jungian terms, every increase in consciousness "habours the danger of *inflation*," as is reflected in Faust's inclination to try and be an *Übermensch*. And for Jung there was a highly personal dimension to this entire Faustian problematic.

---

[52] Is Faust's identification with Paris the "crucial step" in solving the "alchemical riddle," or is it an allusion to Goethe's *Kunstmärchen* entitled "Der neue Paris," included as a *capriccio* in the second book of *Dichtung und Wahrheit* (1811)? In this work, the *Knabe*, who has to choose between three goddesses (Hera, Athene, and Aphrodite), tries to seize the nymph Alerte, and is struck to the ground — just as Faust is when he reaches out for Helena. The "thematic complexities" have been pointed out by C.A.H. Russ, a former Lecturer in German at the University of Glasgow: the fact that Faust is intervening between the spirits of Helen and (the "old") Paris, and the use of the verb *verweilen* to describe how Alerte dances on the fingers of the fascinated *Knabe* recalls the key term in the wager, *Verweile doch, du bist so schön!* (Goethe, *Three Tales*, ed. Russ, p. 15).

In his Tower at Bollingen, Jung carved over its gate the following inscription, "Philemonis Sacrum – Fausti Poenitentia" (i.e., "Philemon's Shrine – Faust's Repentance"). And in a letter to Paul Schmitt in 1942, Jung wrote: "I have taken over Faust as my heritage, and moreover as the advocate and avenger of Philemon and Baucis, who, unlike Faust the superman, are the hosts of the gods in a ruthless and godforsaken age" (L1, 309-310.) Yet to understand what Faust's *repentance* is, we have first to understand what Faust's *sin* is. And in his "Epilogue" to *Psychology and Alchemy*, Jung tells us, explaining that Faust's sin was that he "identified with the thing to be transformed and that had been transformed" (§560), and this led to "his blind urge for superhuman power" (§561), reflected in Part One in his treatment of Gretchen (about which Jung has surprisingly little to say …) and in Part Two in the murder of Philemon and Baucis.

Now the story of Philemon and Baucis can be found in Ovid's *Metamorphoses*, which relates how Jupiter and Mercury, disguised as mortals, went wandering in the hill country of Phyrgia.[53] Turned away from hundreds of homes when searching for somewhere to rest, these divine strangers were welcomed into the humble abode of Philemon and Baucis, an old couple who had happily lived, despite their poverty, together for many years. Their hospitality even went so far as for them to offer to kill their only goose, at which point the two gods revealed their true identities. To punish those who had rejected them, the surrounding countryside was flooded, but the cottage was spared and transformed into a splendid temple. The wish of Philemon and Baucis to serve in this new shrine to the gods was granted, and they lived out their lives together. On their death, both were transformed into trees, in order that they might, as they had done as a loving couple, continue to live side by side even in death.[54]

---

[53] See Ovid, *Metamorphoses*, Book 8, ll. 863-1021; in Ovid, *Metamorphoses: A New Translation, Contexts, Criticism*, ed. and trans. Charles Martin (New York and London: Norton, 2010), pp. 223-226.
[54] For an illuminating discussion of this episode, see Wolfgang Giegerich, "Hospitality toward the Gods in an Ungodly Age: Philemon — Faust — Jung," *Spring*, 1984, 61-

In Act V of *Faust II*, Goethe weaves this Ovidian narrative into the story of Faust. Having embarked at the request of the Emperor on an ambitious program of land reclamation, the aged Faust wants Philemon and Baucis removed from their cottage on land targeted for construction. Mephistopheles is only too pleased to oblige, and he orders three hefty men to burn the cottage — with Philemon and Baucis inside. Although Faust reacts with horror at this deed, it is too late: instead of an exchange, there has been robbery (*Raub*) — the same word used for Paris's seduction of Helena in which Faust intervened (l. 11371, cf. ll 6548-6549). And from the burning ruins of the cottage emerge the four spectral figures of Want, Debt, Care, and Need, who (as we saw above in Chapter 2) torment Faust before his death.

In *Memories, Dreams, Reflections*, we read that Jung felt "personally implicated" in this episode: "When Faust, in his hubris and self-inflation, caused the murder of Philemon and Baucis, I felt guilty, quite as if I myself in the past had helped commit the murder of the two old people," he is recorded as saying (MDR, 261). (Not only is this a "strange idea," but it becomes even stranger when Jung suggests that the "heroic myth" of *Faust* had in some way "prophetically anticipated the fate of the Germans.") As a consequence, we learn, Jung came to regard it as his own personal responsibility to "atone from this crime, or to prevent its repetition" (261).

Hence not simply the inscription above the gate to the Tower in Bollingen but also the role played by the figure of Philemon, Jung's own Faustian figure, in *The Red Book*, where the repentance of Faust is implicitly present in Jung's redemption of God by "healing" him. ("Our God is sick," Jung realizes in the chapter "First Day" in *Liber Secundus*; in fact, he is "dead," with the "venomous gaze of the Basilisk on his face," and so we must "think

---

75; reprinted in *The Neurosis of Psychology: Primary Papers Towards a Critical Psychology* [Collected English Papers, vol. 1] (London and New York: Routledge, 2020), pp. 197-218.

of his healing"; while the transformational events in "Second Day" show how Jung's God "found salvation," becoming a "living fantasy," whose "workings" Jung could feel on his own body; and after the "Incantations" and the "Opening of the Egg," this God rises "in the Eastern sky, brighter than the heavenly host," bringing about a "new day for all the peoples" [RB, 291 and 295 and 316].) And in one of the rooms in the Bollingen Tower, Jung painted a huge mural of the winged Philemon, just as he had imagined him in *The Red Book* and described him in *Memories, Dreams, Reflections*. In his "Epilogue," however, Jung places emphasis on the *metaphysical*, rather than the *political* dimension of the story of Philemon and Baucis. "When the world had become godless and no longer offered a hospitable retreat to the divine strangers Jupiter and Mercury," he says, "it was Philemon and Baucis who received their superhuman [*übermenschlichen*] guests," and when Baucis was about to sacrifice their last goose for them, "the transformation [*die Wandlung*] happened" — "the gods made themselves known, the humble cottage became a temple, and the old couple became immortal servitors at the shrine" (CW 12 §561).

On Jung's account, the problem of *Faust* was taken up again by Nietzsche, as we shall see (in Volume 3); for now, let us note that Jung describes Faust as, like Zarathustra, offering a "not very encouraging example of what happens when we embody this secret" — the secret that the alchemists had "ascribed to matter" — "in ourselves" (*uns selber einzuverleiben*) (CW 12 §564). Instead, Jung urges, we should "repudiate the arrogant claim of the conscious mind to be the whole of the psyche," and "admit that the psyche [*Seele*] is a reality [*Wirklichkeit*] which we cannot grasp with our present means of understanding" (§564). In this sense, the old alchemists were "nearer to the central truth of the psyche [*der seelischen Wahrheit*] than Faust, when they strove to deliver [*erlösen*] the fiery spirit from the chemical elements" and treated the mysterium (*das Mysterium*) — an expression also found in the culminating chapters of *Liber Primus* in *The Red Book* — "as though it lay in the womb of dark and silent nature" (§562).

On Jung's account, Faust's interference in the *coniunctio* of Sol and Luna in the guise of conjuring up Paris and Helena in Act I of Part Two botches the entire alchemical process, and Euphorion, supposed to be the *filius philosophorum*, goes up in flames and disappears in Act III (as do, in their own way, the figures of the Boy Charioteer in Act I and Homunculus in Act II). Hence, in Act V, Faust's final rejuvenation "takes place only in the post-mortal state, i.e., is projected into the future" (§558).

In the final scene of Part Two, Faust is — on Jung's account, for which there is no textual evidence — transformed into Doctor Marianus. Is it a mere coincidence, Jung asks (CW 12 §558), that Marianus is the name of an early alchemist (better known as Morienus), a legendary hermit who lived at the end of the seventh century in the hills around Jerusalem and the author of an epistle to a fellow alchemist, Khālid bin Yazīd?[55] (Of course not; in the world of Jung, there is no such thing as coincidence.) How are we to understand Faust's postmortal rejuvenation? According to Jung, this rebirth and transformation that follow the *coniunctio* "take place in the hereafter, i.e., in the unconscious" — and this leaves the problem "hanging in the air" (*hier blieb ein Problem hängen*) (§559). Here lies, for Jung, the intimate connection between *Faust* and Nietzsche's *Zarathustra* (to which we shall turn in Volume 3).

Mysterium Coniunctionis (1955-1956)

Aside from its significance as an interpretative attempt to understanding a key scene in Goethe's *Faust II*, Karl Kerényi's essay on the Aegean Sea Festival also apparently served as the

---

[55] See the reference to the Byzantine monk Morienus the Greek and his dialogue with Khālid bin Yazīd (or Calid) on the magisterium of Hermes, referred to by Goethe in his *Farbenlehre: Historischer Teil*, "Alchimsten" (*Naturwissenschaftliche Schriften*, ed. Stapf, pp. 325-326).

starting point for Jung's late, great book of his final years, *Mysterium Coniunctionis* (CW 14, p. xiii). In his study, Kerényi had argued that, whatever the mysteries of the Cabiri might have been, they centered — like the mysteries at Eleusis (associated with the cult of Demeter) or those at Lycosura (said by Pausanias to be the oldest city in the world and the site of the sanctuary of the goddess Despoina, the daughter of Demeter and Poseidon) — on the mystery of birth. In the Aegean Sea Festival in *Faust*, this mystery is said to be expressed through the marriage of Homunculus and Galatea.

In Chapter 6 on the alchemical conjunction itself as the union of opposites, Jung explicitly cites Kerényi's work when discussing the role of water as the "sea" where the chymical marriage is celebrated: the "Nile of Egypt," the "Sea of the Indians," and the "Meridian Sea" in the *Tractatus Micreris* (i.e., the *Tractate of Micreris* = *Mercurius*) in the fifth volume of the *Theatrum Chemicum* are Jung's reference points for this observation, as well as the sea journey described by Christian Rosencreutz (see below) — and, of course, Goethe's *Faust II*, where this alchemical motif is said to be "taken up" (CW 14 §658). Jung explicitly praises Kerényi's "brilliant amplificatory" interpretation of the Aegean Festival's "archetypal content," especially for demonstration of how the bands of nereids on Roman sarcophagi reveal "the epithalmic and the sepulchral element," and how "basic to the ancient mysteries [...] is the identity of marriage and death on the one hand, and of birth and the eternal resurgence of life from death on the other" (§658).[56] However, Kerényi's thesis also informs Jung's *Mysterium Coniunctionis* at a much deeper level.

On Jung's account, the "literary prototype" of Goethe's Aegean Festival was provided by the *Chymical Wedding of Christian Rosenkreutz*, a work attributed to Johann Valentin Andreae (1586-1654) and often regarded as one of the great manifestos of the

---

[56] Kerényi, *Das Ägäische Fest*, p. 55.

Fraternity of the Rose Cross (that is, the Rosicrucians).[57] In its turn, Andreae's *Chymical Wedding* drew on the traditional "hieros gamos symbolism of alchemy" (CW 14, p. xiii). Understanding this symbolism was bound up with Jung's project (underway since 1928 and his reading of Richard Wilhelm's translation of *The Secret of the Golden Flower*) of demonstrating that the world of alchemical symbols "does not belong to the rubbish heap of the past," but rather "stands in a very real and living relationship to [...] the psychology of the unconscious" (CW 14, p. xiii). Acknowledging (for once) that his own work builds on the insights in Silberer's *Problems of Mysticism and its Symbolism* (xiv; cf. §792), Jung explained that he had wanted to explore how the so-called "spagyric" art, whose method was captured in the slogan *solve et coagula* (i.e., "dissolve and coagulate"), involved a dual process of separation (or analysis) and consolidation (or synthesis). This process, Jung argued, did not simply offer a parallel to the dissociation of the personality arising from the conflict of the opposites and the subsequent search to resolve this conflict; rather, *it was one and the same process in both cases* (xv).

On this account, the psychoanalytic phenomenon of the transference could be understood in terms of the motif of the "chymical wedding" (and vice versa) (CW 14, p. xv). This motif of the mystical marriage can also be found in the *Aurora Consurgens*, an alchemical work attributed to St. Thomas Aquinas (and which formed the basis of a detailed study by Marie-Louise von Franz, published in the German edition of *Mysterium Coniunctionis* as its third volume and published in English as a separate companion

---

[57] For the text of this work, see "The Chemical Wedding of Christian Rosenkreuz," translated by Joscelyn Godwin, in *Rosicrucian Trilogy: Fama Fraternitatis, 1614; Confessio Fraternitatis, 1615; The Chemical Wedding of Christian Rosenkreuz, 1616*, trans. Joscelyn Godwin, Christopher McIntosh, and Donate Pahnke McIntosh (Newburyport, MA: Weiser Books, 2016), pp. 53-181.

volume).[58] While accepting von Franz's thesis (for which he was, of course, largely responsible) that *Aurora Consurgens* had arisen from an attempt to amalgamate Christianity and the alchemical view (and hence offered an example of "how the spirit of medieval Christianity came to terms with alchemical philosophy"), Jung was convinced there was more urgent, contemporary need to understand alchemy (xvi). For "although contemporary humankind believes it can change itself without limit, or be changed through external influences, the astounding, or rather the terrifying, fact remains" — and we must remember that Jung was writing in 1954 — "that, despite civilization and Christian education, human individuals are still morally as much in bondage to their instincts as animals are, and can therefore fall victim at any moment to the beast within" (xviii), as recent history in Jung's own lifetime had all too tragically demonstrated.

However much Jung may have pivoted away in the 1920s from his work on *The Red Book* toward the investigation of alchemy, he nevertheless sought to find connections between the alchemical tradition and the epic tradition of self-transformation as reflected in Wolfram's *Parzival*, Goethe's *Faust*, and Nietzsche's *Zarathustra*. Hence, Goethe's *Faust* resounds, albeit in a subterranean way, throughout *Mysterium Coniunctionis*. The compositional structure of this work, which might be thought of as analogous to a late Romantic symphony or to a string quartet, is based on a theme — the components of the alchemical transformation — and its variations (example piled upon example of how these ideas are expressed in the form of symbols, emblems, and motifs). Thus Jung considers

---

[58] Marie-Louise von Franz (ed.) *Aurora Consurgens: A Document Attributed to Thomas Aquinas of the Problem of Opposites in Alchemy* [1957], trans. R.F.C. Hull and A.S.B. Glover (New York and London: Bollingen Foundation, 1966); and C.G. Jung, *Mysterium Coniunctionis* [...]: *Ergänzungsband «Aurora Consurgens»: Ein dem Thomas von Aquin zugeschriebenes Dokument der alchemistischen Gegensatzproblematik von Dr. M.-L. von Franz* [*Gesammelte Werke*, vol. 14/iii] (Olten und Freiburg im Breisgau: Walter, 1971).

the components of the *coniunctio* (the opposites, Mercurius, the significance of such symbols as the orphan, the widow, and the moon); the "paradoxa" of the arcane substance, the point, and the scintilla; the personification of the opposites in the figures of Sol, sulphur, Luna, and salt); the alchemical King and Queen (Rex and Regina); Adam and Eve (particularly the "old Adam" versus the "new"); and finally the conjunction itself (its various stages, the production of the quintessence, the psychological significance of the procedure, and the constellation of the self).[59] At important moments (as well as some not-so-important ones), Jung draws on or refers to Goethe's *Faust*, not so much in support of his deliberately contentious thesis that *Faust* is an "alchemical drama from beginning to end" (CW 12 §85), as rather in order to illustrate how this epic work of secular poetry, like the alchemical opus, illustrates the process of transformation.

In the context of discussing the relation between alchemy and Manichaeism, for instance, Jung reminds us how, in the Manichaean system, matter (*hyle*) is "personified by the dark, fluid, human body of the evil principle" (or so St. Augustine presented that system in his *Confessions* [Book 5, Chapter 10]) (CW 14 §33). Thus in his treatise *De Natura Boni* ("On the Nature of the Good") (written in 404), Augustine describes how the Manichaeans (erroneously, in his view) believed that the spirit or divine nature is "imprisoned" by the "princes of darkness" in the body, permeating "all things in

---

[59] Presenting the opposing qualities and principles of the Sun (Sol) as "the male aspect of deity, dawn, daylight, fiery passion, authority, order, discipline, force, militarism, empire, centralization, technology, hierarchy, rationality, practicality, the animus, the phallus" and those of the Moon (Luna) as "the Goddess, twilight, night, emotion, feeling, dreams, intuition, secrecy, moodiness, nostalgia, romanticism, intoxication, ecstasy, mysticism, the anima, the female principle, the womb," Christopher McIntosh notes their proximity to Nietzsche's concept of the Apollonian and the Dionysian; in turn, he suggests, their synthesis in the form of Greek tragic drama find a correspondence with such synthetic symbols as the hermaphrodite (or the androgyne) in alchemy or the symbol of the Holy Grail (*Occult Germany: Old Gods, Mystics, and Magicians* (Rochester, VT: Inner Traditions, 2024), pp. 11-12).

heaven and earth and under the earth" and "found in all bodies, dry and moist, in all kinds of flesh, and in all seeds of trees, herbs, men, and animals." It is "released and set free and cleansed" by "the courses of the sun and moon and powers of light, as well as their elect": assuming alternately male and female form, "by their beauty they inflame the unclean list of the princes of darkness." And "thus the vital substance, i.e., the divine nature, which they say is held bound in their bodies, escapes from their members when they are relaxed in concupiscence, and is thus released, purged and set free."[60] Where Jung euphemistically talks about sweat falling on the earth and fertilizing the vegetation, Augustine has another substance in mind when talking about the Manichaeans ....[61] What interests Jung is the mechanism whereby "the heavenly light-material is freed from the dark bodies and is passed into plant form," because he identifies precisely this dynamic with the scene where Mephistopheles addresses the angels present at Faust's death as follows:

---

[60] St. Augustine, "On the Nature of the Good," §44, in *Earlier Writings*, ed. and trans. J.H. Burleigh (Louisville, KY, and London: John Knox Press, 2006), pp. 325-348 (pp. 339-344).

[61] "At the comely sight ardour and concupiscence grow, and the prison of evil thoughts is broken, and the living soul which was held bound in their members is released and escapes and mingles with the purest air which is its native element. Souls that are completely purified board the shining ships which are prepared to carry them away and to transport them to their fatherland. Anyone who still shows the taint of the adverse race goes down step by step through fiery heat, gets mixed up with trees and plants and the like and is stained with divers colours. Out of that great shining ship the figures of boys and virgins appear to the hostile powers whose home is in the heavens and whose nature is fiery. At the fair sight the part of life which is held bound in their members is released and brought down by heat to earth. In the same way the highest power, that inhabits the ship of vital waters, appears by means of his messengers in the shape of boys and holy virgins to the powers whose nature is cold and moist, which also are set in the heavens. To those which are female it appears in the form of boys, and to males in the form of virgins. By this diversity of divine and beautiful forms the princes of cold and moist stock, whether male or female, are brought to naught and the vital element in them escapes. What remains is brought down to earth by cold and is mingled with all the species of earth" (Augustine, "On the Nature of the God," p. 345). In response to all this, Augustine indignantly cries: "Who could bear stuff of this kind?".

> Damned sprites ye chide us. In your gizzards
> Ye lie, ye are the only wizards,
> For ye seduce both maid and man.
> O cursèd hap! O torment dire!
> Is this Love's element?
> (ll. 11780-11784)

In this part of the scene, Mephistopheles has been distracted from the important business of arranging for Faust to be taken to Hell by an aureole from above, by angels strewing roses, and by other angels that fill the space and crowd him into the proscenium of the stage. In addition, the naked bodies of these young angels arouse his sexual desire, distracting him even further — in this final ironic twist, the great tempter himself is being tempted!

These angels are beautiful (in fact, parodically beautiful) angels, and hence completely unlike (as Jung later observes) the helpful spirits or familiars that assist the alchemist in completing his work in *De Chemia Senioris antiquissimi philosophi libellus* by the Egyptian alchemist Muḥammad ibn Umayl al-Tamīmī, known as Senior Zadith (c. 900 to c. 960 C.E.). (In this work, Senior uses such theriomorphic symbols as snakes and doves for male and female elements to point to the union of unconscious factors in much the same way as they do in *The Red Book*.) In *De Chemia* the angels are "dark messengers of heaven who at this point themselves become white," and Jung goes on to note that, "even in *Faust*, the angels are not entirely innocent of the arts of seduction" (CW 14 §81). (Hence the need for women to keep their heads covered in church, as Jung acerbically remarks, since the angels' inability to sin is "to be taken so relatively" … and one should not underestimate the "moral frailty" of these "winged messengers" [§81] …)

Another element in *Faust* that invites comparison with the alchemical tradition is the reference in the final scene to what Goethe had in his original draft described as Faust's "entelechy,"

which is carried away and aloft by the angels.[62] In his discussion of
the golden, heavenly, hot and dry Sol (CW 14 §110) as one of the
personifications of the opposites, Jung assimilates this problematic
conception with the spark of divine fire implanted in the human
individual, as described by Gerhard Dorn in his *Philosophia
meditativa* as "the true and indubitable treasure, which [...] remaineth
for ever, and is taken hence after death" and of the supreme treasure
which "the animal man understandeth not" because "we are made
like stones, having eyes and seeing not" (cited in §114-§115). By
contrast, Sol's counterpart, Luna — with her characteristics of being
"cold, moist, feebly shining or dark, feminine, corporeal, passive"
(§154) — has a dark side, hinted at by the ancient identification
of Selene as a dog (§174), as exemplified in the *Liber secretorum*
by Khālid ibn Yazīd (c. 668-704 or 709) in the figure of the "son
of the dog" (*filius canis*), which plays the role of a guiding spirit
or familiar found in texts of the Harranite School —[63] just like, of

---

[62] For further discussion, see Paul Carus, "Goethe's Soul-Conception," *The Open
Court*, 21 (1907), 745-751.

[63] The School of Harran or the Harranites seem to have been a Neoplatonic group that
flourished in the 11th century, and who were reputed to consult an oracle of a talking
head they had made (CW 9/ii §193; CW 11 §365-§369). In his account of how Greek
science passed to the Arabs, De Lacy O'Leary writes: "Our knowledge of the ancient
religion of Harran is chiefly gleaned from the observations of ad-Dimishqi, who died
in A.D. 1327, long after the city had passed into obscurity and who could only have
had traditional information about its religion. [...] The people of Harran were not
Gnostics, but they had temples dedicated to the planets, which gave some colour to the
confusion between them and the Mandaeans. Harranite neo-Platonism might possibly
be confused with Gnostic beliefs. It is characteristic that the Harranites claimed that
their religion had come to them from Hermes. It is an interesting instance, though not
a unique one, of the way in which the Muslim law was sometimes evaded" (De Lacy
O'Leary, *How Greek Science Passed to the Arabs* (London: Routledge & Kegan
Paul, 1949), pp. 172-173). According to Walter Scott, "whereas the Neoplatonists
of Athens had ignored the *Hermetica*, the Harranian Neoplatonists of Bagdad
recognized the *Hermetica* as their 'Scripture,' and regarded the Hermetic teaching as
the source whence their philosophy was derived" ("Introduction," in *Hermetica: The
ancient Greek and Latin writings which contain religious or philosophic teachings
ascribed to Hermes Trismegistus*, ed. Walter Scott, 4 vols. (Oxford: Clarenden Press,
1934-1936), pp. 1-111 [p. 104]).

course, the poodle out from which Mephistopheles emerges as the familiar of Faust in his role as alchemist (§177).

For some, such readings may appear to be (at best) arbitrary, or (at worst) completely unfounded. Jung's predilection for the "obscure" (cf. CW 14 §77), the marginal, or the occluded has earned him many enemies in the academy, some of whom bitterly resent such unashamed displays of learning and erudition. Nevertheless, a methodological justification of sorts may be found in Jung's discussion of a passage from a work called *Introitus apertus ad occlusum regis palatium*, published in 1667 and attributed to Eirenaeus Philalethes, now recognized as a pseudonym of George Starkey (1628-1665). Having cited two extracts from this work, Jung takes one of them in order to illustrate how such a text can be interpreted "as if it were a dream" (§189). However "weird and abstruse" alchemical texts may be, he argues, they are no more so than the dreams which are "the daily fare of the psychotherapist" and, like dreams, they can be "translated into rational speech" (§189). Whereas the analyst needs some knowledge of the dreamer's personal situation in order to amplify the dream by this personal history, we need to know something about "the symbolic assumptions" of the alchemists in order to amplify their parables by "statements found in the text" (§189). In short, such texts can be read as *alchemical allegories*, in the sense of using alchemical terms to talk in an allegorical way about the psychological process involved in transformation.

In the case of the text from Philalethes, Jung finds himself turning for amplicatory parallels to Heraclitus (CW 14 §192); to Jean d'Espagnet (§194); to Gerhard Tersteegen (1697-1769), author of the *Geistliches Blumengärtlein inniger Seelen* (1729) and to Angelus Silesius, author of the *Cherubinischer Wandersmann* (§196); indeed, to the mystical language of the Baroque tradition as a whole, including Jakob Böhme (1575-1624) and Abraham von Franckenberg (1593-1652); as well as, of course, to Goethe —

albeit in some interesting and unexpected ways. Philalethes's call
to the alchemist, "If thou knowest how to moisten this dry earth
with its own water, [...] this thief from outside will be cast out with
the workers of wickedness," is glossed by Jung as meaning that
"the enemy is your own crude sulphur, which burns you with the
hellish fire of desirousness, or *concupiscentia*" and that "you would
like to make gold because" — and here follows a reference to a line
from Goethe's poem, *Der Schatzgräber* ("The Treasure Digger"),
"All my weary days I pass'd / Sick at heart and poor in purse. /
Poverty's the greatest curse, / Riches are the highest good!" (§189-
§190). Here the Goethe reference serves to exemplify a kind of
archetypal dimension to desire — in this case, the desire for wealth.

Philalethes's further (and typically obscure) injunction,
about how "the water, by an admixture of the true Sulphur, will be
cleansed from the leprous filth and from the superfluous dropsical
fluid," is read by Jung in terms of "cleans[ing] your interest of that
collective sulphur which clings to all like a leprosy" (CW 14 §192).
Desire, as Jung goes to explain, "only burns in order to burn itself
out, and in and from this fire arises the true living spirit which
generates life according to its own laws, and is not blinded by the
shortsightedness of our intentions or the crude presumption of our
superstitious belief in the will" (§192). And he relates this principle
to those famous lines in Goethe's *West-östlicher Divan* where Hafez
sings, *Das Lebendge will ich preisen, / Das nach Flammentod sich
sehnet* ("Life I praise through all the ages / Which for death in
flames is yearning").[64]

In addition, Jung identifies the figure of the winged youth
in Philalethes's text with the spiritual Mercurius (CW 14 §196)

---

[64] Goethe, *Selige Sehnsicht* ("Blessed Longing"), in Johann Wolfgang von Goethe,
West-Eastern Divan; West-oestlicher Divan, trans. J. Whaley (London: Wolff, 1974),
pp. 24-25. For further discussion, see Katharina Mommsen, *Goethe and the Poets
of Arabia*, trans. Michael M. Metzger (Rochester, NY: Camden House, 2014), pp.
142-144.

and interprets the "central Water" to which he is espoused as the fountain of the soul (or, in the words of the apocryphal Book of Enoch, the "fountains of wisdom" [Enoch 48:1]): if the nymph of the spring is Luna, the mother-beloved, then the winged youth is Sol (that is, the *filius solis*, the *lapis*, etc.), who stands for the "best, the highest, the most precious *in potentia*" (§200). As Sol, however, he can only become "real" (*wirklich*) if he can unite with Luna, whom Macrobius describes as the "author and creator of mortal bodies" (*mortalium corporum et autor et conditrix*) (*In somn. Scip*, I, xi; cf. §155 and §173).[65] If not, then he must suffer the fate of that threefold puer aeternus figure in *Faust* (i.e., the Boy Charioteer, Homunculus, and Euphorion), who "goes up in smoke" three times (§200).

Commenting on Plutarch's conception in his *Isis and Osiris* of Selene as "mother of the world" (μήτηρ του κόσμου) and his account of how, at the time of the new moon in the month of Phamenoth (and Osiris enters into Selene), the Egyptians celebrate a festival called "Osiris's coming to the Moon," thus "mak[ing] the power of Osiris to be fixed in the Moon" (Plutarch, *Isis and Osiris*, §43),[66] Jung further notes Plutarch's remark that "the Moon [...] has a nature both male and female, as she is receptive and made pregnant by the Sun, but she herself in turn emits and disseminates into the air generative principles" (ibid., §43). These comments, Jung argues, shows that the moon has "a double light, outside a feminine one but inside a masculine one which is hidden in it as a

---

[65] Macrobius, *Commentary on the Dream of Scipio*, Chapter 11, §7: "There is no doubt that the moon is the builder and affords the increase of mortal bodies, so that some bodies, at the renewal of her light, experience an increase and diminish again when she wanes" (*nec dubium est quin ipsa sit mortalium corporum et auctor et conditrix adeo ut non nulla corpora sub luminis eius accessu patiantur augmenta et hac decrescente minuantur*) (Macrobius, *Commentary on the Dream of Scipio*, ed. and trans. William Harris Stahl (New York: Columbia University Press, 1990), pp. 131-132).

[66] Plutarch, *Moralia*, vol. 5, trans. Frank Cole Babbitt (Cambridge, MA, and London: Harvard University Press, 1936), pp. 104-105.

fire" (CW 14 §219). To say that Luna is the mother of the sun means, "psychologically" speaking, that "the unconscious is pregnant with consciousness and gives birth to it," and hence that the unconscious is "the night, which is older than the day," or in Faustian terms (and in Mephisto's words):

> Part of the Darkness, whence the Light did spring,
> The arrogant Light, which now for Space doth joust,
> And Mother Night from her old rank would oust.
>
> (ll. 1350-1352)

The idea that the light of illumination, the *albedo*, comes from the darkness of the unconscious, in which the opposites are contained *in potentia* is likewise expressed in the figure of the "Father-Mother" of the Gnostics (see Hippolytus, *Elenchus*, VI, 42, 2), in the vision of Brother Klaus (see CW 11 §485-§486), and in the visionary experiences of the English occultist, Edward Maitland (1824-1897), including an "inner experience" of the "bisexual nature of the Deity" (see CW 11 §47 and CW 13 §40-§42).

Of course, the gender assumptions behind the implications of Sol as masculine and Luna as feminine (or outwardly feminine yet internally masculine) are obviously problematic for us today, and on some level Jung himself seems to be aware of this problem. Perhaps this is why when Jung, in his *Corrected Draft* for *The Red Book*, offers a commentary on the "mystery play" in the chapters "Mysterium. Encounter," "Instruction," and "Resolution" at the end of *Liber Primus*, interpreting the figures of Elijah and Salome as personifications of Logos and Eros (RB, 562-576), this interpretation is later dismissed in *Memories, Dreams, Reflections* as being "excessively intellectual" (MDR, 206). Here in *Mysterium Coniunctionis*, and in the context of his discussion of Sol and Luna, Jung suggests that Logos and Eros are "intuitive ideas which cannot be defined accurately or exhaustively" (CW 14 §224) — an easy get-out-of-jail card! Nevertheless, he accepts Logos and Eros as "intellectually formulated intuitive equivalents of the archetypal images of Sol and Luna," adding that "an archetypal image has nothing but its naked fullness, which seems inapprehensible [*»unfaßbar«*] by the intellect"; in short, "concepts are a coined and negotiable value; images are life [*Leben*]" (§226). In order to convey precisely this "inapprehensibility" of the image, Jung has recourse to Faust's great cry in the "Night" scene at the beginning of Part One, after he has seen the sign of the Macrocosm but before he has seen the sign of the *Erdgeist*: *Wo faß ich dich, unendliche Natur?* ("Where can I grasp hold of thee, infinite Nature?" (l. 455; cf. *Gesammelte Werke*, 14 §222).

In his discussion of salt as the arcane substance, Jung discusses such associated symbols as the "bitterness" of the sea and the baptismal quality of seawater, which in turn relates it to the Red Sea (CW 14 §234). In the course of this chapter, Jung highlights the "mystic peregrination" undertaken by Michael Maier (1568-1622) in his *Symbola aureae mensae duodecim nationum* (or *The Symbols of the Golden Table of the Twelve Nations*) (1617). [67] In this work, Maier describes how he reaches the Red (or "Erythraean") Sea by journeying in four directions: to the north (Europe); to the west (America); to the east (Asia); and finally to the south (Africa), corresponding to the elements of earth, water,

---

[67] For further discussion of Maier's work, see Hereward Tilton, *The Quest for the Phoenix: Spiritual Alchemy and Rosicrucianism in the Work of Count Michael Maier (1569-1622)* (Berlin and New York: de Gruyter, 2003). Methodologically, Tilton undertakes to "reconstruct the worldview of Count Michael Maier via an 'empirical' approach to the study of Western esotericism recently outlined by Wouter Hanegraff" (15) and to "reconstruct the worldview of Maier through a sensitive, non-reductionist approach to the historical data, and to avoid violating the texts at hand by projecting contemporary categories into another time and place" (33); thematically, Tilton identifies the "four key elements of his alchemy," namely: "a doctrine of solar and astral influence; a 'chemical' interpretation of Greek and Egyptian mythology; a 'medicine of piety'; and a Hermetic theory of correspondence, in which the alchemist's spiritual life mirrors laboratory process" (34).

air, and fire, respectively (§276). Taking these four directions and their corresponding four elements as "symbolic equivalents" of the four basic functions of consciousness (i.e., thinking, feeling, sensation, intuition), Africa functions both as the fourth and last or the "inferior" function (that is, the darkest and the most unconscious function), and — precisely because it *is* the "inferior" function — as crucial for the attainment of "Paradise": namely, "the primordial image of wholeness," and "the goal of his journey" which lies in "the attainment of this wholeness" (§276). On the one hand, Africa is described as "uncultivated, torrid, parched, sterile and empty"; on the other, Maier reaches Africa at a time when the astrological signs are at their most propitious: The sun is in its house, Leo, and the moon is in Cancer, the proximity of these two houses indicating "a *coniunctio Solis et Lunae*, the union of supreme opposites, and [...] the crowning of the opus and the goal of the peregrination" (§276).

In other words, Maier's *Symbola aureae mensae* is a kind of alchemical journey in its own right, but for Jung the most noteworthy detail is the fact that Maier reaches the "Erythraean Sea" at precisely the moment when he has completed his journey through the three other continents and is on the point of entering the fourth, and critical, region (given that Africa is both a kind of "hell" *and* Paradise itself). Not surprisingly, this numerical symbolism recalls the motif of the transition from Three to Four that Jung sees thematized in the opening of Plato's *Timaeus* (17a) and in the axiom of Maria, as well as in the Cabiri scene in Goethe's *Faust II* (CW 14 §278).[68] The motifs of ascent and descent in Maier's *Symbola aureae mensae* are highlighted by Jung, who explains "ascent and descent, above and below, up and down" as representing an "emotional realization of opposites" which "gradually leads, or should lead, to their equilibrium" (§296).

---

[68] For further discussion of this motif, see Bishop, *Reading Plato through Jung*, pp. 91-126.

On his account, descent is "analytic," which involves a "separation into the four components of wholeness," while ascent is "synthetic," or a "putting together of the denarius" (that is, a coin), corresponding to the "psychological fact" that the "confrontation of conscious and unconscious produces a dissolution of the personality and at the same time regroups it into a whole" (CW 14 §294). This is, of course, precisely the dynamic that Jung detects as at work in Goethe's *Faust* and which is exemplified in his own *Red Book*; here, as he earlier had in *Transformations and Symbols of the Libido*, Jung turns for an example of how, "in moments of psychic crisis [...] the symbol of unity, for instance the mandala, occurs in a dream," to Hölderlin and his memorable line from the poem "Patmos," "Where danger is, there / Arises salvation also" (*Wo Gefahr ist, wächst / Das Rettende auch*) (§294).[69]

The attempt of the alchemists to attain the *albedo* (that is, "whiteness," the second of the four stages of the *magnum opus*, which follows the initial *nigredo* stage of chaos or *massa confusa*, and precedes the two remaining stages of *citrinitas* and *rubedo*) involves, Jung explains, an *ablutio,* or a washing away of impurities, and the production of an incorruptible, "glorified" body. He notes the need (in the words of Senior) to be "cleansed from the darkness of the soul, and of the black matter, for the wickedness (*malitia*) of base earthiness has been separated from it" (cited CW 14 §319). Jung explains that what Senior calls *terrestreitas mala* is what other authors called *terra damnata* (that is, accursed earth); in the words of the More-Perfected Angels in the final scene of *Faust II*, "Still doth some earth remain, / Still doth arrest us" (*Uns bleibt ein Erdenrest / Zu tragen peinlich*) (ll. 11954-11955), or what Jung calls "that moral deficiency of the mortal human being that cannot be washed off" (*jene nicht abzuwaschende moralische Mangelhaftigkeit des sterblichen Menschen*) (§319).

---

[69] Friedrich Hölderlin, *Poems & Fragments*, trans. Michael Hamburger, 3rd edn. (London: Anvil Press Poetry, 1994), pp. 482-483.

Should, despite all the obstacles, the alchemist nevertheless succeed, the final stage to be achieved is "the union of the spiritual, masculine principle with the feminine, psychic principle" — a goal within Gnosticism (on Iranaeus's account in his *Adversus Haereses* (i.e., *Against Heresies*), I.vi.1), and a goal also echoed in the doctrine of the Assumption of the Blessed Virgin Mary (as dogmatically defined by Pope Pius XII in 1950 and celebrated liturgically on 15 August),[70] in the union of Tiferet and Malkuth in the Kabbalistic tradition (cf. §18), and in the climactic lines of *Faust II*, "The Eternal-Womanly / Draws us above" (*Das Ewig-Weibliche / Zieht uns hinan*) (§327).

Jung's discussion of Rex and Regina, the alchemical King and Queen, is structured around a discussion of a text by the English Augustinian canon and alchemist George Ripley (c. 1415-1490). In

---

[70] Elsewhere Jung argues that the Assumption and Coronation of the Blessed Virgin Mary (two "events" which he conflates) symbolizes the third stage of the *coniunctio*, where the Mother of God represents the body. Thus the dogma of the Assumption serves as a bridge over "a gulf that seems unfathomable: the apparently irremediable separation of spirit from nature and the body" (§664). On this account, the Assumption is really "a wedding feast, the Christian version of the hieros gamos" — an idea whose "originally incestuous nature" is said to have played "a great role in alchemy" (§664). Here Jung defines incest as indicating that "the supreme union of opposites expressed a combination of things which are related but of unlike nature" (§664; but cf. §506, where Jung tells us that "incest expresses the union of elements that are akin or of the same nature"!). Thus alchemy "throws a bright light" over the background to the dogma of the Assumption, inasmuch as the "far-reaching implications" of a marriage of the fatherly spiritual principle with the principle of maternal corporeality (*mater* = matter) cannot be seen "at first glance" (§664). So what *are* those implications? They are that the union of opposites is "incestuous," insofar as it "may begin with a purely intra-psychic *unio mentalis* of intellect or reason with Eros, representing feeling" — just as it does in the chapters "Mysterium. Encounter," "Instruction," and "Resolution" in *The Red Book* —: an "interior operation" which "means a great deal," since it brings about a "considerable increase of self-knowledge as well as of personal maturity" (§664). At the moment, the "reality" (*Wirklichkeit*) of this *unio mentalis* is "merely potential," and it is validated only by a "union with the physical world of the body," hence the alchemists picture the *unio mentalis* as Father and Son, their union as the dove (representing the "spiration" common to both), and the world of the body as the feminine or passive principle, represented by the Virgin Mary (§664).

the next volume in this series, we shall take a closer look at Ripley's *Cantilena* (sometimes called *George Ripley's Song*), which Jung hails as "one of the most perfect parables of the renewal of the king" (CW 14 §463), but for now let us note that Jung finds parallels between the process of transformation as symbolized in this poem and Rosencreutz's *Chymical Wedding* (§404), as well as the *Märchen* or fairy tale called "The Philosophers' Stone" (*Der Stein der Weisen*) by Christoph Martin Wieland (1733-1813) (§406). In this story, part of the collection called *Dschinnistan oder auserlesene Feen- und Geistermärchen* (i.e., *Dschinnistan or Exquisite Fairy and Ghost tales, partly reinvented, partly translated and reworked*) which was published between 1786 and 1789, Wieland revives the motif of transformation that goes back to Apuleius's *Metamorphoses* (where Lucius is turned into an ass), by relating the similar transformation of King Mark (grandson of Isolde's husband) into an ass (§406).

Then again, when discussing the incestuous love of the King for his mother (CW 14 §410), Jung comments that the alchemical consummation of the royal marriage in the *cucurbita* (or glass house) "could be understood as a synthetic process in the psyche 'outside' the ego" (§410) — but where exactly *is* "outside-of-the-ego"? This is an important question, not least because, in recent years, many in the arts and humanities seem to have followed Jacques Derrida (1930-2004) who, in a seminal work of 1967, famously argued that *il n'y a pas de hors-texte* — usually translated as "there is nothing outside the text," [71] but more accurately rendered as "there is no outside-text." [72] Analogously, one might ask, is there any "outside-of-the-ego"? Not the least of the reasons why Jung is so important for us today is because he can help us understand what "outside-of-

---

[71] Derrida, *De la grammatologie* (Paris: Minuit, 1967), p. 227; *Of Grammatology*, trans. Gayatri Chakravorty Spivak (Baltimore: Johns Hopkins University Press, 1975), pp. 158-159.

[72] See J.G. Merquior, *From Paris to Prague: A Critique of Structuralist and Poststructuralist Thought* (London: Verso, 1986), p. 220.

the-ego" or *hors texte* might mean. If "the ego is Here and Now,"
then the "outside-the-ego" is "an alien There, both earlier and later,
before and after" (or, in the parlance of postmodernism, "always
already" there). Hence the various stages in the depiction of the
psyche outside the ego:

- By the "primitive mind" as "an alien country, inhabited by
  the spirits of the dead" (and these spirits of the dead feature,
  as we shall see, in Jung's *Red Book*)
- Its acquisition "on a rather higher level" of the character of
  "a shadowy semi-reality"
- Then, "on the level of the ancient cultures," the conception
  of "the shadows of that land" as "ideas" (*Ideen*) (and as,
  in Gnostic-Christian circles, "a dogmatic, hierarchically
  arranged cosmogonic and chiliastic system")
- Finally, to "us moderns," that Gnostic-Christian system
  appears as an "involuntary, symbolic statement of the psyche
  concerning the structure of the psychic non-ego" (§411).

Jung struggles (as he did in *The Red Book* — and, to be fair, as
probably any of us would —) to make sense of such a "spectral
'land beyond'" which, on the one hand, appears as "a whole world
in itself, a macrocosm," and, on the other, is felt as "'psychic' and
'inside' [...] a microcosm of the smallest proportions" (CW 14
§412). As a microcosm, this region is said to be the equivalent of "the
interior of the *cucurbita* in which the alchemists beheld the creation
of the world, the marriage of the royal pair, and the homunculus"
— or to "the race of dwarfs in the casket," described by Goethe
in his fairy tale *Die neue Melusine* (1807), his own adaptation of
the 14th-century medieval *Melusine* tale, which forms part of his
last great prose work, *Wilhelm Meisters Wanderjahre* (*Wilhelm
Meister's Journeyman Years*) (1821/1829).[73] (A young man — who

---

[73] For further discussion of this work, see Renata Schellenberg, "Goethe and *Die neue
Melusine*: A Critical Reinterpretation," in Misty Urban, Deva Kemmis, and Melissa
Ridley Elmes (eds.), *Melusine's Footprint: Tracing the Legacy of a Medieval Myth*
(Leiden: Brill, 2017), pp. 303-323. See also pp. 317-319 above.

is a bit of a likely lad — meets a beautiful but mysterious young woman traveling on her own at an inn. He falls in love with her and, to prove his love, he must follow these curious instructions: He must travel ahead of her on his own, carry a small casket that she gives him, and keep it locked in a separate room. One day he notices a strange light coming from the casket: Peering in through a crack, he is amazed to see inside his beloved in miniature form, sitting in a miniature hall next to a miniature fireplace. It turns out that she is from a race of dwarfs, in search of a human to marry. He agrees to wear a magic ring that will shrink him in size, but in time, he changes his mind and, removing the ring, returns to the world of human dimensions.)

Stanzas 36, 37, and 38 of Ripley's *Cantilena* bring the work to its conclusion with the apotheosis of the *filius regius* and the reborn king as the "wonder of the world" (as Philalethes puts it in *Introitus apertus*) (CW 14 §460) — symbols which, as Jung argues elsewhere, show that "a new dominant of consciousness has been produced and that the psychic potential is reversed" (§498). Here, he acknowledges that the *Cantilena* is, for stylistic reasons, not comparable with the "much more elaborate" development of the myth in Christian Rosencreutz's *Chymical Wedding*, but nevertheless, he pays it what is in a way an even greater compliment when he compares it to the end of *Faust II*, which contains "the same motif of the transformation of the old man into a boy, together with all the necessary indicia of the heavenly marriage" (§463). (Elsewhere, Jung notes that Ripley's *Cantilena* "includes mother Luna, the maternal aspect of night, in this transfiguration" — that is, "the apotheosis of the king, the renewed rising of the sun," as symbols that "consciousness is no longer under the dominion of the unconscious, in which state the dominant is hidden in the darkness, but has now glimpsed and recognized a supreme goal" — which "reminds us," he says, "of the apotheosis at the end of *Faust II*" [§498].) And Jung rehearses his view, stated earlier in *Mysterium*

Coniunctionis and in the Eranos lectures repackaged as *Psychology and Alchemy*, that the theme of *transformation* "runs through the whole of *Faust* and repeats itself on three different levels (Gretchen, Helen, Queen of Heaven),[74] just as the king's renewal takes a form that was destined to fail three times before Faust's death (the Boy Charioteer, the Homunculus, and Euphorion)" (§463).

Rather than slavishly identifying particular parts of Goethe's work with different stages of the alchemical opus, as subsequent commentators have tried to do, Jung highlights the key motif of *transformation*, a process which begins for the alchemist with "a *katabasis*, a journey to the underworld" — as experienced by Dante (despite his total absence from the alchemical literature), albeit "with the difference that the adept's soul was not only impressed by it *but radically altered*" (CW 14 §493; my emphasis). This is very much the theme of *Faust I*, where it takes the form of the "transformation of an earnest scholar, through his pact with the Devil, into a worldly cavalier and crooked careerist" (§493). In *Faust I*, Mephisto promises Faust, *Wir sehen die kleine, dann die große Welt* (i.e., "The small world, then the great we shall peruse" [l. 2052]), and the counterpart to the transformation of Faust into a

---

[74] Noting that the alchymical marriage is not only older than corresponding formulations in the sacred liturgy and in the Church Fathers, but is based on classical and pre-Christian tradition (§664), Jung cites the alchemist known as Pseudo-Democritus in the first century CE as speaking of a marriage of natures, and points to the conclusion of Goethe's *Faust*, "the last and grandest example of an alchemical opus," as ending with the apotheosis of the Virgin-Mary, Mary-Sophia, queen and goddess (CW 14 §664, fn.). In his article on "Picasso" (1932), Jung notes a correspondence between Gretchen, Helena, Mary, and the Eternal Feminine and the "four female figures of the Gnostic underworld," viz. Eve, Helen, Mary, and Sophia (CW 15 §211); in a letter of 22 March 1939, he refers to "Helena – Maria – Sophia" as a "Gnostic sequence" that stands behind Gretchen, representing a "real Platonic world of ideas," that is, "thinking and sensation on the mystic level" (L1, 265); while in *The Psychology of the Transference* (1946), Jung identified in these figures four stages of the "heterosexual Eros or anima-figure" and, correspondingly, four stages of the Eros cult: from the biological stage (Eve, or Gretchen), through the aesthetic/ romantic (Helena), and the religious (Mary) stages, to the spiritual (Sophia, or the Eternal Feminine) (CW 16 §361); cf. CW 6 §317, cited in Chapter 2 above (p. 271).

rejuvenated rake in Part One is his journey to the Mothers in Part Two, itself a parallel to the way in which Jung reads the motif of incest in alchemy: namely, as expressing "the union of elements that are akin or of the same nature" (§506; but cf. §664).[75] Or put in alchemical terms, "the adversary of Sol is his own feminine chthonic aspect [...] [and] Sol's reflected light is the feminine Luna, who dissolves the king in her moistness" (§506). Indeed, it is as if Sol — like Faust in his journey to the Mothers — has to "descend into the watery deep of the sublunary world in order to unite the 'powers of Above and Below' [cf. §288, §304]" (§506).

Concomitantly, in the *Schlußszene*, the Mater Gloriosa enjoins Doctor Marianus, "Come, soar to higher spheres! Divining / Thee near, he'll follow on thy way" (ll. 12094-12095), reflecting that the transformation of the kingly substance from a lion into a king "has its counterpart" in "the transformation of the feminine element from a serpent into a queen," or in other words, the status of the anima is "raised [...] from that of a temptress to a psychopomp," or a guide of souls (CW 14 §540). These motifs of coronation, apotheosis, and marriage — common to alchemy and to *Faust* alike — "signal the equal status of conscious and unconscious that becomes possible at the highest level" — that is, "a *coincidentia oppositorum* with redeeming effects" (§540). Of course, one might well ask: Why do we need to talk about the *coincidentia oppositorum* in alchemical terms at all? For an answer, one might turn to Jung's conclusion to his chapter on Rex and Regina.

Here he argues that the psychological union of opposites is an "intuitive idea which covers the phenomenology of this process," rather than "an 'explanatory' hypothesis for something that [...] transcends our powers of conception" (§542). So, to say

---

[75] In Chapter 6 on "The Conjunction," however, Jung describes incest as indicating that "the supreme union of opposites expressed a combination of things which are related but of unlike nature" (CW 14 §664) — a definitional contradiction which remains here unresolved.

that "conscious and unconscious unite" is to say that "this process
is *inconceivable*," for the simple reason that "the unconscious *is
unconscious* and therefore *can neither be grasped nor conceived*"
(§542; my emphasis). As a "transconscious process," then, the
union of opposites is "not amenable to scientific explanation," and
so we need symbolism (as in alchemy) or literature (as in Goethe's
Faust) or indeed art *tout court*... Thus the *Rosarium Philosophorum*
records King Solomon as saying (in Jung's paraphrase) that "the
marriage must remain the 'mystery of the queen,' the secret of
the art," and yet the figures of the Queen of Sheba, Wisdom, the
royal art, and the "daughter of the philosophers" are all, Jung
argues, "interfused" in such a way that the following "underlying
psychologem" emerges: namely, that the art (*die Kunst*) is "queen
of the alchemist's heart, [...] at once his mother, his daughter, and
his beloved," and "in his art and its allegories the drama of his own
soul, his individuation process, is played out" (§543).

Thus, alchemy can serve as a template for understanding
Goethe's *Faust* — just as, in fact, it can for understanding the
expression of the "drama" of Jung's own soul, *The Red Book*.
But could it also have served as a template for the *creation*
or composition of *Faust*? Without saying so directly, this is
something at which Jung persistently hints, as when he notes that
Eleazar (Abraham the Jew), the pseudonym of Julius Gervasius of
Schwarzburg and the author of *Uraltes Chymisches Werck* ("Age-
Old Chemical Work") (1735), is a figure who lived in the same
century as the one in which the author of *Faust*, that "momentous
opus," was born. Thus Eleazar's text, a work which purports to be
a translation of a lost text by Nicolas Flamel (c. 1330-1418) about
how to make the Philosopher's Stone, is "nothing but a late echo"
of such "centuries-old events that changed the face of Christianity"
as the Brethren of the Free Spirit, René d'Anjou (1409-1480) (and
his allegorical novel, *Le Livre du Cœur d'Amour épris*, a chivalric
romance written — partly in prose, partly in rhyming couplets — in

the tradition of the *Roman de la Rose*), and the German Minnesänger (the tradition to which, of course, Wolfram von Eschenbach also belonged), yet by the same token this echo is a "premonition of future developments" (CW 14 §646). This claim, while locating the historical significance of alchemy, also situates — *mutatis mutandis* — the historical significance of Goethe's *Faust*.

This sense of historical perspective — and, without history, there can be no psychology of the unconscious — clearly informs Jung's "Epilogue" to *Mysterium Coniunctionis*.[76] Here he argues that, after "alchemy, tapping its way in the dark, [had] groped through the endless mazes of its theoretical assumptions and practical experiments over a course of many centuries," the psychology of the unconscious — beginning with the German Romantic naturalist and landscape painter, C.G. Carus (1789-1869) — had "taken up the trail that had been lost by the alchemists" (CW 14 §791). This shift is said to have taken place — "remarkably enough" — at precisely the historical moment when the alchemists' aspirations had found "their highest poetic expression" in Goethe's *Faust*. This carefully nuanced formulation perfectly captures the breadth of Jung's response to *Faust*: On the one hand, it is the "last and grandest example of an alchemical opus" (§664, fn. 53), a text in which the archetype of the Anthropos — found in the ancient alchemy of Zosimos as well as in Wei Po-yang's notion of *chên-yên* — can be discovered in the figure of Homunculus, just as it "pervades the whole of alchemy" (§748); on the other, it is a *poetic* expression — in fact, the "highest poetic expression" (*höchsten dichterischen Ausdruck*) — with all that this term implies about the presence of rhetoric, irony, and aesthetic sophistication. And

---

[76] In *Memories, Dreams, Reflections*, Jung reminds us that he had grown up in the "intensely historical atmosphere of Basel at the end of the nineteenth century," and had "acquired, thanks to reading the old philosophers, some knowledge of the history of psychology," adding: "When I thought about dreams and the contents of the unconscious, I never did so without making historical comparisons" (MDR, 184).

if, as Jung asserts, even Carus at the time he was writing could not have guessed that he was "building the philosophical bridge to an empirical psychology of the future" (§791), then by extension how could Goethe have guessed that his *Faust* would be interpreted as not just a *magnum opus* but an "alchemical opus" — and indeed as the "last and grandest example"?

In conclusion, Jung reminds his readers of the alchemical dictum that the philosopher's stone "is found in filth" — literally, "you will find it in a cesspool" (*in sterquiliniis invenitur*) or "you will find it in dung" (*in stercore invenitur*) (CW 14 §791; cf. CW 12 §421; CW 13 §209).[77] Nowadays, Jung argues, the "cheap, unseemly substance [...] rejected by all" is not something that could be "picked up anywhere in the street," but is rather something located "in the distressing darkness" of the human psyche, where alone can be found "all those contradictions, those grotesque phantasms and scurrilous symbols" that were so fascinating to the alchemists — confusing and illuminating them in equal measure (CW 14 §791). Access to this psyche can be gained, Jung argued, by "clinical observation," but another pathway into alchemy and into the psychology of the unconscious alike is through those works of art which placed the theme of transformation at the center of their concerns, and, pre-eminently, Goethe's *Faust*.

Conclusion

According to the Seventh Ecumenical Council held in Nicaea in 787, "The Wisdom which is truly according to the nature of God and the Father — our Lord Jesus Christ, our true God — who, by his most divine and wonderful dispensation in the flesh, hath

---

[77] This alchemical dictum often attracts the attention of Jordan B. Peterson (see *We Who Wrestle with God: Perceptions of the Divine* (London: Allen Lane, 2024), pp. 83 and 481); cf. *Maps of Meaning: The Architecture of Belief* (New York and London: Routledge, 1999), pp. 405-406).

delivered us from all idolatrous error: and, by taking on him our nature, hath renewed the same by the co-operation of the Spirit, which is of the same nature with himself; and having himself become the first High Priest, hath counted you holy men, worthy of the same dignity."[78] Building on the notion of σοφία or *sophia* in the "sapiential" books of the Hebrew scriptures and the equation made in the Pauline letters between Christ and the "wisdom of God" (see 1 Corinthians 1:24), there has developed within Orthodoxy a school of theological thought called Sophiology, formulated around the turn of last century in the writings of Vladimir Solovyov (1853-1900), Pavel Florensky (1882-1937), and Sergei Bulgakov (1871-1944).[79] At around the same time, and entirely independently, Rudolf Steiner gave a lecture in Berlin in 1909 titled "Isis and Madonna," in which he pursued the connections between the Egyptian goddess Isis, represented in images of Isis as three Mothers; namely, as Isis with the Horus child at her breast, as Isis bearing two cow horns on her head and the wings of the hawk, offering the "crux ansata" to the child, and as Isis bearing a lion's head — in this respect, reflecting the three natures of the human soul — namely, a "will" nature, a "feeling" nature, and a "wisdom" nature.[80] (In fact, this

---

[78] See the *Medieval Sourcebook: The Second Council of Nicea, 787,* available online HTTP: <https://sourcebooks.fordham.edu/basis/nicea2.asp>. Accessed 25 May 2024.
[79] For further discussion, see Sergei Bulgakov, *Sophia: The Wisdom of God: An Outline of Sophiology* (Herndon, VA: Lindisfarne Press, 1993); Mikhail Sergeev, *Sophiology in Russian Orthodoxy: Solov'ev, Bulgakov, Losskii, Berdiaev* (Lewiston, New York: Edwin Mellen Press, 2007); Caitlin Matthews, *Sophia: Goddess of Wisdom, Bride of God* [2001] (Wheaton, IL: Quest Books, 2013); Michael Martin, *The Submerged Reality: Sophiology and the Turn to a Poetic Metaphysics* (Kettering, OH: Angelico Press, 2015); Judith Deutsch Kornblatt (ed.), *Divine Sophia: The Wisdom Writings of Vladimir Solovyov* (Ithaca, NY: Cornell University Press, 2009); and Henry Corbin, *Jung, Buddhism, and the Incarnation of Sophia: Unpublished Writings from the Philosopher of the Soul* [2014], ed. Michel Cazenave, trans. Jack Cain (Rochester, VT: Inner Traditions, 2019). For a wider historical reader of texts in Sophiology, see Arthur Versluis (ed.), *Wisdom's Book: The Sophia Anthology* (St. Paul, MN: Paragon House, 2000).
[80] See "Isis and Madonna" in Rudolf Steiner, *Isis Mary Sophia: Her Mission and Ours*, ed. Christopher Bamford (Spencertown, NY: SteinerBooks, 2003), pp. 89-103 (p. 99).

volume collects Steiner's numerous writings on Sophia in relation
to Isis and to Mary.)

In Volume 1 in this series, we asked ourselves: What *is* the
Grail? In this volume, the corresponding question must surely be:
What — or who — *is* the Eternal Feminine?[81] One answer can be
found in Jung's letter to an anonymous correspondent, written on
22 March 1939. The immediate context of this letter resides in two
dreams recounted by the anonymous Herr N., in the first of which
the dreamer gives birth to a child, and in the second of which —
standing on a steep cliff, above a deep abyss — he has a small child
in his arms but cannot hold it (L1, 264). The "expression" in the
second dream of an "unnatural and dangerous situation" reminds
Jung — perhaps not unexpectedly, given his interest in Goethe's
Faust in his recent Eranos lectures — of the fate of Euphorion, the
"child of Helen" and "begotten by father Faust," a situation which
Jung describes as "normal."

Jung then turns to *Faust*, declaring that the work involves
"real processes" (*wirkliche Prozesse*) — "real," that is, in the sense
that these "processes" are not "wishful phantasies (*»phantastisch
gewünscht«*), to use a Freudian expression, but are rather "those
matters which, when they ambush someone, can make them insane
[*geisteskrank*]" (L1, 264). (Jung would know all about this; After
all, at "almost every step" of his "experiment" which was *The Red*

---

[81] On Steiner's reading of the Chorus Mysticus, it is the human soul that is the
"Eternal Feminine" that draws us onward to the universal spirit of the world, for
"the soul has sprung from the divine Father-spirit living and weaving throughout the
universe, bearing the Son of wisdom Who is like unto this Father-spirit, of Whom
He is a repetition" ("Isis and Madonna," p. 94). Citing Goethe's maxim that "anyone
to whom nature begins to reveal her open secret feels an irresistible longing for her
worthiest exponent — art" (*Maxims and Reflections*, #201), Steiner claims that when
our gaze falls on such works as Raphael's *Sistine Madonna* or Michaelangelo's *Pietà*
in St Peter's in Rome, the soul "partakes in certain knowledge of the mighty riddle
of the world," for we realize that "in such surrender our soul, seeking in itself for the
eternal feminine, is yearning for the divine Father-Spirit born out of the cosmos, to
Whom as the Sun we give birth in our own soul" (p. 101).

Book, he had "run into" the "same psychic material which is the stuff of psychosis and is found in the lunatic asylum [*im Irrenhaus*]" — that is, "that world of unconscious images which provokes fatal confusion in the mentally insane [*den Geisteskranken*]," but at the same time is a "matrix of mythopœic phantasy" [MDR, 192].)

The same is true, Jung continues, in the fourth stage of the "transformation process" (*Wandlungsprozess*), namely, the "experience of the Beyond," which is glossed by the editors of the *Letters* as Faust's transformation into Doctor Marianus in the last scene of *Faust II*, but which might plausibly also refer to Jung's visions of 1944, which he described in — literally — Faustian terms as floating night after night in a state of purest bliss, "thronged round" — like those mysterious, Faustian Mothers — "with images of all creation" (MDR, 325-326; cf. l. 6289). This Beyond is an "unconscious reality," which was felt as being — "in Faust's case," as the *Letters* say, but according to the *Briefe*, "in Goethe's case" — "beyond the possibility of his time" (*als Jenseits seiner derzeitigen Möglichkeit*), signaled by its separation from his "real existence" (*wirkliche Existenz*) by death (L1, 265). This expresses the fact that he — presumably, Faust — still had to "become a boy" (*»zum Knaben werden«*) and only in this way could he "attain the highest wisdom" (*zur höchsten Weisheit*). In this context, great importance is said to accrue to Euphorion as representing the "future individual" who does not, in an expression we have seen Jung use elsewhere (cf. CW 5 §615), "flee from the bond with the earth [*dem Bund mit der Erde entflieht*] but is dashed to pieces on it," a tragic end which indicates he is "not possible" (*nicht möglich*) in our "present circumstances."

And then Jung goes on to make the following remarkable statement: "Faust's death must therefore be taken as a fact" (*Faustens Tod ist darum als tatsächlich zu verstehen*) (L1, 265), a statement which shows Jung's central hermeneutic move: his identification of *Faust* (as a text or work of literature) with psychological (or

perhaps even metaphysical) "reality." For what kind of reality are
we talking about here? Jung is, it seems, treating *Faust* as *more
than* a literary text *about* transformation, but as *actually enacting*
the very process of transformation — and as having the potential
to work that same transformation in its readers! What other sense
can we give to Jung's next remark, that Faust's death is, "like many
a death, in fact a mystery death [*ein Mysterientod*] which brings
what is imperfect to perfection [*das Unvollendete zur Vollendung*]"
(265)? The "Paris-Helena-Euphorion episode" is said to be "in fact
the highest stage reached in the transformation process [*der höchst
erreichte Grad des Wandlungsprozesses*]," but it is *not* in itself the
highest, since Euphorion as an "element" has not been "integrated"
into the "Faust-Mephisto-Paris-Helen quaternity" as its *Quinta
Essentia* or "fifth essence," i.e., aether, said to be the fifth element
and as such superior to the other four (earth, air, fire, and water).[82]
What is the *Quinta Essentia*?

In *Psychology and Alchemy*, Jung notes the identification
of the quintessence with the aether in Aristole's *De Coelo* and
Meterologica (CW 12 §371);[83] suggests that the Paracelsian term
astrum ("star") means the same as quintessence (§394); and
notes that the geometrical problem of "squaring of the circle,"
i.e., constructing a square equal in area to a given circle — which
is impossible! — "greatly exercised medieval minds" and is a
symbol of the *opus alchymicum* (§165). The *opus* breaks down
the original chaotic unity (represented by a circle) into the four
elements (represented by a square), and then combines them again
in a "higher unity," producing the One from Four by a process of
distillation and sublimation, so that the "soul" or "spirit" — the

---

[82] Raphael Patai, "An unknown Hebrew medical alchemist: A medieval treatise on
the quinta essentia," *Medical History*, vol. 28, no. 3 (1984), 308-323.
[83] See *On the Heavens* (Book 1, §3) and *Meteorology* (Book 1, §3), in Aristotle,
Complete Works, ed. Jonathan Barnes, 2 vols (Princeton, NJ: Princeton University
Press, 1984), vol. 1, pp. 451 and 556.

"quintessence," although "this is by no means the only name for the ever-hoped-for and never-to-be-discovered 'One'" — is extracted in its purest state (§165). And this dual sense of the *Quinta Essentia* can also be found in *Mysterium Coniunctionis*.

On the one hand, the location of the Crowned Maid in the "fifth circle of the mysterie" in verse 30 of Ripley's *Cantilena* is read by Jung as an indication of the quintessence, and as being equivalent to aether, the "finest and most subtle substance" (CW 14 §452); on the other, Gerhard Dorn is said to be tacitly identifying the quintessence with "the sun [as] a single element" when in *Physica Trismegisti* he says that it contains "all the simple elements [...] as they are in heaven and in the other heavenly bodies" (CW 14 §114; cf. "The Production of the Quintessence," §681-§685). Commenting on verse 27 of Ripley's *Cantilena*, Jung rehearses his point about the squaring of the circle (square = quaternio, circle = unity) and about how "the One born of the Four is the Quinta Essentia" (§439); and he returns to this point yet again when commenting on the anonymous treatise "De sulphure," when he says that the male (produced from Sulphur and Mercurius) and the female (produced from Mercurius and Salt) bring forth the "incorruptible One," or the *Quinta Essentia*, and "thus quadrangle will answer to quadrangle" (§655), and that this synthesis of the incorruptible One or quintessence follows the Axiom of Maria (§656). Finally, with reference to Albertus Magnus, Mercurius quadratus is said to "consist of four elements," thus forming the "mid-point of the cosmic quaternity" and representing the "quinta essentia, the oneness and essence of the physical world, i.e., the anima mundi," which itself corresponds to the "modern representations of the self" (§719). (In a footnote to one of these paragraphs, which might well be the most important footnote in the entire *Collected Works*, Jung gives us the key to his understanding of alchemy and its key concepts: Mercurius, he says, is (a) *both* masculine and feminine; and (b) *at the same time* the child born of their union [§655, fn. 16]!)

This failure to "integrate" Euphorion and thus to produce the
Quinta Essentia means that, on this alchemical reading, a sense of
failure is built into the narrative architecture of *Faust*. Now Jung
switches his focus away from the figures of Faust and Euphorion
and toward the notion of transformation itself. Describing Goethe
as having been an intuitive feeling type, the figure of Faust appears
first as Goethe's "shadow," representing the thinking and sensing
functions of Goethe as an "introverted scientist and doctor" (L1,
265). His first transformation is to discover his countertype in the
function of feeling, which "is everything," and at the same time
he realizes — as, apparently, is "invariably the case in analysis"
— the "projection of the anima" (in the figure, one assumes,
of Gretchen). But behind Gretchen is said to stand a "Gnostic
sequence" (*gnostische Reihe*), namely, "Helena-Mary-Sophia,"
representing both "thinking and sensation on a mystical level"
and a "real Platonic world of ideas." (In what sense this sequence
is a Gnostic one, and in what sense it is both Platonically ideal
and typologically-functionally "mystical," is left unexplained.
Clearly, however, Jung *did* consider it to be Gnostic, as he made
the same point about it in identical terms elsewhere [CW 6 §317;
CW 15 §211; CW 16 §361]. Sophia or Mater Gloriosa or "Eternal
Feminine" — all stand as expressions for the final stage in Faust's
development and his ultimate transformational moment.) On
Jung's account, Goethe is said to have intuitively grasped (*erahnt*)
this psychological fact: namely, that "unconscious, undifferentiated
functions" are "contaminated" with the collective unconscious, as a
result of which they are only partially rational and mostly irrational,
or in other words they can be realized as "inner experience" (*inneres
Erlebnis*).

As "inner experience" — but nevertheless as "real"? In
the conclusion to this letter of 22 March 1939, Jung takes his
correspondent to task for having understood the "reality character"
(*»Wirklichkeitscharakter«*) of the "Faustian experiences" in a

merely psychological or even psychologizing way (L1, 266). Here Jung specifically and explicitly rejects Freud's notion of "incestuous wish-fantasies" as a product of his "personalistic psychology of neurosis." On one level, such fantasies, as in the case of his correspondent's first dream of giving birth to a child, are "incorrect" (*unrichtig*), but on another level they are just as "correct" (*richtig*) as Goethe's Paris-Helena experience. (Time and again, we see Jung confusing fact and fiction, or the literal and the literary, or the biographical and the bibliographical; or perhaps rather uncovering and deliberately equating their symbolic dimension.) What might be a "thoroughly morbid affair" from a medical standpoint — such as when a patient claims to be a primordial father, fecundating his daughter for millions of years — can nevertheless, from a psychological standpoint, express an "astonishing truth" (L1, 266). And in the case of Goethe's *Faust* — this remarkable, baffling, fascinating text — Jung would "firmly reject" (*perhorreszieren*, or "anathematize," as Hull translates it) any talk about "incestuous wish-fantasies."

For *Faust* is a "noble," "elegant," or "distinguished" (*vornehm*) affair, and — in the sense that we have seen in the preceding pages — its Second Part is "closely connected" with Goethe's knowledge of alchemy, which no one should "underestimate" (L1, 265). In fact, Jung once again declares himself to have been "amazed" by how much Hermetic philosophy he had found in Part Two, and he went so far as to advocate a quasi-therapeutic use of the work, recommending his correspondent to "consider the thought-processes of alchemy [*die Gedankengänge der Alchemie*] in relation to *Faust*" *for his own benefit* (in German, *zur Ihrer eigenen Klärung*). For the work of Sophia is not complete until we set aside our Faustian desires to *push onward or forward* in the search to discover "the inmost force / That bonds the very universe" (ll. 382-383) and instead allow ourselves to be *pulled onward and upward* as the Eternal Feminine "draws us on high" (l. 12111). Never mind turning base metal into gold, *this* transformation would be a truly epic one! Yet what makes *Faust* such a powerful — and poignant — work is that this transformation is not quite achieved; or, expressed in analytical psychological terms, the "rebirth and transformation" that follow the *coniunctio* take place "in the hereafter, i.e., in the unconscious" — which leaves the problem unresolved (CW 12 §559). This problem, Jung adds, was "taken up" again by Nietzsche in his *Zarathustra*; and it is to this work, the next stage in the epic of transformation, that we shall turn in Volume 3.

Bibliography

Primary Texts and Editions

See *List of Abbreviations, Editions of translations cited, "Faust" editions and commentaries*, etc.

Works Cited

Abrams, M.H. *Natural Supernaturalism: Tradition and Revolution in Romantic Literature* (New York and London: Norton, 1973).

Adorno, Theodor W. and Max Horkheimer. *Dialectic of Enlightenment: Philosophical Fragments* [1947], ed. Gunzelin Schmid Noerr, trans. Edmund Jephcott (Stanford, CA: Stanford University Press, 2002).

Agamben, Giorgio. *Hölderlin's Madness: Chronicle of a Dwelling Life, 1806-1843*, trans. Alta L. Price (London: Seagull Books, 2023).

Alter, Robert. *The Wisdom Books: Job, Proverbs, and Ecclesiastes: A Translation with Commentary* (New York and London: Norton, 2010).

Anderegg, Johannes. *Transformationen: Über Himmlisches und Teuflisches in Goethes Faust* (Bielefeld: Aisthesis, 2011).

Angelus Silesius, *The Cherubinic Wanderer*, ed. Josef Schmidt, trans. Maria Shrady (New York and Mahwah, NJ: Paulist Press, 1986).

Antonelli, Francesca, Antonella Romano, and Paolo Savoia (eds). *Gendered Touch: Women, Men, and Knowledge-making in Early Modern Europe* (Leiden and Boston: Brill, 2022).

Aristotle. *Complete Works*, ed. Jonathan Barnes, 2 vols. (Princeton, NJ: Princeton University Press, 1984).

Aristotle. *On the Art of Poetry*, trans. Ingram Bywater (Oxford: Clarendon Press, 1920).

Arkin, Arthur M. "A Short Note on Empedocles and Freud," *American Imago*, vol. 6, no. 3 (September 1949), 197-203.

Assmann, Jan and Florian Ebeling. *Ägyptische Mysterien: Reisen in die Unterwelt in Aufklärung und Romantik: Eine kommentierte Anthologie* (Munich: Beck, 2011).

Athanasius, *The Life of Antony and the Letter to Marcellinus*, trans. Robert C. Gregg (Mahwah, NJ: Paulist Press, 1980).

Atkins, Stuart. "The Mothers, the Phorcides and the Cabiri in Goethe's 'Faust,'" *Monatshefte*, vol. 45, no. 5 (October 1953), 289-296.

Augustine (St). *Earlier Writings*, ed. and trans. J.H. Burleigh (Louisville, KY, and London: John Knox Press, 2006).

Avenarius, Richard. *Der menschliche Weltbegriff* (Leipzig: Reisland, 1891).

Babich, Babette. "Nietzsche's Zarathustra and Parodic Style: On Lucian's *Hyperanthropos* and Nietzsche's *Übermensch*," *Diogenes*, vol. 58, no. 4 (2012), 58-74.

Baldridge, W. Scott. "The Geological Writings of Goethe: Despite his keen powers of observation, Goethe's ideas on geology reflected the biases of his time," *American Scientist*, vol. 72, no. 2 (March-April 1984), 163-167.

Barnes, John Michael. *Goethe and the Power of Rhythm: A Biographical Essay* [1999] (Ghent, NY: Adonis Press, 2010).

Bartscherer, Agnes. *Paracelsus, Paracelsisten und Goethes "Faust": Eine Quellenstudie* (Dortmund: F.W. Ruhfus, 1911).

Beller, Manfred. *Philemon und Baucis in der europäischen Literatur: Stoffgeschichte und Analyse* (Heidelberg: Winter, 1967).

Bennett, Benjamin. "Histrionic Nationality: Implications of the Verse in *Faust*," *Goethe Yearbook*, vol. 17 (2010), pp. 21-30.

Bennett, Benjamin. *Goethe's Theory of Poetry: "Faust" and the Regeneration of Language* (Ithaca, NY, and London: Cornell University Press, 1986).

Bennett, Benjamin. *The Defective Art of Poetry: Sappho to Yates* (New York: Palgrave Macmillan, 2014).

Benz, Ernst (ed.). *Der Übermensch: Eine Diskussion* (Zurich and Stuttgart: Rhein-Verlag, 1961).

Benzenhöfer, Udo. *Studien zum Frühwerk des Paracelsus im Bereich Medizin und Naturkunde* (Munich: Klemm & Oelschläger, 2005).

Berman, Marshall. *All That Is Solid Melts into Air: The Experience of Modernity* (New York: Penguin, 1982).

Bernadete, Seth. *The Rhetoric of Morality and Philosophy: Plato's "Gorgias" and "Phaedrus"* (Chicago and London: Chicago University Press, 1991).

Bernardini, Riccardo. *Simboli di rinascita nella Basilica di San Miniato al Monte de Firenze: Da Gioacchino da Fiore a C.G. Jung/Rebirth Symbols in the Basilica of San Miniato al Monte in Florence: From Joachim of Fiore to C.G. Jung* (Bergamo: Moretti & Vitali, 2022).

Bertozzi, Alberto. *Plotinus on Love: An Introduction to his Metaphysics through the Concept of "Eros"* (Leiden and Boston: Brill, 2021).

Bett, Richard. "Socratic Ignorance," in Donald R. Morrison (ed.), *The Cambridge Companion to Socrates* (Cambridge and New York: Cambridge University Press, 2010), pp. 215-236.

Binswanger, H.C. and K.R. Smith. "Paracelsus and Goethe: Founding Fathers of Environmental Health," *Bulletin of the World Health Organization*, vol. 78, no. 9 (2000), 1162-1164.

Binswanger, Hans Christoph. *Money and Magic: A Critique of the Modern Economy in the Light of Goethe's "Faust"* [1985], trans. J.E. Harrison (Chicago and London: University of Chicago Press, 1994).

Bishop, Paul. "Adorno and Jung, Bloch and Klages: Disorientation and Reorientation of Consciousness in the Totally Administered Society," in *Eranos Yearbook* 76 (2022-2023-2024) (in press).

Bishop, Paul (ed.). *A Companion to Goethe's "Faust", Parts I and II* (Woodbridge and Rochester, NY: Camden House, 2001).

Bishop, Paul. *Analytical Psychology and German Classical Aesthetics*, vol. 1, *The Development of the Personality*; vol. 2, *The Constellation of the Self* (London and New York: Routledge, 2008-2009).

Bishop, Paul. "Digging Jung: Analytical Psychology and Philosophical Archaeology," *History of European Ideas*, vol. 48, no. 7 (2022), 960-979.

Bishop, Paul. *Jung's "Answer to Job": A Commentary* (Hove and New York: Brunner-Routledge, 2002).

Bishop, Paul. "Ludwig Klages and his philosophy of language," *Journal of European Studies*, vol. 50, no. 1 (2020), 17-29.

Bishop, Paul. *Nietzsche's "The Anti-Christ": A Critical Introduction and Guide* (Edinburgh: Edinburgh University Press, 2022).

Bishop, Paul. *Reading Goethe At Midlife: Ancient Wisdom, German Classicism & Jung*, 2nd edn. (Asheville, NC: Chiron, 2020).

Bishop, Paul. *Reading Plato through Jung: Why must the Third become the Fourth?* (Cham: Palgrave Macmillan, 2022).

Bishop, Paul (ed.). *The Archaic: The Past in the Present* (London and New York: Routledge, 2012).

Bishop, Paul and Heinz-Peter Preußer (eds.). *Eros und Sexus in der Philosophie von Ludwig Klages* (Würzburg: Königshausen & Neumann, 2025).

Bishop, Paul, Terence Dawson, and Leslie Gardner (eds.). *The Descent of the Soul and the Archaic: Katábasis and Depth Psychology* (London and New York: Routledge, 2023).

Bloch, Ernst. *Das Prinzip Hoffnung* [1959], 3 vols. (Frankfurt am Main: Suhrkamp, 1980).

Blondell, Ruby. *Helen of Troy: Beauty, Myth, Devastation* (New York: Oxford University Press, 2013).

Bloom, Harold. *The Western Canon: The Books and School of the Ages* (New York: Harcourt & Brace, 1995).

Boehme, Jacob. *The Signature of All Things* [*De Signatura rerum*, 1622], trans. Clifford Bax (London; Toronto: Dent; Dutton, 1912).

Böhme, Jacob. *Werke: Morgenröte; De Signatura rerum*, ed. Ferdinand van Ingen (Frankfurt am Main: Deutscher Klassiker Verlag, 2009).

Boyle, Nicholas. "Goethe's Theory of Tragedy," *The Modern Language Review*, vol. 105, no. 4 (October 2010), 1072-1086.

Brenner-Eglinger, Hans. "Briefe Jakob Burckhardts an Albert Brenner," *Basler Jahrbuch 1901*, 87-110.

Brown, Robert F. (ed.). *Schelling's Treatise on "The Deities of Samothrace": A Translation and an Interpretation* (Missoula, MT: Scholars Press, 1974).

Bubner, Rüdiger. *Innovations of Idealism*, trans. Nicholas Walker (Cambridge: Cambridge University Press, 2003).

Budge, E.A. Wallis. *The Gods of the Egyptians, or Studies in Egyptian Mythology*, 2 vols (London: Methuen, 1904).

Bulgakov, Sergei. *Sophia: The Wisdom of God: An Outline of Sophiology* (Herndon, VA: Lindisfarne Press, 1993).

Bunnin, Nicholas and Jiyuan Yu. *The Blackwell Dictionary of Western Philosophy* (Malden, MA, and Oxford: Blackwell, 2004).

Burdach, Konrad. "Faust und die Sorge," *Deutsche Vierteljahrsschrift für Literaturwissenschaft und Geistesgeschichte*, 1 (1923), 1-60.

Burwick, Frederick and James C. McKusick. *Faustus From the German of Goethe Translated by Samuel Taylor Coleridge* (Oxford: Oxford University Press, 2007).

Busch-Zantner, Richard. *Faust-Stätten in Hellas: Topographie und Quellenfrage der griechischen Landschaften in Goethes "Faust"* (Weimar: Böhlaus Nachfolger, 1932).

Butler, Elizabeth M. *The Myth of the Magus*, *Ritual Magic*, and *The Fortunes of Faust* (Cambridge: Cambridge University Press, 1948-1952).

Caputo, Giovanni B. "Archetypal-Imaging and Mirror-Gazing," *Behavioral Sciences*, 4 (2014), 4, 1-13.

Cardinal, Roger. *German Romantics in Context* (London: Studio Vista, 1975).

Carus, Paul. "Goethe's Soul-Conception," *The Open Court*, 21 (1907), 745-751.

Cassirer, Ernst. *Language and Myth*, trans. Susanne K. Langer (New York: Dover, 1953).

Cauwenberg, Zoë Van. *Illustrious Providence and the Supernatural Art: A Renaissance Alchemist and his Pursuit of Salvation*, MA thesis, University of Gent, 2016-2017.

Cicero. *The Academic Questions, Treatise de Finibus, and Tusculan Disputations*, trans. C.D. Yonge (London: Bohn, 1853).

Clark, Raymond J. *Catabasis: Vergil and the Wisdom-Tradition* (Amsterdam: Grüner, 1978).

Clement of Alexandria. *The Exhortation to the Greeks; The Rich Man's Salvation; and the Fragment of an Address entitled To the Newly Baptized*, trans. G.W. Butterworth (Cambridge, MA, and London: Harvard University Press; Heinemann, 1960).

Collum, V.C.C. "Die schöpferische Mutter-Göttin der Völker keltischer Sprache," *Eranos-Jahrbuch*, 6 (1938), 221-324.

Colonna, Francesco. *Hypnerotomachia Poliphili: The Strife of Love in a Dream*, trans. Joscelyn Godwin (London: Thames & Hudson, 1999).

Colonna, Francesco. *The Dream of Poliphilo*, ed. Linda Fierz-David, trans. Mary Hottinger (Princeton, NJ: Princeton University Press, 1950).

Corbin, Henry. *Jung, Buddhism, and the Incarnation of Sophia: Unpublished Writings from the Philosopher of the Soul* [2014], ed. Michel Cazenave, trans. Jack Cain (Rochester, VT: Inner Traditions, 2019).

Cottrell, Alan P. *Goethe's "Faust": Seven Essays* (Chapel Hill, NC: University of North Carolina Press, 1976).

Cottrell, Alan P. *Goethe's View of Evil: and the Search for a New Image of Man in Our Time* (Edinburgh: Floris Books, 1982).

Cottrell, Alan P. "Zoilo-Thersites: Another 'sehr ernster Scherz' in Goethe's *Faust II*," *Modern Language Quarterly*, vol. 29, no. 1 (March 1968), 29-41.

Davis, Bret W. (ed.). *Martin Heidegger: Key Concepts* (Abingdon, UK, and New York: Routledge, 2014).

Davy, Ted G. *The Descent into Hades* (London: Theosophical Society, 1983).

Deats, Sara Munson. *The Faust Legend: From Marlow and Goethe to Contemporary Drama and Film* (Cambridge and New York: Cambridge University Press, 2019).

Deleuze, Gilles. *The Fold: Leibniz and the Baroque* [*Le pli: Leibniz et le baroque*], trans. Tom Conley (Minneapolis: University of Minnesota Press, 1993).

Deleuze, Gilles and Félix Guattari. *A Thousand Plateaus: Capitalism and Schizophrenia*, trans. Brian Massumi (Minneapolis: University of Minnesota Press, 1987).

Dell, Katharine J., Suzanna R. Millar, and Arthur Jan Keefer (eds.). *The Cambridge Companion to Biblical Wisdom Literature* (Cambridge: Cambridge University Press, 2022).

Derrida, Jacques. "The Double Session" [*La Double Séance*, 1971], trans. Barbara Johnson (Chicago: University of Chicago Press, 1981).

Derrida, Jacques. *Of Grammatology* [*De la grammatologie*, 1967], trans. Gayatri Chakravorty Spivak (Baltimore: Johns Hopkins University Press, 1976).

Diel, Paul. *Le Symbolisme dans la mythologie grecque* (Paris: Payot, 1970).

Diener, Gottfried. *Pandora – Zu Goethes Metaphorik: Entstehung, Epoche, Interpretation des Festspiels* (Bad Homburg: Gehlen, 1968).

Domandl, Sepp. "Goethe als Paracelsuskenner: Zwei neue Belege," *Jahrhuch des Wiener Goethe-Vereins*, 80 (1976), 41-48.

Doniger, Wendy (ed. and trans.). *The Rig Veda* (Harmondsworth: Penguin, 1981).

Durrani, Osman. *Faust: Icon of Modern Culture* (Mountfield: Helm Information, 2004).

Dye, Ellis. "Sorge in Heidegger and in Goethe's *Faust*," *Goethe Yearbook*, vol. 16 (2009), 207-218.

Dye, R. Ellis. "Goethe's *Der Wandrer*: Portrait of a Modern Man," *Sprachkunst*, vol. 34, no. 1 (2003), 1-23.

Dye, R. Ellis. "Goethe's *Faust* and Heidegger: Commonalities," *Sprachkunst: Beiträge zur Literaturwissenschaft*, vol. 41, no. 2 (2010), 171-192.

Dye, Robert Ellis. "'Unmöglich ist's, drum eben glaubenswert': Paradox in Goethe and Heidegger," *Seminar: A Journal of Germanic Studies*, vol. 50, no. 4 (November 2014), 413-435.

Eckermann, Johann Peter. *Conversations of Goethe*, ed. J.K. Moorhead, trans. John Oxenford [1930] (New York: Da Capo Press, 1998).

Ferenczi, Sándor. "Introjektion und Übertragung," *Jahrbuch für psychoanalytische und psychopathologische Forschungen*, 1 (1909), 422-457.

Fisher, L.A. *The Mystic Vision in the Grail Legend and in the "Divine Comedy"* (New York: Columbia University Press, 1917).

Flax, Neil M. "The Presence of the Sign in Goethe's *Faust*," *Publications of the Modern Languages Association*, vol. 98, no. 2 (March 1983), 183-203.

Fradon, Ramona. *The Gnostic Faustus: The Secret Teachings Behind the Classic Text* (Rochester, VT: Inner Traditions, 2007).

Franz, Marie-Louise von (ed.) *Aurora Consurgens: A Document Attributed to Thomas Aquinas of the Problem of Opposites in Alchemy* [1957], trans. R.F.C. Hull and A.S.B. Glover (New York and London: Bollingen Foundation, 1966).

Franz, Marie-Louise von. *The Golden Ass of Apuleius: The Liberation of the Feminine in Man* [1970] (Boston and London: Shambhala, 1992).

Freud, Sigmund and C.G. Jung. *The Freud/Jung Letters: The Correspondence Between Sigmund Freud and C.G. Jung*, ed. William McGuire, trans. Ralph Manheim and R.F.C. Hull (Cambridge, MA: Harvard University Press, 1988).

Galloway, William. *Dissertations on the Philosophy of Creation and the First Ten Chapters of Genesis Allegorized in Mythology* (Edinburgh, London: Gemmell; Hamilton, Adams, 1885).

Gasperoni, John. "The Unconscious is structured like a language," *Qui Parle*, vol. 9, no. 2 (Special Issue on Lacan) (Spring/Summer 1996), 77-104.

Gay, Peter (ed.). *The Freud Reader* (London: Vintage, 1995).

Gerhardt, Volker. "Übermensch," in Joachim Ritter, Karlfried Gründer, and Gottfried Gabriel (eds), *Historisches Wörterbuch der Philosophie*, vol. 11 (Basel: Schwabe, 2001), cols. 46-50.

Giegerich, Wolfgang. "Hospitality toward the Gods in an Ungodly Age: Philemon — Faust — Jung," *Spring*, 1984, 61-75; reprinted in *The Neurosis of Psychology: Primary Papers Towards a Critical Psychology* [*Collected English Papers*, vol. 1] (London and New York: Routledge, 2020), pp. 197-218.

Girard, René. *I Saw Satan Fall Like Lightning* [1999], trans. James G. Williams (Maryknoll, NY: Orbis Books, 2001).

Godwin, Joscelyn (ed.) *Rosicrucian Trilogy: Fama Fraternitatis, 1614; Confessio Fraternitatis, 1615; The Chemical Wedding of Christian Rosenkreuz, 1616*, trans. Joscelyn Godwin, Christopher McIntosh, and Donate Pahnke McIntosh (Newburyport, MA: Weiser Books, 2016).

Goethe, Johann Wolfgang. *Autobiography of Johann Wolfgang von Goethe (Dichtung und Wahrheit)*, trans. John Oxenford (New York: Horizon Press, 1969).

Goethe, Johann Wolfgang. *Briefe*, ed. Karl Robert Mandelkow, 4 vols. (Hamburg: Wegner, 1962-1967).

Goethe, Johann Wolfgang. *Essays on Art and Literature*, ed. John Gearey, trans. Ellen and Ernest H. von Nardroff [Goethe Edition, vol. 3] (New York: Suhrkamp Publishing, 1986).

Goethe, Johann Wolfgang. *Faust: Part One*, ed. and trans. David Luke (Oxford: Oxford University Press, 1987).

Goethe, Johann Wolfgang. *Faust: Part Two*, ed. and trans. David Luke (Oxford: Oxford University Press, 1994).

Goethe, Johann Wolfgang. *Italian Journey*, ed. Thomas P. Saine and Jeffrey L. Sammons, trans. Robert R. Heitner [Goethe Edition, vol. 6] (New York: Suhrkamp Publishers, 1989).

Goethe, Johann Wolfgang. *Naturwissenschaftliche Schriften*, ed. Paul Stapf [*Werke*, vol. 8] (Berlin, Darmstadt, Vienna: Deutsche Buch-Gemeinschaft, 1967).

Goethe, Johann Wolfgang. *Scientific Studies*, ed. and trans. Douglas Miller [Goethe Edition, vol. 8] (New York: Suhrkamp, 1988).

Goethe, Johann Wolfgang. *Selected Poems*, ed. Christopher Middleton [Goethe Edition, vol. 1] (Boston: Suhrkamp/Insel, 1982).

Goethe, Johann Wolfgang. *Selected Poems*, trans. John Whaley (London: Dent, 1998).

Goethe, Johann Wolfgang. *Three Tales*, ed. C.A.H. Russ (Oxford: Oxford University Press, 1964).

Goethe, Johann Wolfgang. *West-Eastern Divan; West-oestlicher Divan*, trans. J. Whaley (London: Wolff, 1974).

Goodrick-Clarke, Nicholas (ed.). *Paracelsus: Essential Readings* (Berkeley, CA: North Atlantic Books, 1999).

Grätz, Katharina. *Kommentar zu Nietzsches "Also sprach Zarathustra" I und II* [NK, vol. 4/1] (Berlin and Boston: de Gruyter, 2024).

Gray, Ronald D. *Goethe the Alchemist: A Study of Alchemical Symbolism in Goethe's Literary and Scientific Works* (Cambridge: Cambridge University Press, 1952).

Grimes, Pierre and Regina L. Uliana, *Philosophical Midwifery: A New Paradigm for Understanding Human Problems* (Costa Mesa, CA: Hyparxis Press, 1998).

Gsell, Monika. *Die Bedeutung der Baubo: Kulturgeschichtliche Studien zur Repräsentation des weiblichen Genitales* (Frankfurt am Main: Stroemfeld Verlag, 2001).

Guéranger, Abbot. *The Liturgical Year*, vol. 13, *Time After Pentecost: Book* 4, trans. Laurence Shepherd, 4th edn. (Great Falls, MT: St. Bonaventure Publications, 2000).

Guthrie, Kenneth Sylvan. *The Song of Mysticism, Being an Attempt to Solve the Problem: "Which is most Reliable, Facts or Interpretation, Science or Mysticism?"* (Medford, MA: Prophet Publishing House, 1904).

Guthrie, W.K.C. *A History of Greek Philosophy*, vol. 5, *The Later Plato and the Academy* (Cambridge: Cambridge University Press, 1978).

Haar, Stephen Charles. *Simon Magus: The First Gnostic?* (Berlin and New York: de Gruyter, 2003).

Hadot, Pierre. *La Philosophie comme manière de vivre: Entretiens* (Paris: Albin Michel, 2001).

Hadot, Pierre. *Philosophy as a Way of Life: Spiritual Exercises from Socrates to Foucault*, ed. Arnold I. Davidson, trans. Michael Chase (Oxford and Malden, MA: Blackwell, 1995).

Hadot, Pierre. "'The Present Alone Is Our Joy': The Meaning of the Present Instant in Goethe and in Ancient Philosophy," *Diogenes*, vol. 34, no. 133 (1986), 60-82.

Hadot, Pierre. *The Veil of Isis: An Essay on the History of the Idea of Nature* [2004], trans. Michael Chase (Cambridge, MA, and London: The Belknap Press of Harvard University Press, 2006).

Haile, H.G. (ed.). *The History of Doctor Johann Faustus* (Urbana, IL: University of Illinois Press, 1965).

Hall, Manly Palmer. *Neoplatonism: Theology for Wanderers in the New Millennium* (Los Angeles: Philosophical Research Society, 2010).

Hanegraaff, Wouter J. et al. (eds.), *Dictionary of Gnosis & Western Esotericism* (Leiden and Boston: Brill, 2006).

Harpur, Patrick. *The Philosophers' Secret Fire: A History of the Imagination* (Harmondsworth: Penguin, 2002).

Hartlaub, Gustav F. "Goethe als Alchemist," *Euphorion*, 48 (1954), 19-40.

Hartmann, Franz. *The Life and the Doctrines of* [...] *Paracelsus* [1887] (New York: Lovell, 1891).

Hegel, G.W.F. *Aesthetics: Lectures on Fine Art*, trans. T.M. Knox, vol. 1 (Oxford: Clarendon Press, 1975).

Hegel, G.W.F. *Werke in zwanzig Bänden*, ed. Eva Moldenhauer and Karl Markus Michel, 20 vols. (Frankfurt am Main: Suhrkamp, 1986).

Heidegger, Martin. *Four Seminars*, trans. Andrew Mitchell and François Raffoul (Bloomington, IN: Indiana University Press, 2003).

Heidegger, Martin. *What Is Called Thinking?* [1951/1952], trans. J. Glenn Gray (New York: Harper & Row, 1968).

Heidegger, Martin. *Aus der Erfahrung des Denkens, 1910-1976* [*Gesamtausgabe*, vol. I.13], ed. Hermann Heidegger (Frankfurt am Main: Klostermann, 1983).

Heller, Erich. *The Disinherited Mind: Essays in Modern German Literature and Thought* (Harmondsworth: Penguin, 1961).

Heller, Erich. *The Importance of Nietzsche: Ten Essays* (Chicago and London: Chicago University Press, 1988).

Herodotus. *The Landmark Herodotus: The Histories*, ed. Robert B. Strassler (London: Quercus, 2008).

Hölderlin, Friedrich. *Poems and Fragments*, trans. Michael Hamburger, 3rd edn. (London: Anvil Press Poetry, 1994).

Hölderlin, Friedrich. *Sämtliche Gedichte*, ed. Jochen Schmidt (Frankfurt am Main: Deutscher Klassiker Verlag, 2005).

Homer. *The Iliad*, trans. Richmond Lattimore (Chicago and London: Chicago University Press, 1951).

Horace. *Odes and Epodes*, ed. and trans. Niall Rudd (Cambridge, MA: Harvard University Press, 2004).

Horden, Peregrine (ed.). *Freud and the Humanities* (London: Duckworth, 1985).

Hughes, Bettany. *Helen of Troy: Goddess, Princess, Whore* (New York: Knopf, 2005).

Hyde, Maggie. *Jung and Astrology* (London: Aquarian Press; Thorson's, 1992).

Jacobi, Jolande (ed.). *Paracelsus: Selected Writings* [1951], trans. Norbert Guterman (Princeton, NJ: Princeton University Press, 1979).

Jantz, Harold. "Goethe, Faust, Alchemy, and Jung," *The German Quarterly*, vol. 35, no. 2 (March 1962), 129-141.

Jantz, Harold. *The Mothers in "Faust": The Myth of Time and Creativity* (Baltimore: Johns Hopkins Press, 1969).

Johnson, Sheila. "Ideological Ambiguity in G.W. Pabst's 'Paracelsus' (1943)," *Monatshefte*, vol. 83, no. 2 (Summer, 1991), 104-126.

Josephson-Storm, Jason Ā. *The Myth of Disenchantment: Magic, Modernity, and the Birth of the Human Sciences* (Chicago and London: University of Chicago Press, 2017).

Jung, C.G. *Dream Interpretation Ancient & Modern: Notes from the Seminar Given in 1936-1941*, ed. John Peck, Lorenz Jung, and Maria Meyer-Grass, trans. Ernst Falzeder with Tony Woolfson (Princeton, NJ, and Oxford: Princeton University Press, 2014).

Jung, C.G. *Dream Symbols of the Individuation Process: Notes of C.G. Jung's Seminars on Wolfgang Pauli's Dreams*, ed. Suzanne Gieser (Princeton, NJ, and Oxford: Princeton University Press, 2019).

Jung, C.G. *History of Modern Psychology: Lectures Delivered at ETH Zurich, 1933-1934*, ed. Ernst Falzeder, trans. Mark Kyburz, John Peck, and Ernst Falzeder (Princeton, NJ, and Oxford: Princeton University Press, 2019).

Jung, C.G. *Jung on Evil*, ed. Murray Stein (London and New York: Routledge, 1995).

Jung, C.G. *Mysterium Coniunctionis [...]: Ergänzungsband «Aurora Consurgens»: Ein dem Thomas von Aquin zugeschriebenes Dokument der alchemistischen Gegensatzproblematik von Dr. M.-L. von Franz* [*Gesammelte Werke*, vol. 14/iii] (Olten und Freiburg im Breisgau: Walter, 1971).

Jung, C.G. *On Psychological and Visionary Art: Notes from C.G. Jung's Lecture on Gérard de Nerval's "Aurélia"*, ed. Craig E. Stephenson (Princeton, NJ, and Oxford: Princeton University Press, 2015).

Jung, C.G. *Psychology of Yoga and Meditation: Lectures Delivered at the ETH Zurich, 1938-1940*, ed. Martin Liebscher, trans. Heather McCartney and John Peck (Princeton, NJ, and Oxford: Princeton University Press, 2020).

Jung, C.G. and Carl Kerényi. *Essays on a Science of Mythology: The Myth of the Divine Child and the Mysteries of Eleusis*, trans. R.F.C. Hull (Princeton, NJ: Princeton University Press, 1963).

Jung, C.G. and Wolfgang Pauli. *Atom and Archetype: The Pauli/Jung Letters, 1932-1958*, ed. C.A. Meier, trans. David Roscoe (Princeton, NJ, and Oxford: Princeton University Press, 2001).

Kaufmann, Sebastian. *Kommentar zu Nietzsches "Die fröhliche Wissenschaft"* [NK, vol. 3/2.1] (Berlin and Boston: de Gruyter 2022).

Kerényi, Carl. *Eleusis: Archetypal Image of Mother and Daughter*, trans. Ralph Manheim (Princeton, NJ: Princeton University Press, 1967).

Kerényi, Karl. *Das Ägäische Fest: Die Meergötterszene in Goethes Faust II* (Amsterdam and Leipzig: Pantheon, 1941); 3rd edition as *Das Ägäische Fest: Erläuterungen zur Szene "Felsbuchten des Ägäischen Meers" in Goethes Faust II* (Wiesbaden: Limes Verlag, 1950).

Kerényi, Karl. *Humanistische Seelenforschung* (Darmstadt: Wissenschaftliche Buchgesellschaft, 1966).

Kerslake, Christian. *Deleuze and the Unconscious* (London and New York: Continuum, 2007).

Keulen, W.H. and Ulrike Egelhaaf-Gaiser (eds.), *Apuleius Madaurensis Metamorphoses, Book XI, The Isis Book: Text, Introduction and Commentary* (Leiden: Brill, 2015).

Kingsley, Peter. *Catafalque: Carl Jung and the End of Humanity*, 2 vols. (London: Catafalque Press, 2018).

Kirsch, Jean and Murray Stein (eds.). *How and Why We Still Read Jung: Personal and Professional Reflections* (London and New York: Routledge, 2013).

Klages, Ludwig. *Of Cosmogonic Eros*, trans. Mav Kuhn, 2nd edn (Munich: Theion, 2022).

Klages, Ludwig. *Vom kosmogonischen Eros*, 2nd edn. (Jena: Diederichs, 1926).

Kohlschmidt, Werner. "Faustens »Entelechie« — doch der Doctor Marianus?" *Orbis Litterarum*, 29 (1974), 221-230.

Kommerell, Max. "Die letzte Szene der Faustdichtung. Ein Interpretationsversuch," *Zeitschrift für deutsches Altertum und deutsche Literatur*, vol. 77, nos. 2/3 (1940), 175-188.

Koopmann, Helmut and Frank Baron (eds.). *Die Wiederkehr der Renaissance im 19. und 20. Jahrhundert – The Revival of the Renaissance in the Nineteenth and Twentieth Centuries* (Münster: mentis, 2013).

Kornblatt, Judith Deutsch (ed.). *Divine Sophia: The Wisdom Writings of Vladimir Solovyov* (Ithaca, NY: Cornell University Press, 2009).

Kreeft, Peter. *The Platonic Tradition* (South Bend, IN: St. Augustine's Press, 2018).

Kurth-Voigt, Lieselotte E. *Continued Existence, Reincarnation, and the Power of Sympathy in Classical Weimar* (Rochester, NY, and Woodbridge, UK: Camden House, 1999).

Lacan, Jacques. *The Seminar of Jacques Lacan, Book III, The Psychoses, 1955-1956*, ed. Jacques-Alain Miller, trans. Russell Grigg (New York and London: Norton, 1993).

Lacan, Jacques. *The Seminar: Book XI: The Four Fundamental Concepts of Psychoanalysis, 1964*, trans. Alan Sheridan (London: Hogarth Press; Institute of Psycho-Analysis, 1977).

Lacoste, Jean. "«L'œil clairement ouvert sur la nature»: Heidegger et Goethe," *Littérature*, no. 120 [Poésie et philosophie] (December 2000), 105-127.

Lamberton, Robert D. *Homer the Theologian: Neoplatonist Allegorical Reading and the Growth of the Epic Tradition* (Berkeley, CA: University of California Press, 1989).

Lamberton, Robert and John J. Keaney (eds.), *Homer's Ancient Readers: The Hermeneutics of Ancient Greek's Earliest Exegetes* (Princeton, NJ: Princeton University Press, 2019).

Lévêque, Pierre. *Aurea catena Homeri: Une étude sur l'allégorie grecque* (Paris: Les Belles Lettres, 1959).

Lüdemann, Gerd. *Early Christianity according to the Traditions in Acts: A Commentary* (Minneapolis, MN: Fortress Press, 1989).

Luden, Heinrich. *Rückblicke in mein Leben* (Jena: Luden, 1847).

Maatsch, Jonas (ed.), *Morphologie und Moderne: Goethes »anschauliches Denken« in den Geistes- und Kulturwissenschaften seit 1800* (Berlin and Boston: de Gruyter, 2014).

Macrobius. *Commentary on the Dream of Scipio*, ed. and trans. William Harris Stahl (New York: Columbia University Press, 1990).

Manoussakis, John Panteleimon. *God After Metaphysics: A Theological Aesthetic* (Bloomington and Indianapolis: Indiana University Press, 2007).

Marlowe, Christopher. *The Tragical History of Doctor Faustus*, ed. Israel Gollancz (London: Dent, 1897).

Martin, Michael. *The Submerged Reality: Sophiology and the Turn to a Poetic Metaphysics* (Kettering, OH: Angelico Press, 2015).

Mason, Eudo C. *Goethe's Faust: Its Genesis and Purport* (Berkeley and Los Angeles: University of California Press, 1967).

Maspero, Gaston Camille Charles. *Études de mythologie et d'archéologie égyptiennes*, 7 vols. (Paris: E. Leroux, 1893-1916).

Matthews, Caitlin. *Sophia: Goddess of Wisdom, Bride of God* [2001] (Wheaton, IL: Quest Books, 2013).

May, Kurt. *Faust II. Teil: In der Sprachform gedeutet* (Munich: Hanser, 1962).

McGuire, William and R.F.C. Hull, *C.G. Jung Speaking: Interviews and Encounters* (Princeton, NJ: Princeton University Press, 1977).

McIntosh, Christopher. *Occult Germany: Old Gods, Mystics, and Magicians* (Rochester, VT: Inner Traditions, 2024).

Mead, G.R.S. *Simon Magus* (London: Theosophical Publishing Society, 1892).

Meier, Harri and Hans Sckommodau (eds.). *Wort und Text: Festschrift für Fritz Schalk* (Frankfurt am Main: Klostermann, 1963).

Merquior, J.G. *From Paris to Prague: A Critique of Structuralist and Poststructuralist Thought* (London: Verso, 1986).

Michelsen, Peter. "Fausts Erblindung," *Deutsche Vierteljahrsschrift für Literaturwissenschaft und Geistesgeschichte*, vol. 36, no. 1 (May 1962), 26-35.

Mills, Jon and Daniel Burston (eds.). *Critical Theory and Psychoanalysis: From the Frankfurt School to Contemporary Critique* (London and New York: Routledge, 2023).

Milton, John. *Paradise Lost*, ed. Alastair Fowler, 2nd edn. (Harlow: Longman, 1998).

Mommsen, Katharina. *Goethe and the Poets of Arabia*, trans. Michael M. Metzger (Rochester, NY: Camden House, 2014).

Murase, Amadeo. "The Homunculus and the Paracelsian *Liber de imaginibus*," *Ambix*, vol. 67, no. 1 (February 2020), 47-61.

Murray, Gilbert. *Five Stages of Greek Religion*, 3rd edn. (Garden City, NY: Doubleday, 1955).

Nakajima, Tatsuhiro. "Psychology of the 12th Century Renaissance in Wolfram von Eschenbach's *Parzival*," *Studia Hermetica Journal*, vol. 8, no. 1 ("Hermetism and the Underworld") (2018), 23-40.

Neumann, Erich. *The Great Mother: An Analysis of the Archetype* [1951], trans. Ralph Manheim [1955] (Princeton, NJ, and Oxford: Princeton University Press, 2015).

Niazi, Mohammed Nadeem. "Faust's Violence against the Mothers," *The German Quarterly*, vol. 72, no. 3 (Summer 1999), 221-231.

Nievergelt, Marco and Stephanie A. Viereck Gibbs Kamath (eds.), *The Pèlerinage Allegories of Guillaume de Deguileville: Tradition,*

Authority and Influence (Woodbridge and Rochester, NY: Boydell and Brewer, 2013).

Nisbet, H.B. *German Aesthetic and Literary Criticism: Winckelmann, Lessing, Hamann, Herder, Schiller, Goethe* (Cambridge: Cambridge University Press, 1985).

O'Leary, De Lacy. *How Greek Science Passed to the Arabs* (London: Routledge & Kegan Paul, 1949).

Olney, James. *The Rhizome and the Flower: The Perennial Philosophy — Yeats and Jung* (Berkeley, CA: University of California Press, 1980).

Oort, Henk van. *Anthroposophy: A Concise Introduction to Rudolf Steiner's Spiritual Philosophy* (Forest Row, UK: Temple Lodge, 2008).

Otto, Walter F. *Mythos und Welt*, ed. Kurt von Fritz (Stuttgart: Klett, 1962).

Ovid. *Metamorphoses: A New Translation, Contexts, Criticism*, ed. and trans. Charles Martin (New York and London: Norton, 2010).

Pagel, Walter. *Paracelsus: An Introduction to Philosophical Medicine in the Era of the Renaissance*, 2nd edn. (Basel: Karger, 1982).

Pagel, Walter. *The Smiling Spleen: Paracelsianism in Storm and Stress* (Basel: Karger, 1984).

Paglia, Camille. "Erich Neumann: Theorist of the Great Mother," *Arion*, vol. 13 no. 3 (Winter 2006), 1-14.

Palmer, Philip Mason Robert Pattison More, *The Sources of the Faust Tradition: From Simon Magus to Lessing* [1936] (London and New York: Routledge, 2013).

Panofsky, Erwin. *Hercules am Scheidewege und andere antike Bildstoffe in der neueren Kunst* (Leipzig and Berlin: Teubner, 1930; reprinted Berlin: Geb. Mann Verlag, 1997).

Paracelsus (Theophrastus Bombastus von Hohenheim, 1493-1541). *Essential Theoretical Writings*, ed. and trans. Andrew Weeks (Leiden and Boston: Brill, 2008).

Patai, Raphael. "An unknown Hebrew medical alchemist: A medieval treatise on the quinta essentia," *Medical History*, vol. 28, no. 3 (1984), 308-323.

Patai, Raphael. *The Jewish Alchemists: A History and Source Book* (Princeton, NJ: Princeton University Press, 1995).

Peterson, Jordan B. *Maps of Meaning: The Architecture of Belief* (New York and London: Routledge, 1999).

Peterson, Jordan B. *We Who Wrestle With God: Perceptions of the Divine* (London: Allen Lane, 2024).

Picard, Charles. "Die Ephesia von Anatolien" and "Die Große Mutter von Kreta bis Eleusis," *Eranos-Jahrbuch*, 6 (1938), 59-90 and 91-119.

Pindar. *The Odes of Pindar, including the Principal Fragments*, trans. John Sandys (London; New York: Heinemann; Putnam, 1927).

Plato. *Collected Dialogues*, ed. Edith Hamilton and Huntington Cairns (Princeton, NJ: Princeton University Press, 1989).

Plotinus, vol. 1, *Porphyry on Plotinus; Ennead I*, trans. A.H. Armstrong (Cambridge, MA, and London: Harvard University Press, 1995).

Plutarch. *Moralia*, vol. 5, trans. Frank Cole Babbitt (Cambridge, MA, and London: Harvard University Press, 1936).

Preminger, Alex and T.V.F. Brogan (eds). *The New Princeton Encyclopedia of Poetry and Poetics* (Princeton, NJ: Princeton University Press, 1993).

Prokhoris, Sabine. *The Witch's Kitchen: Freud, "Faust," and the Transference* [1988], trans. G.M. Goshgarian (Ithaca and London: Cornell University Press, 1995).

Raffoul, François and Eric S. Nelson (eds), *The Bloomsbury Companion to Heidegger* (London and New York: Bloomsbury, 2016).

Rätsch, Christian. *Walpurgisnacht: Von fliegenden Hexen und ekstatischen Tänzen* (Baden: AT Verlag, 2005).

Rather, L.J. "Some Reflections on the Philemon and Baucis Episode in Goethe's *Faust*," *Diogenes*, vol. 7, no. 2 (March 1959), 60-73.

Rendall, Thomas. "Goethe's *Faust* and Heidegger's Critique of Technology," *ISLE: Interdisciplinary Studies in Literature and Environment*, vol. 22, no. 1 (Winter 2015), 115-131.

Resenhöfft, Wilhelm. *Goethes Rätseldichtung im "Faust": Mit Hexenküche und Hexen-Einmal-Eins in soziologischer Deutung* (Berne: Lang, 1972).

Rosen, David. *The Tao of Jung: The Way of Integrity* (New York: Viking Arkana, 1996).

Rowland, Susan (ed.). *Psyche and the Arts: Jungian Approaches to Music, Architecture, Literature, Painting and Film* (London and New York: Routledge, 2008), pp.107-116.

Rudolf, Adalbert. "Abgerissene Bemerkungen zu Goethes Faust," *Archiv für das Studium der neueren Sprachen und Litteraturen*, 37. Jahrgang, vol. 70 (1883), pp. 462-473.

Russ, C.A.H. "Introduction," in Goethe, *Three Tales* (Oxford: Oxford University Press, 1964), pp. 7-41.

Sandy, G. "Knowledge and Curiosity in Apuleius' *Metamorphoses*," *Latomus*, vol. 31, no. 1 (January-March 1972), 179-183.

Saul, Nicholas and Ricarda Schmidt (eds). *Literarische Wertung und Kanonbildung* (Würzburg: Könighausen & Neumann, 2007).

Sayapova, Albina and Oksana Amurskaya, "Symbolic Interpretation of the Image of Goethe's Faust in the Context of Heidegger's Notions 'The Earth' and 'The Sky,'" *Mediterranean Journal of Social Sciences*, vol. 6, no. 6 (December 2015), 43-49.

Schärf Kluger, Rivkah. *Satan in the Old Testament*, trans. Hildegard Nagel (Evanston, IL: Northwestern University Press, 1967).

Schärf, Rivkah. "Die Gestalt des Satans im Alten Testament," in C.G. Jung, *Symbolik des Geistes* (Zurich: Rascher, 1953), pp. 151-319.

Schelling, F.W.J. *Ueber die Gottheiten von Samothrace* (Stuttgart and Tübingen: Cotta, 1815).

Schiller, Friedrich. *On the Aesthetic Education of Man*, ed. and trans. Elizabeth M. Wilkinson and L.A. Willoughby, 2nd edn. (Oxford: Clarendon Press, 1982).

Schleiermacher, Friedrich. *Über die Religion: Reden an die Gebildeten unter ihren Verächtern*, ed. Rudolf Otto [1899] (Göttingen: Vandenhoeck & Ruprecht, 2002).

Scholem, Gershom G. *Jewish Gnosticism, Merkabah Mysticism, and Talmudic Tradition* (New York: Jewish Theological Seminary of America, 1960).

Schopenhauer, Arthur. *The World as Will and Representation*, trans. E.F.J Payne, 2 vols (New York: Dover, 1966).

Schulte, Hans, John Noyes, and Pia Kleber (eds), *Goethe's "Faust": Theatre of Modernity* (Cambridge: Cambridge University Press, 2011).

Seiling, Max. *Goethe als Okkultist: Komme, folge mir ins dunkle Reich hinab!* (Berlin: J. Baum, 1919).

Seppänen, Lauri. "Goethe und seine *Entelecheia*," *Neuphilologische Mitteilungen*, vol. 84, no. 1 (1983), 126-131.

Sergeev, Mikhail. *Sophiology in Russian Orthodoxy: Solov'ev, Bulgakov, Losskii, Berdiaev* (Lewiston, NY: Edwin Mellen Press, 2007).

Shamdasani, Sonu. "Who is Jung's Philemon? An Unpublished Letter to Alice Raphael," *Jung History*, vol. 2, no. 2 (Fall 2007), 5-7.

Sheppard, Richard (ed.). *New Ways in Germanistik* (Oxford: Berg, 1990).

Siebert, Gustav. *Das Hexeneinmaleins, der Schlüssel zu Goethes Faust* (Münster: Aschendorff, 1914).

Silberer, Herbert. *Problems of Mysticism and Its Symbolism* [1914], trans. Smith Ely Jelliffe (New York: Moffat, Yard, 1917).

Skelton, Ross. "Is the Unconscious structured like a language?", *International Forum of Psychoanalysis*, vol. 4, no. 3 (1995), 168-178.

Spitzer, Leo. "Wiederum Mörikes Gedicht «Auf eine Lampe»," *Trivium*, vol. 9, no. 3 (1951), 133-147.

Staiger, Emil. "Zu einem Vers von Mörike: Ein Briefwechsel mit Martin Heidegger," *Trivium: Schweizerische Vierteljahrsschrift für Literaturwissenschaft*, vol. 9, no. 1 (1951), 1-16.

Staiger, Emil, Martin Heidegger, and Leo Spitzer, "A 1951 Dialogue on Interpretation," trans. Berel Lang and Christine Ebel, *Publications of the Modern Language Association*, vol. 105, no. 3 [Special Topic: The Politics of Critical Language] (May 1990), 409-435.

Steiner, Rudolf. *Anthroposophy in the Light of Goethe's "Faust": Volume One of Spiritual-Scientific Commentaries on Goethe's "Faust"* [*Collected Works*, vol. 272], introd. Frederick Amrine, trans. Burley Channer (Hudson, NY: Steiner Books, 2014).

Steiner, Rudolf. *Aus dem mitteleuropäischen Geistesleben: Fünfzehn öffentliche Vorträge gehalten zwischen dem 2. Dezember 1915 und dem 15. April 1916 im Architektenhaus zu Berlin* [GA 065] (Dornach: Rudolf Steiner Verlag, 2000).

Steiner, Rudolf. *Die Geheimnisse: Ein Weihnachts- und Ostergedicht von Goethe* (Dornach: Philosophisch-Anthroposophischer Verlag am Goetheanum, 1931).

Steiner, Rudolf. *Geisteswissenschaftliche Erläuterungen zu Goethes «Faust»*, 2 vols (Dornach: Rudolf Steiner Verlag, 1982).

Steiner, Rudolf. *Goethe und die Gegenwart: Fünfunddreißig Vorträge in verschiedenen Städten 1889-1912*, ed. by Monika Philippi (Basel: Rudolf Steiner Verlag, 2017).

Steiner, Rudolf. *Goethe's "Faust" in the Light of Anthroposophy: Volume Two of Spiritual-Scientific Commentaries on Goethe's "Faust"* [*Collected Works*, vol. 273], introd. Frederick Amrine, trans. Burley Channer (Hudson, NY: Steiner Books, 2016).

Steiner, Rudolf. *Goethe's Standard of the Soul* [*Goethes Geistesart in ihrer Offenbarung durch seinen Faust und durch das Märchen von der Schlange und der Lilie*, 1918], trans. D.S. Osmond (New York: Anthroposophic Press, 1925).

Steiner, Rudolf. *Isis Mary Sophia: Her Mission and Ours*, ed. Christopher Bamford (Spencertown, NY: SteinerBooks, 2003).

Steiner, Rudolf. *The Mysteries: A Poem for Christmas and Easter by J.W. v. Goethe*, trans. Marianne H. Luedeking (Great Barrington: SteinerBooks, 2014).

Stokes, Richard. *The Book of Lieder* (London: Faber and Faber, 2005).

Storl, Wolf-Dieter. *Pflanzendevas* (Aarau: AT-Verlag, 2002).

Stroumsa, Guy G. *Hidden Wisdom: Esoteric Traditions and the Roots of Christian Mysticism*, 2nd edn. (Leiden and Boston: Brill, 2005).

Sudhoff, Karl. "Paracelsus und Goethe," *Die medizinische Welt*, 6 (1932), 1409-1412.

Sulger-Gebing, Emil. *Goethe und Dante: Studien zur vergleichenden Literaturgeschichte* [1907] (Hamburg: Severus Verlag, 2013).

Tarnas, Richard. *Cosmos and Psyche: Intimations of a New World View* (New York: Plume, 2007).

Tarnas, Richard. *The Passion of the Western Mind: Understanding the Ideas That Have Shaped Our World View* (London: Pimlico, 1996).

Tilton, Hereward. *The Quest for the Phoenix: Spiritual Alchemy and Rosicrucianism in the Work of Count Michael Maier (1569-1622)* (Berlin and New York: de Gruyter, 2003).

Tourney, Garfield. "Empedocles and Freud, Heraclitus and Jung," *Bulletin of the History of Medicine*, vol. 30 no. 2 (March-April, 1956), 109-123.

Travers, Martin ."Trees, Rivers, and Gods: Paganism in the Work of Martin Heidegger," *Journal of European Studies*, vol. 48, no. 2 (2018), 133-143.

Travers, Martin. "The Happening of *Ereignis*: The Presence of Greek Ritual in Heidegger's Concept of Enowning," *Seminar: A Journal of Germanic Studies*, vol. 51, no. 1 (February 2015), 1-9.

Trevelyan, Humphry. *Goethe & the Greeks* [1942] (New York: Octagon, 1972).

Ugrinsky, Alexej. *Goethe in the Twentieth Century* (New York: Greenwood Press, 1987).

Urban, Misty, Deva Kemmis, and Melissa Ridley Elmes (eds.). *Melusine's Footprint: Tracing the Legacy of a Medieval Myth* (Leiden and Boston: Brill, 2017).

Valdey, Damian. *German Philhellenism: The Pathos of the Historical Imagination from Winckelmann to Goethe* (New York: Palgrave Macmillan, 2014).

Versluis, Arthur (ed.). *Wisdom's Book: The Sophia Anthology* (St. Paul, MN: Paragon House, 2000).

Vietor, Holger. "Das Hexen-Einmaleins — der Weg zur Entschlüsselung," *Goethe-Jahrbuch*, 122 (2005), 325-327.

Wallis, Richard T. and Jay Bregman (eds.). *Neoplatonism and Gnosticism* (Albany, NY: State University of New York Press, 1992).

Weeks, Andrew. *Boehme: An Intellectual Biography of the Seventeenth-Century Philosopher and Mystic* (Albany, NY: State University of New York Press, 1991).

Weeks, Andrew. *Paracelsus: Speculative Theory and the Crisis of the Early Reformation* (Albany, NY: State University of New York Press, 1991).

Wehr, Gerhard. *Jung & Steiner: The Birth of a New Psychology* [*C.G. Jung und Rudolf Steiner: Konfrontation und Synopse*, 1990], trans. Magdalene Jaeckel (Hudson, NY: Anthroposophic Press, 2003).

Wesche, Ulrich. "The Spirits' Chorus in *Faust*: A Jungian Reading," *Germanic Notes*, vol. 14, no. 4 (1983), 49-51.

Whiton, John. "Reading Goethe's *Faust* from a Catholic Perspective," *Faith & Reason: The Journal of Christendom College*, vol. 22, nos. 1-2 (Spring-Summer 1996), 1-6.

Wilkinson, Elizabeth M. and L.A. Willoughby. *Goethe: Poet and Thinker* (London: Arnold, 1962).

Wilkinson, Elizabeth M. and L.A. Willoughby. *Models of Wholeness: Some Attitudes to Language, Art and Life in the Age of Goethe*, ed. Jeremy Adler, Martin Swales, and Ann Weaver (Oxford: Lang, 2002).

Willard, Thomas. "Beya and Gabricus: Erotic Imagery in German Alchemy," *Mediaevistik*, 28 (2015), 269-281.

Willoughby, L.A. "The Image of the 'Wanderer' and the 'Hut' in Goethe's Poetry," *Etudes germaniques*, 6 (1951), 207-219.

Wilpert, Gero von. *Goethe-Lexikon* (Stuttgart: Kröner, 1998).

Wycherley, R.E. "The Scene of Plato's 'Phaidros,'" *Phoenix*, vol. 17, no. 2 (Summer 1963), 88-98.

Xenophontos, Sophia and Katerina Oikonomopoulou (eds.). *Brill's Companion to the Reception of Plutarch* (Leiden and Boston: Brill, 2019).

Zaehner, R.C. (ed. and trans.). *Hindu Scriptures* (New York: Knopf, 1992).

Ziolkowski, Theodore. *The View from the Tower: Origins of an Antimodernist Image* (Princeton, NJ: Princeton University Press, 1988).

Žižek, Slavoj. *The Indivisible Remainder: An Essay on Schelling and Related Matters* (London and New York: Verso, 1996).

www.ingramcontent.com/pod-product-compliance
Lightning Source LLC
Chambersburg PA
CBHW020331270326
41926CB00007B/130

* 9 7 8 1 6 8 5 0 3 5 9 5 2 *